WOMEN & SUCCESS

WOMEN & SUCCESS

THE ANATOMY OF ACHIEVEMENT

Originally published under the title SUCCESSFUL WOMEN IN THE SCIENCES

edited by Ruth B. Kundsin, Sc.D.

WILLIAM MORROW & COMPANY, INC., NEW YORK
1974

"I think success is defined in terms of whether or not people get to do what they perceive as their work. There are so many persons who are females who have not been able to do their work."

JO-ANN EVANS GARDNER

CONTENTS

TO AUTONOMOUS WOMEN: AN INTRODUCTION

Ruth B. Kundsin, Sc.D.

Surgical Bacteriology Laboratory
Peter Bent Brigham Hospital
Boston, Massachusetts 02115

If a female Einstein existed in the United States today, would she be recognized? Would she be a professor at the Princeton Institute for Advanced Studies? Would she get a National Science Foundation Grant? Would she be listed in *Who's Who?* Or would she be found in a neat suburban house washing her husband's socks, practicing Craig Claiborne's recipes and imbibing dry martinis in the afternoon with anger mounting in her heart toward her family, her friends and the faculty at the college where she majored in physics?

Despite Women's Lib, consciousness-raising and the Equal Rights Amendment, the answer, most probably, is that our female Einstein would be in the suburbs with the socks, the recipes, the martinis and the anger. For reasons deeply rooted in our history and culture—though not in our respective genders, as these studies show—potential Einsteins (or Picassos, Salks, or Lincolns), if they happen to be born female, rarely achieve their highest potentials.

Occasionally, however, a few women can be seen pursuing professions and reaching remarkable degrees of success despite the obvious obstacles. This fact raises a number of questions. What is the source of their motivation? What factors influence their performance? How do these women look at themselves with regard to the traditional female roles of wife and mother? How are they able to achieve—and how do they feel about their achievements—in the context of an ambivalent, and often hostile, environment?

Deep concern for the sparsity of professional women in our society, coupled with the questions arising from the fact that *some* women do achieve varying degrees of professional success, prompted the New York Academy of Sciences, in May, 1972, to conduct a conference to explore the subject of women and success. This book is a compilation of the papers presented at that conference.

The original conference was organized by Dr. Jane Anderson, a psychiatrist at the Harvard Medical School, Dr. Mary G. Ampola of the Tufts Medical School and the New England Medical Center, Dr. Iolanda E. Low, also of the Harvard Medical School, and myself. We met for two hours every week for one year to plan the structure of the conference, and while part of the time was taken up with the business of the conference, inevitably we shared some of our frustrations, both professional and personal. A bond of loyalty developed between us. A professional setback to one disturbed all of us, while recognition of some sort—a promotion or a professional compliment—was shared by all with joy untinged with envy.

Because the purpose of the conference was to explore the topic of women and success, we found it necessary to establish a working definition for "success." We finally concluded that "success," in the context of the conference, should be defined as the ability to function in a chosen profession with some measure of peer recognition. Although the conference was sponsored by the New York Academy of Sciences and we ourselves were all scientists, we looked for participants from a wide range of professions. Ultimately, in addition to women from the hard-core sciences, such as chemistry, physics and mathematics, women were included from the fields of education, government, architecture

9

and horticulture to give their individual life experiences. In general, we sought women who were active in professional careers and, in keeping with our definition of success, were considered outstanding or successful by their colleagues. We selected women who, in addition to having a career, were also married and had children because we felt that having a family was a complicating circumstance that made pursuit of a career that much more difficult.

Finding professional women who wished to participate in a conference on the subject of successful women was more difficult than we had anticipated. First we had difficulty finding women in top-status positions, particularly in academic life where most were research associates rather than full professors. A number of women who were suggested to us had become known because they were associates of their husbands rather than independent investigators in their own right. Successful women in the sciences, professions known to be dominated by men, were the most difficult to find. One woman whom we consulted had a doctorate in chemistry and had been the first woman assistant professor of chemistry in a large university. However, she had abandoned her career with the firm conviction that a career and a family each demanded total commitment, and therefore, the combination was incompatible with reality.

We planned the conference in sections. The first part consisted of twelve brief life histories of women who not only fit our general definition of success, but were and are extremely successful by any standards. These twelve autobiographies appear in full in this volume. Besides success, a number of qualities were similar about these women, although, by design, they represented a variety of professions. They all were successful in fields ordinarily dominated by men: architecture, physics, government, chemistry, economics. Secondly, they all were or had been married and had reared families. They all began their careers before the term "women's liberation" became part of our language. In fact, for the most part, they established and pursued their careers at a time when societal support was virtually nonexistent. On the whole, their life goals were hard work and achievement. Being pretty and popular was not important; they were inner-directed, supercharged women.

The second section of the conference consisted of three simultaneous workshops dealing with family attitudes and relationships, the impact of education and economic factors affecting women, and the influence of these parameters on women who wished to pursue careers. (The papers presented in these workshops appear in Parts II, III and IV of this volume.)

Influences which emerged consistently in the twelve autobiographies, such as parental support or educational influences, were isolated and analyzed in the section entitled *Determinants in Individual Life Experiences* (Part V). Individual life histories were studied for common determinants by a psychiatrist, Dr. Jane Anderson, a sociologist, Dr. Arlie Hochschild, and an educator, Dr. Mary Bunting. Historical perspectives of professional women were presented by Dr. Barbara Solomon.

The last part of the conference consisted of discussions of the problems of professional women in relation to others, particularly husbands, children and professional colleagues. In this section we also discussed such varied topics as the hormonal differences between men and women and their effect on a woman's ability to function in a career, and the implications of pregnancy and abortion on working women.

We constructed the conference proceedings in this way very deliberately. We chose to open the conference with the twelve life histories in order to get a varied and subjective view of the influences and motivations behind the professional pursuits of a number of women. We then wanted objectively to glean and isolate the influences that were consistent in each of these lives. These influences were appropriately analyzed by experts in the fields of psychiatry, sociology, education and history. Since these influences also involved personal and human ramifications, we structured the final part of the conference to explore the human element of career pursuit more closely.

The conclusions that emerged from both our planning of the conference and the conference itself were fascinating, sometimes discouraging, sometimes encouraging and often surprising. While planning the conference, we inevitably confronted barriers, sometimes from men, and surprisingly often from women. When we presented the conference to the New York Academy of Sciences for acceptance, we anticipated opposition to this predominantly female conference. Dr. Jane Anderson, a psychiatrist, suggested that we allow all opponents full expression of their ideas to help dissipate hostility. This was a wise decision. My intuitive feeling would have been to answer any objection immediately and to the point, regardless of the fact that it would be, probably, an emotional rather than a factual response.

The presentation meeting, on the whole, went very smoothly. However, one prominent senior member of the advisory board at the Academy suggested that the conference be opened and closed by a male speaker to give the conference "status." But encouragingly, a male member of the Academy's editorial staff, sensitized to the situation, immediately pointed out that a man opening and closing the conference would not give it "status." On the contrary, it would only imply that women, and successful women at that, could not handle their own conference.

Several women who were invited to participate objected to the idea of having a conference dedicated totally to the subject of "successful women." The idea of "success" was objectionable to some women; one distinguished woman refused to participate, saying, "I find myself somehow or other turned off by the aura of elitism." The reluctance of these women to be considered successful was a pathetic revelation. As Matina Horner points out in her study on the psychological barriers to success in women, women are basically afraid of success. In a woman, and apparently to many women invited to participate in our conference, success is considered deviant behavior.

Discussions at the conference itself went far beyond consciousness-raising. Opinions emerged that reflected the complete range of women's liberation philosophy—from traditional to radical. However, most of the discussions centered around the positive factors that made careers possible for women. A basic point of departure was the "fear of success" experienced by many women, a fact that Matina Horner firmly documents in her study. This fear, like most other fears, is established at a very young age, and evidence presented at the conference proved that this fear lies at the core of most women's inability to pursue and accept professional success.

Some conclusions that were established at the conference included the fact that a real need for parental support, from both fathers and mothers, is imperative for developing the confidence and self-esteem needed to prepare for a career. A husband's support is essential later in life, though we found in some studies that a man's support is often helpful for the wrong reasons. We also discovered, interestingly, that the support of teachers and colleagues is not as essential as the support of parents and spouses. A sad revelation was that women rarely find support among their female peers. It is noteworthy that five of our twelve women attended strong women's colleges, a factor which is thought to provide opportunities for leadership. Seven had either foreign backgrounds or considerable exposure to other cultures.

One of the most interesting conclusions drawn from these studies was that it is not only possible for a woman to have both a career and a family, but it is beneficial to all concerned. Dr. Aronson's essay on "Marriage with a Successful Woman" explains how a woman's career can add an exciting dimension to a marriage. Dr. Lois Hoffman's discussion, "The Professional Woman as Mother," stresses the positive effects of a mother's career on her daughters, and later discussions revealed that it was beneficial to her sons as well. The general conclusion seemed to be that accomplished women of today are not deviants. They are precursors indicating the profound change of direction of the role of women in our society.

This conference was a tremendously exhilarating experience for me, and I am sure it was for all the other women who attended it. There emerged a solidarity and a unique communion that many of us had never sensed before, as if each one of us personally heard ourselves saying "Right on!" What a rare commodity female friendship is!

Many individuals contributed to the success of our conference and, in turn, to the success of this volume. I am sure that without the sensitivity, understanding and warmth of my three fellow-planners, Drs. Anderson, Ampola and Low, we could never have been able to organize the conference initially. Participants whose papers are included in this volume worked long and hard, and to them I am grateful. Session chairpersons and discussion leaders were confident, outstanding women, all well-qualified autonomous professional women: Wilma Scott Heide, President of the National Organization for Women; Dr. Martha Berliner, Associate Professor of Microbiology at Simmons College; Dr. Jo-Ann Evans Gardner, of KNOW, Inc.; Dr. Rita Arditti, Assistant Professor at Boston University; Dr. Rosa Lee Nemir, Past President of the American Medical Women's Association.

All of the women who participated in the conference feel deeply indebted to Admiral L. R. Neville of the New York Academy of Sciences for his advice and help, and also to Beatrice H. Radin, who prepared the original monograph of this volume for the Academy. Her personal involvement in the subject of the conference equipped her with a profound sensitivity to the issues. This quality helped her to transform a large quantity of disjointed data into a cohesive, meaningful whole. Finally, much gratitude goes to Pamela Hatch of William Morrow and Company. As a result of her interest and concern, a scientific monograph evolved into a volume for the thoughtful women of our time.

Editor's Note: For this edition, it has been necessary in the interests of space to exclude some of the fine discussions and summaries originally prepared for the conference. The women who contributed this material, however, must not go unrecognized. They are Wilma Scott Heide, Loretta McLaughlin, Jo-Ann Evans Gardner and Rosa Lee Nemir.

BRINGING WOMEN IN: REWARDS, PUNISHMENTS, AND THE STRUCTURE OF ACHIEVEMENT

Cynthia Fuchs Epstein

*Queens College of The City University of New York, Flushing, New York 11367
and The Bureau of Applied Social Research, Columbia University
New York, New York 10027*

I have found it curious that merely pondering the issue of "women and success" has seemed to raise personal anxiety among my female colleagues as well as in myself. Only recently it occurred to me that this distress was probably a variation of the process that Matina Horner has identified as the motive to avoid success,[1] a syndrome to which women especially fall prey, in this case from simply *thinking* about women and success.

This analysis will not, however, deal with the psychological dimension of success. It will be restricted to a set of sociological explanations of the processes that I believe lead to success, or rather, the processes in the society—and thus in the minds of women—that place severe limits on their attainment of success.

It is my conviction that anxiety about success is not the major problem. Although the dynamics of the achievement motivation process remain unclear, we see that while at some levels anxiety destroys motivation, at other levels it drives individuals toward achievement. The far greater problem, I believe, is the general statistical reality that women do not have much success. Perhaps the anxiety that Dr. Horner has so ingeniously identified arises because women's success is in such short supply, and, as with all scarce commodities that we value, we worry about wanting it, feel guilty about having it, and don't quite know how to cope with it when we get it.

From one analytic perspective, the low incidence of success among women is a pathological state in the society, a state of structural imbalance. Considering the vast participation of women in the occupational sphere and their infinitesimal degree of success, it is apparent that a large investment must be made on their behalf to create even a modest ratio of input to payoff. Until some reasonable ratio is developed, the tiny number of women who have been successful are destined to be regarded as pathological and gender anomalies. In addition, because women are not generally counted among the successful, *all* women are regarded as deficient. Thus, women outside as well as inside the professions and occupations are regarded as second-class citizens, as incompetents dependent on males to make the important decisions; as giggling magpies who will contaminate the decorum of the male luncheon clubs and bars; as persons who can't be trusted to be colleagues.

I do not think that these last observations are antiquated. Contrary to the beliefs of many, the world has not changed much in the last five years or two years or two months—in spite of the recent legislation aimed at guaranteeing women and other success-deficient groups a larger share of the places at the top. Informants who wish to remain anonymous report that the male gatekeepers of the channels and the structures of success commonly voice strong objections to bringing women in, suggesting that standards of performance will surely be diminished by their presence. Somewhat contradictorally, these same gatekeepers

* This paper was prepared with the support of a grant by the Research Foundation of the City University of New York.

believe that bringing women in poses *unfair* competition to the special needs of men: economically, as dutiful providers for the family; and psychologically, because their fragile egos would be impaired. The mixed bag of accusations against women and assertions about their incapacities or special strengths; the images, models of human nature, and the nature of man—all seem to have the consequence of assigning women (and resigning them) to supporting roles in the human drama. They are almost never heroes.

The topic around which the papers in this volume is organized—successful women—is not a simple one; it calls into question the entire set of standards used in assessing women's accomplishments in this society. The underlying assumption in this assessment is the use of occupational criteria of success, the dominant standard in the culture. But in American Society there is actually a double standard of success: one for males, another for females.

Although this forum is directed at examining determinants of success of women in the sciences, it is probably reasonable to assume that similar processes affect women's success in almost any domain.

One thing is clear about those women regarded as successful in the United States. Women at the top are at the *bottom* of the top, just as they are at the bottom of any stratum in which they happen to be represented. The occupational spread of women is bottom-heavy. As service workers, women cluster in the lowest paying domestic jobs, ranking lower even than porters and janitors (male jobs); as clerical workers, they hold the lowest ranking jobs as file clerks and typists; in the school system, the women teach and the men administrate. Women lawyers still seem to be found primarily in the specialties considered low ranking, such as matrimonial and real estate work; women doctors cluster in the lower-ranking areas of public health and psychiatry (see Ref. 2, p. 163). In the university, women are most often found in the ranks of lecturer and assistant professor, and fade into statistical obscurity as one goes to the top. The best-situated women, those who hold top ranks as professors or lawyers in Wall Street firms, are not really in and of their elites. Even the most talented and productive are balanced at the outer edge or hold ancillary posts as special assistants to the presidents of prestigious institutions, as adjunct or visiting professors. A striking example is the Noble Laureate Maria Mayer, who held auxiliary and adjunct posts for many years of her career, not becoming a full professor of physics (at the University of Chicago) until 1959, when she was 53 years old. Even today, bringing women into elite structures means creating special posts for them, not in the mainstream of a field but often in the newly created women's specialties—women's studies in English and sociology; the first law professors appointed in the law schools tend to teach courses on women in the law.

Of course, in the natural sciences women are so few and far between that it is hard to assemble statistics about their specialties. Chance seems to play a big role. I understand, for example, that there are women crystallographers in England who have achieved some distinction and whose careers were developed partly through the sponsorship of Dame Kathleen Lonsdale. Lonsdale herself would have settled down to become a "good wife and mother" after her marriage (as she reports in an article of "reminiscences",[3] except that her husband pushed her to return to science and Sir William Bragg persuaded the managers of the Royal Institution to provide her with £50 to pay for the services of a daily domestic helper.† This was in 1929, and one may assume that not many such fellowship

† I am indebted to Professor Harriet Zuckerman for passing on this reference, as well as for the note on Maria Mayer, from her substantial knowledge of Nobel Laureate lore.

awards for the services of a domestic helper have been granted since or are being considered.‡

The chance award, the especially sensitive husband, the protected work situation,[4] a high degree of accident (see Ref. 5, p. 403), the crisis of war—all these idiosyncratic elements have resulted in the success patterns of the few women whom we rate as successes. But there are some more general patterns, as well. Successful women tend more than men to come from higher-income families and to have mothers who have been professional workers. Yet this is not so surprising. The women who come closest to belonging to elites could never have surmounted all the obstacles in their way had they not had some special benefits, had not some of the barriers been lowered. Yet "drift" characterizes even successful women, and their lack of long-range career strategy processes is documented by the studies by Fogarty and the Rapoports of women in top jobs in England[6] and in all the available American literature.

The pressures on American women *not* to achieve (in the *normative,* not the psychological dimension) are strong and more complex than has been realized. Although we have become very sophisticated about early socialization and its clear and present danger to women's careers, there is less cognizance of the *later* dangers to girls' self-images. The fact that girls do not aspire is not just linked to early socialization and the fact that the mothers in children's primers are never seen reading a book or a newspaper, much less scouting adventure. Long after their earliest influences, girls and women are constantly encountering pressures directing them toward the home as a compelling and socially legitimated activity. No balancing pull exists to keep them in the occupations. My studies on women's careers in law indicated that women were as likely to drop out at the peak of their careers as at the start. The late dropouts were clearly engaged in rather successful and rewarding activities and usually no longer had young children demanding constant attention. These women had surmounted the obstacles of the early professional years to drop out at a time when they were supposed to have increased career commitment.

Why?

I think that it comes from the general orientation of girls, young women, and even older women, toward "others" (in David Reisman's sense of being "other directed"). Women are constantly urged to consider "Am I doing the right thing?" and "What shall I be or do that will please my husband, children and parents?" Occupational success never comes out as the positive answer to these questions. Pleasing others and doing the "right thing" always means holding back, and retreating from a position of strong ambition and career commitment.

Black women, ironically, are getting subjected to a strong dose of this orientation today as an outgrowth of the black political movement. They are asked to weigh their life choices from the perspective of how their actions will be viewed by black men, rather than from the perspective of how their choices will give them a richer life or a wider set of options.

Men also face the problems of making important life decisions and experience anxiety about competition and the drive to success, but they have the firm approval of a society that says, "Yes, you are a person, a potential contributor to society; you are on the right course, aim high, be something!" That's quite different from

‡ There is a further footnote to this apocryphal tale. Dame Lonsdale's housekeeper was a woman named Mrs. Snowball, and through her efforts, certainly a kind of "snowball effect" was produced that created careers for a number of women crystallographers in Great Britain.

the message given women: "Explain why you want to be something or somebody and make sure your reason is a good one."

Women do not hear insistent voices saying they *must* do, as do men.

Both men and women are probably afraid of the heights of ambition, achievement, and accomplishment; all these have their costs. But men are forced to face their fears. For those who are successful in conquering them, the lives they chart may be rich and meaningful. Women are not challenged to face their fears and thus never lose them, and remain self-doubting. Without the support to do their best, to be their best, and to enjoy doing well, most of those who could "make it," don't.

It was curious to find in my research on black professional women that in spite of enormous obstacles, they could often be their own person, depending on their own resources and not on the coattails of a husband or a mentor, as do so many women of the white middle class, not because black men don't wish to supply the coattails (it is probably gratifying and power-affirming for the male to know he can carry himself and also his wife and family), but because white society makes it impossible for them to do so.

Why could black women be their own persons? Not because there is anything unique about their sense of competence. In fact, they were behaving much like women lawyers I interviewed earlier who came from white immigrant families, who also went to work with enthusiasm and a sense of commitment and purpose. The thread that connected them was the fact that they *had* to work. That is, the *economic* rationale—the most legitimate in American Society—gave them the answer to the question that all women face: "Why aren't you at home, and aren't you denying your family something by not being there?"

As a footnote to the question still asked in America about women's capacities for distinction in work, some further data on the black women is instructive. Considering the tiny total pool of black women in the prestigious professions (less than 1,000),§ of the eleven doctors I interviewed, two had performed ground-breaking research: one in kidney disorders and the other in pediatric blood disorders. Clearly, this indicates that once women get a foot in the door, quality is not a problem.

A further deterrent to women's success stems from the fact that they are asked to demonstrate competence in a *range* of roles, their female roles as well as their occupational roles, in order to be deemed successes. Occupational excellence is not sufficient for them to be considered really successful. In exchange for this multirole achievement, women are permitted to perform somewhat less than men in their occupational roles and still be considered a success ("for a woman"). Men, on the other hand, must succeed or fail primarily on the basis of occupational achievement. They get few extra credits for being good husbands and fathers.

Does society grant women permission to perform less well than men occupationally because of the awareness of the other crucial societal functions women perform? Or is lower performance structured and guaranteed for women, making it idiosyncratic for them to aim for the top and become professional stars?

Consider some of the dimensions of the problem:

There is probably far more compatibility and structure to the performance of women in the institutions of the family and work than appears on the surface.

Each institution supports the other. The demands by the family on the woman keep her out of real competition in the occupations; reciprocally, the lack of

§ According to the 1960 Census, there were 222 black women lawyers, 487 black women physicians.

positive reinforcement she faces in the occupations sends her back to the home to seek rewards there. This may not be the manifest intent of decision-makers in these institutions, but the consequences are the same.

Part of this is a phenomenon of simple definition. Although 40% of the work force is composed of women, the cultural view is that women do *not* work and are in the home. It is an ideal view and not a real one; but it serves the purpose of forming images and placating discontents. Even the women who are working are convinced that they are not really "workers" and do not think in terms of ambitions, goals, demands, and rights. They may be pleased that they are permitted to work at all, particularly at interesting work. Consider the professors' wives who have been teaching and research assistants on college campuses through the years. Many or most of these held low ranks but were uncomplaining, aware that many others in their position couldn't get jobs at all.

Women's success also is directly affected by the general system of social control in the occupations. The social control system typically operates to undercut the sense of commitment and ambition of those persons not considered potential members of the elite; it acts to make the route to the top clear only to those deemed the preferred candidates.¶

Further, it is characteristic of the world of work that the rewards and punishments are supposed to be clear. A man is supposed to feel that if he is clever enough and hard-working enough, he can "make it." True, there are obstacles, and not everyone possesses talent. But there does seem to be some rationality and coherence about the whole process: reward for performance; punishment for failure.

The messages are shaped to be direct, instructive, and motivating for the person who will be brought inside, and to be confusing and exclusionary for women, blacks, and others regarded as outsiders.

The problem of *demonstration* of competence is in itself a problem, which, once recognized, can be justly rewarded and lead to success.

It is often impossible for the aspiring elite recruit who is unwanted to acquire competence, especially the competence learned after formal training, in an informal professional setting. This later training is necessary if the professional is to operate at the highest levels.

There are a number of dimensions to the creation of competence. One was long ago identified by the sociologist Max Weber as "charismatic education," the education of persons selected to assume leadership roles. Weber included in his description not only the technical knowledge necessary to become warrior, medicine man, priest or legal sage, but the *secret* know-how, and the creation of a sense of distinction by passing through often torturous initiation ceremonies.[8] But who gets this elite education? What are the selection criteria? Who is permitted to learn the secret chants, the etiquette, the names of the gods, to become able to perform miracles, make discoveries, or heal the sick?

The standard selection criteria for graduate education and professional education are fairly well known. But less information is available about the ways in which senior scientists pick members of their research teams, the ways in which authors select collaborators, or how chiefs of staff are chosen. There are no civil

¶ This section is drawn largely from my analysis of social control in the professions reported in two papers: Ambiguity as social control: consequences for the integration of women in professional elites. *In* Varieties of Work Experience. Stewart & Cantor, Eds. Schenkman Publishing Co. Cambridge, Mass. In Press. Women lawyers and their profession: inconsistency of social controls and their consequences for professional performance. *In* The Professional Woman. Athena Theodore, Ed. Schenkman Publishing Co. Cambridge, Mass. 1971.

service exams for any of these elite statuses; entry to structures from which success emanates is problematic.

A degree from a good school will not guarantee that the doctor who graduates high in his class is a brilliant diagnostician, nor can a recently graduated lawyer become a persuasive courtroom advocate through courses in litigation. There are no objective tests for competence at high levels. Here the status-judges of the profession and, to some extent, one's clients bestow the crown of competence. The lawyer doesn't really learn law until he has had the experience of handling actual cases and courtroom situations. He learns partly by trial and error, but better, he learns from the tutoring of an older partner who sees it his duty to guide the neophyte through the maze.

In science, medicine, law, and the academic world (and this is true for business as well), competence is created by exposing the new professional to the tasks, giving him the opportunity to learn the techniques and avoid the pitfalls. He must be given access to persons who can help him, and to information about the important people in the system. The accepted newcomer learns by observing and performing because he is put in a position where he can observe and *must* perform. His important colleagues will watch how he does and give him feedback vital for his improvement as a professional.

Those who teach the young professional and those who lead the profession usually agrees that the "appropriate" candidates are competent and will later become more competent in important ways beyond their talents and formal training. They agree, too, that the "inappropriate" candidates cannot become competent. It is believed that those with the "wrong" statuses cannot be part of the subtle, informal collegial system, will be unable to catch the messages, will be ill-prepared in the necessary etiquette of professional behavior and rules of reciprocity, and will be incapable of proper behavior toward a hierarchy that may not be clearly labeled—for them.[2] Cleverness is not sufficient, nor is a professional degree. Because failure is presumed, few act as sponsor for the *unwanted* professional. "The creation of competence" is a result of on-the-job training given only when important gatekeepers decide that a person has talent that will develop and that he or she will continue to perform well. Residents in hospitals are picked partly because of their past records as medical students and interns, but mainly on the judgment of potential by senior staff members. The new assistant professor is hired because it is believed that the person will later produce competent works and be a colleague of worth.

In short, gatekeepers can structure success for those whom they judge will become competent. Because they are usually men, no one at the gate asks about their hormones, whether they have lovers, children, or spouses. The man of erratic flashes of insight and emotion often will be said to have an interesting mind or a creative nature. He will be told that great things are expected from him and he will be protected from the mundane routines. The woman who is erratic may be labeled muddleheaded. Consider the disesteem suffered by Rosalind Franklin, even though her contributions to current genetic theory were of prime importance. She was considered more odd than a usually "eccentric" scientist.[9]

Women do not fit the *image* of competence held in the society. The woman's commands are heard as shrill. The study by Fogarty and the Rapoports of English women managers[5] reports that women's managerial styles are not thought to be successful. Women are said to be more liable than men to nag, to whine, to "flap like wet hens" when something goes wrong, to be unaware of how to handle colleagues, or to react to extremes: "dragons in an older generation, ineffectual nice mice" in the present one; in any case, ineffective as managers, whatever their style (see Ref. 5, p. 403). There is a self-fulfilling prophecy in this. *Any* female command style is interpreted as inept.

Are men constrained to be so perfectly balanced?

But what of the women who do manage to pass the gatekeepers and are judged to be among the potentially competent? For them the key question is whether they are truly brought into the inner core of professional elites.

As we know from early childhood studies, belonging is as much geared to the discipline structure as to the reward structure. It is my hypothesis that women are often not subjected to the disciplines of their professions as are the men, and thus do not learn how to improve or refine their behavior. Often they are rewarded for merely adequate performance (*any* performance by a woman is considered unique), or their deficiencies are attributed to women as a class of persons, rather than to the individual. What I am pointing to here is a structure of ambiguity. Women don't know where they stand and may not find out until they realize they are out of the picture entirely. As a *class of persons* they are subject to the subtle cooling-out process that men also experience, but the latter undergo it as individuals. Women are rewarded for irrelevant performances or ignored entirely.

Furthermore, I believe that knowledge that they stand in peripheral places undermines women's motivation. Again, we can draw on numerous studies indicating that persons who feel they do not have a stake in an organization have less commitment to it and are more likely to leave.[10],** Women are often seduced into a type of high commitment by rewards directed at their sex status (such as affection and attention) rather than their occupational status,[11] money, rank, and coauthorship. It is doubtful that the resulting commitment will lead to the major contributions that result in success. The inappropriate rewards women get generate commitment directed to a person, a set of persons, or an institution, rather than more diffusely, to the profession or the discipline.

The secondary rewards women typically receive also pull them off course. They do not compete, nor do they ever put their capacities and talents on the line. Women do not expect or believe that there are *tests* for them as there are for men, and that, like men, they can succeed or fail in the society on the basis of their occupational contributions.

Were this to happen, they would expect that if they did contribute, they would rise in rank and be paid accordingly; they would expect deference and respect. On the other hand, if they did not do well, they could expect the same loss of face that men suffer.

Equality for women means that they should no longer be judged by a different set of standards, because this has typically meant *no* standards at all or debilitating ones.

Equality means the right to the same sanctions, fears, and punishments: the same set of forces that drive men within the reward structure. Where merit is at issue, there must be one standard for all.

I am suggesting that until now there has been virtually no success for women; not that women have not performed well, but because of the multiple standards, the acceptance of a different set of measures that have cheated them of their due. The work of great women painters is often assessed in comparison with other women painters, and not with *all* painters. Women writers suffer the same fate.

** See also the testimony of Judith Long Laws before the Federal Communications Commission, Washington, D.C. 1971 Docket No. 19143. Causes and Effects of Sex Discrimination in the Bell System.

I don't think women have ever had much of a chance to demonstrate greatness in architecture, or as jurists. Uniquely in science, the work of women that has surfaced has been given the same assessment as the work of men, because contributions in science defy sexualizing.

More typically, however, women are encouraged to fail. The "new" woman is a perfectly balanced person who does a little of everything—a little writing and research; a little gourmet cooking; a little loving; a little mothering. But nowhere is she expected to rise to the top of her profession or field of work.

Occupational success probably is a developing phenomenon for women. We will probably witness less fear of success and more movement toward success.

A hypothesis has grown out of my research, which can easily be summed up by the old homily that "nothing succeeds like success!"

Women who have had any success find that in fact it is more pleasant than failing. Women who fear taking jobs with authority find that people will listen to them, and that they *can* be effective task leaders and administrators.

Too often we explain phenomena in terms of the charisma of the leader and not the charisma of the office. The person who is given a role with high ranking attached finds that he (or she) is more successful in effecting changes than the person who has a low-ranking position. Success breeds success. Once we cast the mantle of success on a person, the wheels are set in motion for greater authority. (How much more noble is the judge in his robes than in his golf jacket; how much more sage he is on the bench than at the breakfast table.) Women have always been denied this charisma of office, the halo effect of *place*. (Male colleagues may not hear the wise comments of the female member of the department, but if she is made chairman, their hearing will become more acute.)

I do not anticipate rapid change toward admission of women to the true in-groups of elite structures and stimulation of competence for women at the top. Opening the doors to some women somehow seems to create more apprehension in the hearts of men than opening the doors to members of minority groups. Some of these fears are real, of course. It is certainly true that women, who constitute a substantial pool of the educated and professionally acculturated, could take over a good proportion of men's jobs tomorrow, if they were so inclined and were given the opportunity.

I think that given the taste and experience of success, women will not only not fear it any longer, they will actively seek it and enjoy it. Certainly the women in the sciences have proved that as a class of persons, women can do work that meets the criteria for success in this society. Furthermore, the inclusion of more women in the elite sphere will probably do much to raise the general level of talent and discovery in the society.

The stimulation of the intellectual arena comes from the challenge and confrontation of good minds. Bringing women in is likely to make it more productive for the entire society.

References

1. HORNER, M. 1969. Psychology Today 3(6): 36. November.
2. EPSTEIN, C. F. 1970. Woman's Place. The University of California Press. Berkeley, Calif.
3. LONSDALE, K. 1962. Reminiscences. *In* Fifty Years of X-Ray Diffraction. : 598. P. P. Ewald, Ed. International Union of Crystallography.
4. EPSTEIN, C. F. The Woman Lawyer. University of Chicago Press. Chicago, Ill. To be published.
5. FOGARTY, M. P., R. RAPOPORT & R. N. RAPOPORT. 1971. Sex, Career and Family. Sage Publications. Beverly Hills, Calif.

6. FOGARTY, M., A. J. ALLEN, I. ALLEN & P. WALTERS. 1971. Women in Top Jobs. George Allen & Unwin Ltd. London, England.
7. EPSTEIN, C. F. 1973. Positive effects of the multiple negative: explaining the success of black professional women. Am. J. Sociol. Jan. In press.
8. WEBER, M. 1968. Economy and Society. : 1143. Bedminster Press. New York, N. Y.
9. WATSON, J. D. 1968. The Double Helix. Atheneum Press. New York, N. Y.
10. BLAUNER, R. 1964. Alienation and Freedom: the Factory Worker and his Industry. The University of Chicago Press. Chicago, Ill.
11. EPSTEIN, C. F. 1972. Sex Role Stereotyping, Occupations and Social Exchange. Paper presented at the Radcliffe Institute Conference. Radcliffe College, Cambridge, Mass. April 18.

PART I

Individual Life Experiences

ARCHITECT

Gretchen Minnhaar

505 Waters Building
Grand Rapids, Michigan 49502

Although each of us would like to believe that we are completely the masters of our life patterns, indelible influences are impressed on our development by the circumstances of our youth. These circumstances create an environment that engenders an attitude and an approach to life's opportunities and challenges. My own early background is inextricably woven into the course of my professional life, and this fact is particularly noticeable to me because I left behind the powerful and elaborate influences of an entirely different life-style in Argentina.

To a world that has somehow been divided into over- and underdeveloped countries, Argentina is included in the latter. Undoubtedly, this classification has more to do with the country's gross national product than with the spirit of its people.

Argentina is a rather underpopulated country of only 22 million; a third of them live in Buenos Aires, which was colonized by the Spaniards and the Italians who came to the "Promised Land" in search of wealth. They brought with them little or no education or skills; however, a small minority of Germans and English provided the leadership needed to transform the raw land into a productive country.

I am the result of these two currents. My maternal grandfather was Italian. Although he had only an elementary school education, during his long life he acquired great economic and social success and he accompanied it with the accumulation of a vast cultural knowledge. Since I was his oldest grandchild, we were the best of friends and traveled together extensively. His sons did not fulfill his dream of a college degree; I was then a new hope.

His dynamic approach to life, his charm, his never-give-up attitude, and his generous devotion of time and attention to friends left a great impression on me. Unfortunately, he could not share with me the longed-for degree.

My paternal grandfather was German; he arrived in Argentina as a chemical engineer and worked as such until the end of the Second World War. At that time all German holdings were confiscated, and, as a result, he lost his job at an age when starting again was, at least for him, impossible. In spite of his excellent training, it apparently gave him only one tool with which to work.

But the German tenacity bloomed in my father, who became a medical doctor and after specializing in Germany, returned to Argentina to start his practice as an internist. It wasn't easy at first, especially since he had married a woman who came from a much higher social level and was accustomed to all the luxuries of life. I doubt that he ever accepted financial help from his father-in-law, and I am sure that only his youth and the total devotion to his profession made it possible for him to work long hours and be able to attain a comfortable economic position, always finding time for study and research. Father is still very active in his practice, which is primarily devoted to hematology. He has recently been honored by being named a member of the National Academy of Medicine for his contribution in research and teaching.

I'm sure that Mother understood, in her own way, his unquestionable need for fulfillment, but her needs were diametrically opposite to Father's. She was a beautiful woman who had finished high school and expressed the desire to study dentistry. This was not encouraged by her parents, and after several long trips to Europe, a rather active social life, and an early marriage, her goals changed. Mother is a talented woman and has exquisite taste and unlimited energy, which she uses in humanitarian endeavors.

I have a brother who is a physician; he works with Father and, I am sure, will eventually take over his practice.

Our household was efficiently run with the help of a permanent staff. Until the age of 14, my brother and I had German governesses who stayed with us after school hours. Although they attended to all our physical and emotional needs, my brother and I felt extremely close to our parents, though later my rapport developed better with Father than with Mother, with whom I have had violent discussions. In addition to school, we were exposed to many other disciplines, such as languages, music, and art, which we learned from private tutors.

During my early childhood my maternal grandparents lived with us, so that I spoke first German, then Spanish. I must add that German was always the language we spoke to Father, encouraged by my mother, who couldn't speak it. I attended nursery school from the ages of three to six, at which time I started first grade. It was a private German school; 90% of the teaching staff were natives of Germany. I still recall the superb education we received. In addition to the usual academic subjects, we were exposed to German history, mythology, music, and a rigorous program of gymnastics. I could complete only sixth grade there because the termination of the Second World War forced the close of the school under the false charge that we received a Nazi-oriented education.

Seventh and eighth grades were completed in an English school. Our school day was divided into Spanish in the morning and English in the afternoon. With that degree of concentration I learned to speak English in a few weeks.

For high school I was transferred to a Catholic academy, my mother's Alma Mater. Since I found the curriculum rather easy, I completed the four-year course in only three.

I was brought up as a Catholic and went through the whole series of indoctrinatory classes. It was during my years with the nuns that my understanding of my religion widened. The emphasis was in following the rules as contrasted with a full awareness of their philosophical impact. A great number of those regulations have now been lifted, but at that time I rebelled furiously against them, believing basically in a god without the elaborate mysticism of the traditional Catholic Church. Today, although I call myself a Catholic and sporadically attend Sunday Mass, my line of thought is totally liberated from the dogma and rulings of the Church.

My grades were very good, but I must say that I worked hard for them. At 15 an illness kept me in bed for a long time. It was a trial, not because of physical pain or discomfort, but because I was restricted in my activities. During that period of time I was the center of the household, which, in so many ways, tried to fulfill my selfish demands. Books and studies furnished me with the stimulus I needed. I read everything that I could get, from the classic to the bestsellers, from pornography to comics. The unreal world that I could create through them helped me greatly during those long months. This occurrence made me reconsider the meaning of life and the extent of my controls over it; this period of physical inactivity also gave me great strength in the knowledge of an inner power that can turn negative situations into positive assets.

It was during this time that I met the man who was to become my husband.

At the time, he was a medical student almost ten years older than I. He spent a great deal of time with me even when he recognized that my thoughts were elsewhere. If popularity with boys is to be measured in direct relation to invitations and dates, I must say that there was always somebody waiting, but my hours were devoted first to study and then to fun.

Argentina is a country in which suburbia is used only for weekends. We lived in an apartment in downtown Rosario, a port city of almost one million inhabitants. It is customary, because of the proximity of all places of recreation, to walk everywhere; the highlight of a Sunday afternoon, after the movies at eight p.m., was to walk up and down the main street in the middle of a multitude of other people who were doing the same, to meet and chat with friends.

I recall that at this time I was strongly influenced by the father of a good friend. He was an architect, and, through him I came to know several people in that profession. My enthusiasm for architecture was aroused when I marveled over the intricate drawings that he was doing. Some of the most simple elements of the profession became familiar to me. All careers appeared very exciting, primarily the fascination of new knowledge, and the search for different goals left no doubts regarding the pursuit of a higher education.

Medicine, of course, was one strong consideration; I thought of it as a rewarding career because of the great satisfaction that Father derived from it, more than because of my actual knowledge or information about the profession.

Luis, my future husband, whom I dated off and on, was still a very good friend; he, together with my father, influenced my decision. Architecture would give me the opportunity to translate my creativity into reality. Painting was my hobby and mathematics my favorite subject.

Universities in Argentina are not organized as in the United States: there are no campuses; colleges are sprinkled all over the city. I lived at home while attending college. The choice of fields to select from is very much the same as in the United States, and in all of them, women and men are accepted with no sex distinction. There are, of course, some fields that tend to attract a larger number of women than do others. Women are usually found in large numbers in the fields of law, philosophy, dentistry, biology, chemistry, medicine, and architecture. My decision, then, was not unusual.

The universities are organized into colleges of specialized fields. There are no liberal arts schools and no transfers of credits. My curriculum was divided into a six-year program, with no electives, and was devoted only to subjects related to architecture: mathematics, history of architecture, structure, mechanical and electrical, building system, and so on. All examinations there are oral, although for some subjects, there are also written ones.

The universities were a significant political influence during my college years. When I entered college in 1953, Argentina was living under the increasingly intolerable rule of a dictatorial government led by Juan Peron. This government had spawned corruption not only in affairs of state but also in business and education. This led to the development of a strong underground movement of which my husband and I were a part.

In fact, most college students were either actively engaged in the rebellion or at least provided passive support; very few students were Peronists. At the risk of expulsion from college and even at the risk of their lives, students let their discontent be heard. We printed newspapers, pamphlets, and posters, and wrote our message on walls all over the country. Our aim was to inform the public of the hidden realities of our universities. Most professors with tenure had refused to join the Peronist Party and had therefore summarily been relieved of their positions. They were replaced by incompetent Peronists. Freedom of speech was curtailed; the press, radio, and television were under government control. The Peronist Party was the only one accepted. There was no room for opposition, not only in the political field, but also in education. Father lost his teaching position in the School of Medicine because he refused to join the party.

In September, 1955, the Peron regime collapsed, and today the country, after almost 20 years, is still slowly trying to find some political, social, and economic stability. The harm done was not only the emptying of the national treasury, but also the creation of an entire generation of young people who were brainwashed into a false sense of Utopia in which all their physical needs would be provided by the government in a classless society without the expenditure of any effort on their part.

Shortly after this, Luis, my husband today, became my steady date. He was practicing in Buenos Aires and planning to come to the United States for a few additional years of training. This meant losing him. So in three months, and though I still had three more years to go for my college degree, we were married. Knowing how much my work meant to me, he reassured me of his help. We lived for three years in the United States, a country that, for the first year, certainly didn't appear to be as glamorous as I had expected.

It was a difficult adjustment, brought about by a combination of factors: the new life-pattern of marriage to a stupendous person, who spent 90% of his time in the hospital, fighting his own battle of adjustment; loneliness, in surroundings that did not have the luxury of my home; and the responsibility of running a house with no staff.

Luis' day was spent in the hospital; for him it was a different kind of adjustment, because he spoke very little English. Patiently he coped with his problem and mine, but the difficulties became further complicated when, after three months, I became pregnant. To return to the security and tranquility of Argentina at that time, however, would have been an admission of defeat, which I could not accept.

I found a job in a architectural office as a draftsman. I must add that I never had any difficulty getting a job. Initially my duties did not involve great responsibility, but later, when it was evident that I was very serious about the profession, I was given a great many opportunities.

We remained in Detroit for two years longer. More adjusted, we could profit greatly from the array of alternatives we found to expand our field.

As we had planned, we returned to Argentina and remained there for three years, during which time I completed my education. Meanwhile, my husband was searching for a place in which he could apply his newly acquired specialization, but since Argentina was not ready for such highly trained specialists, we returned to the United States.

Again, it was Detroit, but we were older and already in familiar territory, and things worked out much better. The adjustment was less painful. I worked in one of the largest architectural firms in the country for three years and was given ever-increasing responsibility. The firm has broad hiring policies, since they recognize that they too profit from the varied backgrounds of their people.

At that time my mother-in-law, then a widow, came to live with us. Since then she spends 80% of her year with us. A superb woman, who despite her different outlook on life, accepts my life-pattern and in all possible ways tries to take off my shoulders the everyday, mundane decisions, she is now definitely a part of our lives; our relationships are peaceful, since we three enjoy the great comforts of her love and thoughtfulness.

When we moved to Grand Rapids, I joined a small firm of five architects. After working with 500 specialists, I had to see the profession from another point of view. I worked with this group for five years, doing primarily design. During this time my contact with clients increased, with almost no unfavorable response. I recall only one with whom I could not communicate, and he was very short! (I am tall.) This direct client relationship gave me a professional maturity that I had previously lacked, and this helped me to extend my activities beyond office work. I am deeply involved in the planning of the city in which I live; I am active in the local chapter of the American Institute of Architecture, and now also in the National Institute of Architecture.

Being a woman in a liberal profession is really an asset; it opens doors that a man with the same background would find difficult. People remember you and find you stimulating company. It seems that so very little is expected from us that our level of "success" is achieved with little effort. The small town doesn't curtail my activities, perhaps because I always try to be just me. From the day we arrived we brought with us a certain philosophy and way of life. I did not change my philosophy of the consistency of my life activities in order to adapt to the more conservative standard of the community. As might be expected, there was criticism. I did not pay attention to it, and not doing so paid off. There is little room for mistakes; it takes hard work, long hours in the office, time to give something back to the city that welcomed you, time for your family and a very busy husband, who doesn't demand much. There is teenage daughter who looks at me more as her best friend than a mother. Also, I must find time to be just me, doing the things in which I can just give—pour out some of my uncontrolled, impractical, senseless creativity. Painting gives me the release, the opportunity to do, with no plan and no explanation.

I inadvertently convey to my daughter, very strongly sometimes, some of the basic elements of my philosophy of life. In many ways she reflects some of my actions, but, as is to be expected, in other ways she reacts against it. We are good friends; there is a great line of communication; no subject is taboo. I feel she enjoys having a mother who is different; she sometimes basks in this small glory. She is extremely independent and very much at ease with all age groups. As an only child, she is an active participant in our leisure hours.

Although my daughter and I are a very important part of my husband's life, he is absolutely devoted to his profession, to which he gives the best of himself with a great deal of success, success not only measured by money. That, though important, is certainly not his primary concern; rather, it is the achievement of his goal. Very well informed in all subjects, he is the epitome of a man who knows where he's going. Even-tempered, he always finds time to make this party or that meeting. Time is very relative to him, so there is an abundance of hours devoted to the psychological well-being of his patients, who find in his word as much healing power as in his scalpel. In the six years we have been in this community, he has made of his hospital a well-known heart center. Patients come from all over Michigan; because of these accomplishments we are highly regarded. His constant support and understanding make my professional life very easy.

The daily contact between the three members of my family is sometimes very brief, but we find that long vacations together away from all of this, usually in some foreign country, give us the possibilities to touch base, to reevaluate our goals, and just to rejoice in each other's company.

The enviable financial security that my husband provides gives me a freedom of action that would otherwise not be possible. Released from the economic burdens, I can choose how and to what I am going to devote my talents and skills.

Knowing that my earnings are an extra to our income makes my approach to business very loose. On many occasions I share my talents and experiences without thinking that these are the wares that I have to sell. Business undoubtedly is not my forte, but now, running my own office will help me think in a more practical way. To this point in my career I have encountered but few restrictions in my practice, principle among which has been location. I cannot look for a more interesting job in another city, since my husband has first choice; however, I feel that even a small town gives enough opportunity and exposure to enable me to use my knowledge and fulfill my present goals. I must admit that the possibility of getting great commissions is curtailed because of my sex, a limitation brought forth by this society, which still sees the woman only in the role of homemaker. In Argentina, where traditionally this activity was hired out, women are active members of the professional community.

Presently I am working alone, sharing office space with other architects. Through an association with an architectural-engineering firm in Indiana, I have the opportunity to be involved in large jobs. This firm works primarily in precast concrete systems, and we are presently building two high-rise buildings in Grand Rapids.

When working with my colleagues or with contractors, or when supervising the job site, I have never encountered any resistance. Granted that at first the workmen are surprised to see a tall blond trotting through the mud, once I'm part of the team, my orders are accepted with respect.

My association with men is easier with those who are sure of themselves; others simply remain competitors. After all, we cannot be liked by everybody.

In my work I wear tailored clothing, but always very feminine. I find that it's not necessary to shout or to sprinkle my order with foul language, which is used constantly during our meetings. At the end, when somebody must make the final decision and assume the responsibility, there are not too many competitors.

During past years I have attended several seminars in Europe, studying city and land planning, a field in which I would like to devote my practice. I should like to expand my firm to a staff of approximately 20 professionals. This would allow me to get involved in larger jobs, and, on the other hand, still become personally involved in the creative part of the process, instead of being bogged down in the business part of the practice.

Occasionally the opportunity comes along to design a house. Although this requires a great deal of time, there is a tremendous personal satisfaction when you are able to translate the wishes of your clients into the proper environment in which they are going to live.

Unfortunately, there is no school of architecture in Grand Rapids, because I would very much like to complement my practice with teaching. Concurrent with my professional career, through all these years, I have continued my painting education, in classes both in the United States and Argentina. In addition to oil, I've become fairly proficient in watercolor, etching, engraving, and lithography. I have received several awards and mentions in state and local shows. I devote as many hours as I can find, always with the thought of achieving a certain mastery that will allow me to compare favorably in the rather close circle of the art world.

To work outside my home in a liberal profession implies extra effort but never a sacrifice, since this is what I want to do. If I could start all over again, my choice would be the same, but I would devote a few more years to study before starting to practice.

I had a need and searched for fulfillment. Selfishly, life approached this way is easy; but you must ask some sacrifice from the ones who will share it with you. On the other hand, you are better able to give in return, with all the richness and fullness of your accomplishments, in a relaxed and joyful personality.

There are no more frustrations for a woman in a job than for a man; we may have to try harder and are allowed fewer mistakes, but we get the job done.

My self-established rules of life are very strict. An urgency to do things and not lose time, and a need of continuity are impelling forces.

Now, unwilling, I seem to be part of the Women's Liberation Movement, a fact that I resent because I refuse to be bunched up under the heading "women" and then see all the things that I must be or do. There are no formulas and no advice, only that when I chose my way, I never thought that my sex made me different. It was not until I came to the United States that I realized that from a mundane architect, I was transformed into a pioneer.

CRYSTALLOGRAPHER

Isabelle L. Karle

Naval Research Laboratory
Washington, D. C. 20390

Background

My parents emigrated from Poland and settled in Detroit, Michigan, where I was born. They had very little formal education but were self-taught through reading a great deal, both in Polish and in English. My mother was a seamstress and my father a painter. They were thrifty and capable people who lived much better than people with comparable incomes because of good management and do-it-yourself projects. Although both came from large families, they limited their children to two. Even through the depression days, they managed to save enough money for vacations in the country and at the beaches in Michigan, to visit friends and relatives in Wisconsin, Minnesota, and Ontario, and even for a trip to Florida and to New York City.

We lived in a new suburb where the majority of people were immigrants, from a number of Europeon countries. Thus, by contact with neighborhood children, I was introduced to many European cultures. There was little opportunity to observe life as lived by American families whose forebears had lived in the United States for a longer time. Only Polish was spoken in my home. I learned to speak English in school. By the time I entered elementary school, my mother had already taught me to read and write in Polish and to do the basic operations in arithmetic. School work was interesting and easy, and I progressed rapidly. Fifteen and one-half years elapsed between my entering first grade and being awarded the Ph.D. degree.

My parents constantly encouraged my younger brother, who is now an engineer, and me in our school work, even though they understood very little about science. They would have preferred, at the time, that my goal in life would be teaching or law. My first encounter with chemistry was in high school. One year of science was required for a college preparatory course, and chemistry was chosen by chance. The subject fascinated me, and I decided to pursue the study of chemistry in college. When I mentioned my intentions to my high school chemistry teacher, he tried to discourage me by saying that chemistry was not a proper field for girls. I was awarded a four-year undergraduate scholarship to the University of Michigan and further augmented my finances by obtaining an assistantship in the chemistry department. Although I graduated with highest honors, I was not encouraged in graduate studies at the University of Michigan. The usual manner of supporting graduate students in chemistry, then as now, was by awarding teaching assistantships, and none were available in the chemistry department for girls; however, the American Association of University Women graciously awarded a fellowship to me, and the following year I received a Horace H. Rackham Fellowship. My financial problems were solved partly by good fortune, but mostly by being able to maintain a top-ranking scholarship position and to qualify for the few fellowships that were available.

While I was in graduate school, I married a fellow graduate student in chemistry. In 1946 we were seeking permanent professional positions. Although academia appealed to us, there were no opportunities for women in institutions with reasonable research facilities. We both joined the Naval Research Laboratory, a government institution. The decision has proved to be an excellent one. I have been well supported in research, given opportunities for development, encouraged to attend national and international meetings, and given the opportunity to present the results of my investigations, both in lectures and in publications.

Management of Career and Children

My husband and I have three daughters, born in 1946 (before the beginning of my career with the government), 1950, and 1955. From 1946 to 1959 we had live-in housekeepers for household duties, with emphasis on child care. The housekeepers were generally widowed women from the mountain regions of Virginia whose grown children had come to the Washington, D.C., area. One woman stayed with us for seven years, and the others, for periods of two years each. The eldest daughter began attending nursery school at age three and the youngest, at age four. They liked the companionship of many children, the activities of the schools, and the animals, including a goat, kept by the schools. The middle daughter preferred to stay at home with the housekeeper, who spent several hours a day reading to her.

Since 1959 we have managed without outside household help, except for a woman who comes to clean the house once a week. Accordingly, a reasonable amount of organization has been needed, as well as cooperation from all members of the family. My husband approved of my career and my professional aspirations and offered help with household duties. By nature, both of us are reasonably neat and orderly people, and the children are taught not to scatter their belongings. The children had small responsibilities, which increased with age. They were taught to look after each other's needs. Clothes, books, lunch money, and any other items needed for school were laid out the evening before, in order to avoid a rush in the morning. Clothing was selected with an eye toward minimum care. If the girls wanted blouses or dresses that required ironing, that was their own responsibility. Grocery shopping was limited to once a week, usually Thursday evening, when the supermarkets had already received their weekend supplies but before the markets became crowded with weekend shoppers. My husband selected all the meat and fish products, one of our daughters would select the staples, and I would choose the fresh produce and dairy products. A list is always kept in the kitchen, so that grocery items are recorded for the next shopping trip as they are used up.

Twenty years ago we purchased a plot of land in Virginia and had a house built of brick and thermally insulated aluminum windows for minimum maintenance. All the modern conveniences were included: automatic dishwasher, automatic clothes washer and dryer, garbage disposal, freezer, and oven with automatic controls. The latter is very important for preparing meals in absentia. A roast, potatoes, and/or casserole can be placed in the oven in the morning and the cooked food will be ready at the appointed hour in the evening. One daughter would prepare a salad and another one the dessert, and the youngest would set the table. The lake adjacent to the house has provided recreation such as swimming, boating, fishing, and ice-skating.

All members of the family have been quite healthy. Since there has been little illness, I have not had to spend time and energy in nursing duties. Although there has been adequate social life, I have not participated in bridge parties, bowling teams, women's social and philanthropic organizations, cocktail parties, or neighborhood coffee socials. Since many women in our neighborhood have careers such as teaching, nursing, economics, and so on, we understand each other's need for private time and are not offended by any superficial appearance of lack of neighborliness.

Relationship with Children

During the school year, I had restricted travel to one conference, in order not to be absent from home for too long a time. During the summers, as soon as the children reached the age of five, they have accompanied my husband and me to conferences held in various parts of the United States and in foreign countries. The children have been sufficiently independent and knowledgeable to occupy themselves with local museums, parks, and other activities while I was occupied with the business at hand. In this fashion, they have seen most of the United states and are familiar with half the countries in Europe.

Evenings have been and generally are spent at home with the children. My husband and I have always made ourselves available to them. When needed, help was offered with homework, school projects were discussed, their cultural education was augmented at home, and transportation was provided for evening activities. We have had many cooperative projects at home. The girls have become accomplished seamstresses, cooks, and home decorators.

Our daughters are now old enough so that some assessment can be made of the effect of their home life on their future careers. Each of the girls has been an excellent student. The eldest, who is married to a scientist, is in graduate school at the University of Washington, in Seattle. This summer she expects to complete her requirements toward a Ph.D. degree in physical chemistry. She has already published several scientific papers. Her interests and hobbies, however, encompass a rather wide field of activities. They include playing the piano and clavichord, hiking, ocean sailing, photography of alpine plants, archaeology, and local politics. The middle daughter is a graduate student at Duke University and has begun her research toward a Ph.D. degree in organic chemistry. She also is an author of several scientific publications. Her other interests include sailing, swimming, photography, knitting, and mathematics. The youngest daughter will be a senior in high school. She plans to study some field of science in college. She is otherwise occupied with gymnastics, swimming, and sewing, and being a student aide in the Guidance Office at school.

There is a close family spirit. The older girls visit home often. They write, keep in contact, and visit, when possible, with their surviving grandparents (who live in Detroit and New York), with other close relatives, and with each other.

Professional Relationships

Recognition in the laboratory and in the scientific community was dependent upon ability, perserverence and productivity in terms of scientific publications, oral presentations at technical meetings, and invitations to lecture nationally and internationally. In the laboratory I did not feel discriminated against because of sex. There was adequate support for my own research program and for travel to scientific conferences. My goals were directed toward being a research scientist. I have not desired and do not seek administrative positions.

In the scientific community in the field of crystal structure analysis, there have been a number of well-known female predecessors, including Dorothy Hodgkins (Nobel laureate), Kathleen Lonsdale (England), Caroline MacGillavry (Netherlands), and Dorothy Wrinch, Rose Mooney, and Elizabeth Woods (U.S.). These women have been professors or have held responsible research positions in their institutions. In addition, there are a number of active female contemporaries.

Thus the conclusion can be drawn that gender is not a particular problem, although recognition was accorded to these women somewhat more slowly than to their male counterparts. The main problems that arose in my career are common to scientists of both sexes who propose unusual or radical solutions to problems. Much perserverence was needed to prove that the innovations were correct in two different fields of structure analysis.

A large amount of current scientific work is collaborative, in which specialists from different disciplines each contributes his or her special knowledge and abilities to a common problem. My husband has been among my collaborators. We have found it convenient and profitable to divide our labors so that he contributes most of the theory, whereas I concentrate on the practical aspects of application. Currently, a large amount of collaboration exists with other institutions. In one recent problem concerned with the isolation, characterization, synthesis, and possible medical application of a South American frog venom, the cooperating scientists included a herpetologist from the Museum of Natural History in New York, and an organic chemist and biochemist from the National Institutes of Health in Washington and one from the University in Osaka (Japan), chemists involved in syntheses from the technical university in Zurich, (Switzerland), and a pharmacologist at the University of Rochester, as well as myself. Although my collaborators have generally been men, there has always been a spirit of friendly cooperation with no apparent sex discrimination. Among my younger associates at my laboratory, there are both young men and young women. At the beginning, my chief relationship with them had been that of an instructor, until they attained a level of independent research. Some have remained in our laboratory; others are now on the faculties of colleges and universities.

My advice to young women who are ambitious, capable, and truly interested in scientific work is to approach their education and their future scientific efforts with quiet determination but without belligerence. Quality leads to success in the long run, resulting in a firmly established basis for recognition. Demands for equality on the basis of sex without full qualification may bring temporary gains but will eventually prove to be a detriment to a complete acceptance of women in the scientific fields.

Employers should recognize that marriage and children are not necessarily deterrents to full-time careers for women. Many older women have managed successful careers along with gracious and satisfying private lives as wives and mothers. Increasing numbers of younger women appear to be succeeding in combining careers with the traditional role for women.

DISCUSSION

WILMA SCOTT HEIDE (*president, National Organization for Women, session chairman*): Whatever your intent, quite obviously you have been a role model, and, I suspect, for more than your daughters, as well as an excellent one. I am sure our audience would like to know what a crystallographer is, Dr. Karle.

DR. KARLE: A crystallographer is one who studies the interior of crystals, determining which atoms are connected to which, and how they are arranged with respect to each other in the crystal lattice. The work encompasses many fields and the results are used by many types of scientists — physicists, photochemists, and biochemists, for example.

MATHEMATICIAN

Marian Boykan Pour-El

School of Mathematics
University of Minnesota
Minneapolis, Minnesota 55455

As a woman mathematician — a mathematical logician — my existence apparently refutes a commonly held conviction. It is generally believed that a woman is not logical, but acts on the basis of intuition alone.

Why am I in this field? Because I like it. This was not considered sufficient reason for a woman to enter the mathematical field when I received my education. At that time a woman's goal was to marry and raise a family. She went to college primarily to meet her future husband and to obtain an education so that she could raise her family intelligently. Desire for financial security and status through marriage were additional considerations. To sum it up, it was quite clear that she conceived of her role in life as secondary to her husband's, her status achieved as a reflection of his status, her success dependent on his success and that of her children, particularly her male children. I know this because I went to a girls' high school and an all-girl college, where this was discussed many times. Although I did not emphasize it, I did not agree with this point of view. Nevertheless, I still had many good friends throughout my high school and college life. In fact, I acted as bridesmaid at their weddings.

This point of view, so prevalent during the fifties and early sixties, was reinforced when I went from an all-female environment to an all-male environment when I enrolled in Harvard University Graduate School. I recall very vividly my first day in class: three seats in front of me, three seats in back of me, and two seats on either side were left vacant. I was a complete pariah in that social setting. The reason was quite simple. The men were positively unable to interact with me. They were accustomed to dating girls and talking to them about sweet things and even speaking to them about more intellectual subjects such as politics, history, and sociology. But to converse about a purely masculine subject such as physics or mathematics as one equal to another was something they had not previously experienced.

The faculty members also were surprised at the presence of a woman in their midst, in spite of the fact that they had awarded me a fellowship. They had assumed, before I arrived, that I was some sort of misfit, a woman who was substituting mathematics for the normal womanly attributes leading to marriage and family rearing.

My first colloquium at Harvard University was a memorable event. The tea, which preceded the actual lecture, was held in the library and was a rather formal affair. As I entered, all eyes sank lower into the teacups in a great effort not to seem to notice me. Needless to say, no one talked to me at all. At the end of the tea the chairman flipped the light switch up and down as a signal for the colloquium to begin. As he did so he turned to me and said, with a twinkle in his eye, "Your presence is noted here."

It was not long before normal interactions between myself and my fellow students developed. We used to spend long hours at the graduate dining-hall table discussing a variety of topics, including mathematics. Every once in a while, someone would say, "Let's not study tonight, let's go to a movie," or "Let's go to a concert." I wanted the privilege, which all the men had, of making the same suggestions without seeming to ask for a date. So I insisted that I be allowed to pay my own way at all times. This was, of course, against the gallant habits of the men there, but they finally got the point, and many jokes were made as they laughingly tried to overrule me. This interaction also brought mutual respect for each other's mathematical abilities, which had no basis in sex. In a sense I was 'one of the boys' as far as mathematics was concerned. Yet they never forgot that I was a woman.

In the normal course of events, I married a biochemist and we had a child. We were still students, both studying for our Ph.D. degrees. Needless to say, our finances were extremely limited. I did all my own housework, my own cooking, and even my own washing. Oh yes, every once in a while I would lug my clothes to the local laundromat and have them done there. There was no dishwasher or washing machine.

My thesis was finished when our daughter was at the awkward age of two and a half, in 1958. My first position was that of assistant professor at a large State University. Thus I was initiated into the mathematical community and took part in its activities: research, teaching, and going to meetings. At my first few meetings I experienced the same phenomenon I had experienced with the men students at Harvard University. The men were unable to interact with me mathematically because they had no social practice in doing it. Gradually, after they noticed that I had research results that were of interest to them, they became interested in what I was doing as a colleague, and the fact that I was a woman played essentially no role in the relations between us.

Today I am completely assimilated in the mathematical community. My presence as a woman, although noticed, virtually plays no role in the professional relations between myself and my colleagues.

In the normal course of my mathematical life I have been invited by my colleagues to lecture at various institutions and at various international congresses. I have always been treated with the traditional respect. There is the talk, then the dinner, and afterwards, the party that goes with it. This party is usually given by the host and is organized by his wife. There has never been any friction or any estrangement in these situations, so far as I can remember.

This article may be conceived of as a mere summary. It touches only briefly upon my educational experiences and the scholarly interactions in my professional life. In particular, no attempt has been made here to discuss the problem of rearing a child, playing the role of wife, and interacting in the community — P.T.A., and so on. More generally, no analysis has been given of the careful investigations and deliberations that led me to the conclusion that the triple roles of mother, wife, and professional could be carried out successfully in a society alien to these ideas.

DISCUSSION

DR. POUR-EL: I might add that I have always wanted a career, as long as I can remember. I was unconcerned that there might be obstacles, and that some people might react in a negative way. I am still married, still have my child. In my professional life it has been advantageous for my husband to be in one place and for me to be in another. This year he is in Illinois and I am in Minnesota. A couple of years before that I was on an extended lecture tour in Europe for a whole year while he was in the United States. Before that, I was at the Institute for Advanced Study, he was in Pennsylvania. We don't like it — but we have done it. He respects my commitment as a professor of mathematics and I respect his work.

ELECTRICAL ENGINEER

Mildred S. Dresselhaus

Electrical Engineering Department and
Center for Materials Science and Engineering
Massachusetts Institute of Technology
Cambridge, Massachusetts 02139

I would consider my own life experience to be quite atypical for women who have "made it" in the fields of science and engineering. Nevertheless, looking back upon my history, it is clear that this atypical background has provided me with certain habits and attitudes that have been helpful in my professional life.

I come from a background of extreme poverty and disadvantage. My parents were immigrants who had little education or understanding of the possibilities of life in America. They came to the United States as to a land of opportunity, and their two children were raised with that concept as a guiding principle. I found out early enough that in this country, opportunities did present themselves — perhaps unexpectedly and in singular fashion — but opportunity was present, and one had to take the initiative to find these opportunities and to exploit them. This attitude has proved very helpful to me and has provided me with a positive, constructive, and rather pragmatic approach to life. There is nothing in life that is impossible to accomplish; it is largely a matter of effort and perserverance that produces results.

Life in the ghettos of New York City was difficult during the years of the depression. I can remember clearly the times I had only one set of clothes and went to bed at night not fully fed. From this experience I learned not to expect much from life. If you want something to happen, you must go out and perservere. This background also provided me with an appreciation for hard work. The most difficult job I ever had in my life was teaching a mentally retarded child to read and write. I was eleven years old at the time and worked three hours a day, five days a week for 50¢ a week. What I am most proud of today is that I stuck to this job for the whole school year. As I got older, I worked in factories and sweat shops. Since I was always under the legal working age, I had to suffer a great deal of personal abuse as well as a very low pay rate. Nevertheless, I always tried to do my best on the job, no matter how difficult or unpleasant the work. I needed the paycheck, and I wanted to succeed in whatever I tried, for my own personal satisfaction. I learned a great deal from these work experiences. I came to realize at an early age that an education was imperative to overcome this poverty syndrome. Although I had no idea what sort of work I wanted to do in later life, one thing I did learn was that factory work was not for me. All this work experience also taught me a great deal about utilizing my time effectively.

One other factor that influenced my early life was my musical education. My older brother was bestowed with a remarkable intellect and musical talent. At the age of 3½ he took his first violin lessons at a neighborhood settlement house, and he was so outstanding that everyone wanted to teach him. By the age of six he was playing concertos with community orchestras. As a consequence of his success, his music teachers were anxious to teach me, too. Although I did not have quite as much talent as he did, it was adequate to enable me to have a very extensive musical education at no cost to my family. Through this musical education, I came in contact with children from the "other side of the tracks," and learned how people of the middle class lived. These other children and their parents became my role models and raised my aspiration level.

As a consequence of my desire to climb out of the confines of my ghetto environment, I aspired to gain entrance to the only good school that was available to me — Hunter College High School, a special school for talented girls in the Greater New York area. No girl from my junior high school had ever passed the entrance exam, and the teachers laughed at me for even thinking of applying. I never worried too much about what people said and, if anything, discouragement from well-meaning people always left me with increased determination to succeed in things that were supposed to lie beyond me. At any rate, in school, my job, and music school, I found bits of time here and there for study. Without really knowing what I was doing, I prepared myself for the entrance exam completely on my own. My achievement in passing the entrance examination to Hunter College High School is the greatest achievement in my life, and everything since then has been easy. In passing the exam, I earned a perfect score on the mathematics portion. This accomplishment meant a great deal for my self-confidence.

My first few months at Hunter High were an uphill struggle. I worked like a Trojan to overcome the handicap of years of ghetto schooling. When exam papers came back with grades below zero and filled with derogatory comments, my fighting spirit was aroused. It was not long before good papers started coming back, and I was in the top group of my class. Before the end of my first year at Hunter High, I was clearly a highly respected math-science student. There were other uphill battles along the path of life, but in some of these later battles, never did I have doubts about my ability to succeed.

My high school days were happy days. I loved the intellectual stimulation of this wonderful school and was completely happy doing my daily routine — school, my job, music school. I gave no serious thought to a professional career. Because of my very modest circumstances, the school guidance counselor offered me no career counseling, nor did I seek such counseling. Perhaps others would have found such treatment discriminatory with respect to socioeconomic class structure, but I accepted it. Even without guidance, I had many attractive college offers coming in the mail, but I could not exploit any of these for lack of means. None of this worried me in the least. I had decided to go to Hunter College, to which my high school was attached, and that seemed good enough for me. I was going to major in elementary school teaching, and to me at the time, this seemed to be a realistic and rewarding goal in life. All the wonderful things that have subsequently happened to me have just been like frosting on a lovely cake.

My professional career can be said to have started with freshman physics. My performance in that class impressed my teacher enough so that she, on her own, started to offer me professional counseling. She suggested that a career in science would be more suitable than elementary school teaching; this professor maintained an interest in me throughout my undergraduate days at Hunter College and broadened my horizons by many orders of magnitude. While at Hunter College, I took essentially every course that was offered in physics, chemistry and mathematics. These courses were not very sophisticated or advanced, and were in many ways an inadequate preparation for a top-flight graduate school program; however, I didn't find this shaky preparation a serious obstacle in my career. Being a star at a less prestigious woman's college had its benefits in terms of guidance, encouragement, and financial reward. In fact, I earned enough money as an undergraduate to pay not only all undergraduate costs, but also enough savings to finance most of my graduate education. At the time, I didn't realize that a graduate education would not cost me anything.

As for encouragement, it came from many directions. Of particular significance were some kind words said to me by a famous woman mathematician who spoke at my college graduation. I was very much impressed that she singled me out to tell me these kind words.

The people at Hunter College were very supportive and encouraging, and rather pushed me into the "big time." From Hunter College I was awarded a Fulbright Fellowship to study for a year at the Cavendish Laboratory in Cambridge University, England. For someone whose experience hardly extended beyond the confines of New York City, this opportunity was so far beyond expectations that I had real difficulty in comprehending what was happening to me. I was determined to take full advantage of this magnificent opportunity and to succeed at a major university. I worked hard at Cambridge and had a great time, both professionally and socially. I used this year to overcome some inadequacies in preparation and to learn what science was all about. I found that I could compete successfully with the very talented people at Cambridge. Being an American helped greatly with the social side of life; my strong liberal arts background and my extensive musical education disguised my humble background, which would have otherwise been a serious obstacle in the class-conscious England of the early 1950's.

From Cambridge, England, I went to Cambridge, Massachusetts, to study at Radcliffe College, and it was here that I completed most of my graduate coursework in physics. My study at Radcliffe was very rewarding; the professors were outstanding and encouraging. In my class at Radcliffe was Laura Roth, who has since then developed into a most distinguished woman solid state physicist. There was no question that we two girls could take care of ourselves, both academically and socially. For personal reasons, I left Radcliffe after one year with an A.M. degree to continue my studies at the University of Chicago, which at that time was perhaps the top physics school in the world.

My career at Chicago was intellectually most stimulating. Being a woman always seemed to help my career, insofar as I was more easily identified by the men professors and students, and special opportunities somehow used to arise because of my sex. At the University of Chicago there were a number of outstanding women faculty members: Maria Mayer, Margaret Burbidge, Leona Marshall. Women students had gone through the mill before me, and had been successful. Being a woman and of exactly the same age as Nella Fermi (Enrico Fermi's daughter) resulted in my becoming very friendly with the Fermis; through the Fermis I became acquainted with many other inspiring professors. Because the University of Chicago was in such a rough neighborhoood, the university people were very warm and friendly, and this probably also helped students to feel at home.

I developed a great deal of professional independence and self-confidence at the University of Chicago because of its emphasis on individual and independent thesis research. Although my thesis advisor was totally unsympathetic to career women, this had very little effect on me, because I did my thesis work pretty much on my own with essentially no help from him. This was not particularly a matter of planning; it just happened that way. I started working on a problem on the high frequency behavior of a superconductor in a magnetic field and there was nobody around that could provide me with much help. So I had to depend on myself, which was fine with me. Consequently, I really felt like a professional when I was still a graduate student. This was also partly due to the success I had experienced as a teaching assistant in the elementary physics course.

My teaching career started with my first job, that of teaching a mentally retarded child to read and write. Throughout high school and college, I did a vast amount of tutoring. In those years, I tutored anything that was needed and was very successful at it. This work not only provided me with a plush income but gave me extensive teaching experience. When there was a need for a teaching assistant at the University of Chicago, I volunteered because of my own interest, and not for any financial reward. I loved this job and was especially good at it. It helped my ego to have all these men students coming to my recitation sections rather than to sections run by the male teaching assistants. I found that I could be natural, friendly, and relaxed with men students. This experience turned out to be very valuable later on.

When I took my Ph.D. degree at Chicago, I had all kinds of professional opportunities. I have no idea whether the men had better opportunities than I did, but I could, basically, choose what I wanted to do. I decided to go to Cornell University as a National Science Foundation postdoctoral fellow for personal reasons. It was at this time that I married Gene Dresselhaus, a theoretical solid state physicist who was a junior faculty member at Cornell. During the two years at Cornell I did some research and undergraduate teaching, but my performance was not outstanding. During that period my first child arrived. I was, in part, learning how to manage a family and career, and I never did get things organized particularly well. Because it was clear that both my husband and I didn't have a promising professional future at Cornell, we decided to go to a place where both of us could get good jobs and do research work together.

We found such an opportunity at the MIT Lincoln Laboratory. My seven years at Lincoln Lab proved to be the most productive years of my research career. The research facilities here were excellent, and I was given a great deal of encouragement and support. These were years when the children were coming thick and fast; my four children came in less than five years. By working on a number of research problems with my husband, the mechanics of running an active research career and a home were easily solved. Dr. Benjamin Lax, who headed the solid state division at Lincoln Lab, had a very enlightened view toward women scientists and was very proud to have both Laura Roth and me in his research group.

Although women were treated very well at Lincoln, there was one constant source of harassment that Laura and I faced, and that had to do with our working hours. Nobody doubted that we were among the most hardworking and productive people in the lab, but, we always arrived at least one hour late for work because of our commitments to our young children. Although this time-clock routine was very irritating to me, I refused to change my ways. This was going to be my life-style, and the administrators had to accept it. If they thought they could manage my life better than I did, I told them I would switch jobs with them for a while! Laura took this harassment very personally and, before long handed in her resignation. This must have been a terrible blow to Lincoln Laboratory, because I don't think they ever again did get such a talented and productive scientist to join their staff.

Some of my research activities brought me to the MIT campus and to the National Magnet Lab. As a result of this interaction with the solid state research groups on campus, I was offered a visiting professorship in the Electrical Engineering Department under the auspices of the Abby Rockefeller Mauzé chair. To me this was an unbelievably wonderful opportunity, and I though I would try the life of a professor for a year in order to see what it was like and, in general, to have a good time. I was fortunate in having an active research program in progress, and this gave me some time to do other things. There seemed to be a need for a more comprehensive solid state graduate course and I began to teach such a course.

I sensed a need for an interdepartmental student research seminar in the solid state area and organized that, too. I got much student support and enthusiasm for these efforts. In addition, I ran a little discussion group for women students that addressed itself to problems faced by career women. I really loved this year at MIT, and I suppose that my enthusiasm attracted the attention of some of the important people of the department. I have always felt that the department could have found a more talented person than I for the job, but the Electrical Engineering Department did offer me a permanent job when the visiting appointment expired, and I accepted with humility and the determination to prove that they had not made a bad investment in me. Never in my life did I put forth so much effort into my job; fortunately, it was a labor of love. People everywhere seemed appreciative of my efforts, and this provided me with the motivation to continue in the same zealous way. I have been completely happy and content with everything I have been doing these last four and one-half years as a professor of electrical engineering — directing a fairly extensive research group of graduate students, teaching graduate courses, running the research seminar, doing service around MIT, and so on.

Very recently a new opportunity presented itself: becoming associate department head of Electrical Engineering. This position, being second in command in a very prestigious department of 100 faculty and nearly 1,100 students, was not anything I had ever imagined myself capable of doing. Nevertheless, when the opportunity presented itself and I was asked to serve, I did not refuse. I felt I could never refuse my services to a department that had been so considerate and trusting. I furthermore felt that this was an opportunity to do something for women at MIT. This is the position I currently hold.

While at MIT, I have felt a need to serve our women undergraduate and graduate students. My earliest effort was in the form of a discussion group. I had about ten student participants in this group. It may have been useful to them; at least, they came back, week after week, for more. When the year was over, I tried a new approach to women's affairs and became active in the undergraduate women's admission program. The years that I worked on this program saw a huge increase in the number of women applicants and admissions. This admission committee work turned out not only as serving the women students, but as having an impact on the whole admissions policy at MIT. After a few years of this, I turned again to a more interactive participation in women's affairs. With the doubling of women students during the time I had been at MIT, it seemed that various women's problems were developing. To identify the problems and to suggest solutions, I started a Women's Forum. This forum has enjoyed extraordinary popularity and has provided women with a new feeling of community and awareness. The seriousness of purpose of this forum has drawn the attention of the entire MIT community to women's affairs. I anticipate that this forum will have an important and constructive impact on the MIT scene.

The above description of my life experience deals with the most essential factors. I cannot say that I face any unique problems in the profession because of gender. I love my work intensely and am thankful for the opportunity to pursue my profession. I am and have always been well respected by my colleagues, both men and women. Social situations seldom present obstacles, since I have learned over the years how to take the initiative with men who are startled to find that they must deal with a woman in authority. I have learned how to appear technically competent, yet feminine, and how to get away with it. My marriage has been an exceedingly happy one. My husband is deeply interested and supportive of my career, and my children have also been raised to enjoy the benefits of a working mother. They are ardent enthusiasts of the MIT day camp, of the swimming pool, of the skating rink, all of which they consider fringe benefits for them because of my professional position. They are enthusiastic about the exciting and extensive travel opportunities my career has provided for them. To manage my home, I have had the same baby-sitter for nearly 11 years to care for the needs of the children while I am gone. This woman is thoroughly dependable, loving, and devoted. She has been a most satisfactory mother substitute in every way. She too loves her job and my children and is in a very real sense a part of our family. When I must work on a lecture or on a paper, my children always offer a helping hand in getting the household chores done quickly. I spend three hours each evening interacting intensively with my children. One activity that takes most of this time is our extensive musical commitment, and I personally assist each child daily with practice on his string instrument, my husband taking charge of the supervision of piano practice. I would say that my children have gained more than they have lost because of my professional career; they seem like a happy enough bunch.

As for personal ambition, I can only say that what I am doing now is vastly more exciting than anything I could ever imagine as a child; my accomplishments have gone greatly beyond my aspirations. My salary as a professional has always far exceeded my needs, and consequently my salary has been of little interest to me; I really work for love, and not for money. My salary is, I am sure, comparable with that of men of my age and in my position. My husband has no particular interest in money or in my salary. I am exceedingly happy about the outcome of my life; I would find it hard to think of additional desires, except perhaps for a 30-hour day! I cannot honestly say that I ever sacrificed anything for my career. I always did pretty much what I wanted to do, subject to family obligations, which have always come first. I do not feel any conflict of interest between family and career, since I always think of them as an integrated package.

My advice to women starting careers and to women in careers is: Relax, enjoy every moment of life, act and be yourself, exploit every opportunity that comes your way, stick up for yourself, arrange your personal affairs so that you can succeed in your professional activities. My advice to the men associated with professional women is: Act supportively and encouragingly to your women colleagues; invite them to share in the action and in the social life of the group; do not assign a woman a job that is so difficult that few men would succeed at it; nor should she be assigned a job that she is not qualified to do. Men should consult with women directly about women's affairs, and should not assume to know all the answers prior to such consultation.

In conclusion, I doubt that my story provides much insight into what it takes to be a success in science or engineering. All the hardships that I encountered in early life provided me with the determination, capacity for hard work, efficiency, and positive outlook on life that have been so helpful to me in realizing my professional career.

PHYSICIST

Betsy Ancker-Johnson

Seattle, Washington 98124
The Boeing Company and The University of Washington

With considerable hesitancy, I have decided that the best way for me to address the topic of women in physics is to say frankly what it is like to be a member of this tiny minority. I would prefer to wait until I have retired before speaking out so personally (or to do so anonymously, a feat that is rather difficult as a panel member), for the obvious reason that I should like to be known, if I'm known at all, for my contributions to physics research, teaching and management, and not for being "a woman in physics." Problems, however, are seldom solved by delay, nor is it admirable to let someone else take the brunt of this type of publicity, a type which I'm sure 99.9% of you would avoid in the absence of compelling reasons for being in this limelight. So, I'll be personal and frank.

My undergraduate years at Wellesley College, during which I became increasingly fascinated with physics, were idyllic. No professor, either male or female, ever told me a woman can't think analytically. It did happen that some of my MIT and Harvard dates, upon learning of my major and my interest in going to graduate school, dutifully informed me that my chances of finding a husband were nil. Since I wasn't husband hunting, contrary to the assumption of these dates and of so many other egotistical men I was to meet later, I wasn't alarmed or deterred. It occurred to me later that I might have done these men some good if I had said what I was thinking: "Buddy, who wants one like you!"

As a result of this idyllic climate for learning, I was totally unprepared psychologically for what followed. I chose a German university for graduate work, partly because my interests were (and are) much broader than physics (e.g. cultures and peoples alien to me, Christianity at home and abroad, art, architecture) and partly for reasons I can't even explain well to myself, such as love of adventure and my guardian angel's making special plans for my future. I'll explain these plans later.

During my first year of graduate school, what seemed to me like an infinite number of professors, teaching assistants, and colleagues, none of whom were women, told me that women can't think analytically and I must therefore, be husband hunting. Consequently, I was never involved in the informal study groups that graduate students form and find so very helpful in the learning process. By the time I had made friends with fellow students who accepted me for what I was, another student, I was past that stage. The resultant discouragement was as great as or greater than any I've known since; hence the solid determination with which I emerged with my Ph.D. to go on in research. It needed to be solid, because it seems that a woman in physics must be at least twice as determined as a man with the same competence, in order to achieve as much as he does.

You may be thinking that my graduate school experience was extreme. It is true that being a foreign student has its special trials, but for me it had a special advantage: being strange because I was an American occasionally overshadowed my being a "weirdo" because I was a woman studying, of all things, experimental physics. Don't be fooled: blatant prejudice is no harder to bear than covert. The essentially universal experience of your female colleagues, my esteemed male

---

* A talk prepared as a contribution to the "Panel on Women in Physics," at the Annual Meeting of the American Physical Society, New York, N. Y., 1971.

colleagues, includes unnecessary, painful periods of isolation and suffering from the stereotype many of you have regarding women.

Since finishing graduate school I have been employed by two universities and three industrial research laboratories. Along the way, I've acquired a husband and four children and five German "little sisters" (in series, not parallel!) who have cared for our brood during my absences. Let me begin with the jobs. I'm lucky enough to have one, even now, or at least I did on Monday, when I talked on the phone with my boss. But let me tell you what it was like to job-hunt as a new, female Ph.D. in physics. There were openings galore (imagine that, you younger colleagues!) and arranging interviews was trivial, but the jobs I was offered were second-rate. I desperately wanted to do research, not to help somebody write his handbook, or the like. My record was good; why was I having so much trouble even being interviewed for the right kind of opening? Those of you who have recently obtained your Ph.D.'s or who have been laid off and can't find suitable jobs can understand something of my frustration — *except* that I wasn't being treated like everyone else in my set. I was in a special subset that employers had decided was not dependable; i.e., a woman will marry and quit, and what is invested in her goes down the drain. Not one interviewer ever leveled with me; I had to bring up the subject of my sex to get the issue into the open. This was the worst prejudice I've ever encountered. In graduate school the psychological put-downs were hard to bear, but I was allowed to study. As a job-hunter I was not being given an opportunity to show I could succeed, and not even being told why the opportunity was being withheld. How can you solve a problem you can't get your teeth into?

The University of California, Berkeley, study[1] on the status of their academic women says, "The attrition rate among women once established on the academic ladder is less than that for men." A survey of women engineers in industry[2] shows they are paid less than their male counterparts, usually with the old excuse that they'll catch a man and quit. The same survey shows that most male engineers leave their first jobs within three years, presumably for a better one, and the turnover rate is lower for women. Since the excuse for discrimination is clearly not grounded in fact, it must be viewed as another example of male chauvinism.

Obviously, I found an employer who was willing to take the risk I represented, but my first job was a nonladder academic one of the kind to which women are so frequently relegated. But I'm not knocking it; as a first job it was all right, much like a postdoctoral.

With time it became easier to convince employers that I was an acceptable risk. But by then I was job-hunting as part of a couple. Now everybody knows that a many-body problem is much harder to solve than a single particle problem. Job-hunting as a couple can be extremely difficult, even in a seller's market. The University of Chicago department chairmen were asked[3] about this, and here is what the investigating commission learned: "The cases are increasing where the acceptance of an academic appointment by a man hinges on a job for his wife. Chairmen themselves have been and presumably will continue to be the most motivated and talented employment agents in such situations. There is also a small but growing number of cases where a woman is sought and her husband must be accommodated. (The latter instances are probably more frequent than is immediately apparent. They may not materialize as 'cases' because chairmen, following a practice unlike the one they follow in the case of a man, may hesitate to offer an appointment to a woman unless a position for her husband is already in prospect.) The subtlety of this practice is well illustrated by one chairman's comments about a prominent woman scholar in his field whom he would like to have on his faculty. He reported that the department had never even considered trying to recruit her because they assumed that her husband, also an academic, would not want to move.

"In instances where it is a woman who is wanted, it is not unkown that a chairman is worried about precipitating a family crisis should the husband receive a less satisfactory offer than his wife. We assume that the cultural norms in this connection are in flux. Although chairmen and deans must be responsive to the human needs in each situation, we suggest that the chairmen make sure to consult the woman in each such instance, lest he foreclose his recruiting opportunities and lose talent for the university by presuming in advance what the woman's, or her husband's, response will be.

"Beyond this, the committee urges chairmen and deans to put forth the same effort when it is a married woman who is being recruited as when it is a married man, and that chairmen's talent as employment agents for spouses be exercised as vigorously in the one direction as in the other."

That, at least, is a good beginning, but I think part of that comment is insulting to husbands who, after all, chose as wives the able women under discussion. These men are of such a caliber that they hardly need to be protected from "family crises," or whatever, by chairmen and deans, as this report implies.

As I said, it became easier, with time, to convince employers that I was an acceptable risk, but trauma still lay ahead. I had my first baby as an industrial research physicist, and it was an unnecessarily unpleasant experience. My private life was delved into by half-a-dozen executives in interviews that no one should have to endure. Finally, I was told, perhaps in jest, that the decision to lay me off over my protest went all the way to the Board of Directors of this large corporation. I'm sure you will all agree that nothing is so conducive to success in research as having a group of people pry into your personal affairs. I wasn't even allowed to enter the laboratory building for three months before the birth to hear a talk or get a book out of my private collection without special permission of the laboratory director. In order to understand something of how I felt, a member of the majority would have to have an advanced case of leprosy.

My colleagues, I will say in your support, apparently did not think my ability to do physics had been temporarily or permanently damaged by pregnancy. Just before I was laid off, one dropped by to discuss something that required my getting a sample off the back of a very low shelf. As I got up, puffing, I said, "It's a good thing you didn't ask me for this after I gained another pound." He replied that I shouldn't eat so much lunch. My startled expression and patting my profile made this grandfather recall what he knew about the birds and bees. The incident reassured me that pregnancy is not damaging to the brain, so I wrote a paper at home while laid off. Also in defense of the majority, my boss hired me as a part-time consultant during those three months and promptly rehired me when I returned two or three weeks after the baby arrived.

My second baby was born while I was employed in a research lab of another industry, one that possessed considerably more enlightened management. My paycheck stopped eight weeks before expected delivery (a company rule) and resumed six weeks after (a state law). However, no one cared that I went right on working. On a Friday shortly before I expected the baby, I was having a wonderful time tracking down an apparently new effect. Because it wasn't clear just what parameters influenced these oscillations and I couldn't produce them at will, I suggested to my willing technicians that we carry on Saturday while we had the effect. Saturday morning I went to the hospital instead of the lab, and a couple of weeks later, sure enough, the elusive oscillations were not to be found, but never mind; other equally fascinating effects were found. I must say I thought it a bit perverse, though, when the wife of one of my assistants had a baby a few weeks later and he was given a week's leave *with pay*.

Yes, a woman physicist suffers some prejudice. On the other hand, I've certainly had my fair share of opportunities. Furthermore, I wouldn't be giving a fair picture if I didn't tell you that sometimes prejudice works in reverse. Let me illustrate by describing some of my relations with machine shops, clearly a vital link in any experimental program. In graduate school, I think I got parts faster than my colleagues because I was a novelty. Shortly after starting my first job, a colleague offered me a cigar when he became a father, with an intentionally depreciating comment like, "Oh, I forgot about you." I took the cigar and later in the day swapped it for a well-smoked butt. This I stuck between my teeth and marched into the shop. The machinists gaped, and the head rushed to me, yelling, "You're costing us hundreds of dollars — these machines are running past the tolerances!" He had his exaggeration and I had my amused machinist friends, who, I daresay, gave me what I needed a bit ahead of my uppity colleague.

On another occasion, I thought I was really wiped out on my first day at another job when my immediate supervisor and I met. (His boss had hired me.) He told me the last woman they'd had (during World War II, and not well prepared) had asked a machinist for a brass piece $2 \times \frac{3}{4} \times \frac{1}{4}$ inches, plane and parallel to one thousandth. After two weeks, when he finally had a sample within tolerance and urged her over the telephone to come quickly and get it, she said upon seeing it: "Oh, it's lovely. Now would you please cut it in half." That story passed through the building with the speed of sound, and its half-life — well, for all I know there hasn't been enough decay yet for the half-life to be estimated. After this painful interview, the only thing to do was take direct action. I got a colleague to introduce me at once to the machinist who was to do my work. After a little conventional chitchat, I said, "Say, the first thing I need is a brass piece $2 \times \frac{3}{4} \times \frac{1}{4}$ inches, plane and parallel to a thousandth." We eye-balled each other for several seconds while his memory flipped through its storage and then he roared. I was one of the few physicists the machinists let use the machines for little jobs, a privilege that saved me lots of time. Seldom can a member of the majority capitalize on an error made by one of his group; the error is hardly noticed. I think you'll all agree with me, though, when I say that ideal conditions for doing research seldom exist under a microscope. And surely a researcher shouldn't be put into a position where he is afraid to make some mistakes.

So much for jobs. As I said, along the way I've acquired a family and a series of young German girls as babysitters. Now you see an unplanned benefit of my choosing Germany for graduate work and making friends there. These German girls didn't dream of traveling to the U.S. until offered the opportunity to join our family for two years. Each, it is fair to say, has given and received much through the experience. Without the assurance that my children were being competently and lovingly cared for in my absences, sometimes for weeks at a time, I could never have made the commitment necessary for research. Alas, this method of child care is no longer possible because of the new immigration law, which, in my opinion, should be modified to leave this avenue of child care open. I have no idea how I'd arrange child care if I still had preschoolers. I believe this is the most difficult barrier to serious careers for women. No one should be forced into the position of having to choose between children and career. Obviously there are times when a child essentially consumes his parents, e.g. during a serious illness, and everyone, including employers, are understanding of such problems. It is quite another matter, however, if a constant, nagging worry about the welfare of her or his children incapacitates the concentration anyone requires to be a physicist.

And now, finally, about the husband — last in this list of topics but not least. My husband is man enough not to be threatened by his wife's awareness of electrons; indeed, he takes for granted that her interest in them can be just as deep as his in differential geometry, without its adversely affecting her femininity nor disqualifying her for the role of wife and mother. Clearly his attitude and encouragement have played a key part in making possible the life I lead. Through the years I've met more men of his caliber. And I'm delighted to observe, from the Berkeley report, that some exist there. Let me give you two short comments made by such men:[4]

"The university nepotism rules bar her employment here, and so she is consigned to a job vastly inferior in all ways, though her qualifications are equal or superior to my own . . . and better than many of the people the department does hire."

"She is employed here, at a lower level than in her previous position and in a 'temporary' position . . . . She has no facilities for research or support for research here and is forced to use my lab, where she has an established reputation as an independent investigator."

Our four children range in age from eight to twelve years. (Incidentally, they have necessitated my taking about eight weeks of actual leave from research, five for delivering and three following simultaneous adoption of two of them.) My husband is also secure enough in his masculinity to share the responsibility of our children completely, and to enjoy doing so. I think our children are exceptionally fortunate to have such a father.

I have more things on my mind than most males with whom I must compete; I say "must" because, as we all know, that is the way the research and management games are played. I do research and management for fun, but nevertheless, I compete vigorously. And here again a woman is in trouble. She's damned if she does and damned if she doesn't. If she does not compete, it proves women can't do physics; if she does compete, she isn't feminine and hence, presumably, is some sort of a freak. One might be led to conclude that my career has been adversely affected by too many responsibilities outside physics and management; in particular, so many children. I don't think so. I find it appalling that some men think they can pursue several interests simultaneously, but women cannot. Most often, men apply this absurdity to women with regard to career versus motherhood. Well, my four kids are still very young, eight to twelve, as I said, so it's too early to tell if they'll turn out to be psychological disasters. I hope to live to prove not only that it's not impossible to be totally committed to several goals, but that one can also have fun in the process. Incidentally, my esteemed male colleagues, if you are guilty of holding this absurdity that women can't be successfully committed to more than one goal, may I inform you that you are terrible bores.

Before I summarize briefly, I want to emphasize quickly how hard it is for the majority to recognize prejudice. Sometimes it is expressed so subtly that it may be unintentional. That doesn't make it any less painful. Let me illustrate. The huge, three-story physics building in my graduate school had no women's restroom. The secretary explained to me that she and I were to share the private facility reserved for the head of the institute. She, of course, always knew his whereabouts, but, one day when I didn't, he absent-mindedly failed to lock the door. The very next day workmen began to install what my colleagues immediately labeled "Betsy's." Years later, on my way to an international meeting, I gave a colloquium talk at my graduate school. I was rather disappointed on observing that perhaps my major contribution to physics was no longer recognized as such; there was only "Ladies" on the door, and no plaque commemorating my victory for my sex.

In summary there are four points:

1. Treat each woman on her own merits, abandoning stereotypes.
2. Abolish discriminatory practices in industry and nepotism rules in universities in favor of conflict of interest clauses; i.e., that spouses abstain from voting *re* each other's promotions. Surely no one can seriously fear that such a change will jeopardize our universities.
3. Don't take advantage of the many-body problem couples represent by withholding earned promotions, because it's harder for them to fight back by finding other jobs.
4. Give maternity leaves without penalties and help with child care. Universities and industry should establish child care centers or simply be clearing houses for baby-sitting help, at the expense of the users.

But please note that we women physicists are not asking for the lowering of any standards!

References

1. SUBCOMMITTEE ON THE STATUS OF ACADEMIC WOMEN ON THE BERKELEY CAMPUS. Academic Senate of the University of California, Berkeley Division. May 19, 1970: 9.
2. WOMEN IN THE WORKFORCE. Management Review. November 1970: 20–23.
3. WOMEN IN THE UNIVERSITY OF CHICAGO. Report of Committee on University Women. University Senate, University of Chicago. Chicago, Ill. May 1, 1970.
4. See Ref. 1, pp. 11–12.

EDUCATOR

Millicent C. McIntosh

President Emeritus, Barnard College, New York, New York
Tyringham, Massachusetts 02164

I was born in Baltimore at the end of the Victorian age—two circumstances that made it difficult for a girl to become self-directed and independent. For Baltimore was an aristocratic southern city in which the daughters of the old families were expected to learn to be charming, to make their debuts, and to get suitably married. My father's ancestors had come to Maryland in the eighteenth century, but they were Quakers, as were my mother's Philadelphia family. So although we were part of the Baltimore inner group, we were different. My mother went to the newly opened Bryn Mawr College in its first class. She was a minister in the Friends Meeting, and had an extensive career as a volunteer public servant.

It was she who was the earliest and most profound influence on my life. Although we all loved our handsome, gentle, idealistic father, he left to Mother the bringing up of their six children. Her energy, her hard work in behalf of unpopular causes (women's suffrage, peace, prison reform, racial equality) made the deepest impression on me. I can't remember a time when I didn't expect to go to college to prepare myself to save the world.

I was lucky in my education. The Bryn Mawr School in Baltimore was founded by a group of ladies, chief among whom was M. Carey Thomas, my mother's oldest sister, who at that time was dean and later president of Bryn Mawr College. Their purpose was to provide Baltimore girls with an education equal or superior to that of their brothers. An extraordinary young woman, Edith Hamilton, became headmistress; and in 1905, when I entered the school, she and Miss Thomas between them had collected an unusual faculty. We were given a rigorous education in preparation for passing the entrance examinations to Bryn Mawr College, a requirement for the diploma.

Modern psychologists often claim that you cannot transfer learning skills; that sweating over Latin and math does not help you master other difficult tasks. I simply do not believe it; I am absolutely sure that the stiff requirements of my school and college made it possible for me to meet the arduous schedule I followed in my subsequent life. I feel grateful to the young Greek Ph.D. who made us learn by heart the principal parts of fifty irregular Greek verbs, and to the highbrow English teacher who gave us endless lines of difficult English poetry to memorize.

At Bryn Mawr College, along with all other students of my generation, I came under the powerful influence of M. Carey Thomas. She spoke to us in chapel three times a week and shared with us her delight in reading and the world of scholarship, her passion for travel and politics. She impressed on us our responsibility as educated women not to be submerged by our parents or our marriages, but to accept a commitment to leadership in the society for which we were preparing. We were told that if we *must* marry (!), we could plan to have our babies in August, presumably so that we could continue in our teaching careers. Miss Thomas introduced us to many areas of her own concern: women's suffrage, the infant trade-union movement, progressive education. As her niece, I shared her more private views which she was wise enough not to expound in chapel—on birth control, on her loss of belief in orthodox religion.

Few Bryn Mawr students escaped the impact of Miss Thomas's ideas. A large proportion of us, supported by our professors, were inspired to go on to graduate school, to enter various professions, or to undertake important community leadership. Moreover, some of my generation continued with our careers after we were married. A few entered the law and several became judges; even more were doctors and research workers. But most of those who survived were in the school and college field.

Our success depended not only on our own determination but on the open-mindedness of the institutions in which we worked. The Brearley School, where I was headmistress for seventeen years, urged me to continue in my job, and encouraged married teachers to stay after they were pregnant or had children. The women's colleges made it possible for married professors to teach along with their academic husbands, whereas the universities prevented this, especially if the two were in the same department.

It is no secret that the basic factor in the success of married women in careers is the cooperation and support of their husbands. It was unusual in the '20s and '30s for men to accept equal professional rights for their wives, and those of us whose husbands did so were fortunate beyond belief. Dr. McIntosh was a professor at the Columbia College of Physicians and Surgeons when we were married; but while practicing pediatrics earlier, he had become convinced that the 24-hour mother was not necessarily a good mother. He accepted women as equal to men (except women drivers!), and he encouraged and helped me to continue my work after our children were born. He shared the household tasks and made us able to have a truly "liberated" marriage—an ideal that our married children are now perpetuating in their own families.

A number of other factors should be mentioned as to what makes for success in a dual role. Good health is almost essential to the relaxation necessary for carrying a heavy, complex schedule. I found that my own physical strength made it possible to work on the job from 8:30 to 4 or 5, to come home and feed, bathe, and read to the children before putting them to bed; then, after our dinner, to put in an evening's work on correspondence or reports or on preparation for my own classes. A mother who is exhausted is beaten from the start. On the other hand, many working mothers have mentioned the fact that their two roles contribute to each other; that they feel refreshed when they make an exchange between them.

Another important factor is, of course, the availability of good help in the home. In the '30s, when I was married, the depression made it easy to find such help. We had a wonderful Scottish couple who filled in all the gaps and stayed with us for ten years. But I feel sure that even now, if one has determination and ingenuity, this problem can be solved. The use of students where these are available can be expensive, but works well. One of my daughters-in-law uses three students for three different purposes in her home. Teaming up with other families was common during the Second World War but apparently seems too complicated now to many young parents. Why can't we go back to it? As day care centers are expanded and improved, there is no doubt that they will be a great support to the professional woman.

Those of us who have been fortunate enough to do congenial work throughout our married lives are aware of the many benefits resulting from our dual status. We enjoyed our children greatly, and longed to spend every spare moment with them. We realized that our homes were not as well kept and beautiful as they might have been, but at least we were not bowed down with housekeeping details and absorbed in minutiae. As a result, and because we, like our husbands, were working, we had many interesting things to talk about, and interesting friends to bring home.

We're grateful to Women's Liberation for working to solve lots of sticky problems that remain, and most of us try to help when we can. But we feel that the querulous members of the movement have failed to recognize one basic fact about women: provided that they are willing and able to work hard, with self-discipline, they can do anything they *really* want to.

HORTICULTURIST

Ernesta Drinker Ballard

Pennsylvania Horticultural Society
Philadelphia, Pennsylvania 19106

I am a horticulturist, which means that I have two funds of information. The first is an elementary knowledge of the science of plant growth. The second is a much larger store of practical knowledge about how to grow plants and how to use them for ornamental purposes.

I am also an organization executive. I run the 5,000-member Pennsylvania Horticultural Society, a nonprofit organization that collects and disseminates horticultural information and conducts horticultural activities. It is a full-time job, spilling over into many evenings and weekends. It carries a good salary.

My profession is one of comparatively low prestige, not overpopulated with brilliant or aggressive people. The fact that I have one of the top horticultural jobs in the country with no academic credentials beyond the degree of associate in science shows that horticulture holds out rewards to anyone with above average ability, a determination to work harder than most people, and a basic knowledge of the subject.

Horticulturists can be divided into three groups: academic horticulturists (teachers at land grant colleges and researchers at the U. S. Department of Agriculture), commercial horticulturists (nurserymen, greenhouse operators, landscapers, and fruit and vegetable growers), and horticulturists who provide educational and informational services to people, often through an institution such as an arboretum, a horticultural society, or a publication. The three groups have frequent professional meetings, and it is part of my job to go to these affairs and find out what is going on. As a result, I know literally hundreds of horticulturists in this country and quite a number abroad. From my own experience I can tell you that horticulture is populated 90% by men. Outside of writers of popular gardening texts, I know of only two other women who have attained a position equal to mine in salary and responsibility.

Associated with horticulture are vast numbers of garden club women—more than 500,000 in clubs throughout the country. They are to the professionals as grey ladies are to doctors, yet their activities receive highly disproportionate attention. It took me fifteen years to convince people that I was not a super garden clubber. From the very beginning I intended to be a professional, a fact impossible for most of my social peers to understand.

I chose horticulture because it offered practical opportunities for a business or professional career at the time when I first realized I wanted to stand on my own feet, earn money by my own efforts, and achieve recognition for my own accomplishments. This happened when I was 31 years old. I was thoroughly married to a very bright lawyer and had four children—a boy and three girls—all planned, all wanted, all healthy, happy, and successful in their ways. We had a lovely house in the suburbs, a car, a live-in mother's helper, a normal social life, and everything else included in the American dream. I filled the role of wife, mother, and housekeeper with no strain. In fact, for ten years, I enjoyed it. In addition, I was involved in social work and had been president of the local visiting nurse society before I was 28 years old.

Suddenly the dream ended, and I realized that I would never be satisfied until I proved to myself and to the world that I was not just someone's wife or someone's mother but a capable person in my own right. *By this I meant earning money.* It was not that I needed it; my husband's earnings were quite satisfactory, and I could always look to my father if my husband disappeared from the scene. No; the reason I wanted to earn money was that being paid for my work was a form of recognition. It was tangible evidence that the world appreciated my efforts. No expressions of gratitude to a volunteer carry the same solid conviction of worth as a royalty check or an increase in salary.

The basic questions that I am supposed to answer for you today are: Why did I suddenly decide to become a self-reliant human being? What motivated me to break out of the mold and seek independence? And what enabled me to achieve my goals to the extent that I have done so?

I think the answers to these questions can be found in my family background. My father was one of six children, four boys and two girls, all but one markedly successful in either the arts, science, or law. (The "unsuccessful" brother was the nicest.) The mother of these six, my paternal grandmother, never had any role outside her family, but she constantly encouraged her daughters to take on the world, assuring them they could do anything any man could do. Her sister, my great-aunt, was a renowned portrait painter, the prototype of today's liberated woman. As far as my father's family was concerned, I was exposed to models of achievement, women as well as men. I was also exposed to the intense, dedicated effort that leads to achievement.

My mother's family was less accomplished but much more social. The best clubs, the right schools, the so-called right people were hugely important to them. I grew up believing that to practice ladylike skills, to "marry well" and to raise well-bred children were goals enough for a girl.

In my own immediate family I was the fourth of five children. My father paid little attention to me; he took my brothers on hunting and fishing trips. My mother read to us at teatime and always came upstairs to kiss us goodnight. We never doubted that she loved us, and we knew she was very busy managing her household and her servants, keeping up with her vast array of cousins, and discharging with great reliability the burdens of charitable, cultural, and social activities. She also pursued an interest in music, partly as a matter of self-defense against my father, who was one of the most eminent amateur musicologists of his time.

My father worked all the time, either at the law or on his music. Indeed, my picture of both my parents is one of incessant work. They never relaxed. They never wasted time. They rarely joined or arranged social gatherings (except with relatives or musicians), rarely indulged in conversation, never did the things that most people classify as "fun." When I was 12 years old my father decided to teach me to sight-read music. I had to be at the piano at 6:45 each morning, and our sessions lasted precisely 45 minutes. In this fashion we worked our way through all of Schubert's songs, 700 of them. He played, I sang. He took satisfaction in telling his associates that his daughter could sight-read anything. I did not enjoy it, although subsequently I was glad to have the skill.

Career aspirations for me, or for my sister, were never mentioned in my family. When, at the age of 13, I announced that I wanted to be a lawyer, my father smiled and told his acquaintances. But he never took me to his own law office or gave me any idea what the legal profession was all about.

When I entered adolescence, there was constant talk about the right kind of people for me to associate with, the necessity of coming out to meet my mother's friends and their eligible sons, and the ultimate goal of a proper marriage. At 15 I was sent off to a fashionable boarding school, the same one my mother had attended, and after three years, became what my husband later called the least-educated person he knew.

While I was at school, something happened to my mother; perhaps a psychiatrist could explain it. My mother's own version, as definite as most of her rare self-analyses, was that because she had a hysterectomy, right away she began to think. In a remarkably short time she became a fanatical feminist and wrote and published four books about women. By then, however, I was cast in the mold she had made. It was too late for me to learn feminism from her. I was embarassed by her feminist ideas and did not see their implications for me.

My mother was never an activist. She just read, and wrote and talked about women to anyone who would listen—and to some who would not. My father was amused by it all. It didn't threaten him.

At 18, I did what had been planned all my life. I "came out," made my Philadelphia debut, did some volunteer work, and married. I was still ten years away from liberation.

The man I married was 21 when we fell in love. The attraction was about 99% physical. We had practically nothing in common. I was not even going to college; he was preparing for a career in law. I had no commitment to anything; he had many. He was a sufficiently serious student and athlete to be awarded a Rhodes Scholarship. And he found time for sailing, polo playing, fox-hunting, skiing and having fun. As it turned out, none of these things has played any real part in our life together.

There you have my little autobiography, the not-quite typical story of a debutante. Now, I will try to pick out the factors that led me to a *second coming out*, ten years after the first:

First, I inherited from my father's family an overabundance of nervous energy, a great capacity for detail, a good memory, and the ability to make up my mind. No wonder I became restless and dissatisfied with being a housewife.

Second, the fact that my family were achievers gave me confidence in my own ability. Once I saw where I wanted to go, I was able to set out on my own, without waiting for guidance that might never have been forthcoming. I wrote two books, gave hundreds of lectures, and ran my own business. The first and only job I have ever had was as chief executive.

Third, I had the examples of my three aunts. Unconsciously, I think, I wanted to prove that I was as good as they were.

Fourth, I resented my father's refusal to appreciate what I could do, a refusal traceable not to his appraisal of me as a person, but to his appraisal of women generally. From the time I learned to talk, my father made it plain that women were clever and lovable and might be useful, but they did not have men's brains or men's capacity for objective achievements. After living with this view of my sex for thirty years, I became determined, first at the subconscious level and later consciously, to prove him wrong.

Fifth, I had a husband who believed as a fundamental article of faith that every person—a woman as well as a man—has the right to become an adult human being, and to be treated as such.

When I decided to have a life of my own, I realized that the first step would have to be at least a rudimentary education in the field in which I would work. One of the reasons I picked horticulture was that there was a good practical school twenty minutes away. Finances were no problem, nor were the domestic arrangements. The children were intrigued with the idea that their mother was studying too. It all seemed unbelievably easy.

Then came the reaction. Six weeks after I began my studies, I started to feel miserable. Soon, I couldn't swallow. I could scarcely get up in the morning. I was convinced that I was desperately ill.

After undergoing the usual medical tests—with negative results—I was finally referred to a psychiatrist, a woman. My mother, who was at this point going through a horror-of-Freud stage, was appalled.

I don't think anyone except my husband realized at that juncture that my motive for going to horticultural school was not simply to pass the time, but rather, to prepare myself for independence. The secret knowledge that I was about to repudiate many of the goals I had been brought up to accept and the dawning realization of the deep wounds inflicted on me by my father's view of me as a woman were the roots of my physical symptoms. I felt selfish and guilty because I was pursuing my own goals and rejecting my father's beliefs. When my doctor helped me to understand these things, the sense of selfishness and guilt receded and my ailments gradually went away.

Throughout all this I was able to say whatever was on my mind to my husband. There are many things that happen to him that he does not share with me, but little happens to me that, sooner or later, and usually sooner, I don't tell him about. He never seems bored. With me and with our children, particularly our three girls, he has always made it clear that what we thought, what we wanted to do, and what we did was of interest and importance to him. To use his own phrase, he has always treated us as "adult human beings."

With a husband who believes in the rights of women as adult human beings, there has never been any suggestion that permission was needed for anything I wanted to do. My husband has, in fact, sometimes pushed me beyond where I thought I wanted to go. The limitations on what I attempt are, to a large extent, self-imposed for reasons all of you can understand—a realization that no matter how capable a woman may be, the world does not take her at face value. The world expects us to lose interest and to fail.

So much for how I got out into the world. Now that I am there, what kind of treatment do I receive? My colleagues (mostly men, remember) are very respectful of my horticultural competence. They acknowledge that my books are sound and sensible, that my plants are beautiful, and that my horticultural advice is good. But they react quite differently to my administrative and organizational activities. This is the area where I think I excel, but where I have had to work harder and accomplish considerably more than my masculine peers in order to gain recognition. For years I was paid less than my male confreres, although now, finally, that gap is closing. Over and over again, I have experienced hostility from men who resent every step I take up the ladder of organized horticulture; all of which goes to prove that it is much easier for a man to acknowledge the worth of a book written by a woman than it is to acknowledge the worth of a woman who matches her judgment against his, or competes with him for an office or a title.

I feel that my greatest contribution to the women's movement is my exemplification of a role for my daughters and for other women with a background similar to mine. My oldest daughter is a hematologist and is married to an internist. My second daughter is a graduate of the Harvard Business School, is married to a classmate at that institution, and is presently both pregnant and starting a travel business. My youngest daughter is in her second year at Harvard Law School, is an activist for women's rights, and is not going to let marriage interfere with her efforts to improve our society. Not long ago she paid me the ultimate compliment. After a supper at her house in Cambridge, attended by me and her and by four other women law students, she reported that her friends were amazed that they could talk unreservedly to her mother.

As I look toward the future, I think it will be easier for women to become full-fledged people. More of us are getting good educations. Fewer of us are burdening ourselves with large families. A growing number of us will find understanding men to share our lives. The one place where progress is so slow as to be almost imperceptible is in acceptance at the top. The men who run the world are not ready to see us as people. And I'm afraid it will be at least another generation before they do.

PEDIATRICIAN

Gertrude T. Hunter
Regional Health Director
Health Services and Mental Health Administration
U.S. Department of Health, Education, and Welfare, Region 1
Boston, Massachusetts 02203

The conference on successful women in the sciences, on which this monograph is based, is subtitled: "An Analysis of Determinants." What determines the success of the woman scientist?

I have no particular analyses—no graphs and no statistics that will shed much light on this important question.

Yet it would seem to me appropriate that I should, in this instance, reduce my assessments of the question to quantifiable, scientifically documented, and validated data.

My presentation here will not withstand such scientific scrutiny. I have no such data to share with you. Instead, I trust that you will bear with me through a rather anecdotal, impressionistic recollection of my life experience. Somewhere in there, I believe, will be found the answer—or at least some few tentative answers—to the question as it pertains to me.

You will understand that my career is scarcely yet at midpoint. Just now, it is difficult for me to assign final value judgments to these recollections. Some that seem to me important may be in fact extraneous. Others that seem fleeting and chimerical may be all-important. I suggest, then, that there is a system of interconnections among my professional career, my family, my womanhood, and my Blackness. All these elements are important in the formulation of such success as my career has attained to date.

I should like to discuss with you those interconnections. They may contain some useful material not to be found in the simple discussion of a successful scientific career.

I was born in Boston, and in my first year moved with my family to a middle-sized residential community on the south shore of Massachusetts—a community that was, in its culture and attitudes, determinedly middle class.

My father was an immigrant of Portuguese extraction, my mother a native Bay Stater. They believed in some things that have had a tremendous influence on my life ever since.

To my father and mother, it was important that people are what they are—and that being who and what I was was good. As a woman, I was told, I would be able to do whatever I wanted. I was taught that my skin had a beautiful color.

This constant, implicit reinforcement of positive self-image was my parents' most valuable gift to me. I grew up loving my color and enjoying the fact that I was a woman.

The Women's Liberation movement tends to scoff at the imprinting that tells a girl that she is a woman and programs her in that direction. But what kind of liberation requires that an individual be something other—or less—than what she is in order to be free? My daughters are being programmed to womanhood just as I was. It would seem important that women be successful *because* they are women, not in spite of the fact. In school, I performed well because my mother and father expected it of me. When I entered high school, I elected the college preparatory program as a matter of course.

What happened next is, tragically even today, all too familiar to Blacks. A faculty adviser called me in. In her hand was the paper on which I had signified my desire to take college prep courses. The courses I had elected were crossed out, and substituted with a Home Economics curriculum. I took the paper home, a little dazed by this turn of events. When my mother saw it she was outraged. Together, we went back to the school to face the adviser. The adviser attempted to placate my mother. "Mrs. Teixeira," she pleaded, "what is a colored girl going to do with college? If she learns cooking and sewing, she can always get a good job."

But when we left the office, I was enrolled in the college course.

Looking back on that incident, I see it, of course, as an expression of racism in the fact that the faculty adviser had no expectations of me as a "colored girl."

This racist presumption of failure is still too often crippling the aspirations of young Blacks who encounter it.

It should be noted, however, that once the problem of the faculty adviser was overcome, I experienced no discrimination in school, nor did I ever feel stifled, oppressed, or rejected.

I attended Boston University for two years after high school but transferred to Howard University in Washington, D.C., at the end of my sophomore year, intending to major in chemistry. At Howard, purely by chance, I made a decision that dictated not only my professional, but also my marital future.

A friend had signed up to take an aptitude test to determine whether she was qualified for the premedicine curriculum. Having a bad case of nerves about the test, she persuaded me to sign up for it and accompany her. I was well settled into my chemistry studies at the time, but to accommodate her, I went along. The test interested me, and I felt secure in the fact that I had done well in it. After some consideration, I decided to switch over to the premed course. By a strange coincidence, another aspiring young scientist, Charles Hunter, was at the same time signing up for a medical education at Howard, having altered his career plans to accommodate a friend. I am now, in addition to being Dr. Gertrude Hunter, Mrs. Charles Hunter.

Perhaps what this proves is that in every career and in every marriage there is a component of happenstance. I am at a loss to quantify this component, but there it is.

I would wish to mention one other factor that I found at least interesting, and possibly also significant to any discussion of determinants of success for women. In the Black world of Howard Medical School, I was not aware of any sexual discrimination. Perhaps 25% of my classmates were women. They emerged from the medical school experience as feminine women and competent physicians. Without personal knowledge, I would not wish to libel any predominantly white medical school as sexist, but I am pretty certain that the supportive milieu of Howard was instrumental in the eventual success of the females in my class.

An obvious determinant of success for any professional is the appropriate choice of career. Pediatrics is one specialty into which many women tend to gravitate. It is seen as a sort of women's job. Obstetrics-gynecology may be another. Yet my reasons for choosing pediatrics had little to do with any stereotype. I was about equally pulled among internal medicine, surgery, and pediatrics. But I had long-range plans for a home and family, and I love children. Pediatrics was compatible with that set of facts. It was a perfectly conscious decision.

Thus it would seem that a woman's domestic needs and proclivities do have a powerful determining influence on her career choice and are thereafter a large factor in her successful functioning in that career.

As a resident in pediatrics at Homer G. Phillips Hospital in St. Louis, Missouri, I found that my newly acquired husband had expectations of me. He always expected people—and especially me—to perform at the very highest level of which they are capable. He would have been ashamed of me in the role of an inept, inadequate physician. I learned to balance this expectation off against my need to lead a domestic life. (I love to cook, for example.) So, early in my professional life, I discovered the need to find a rational accommodation between two careers, and insofar as possible, combine them into a single life.

The modality I settled upon was to pursue my professional career in increments. When my first child came along, I had no problem at all about giving up my professional interests for six months, and this pattern repeated itself as my younger children arrived.

The positions I held in the interim periods were always in areas where people understood and were not uncomfortable with my home responsibilities. For example, at the Head Start program, where I served as Medical Director, my co-workers exhibited no discomfort if I was suddenly called away from the office to handle some family responsibility. In turn, there was no stress or conflict on the part of my children, who felt at home with my office associates.

All of this brings me to a philosophical point about women. Basically, the successful woman professional must acknowledge the mutual dependency of women—a point most women do not recognize. You cannot talk about the successful professional woman without considering the support she has received from (and, hopefully, given to) other women.

This mutual dependency exists all the way across the board from the housekeeper to whom she must entrust her children several hours each day to her fellow professionals.

There are reasons for this fact that are well based in the sociology of discrimination. In some Black circles, this is known as "getting our thing together." It is a recognition that in an area where there has been a historic attitude of exclusion, all the excluded must come together for their mutual benefit. This factor has operated throughout history. The early Christians in Rome, the Jews in the Warsaw ghetto, present-day Blacks striving for unity without unanimity, and women in a "man's world" are only a scattered few examples.

A recognition of mutual dependency is helpful to all people. To the woman in the professions it is an absolute necessity. Part of the answer to our question about how determinants of success for the woman professional must be found therein.

These, then, are some rather episodic and, of necessity, fragmentary thoughts about the meaning of one professional woman's life.

Perhaps the real lessons to be derived from this examination are rather ordinary, derived as they are from the commonplaces of life in the United States today. I would plead, in summary, that some of the old-fashioned virtues are still valid: being proud of what and who you are; being willing to share responsibility; being acceptive to change; and, perhaps most of all, knowing what you want and being willing to hang in there until you get it.

And, as I hope I have demonstrated, much depends on pure luck.

It is, as I have suggested, impossible for me to predict success for myself. Success is a subjective thing, depending as it does on one's own definition of what constitutes a full life. But to date, I have been able to progress in my chosen profession, and to do so in a manner consistent with a happy and satisfying domestic life. If that is success, I suggest that the determinants are to be found somewhere among the clues I have tried, in this brief space, to suggest.

METEOROLOGIST

Joanne Simpson

Experimental Meteorology Laboratory
Coral Gables, Florida 33124

Introduction

I was the elder of two children in an intellectual but unhappy home. Early influences were a wonderful private school with high scholarship standards, my mother's feminism and my father's interests in aviation. On school graduation, I left the eastern seaboard establishment for the University of Chicago near the beginning of the American involvement in World War II.

The war and my aviation background motivated my choice of meteorology, in which my war service consisted of training military forecasters. At the end of the war, already married, I entered graduate school in meteorology, encountered obstacles and finally became the first woman in the field to obtain a Ph.D.

I have devoted 30 years full time to the profession, about half in university teaching and research, the other half in research organizations. I have published 80 papers and received some honors and opportunities for world travel and public service. The most costly of the many sex-linked obstacles I have encountered have been the nepotism rules enforced by employers. My personal and married life and child raising have surely suffered for the professional attainments I have reached, while my career, in turn, has been severely limited by my sex. I am currently not convinced that either the position, rewards or achievement have been worth the cost. In the current culture, I think that the difficulties faced by a woman trying to combine top-level achievement with successful marriage and motherhood are close to prohibitive, although I have attempted to build on my experience to advise young women determined to seek these goals.

Life History

I am 48 years old and have devoted 30 years, full time, to my work in meteorology. I am presently the director of a small government research laboratory and an adjunct professor at a middle-sized private university. I have published 80 research papers and collaborated on two books. I now serve (one day per month) on an Environmental Council appointed by the governor of my state. My husband is the director of an important weather forecast center, and between us, we have five children, all of whom are adults except my ten-year old daughter who is with me only during the two summer months.

I have experienced three different classes of sex-linked problems in my lifetime. The first is discrimination simply from being a woman. The second comprises difficulties from being a married woman. The third arises from being a mother.

Sex discrimination first struck me as a graduate student, when my department declined to recommend me for any fellowship support whatever on grounds of sex alone (my grades were at or near the top of all the graduate students in meterorology). Since then the disadvantages have ranged from the ego-bruises of not being taken seriously by both men and women, most well meaning and largely subconscious in their prejudice, to being fired summarily on one occasion and on many others missing opportunities for productive employment for which I have been better qualified than the competition.

The problems of merely being a woman, however, are virtually nothing compared with those of being a married woman. Firstly, a married woman must find work where her husband has or can find work. She is therefore trapped in space. Secondly, married women are not expected to place their own careers on an equal or higher priority level than that of their husbands. On the contrary, they are cruelly criticized if they do not patently place their husband's careers first. Thirdly, "upward mobility" is seriously restricted for both partners in the marriage, and the restriction tightens in direct proportion to the level of success already achieved, since two high-level jobs in the same institution, university, or even city are hard to come by in most professions or in most combinations of two different professions.

And fourthly, there are nepotism rules. I believe I have actually suffered more grief and loss of potential productivity from this source than from any other sex-related restriction. I lost my first job (as a university instructor) when I married my first husband. The struggle I had to go through to create myself another job at another university was not compatible with preservation of that frail marriage. With my second husband, we jointly played a major role in breaking the nepotism rule at a great university, where we both became full professors. For a time it appeared that my career problems were ideally solved. But after 17 years of increasing conflict, that marriage broke up, too.

The professional golden age ended when I married my present husband and took my present job. My husband and I met on a professional association and developed — before we were married — into a terrific research team with complementary skills. Where I was weak, he was strong, and vice versa. The two of us together were able to create more than twice as much as the sum of our individual efforts. In part we married because we looked forward to a long life of working closely together. That was the daydream. The reality is that our collaboration has been virtually 100% destroyed by the nepotism rule in the federal Civil Service. Unfortunately, our work interests are now somewhat in conflict. The conflict is compensated for in part by the common language, the associates, and the intellectual interests which we share. In this marriage my major problem is that guilt from the previous failures has driven me to try too hard to be a "good wife." These efforts have often boomeranged; in some I have forced myself into actions later regretted or even resented.

In raising my children, I had fewer obvious difficulties than most working mothers I have known. I got ahead fast enough at work to afford expensive child care, and both my sons were outwardly adaptable to changing faces and early schooling. Inwardly, I am sure now that they both suffered from my deep absorption in my work. In an angry outburst a few years ago, my younger son charged that I had never been more than a "distant figure" in his life.

By the time of the second divorce, I had sufficiently lost confidence in myself as a mother so that I relinquished custody of my little girl, perhaps too readily, to a stepmother who is a stable, loving, and outgoing housewife. I realized that, like myself, my Karen is a hypersensitive child, without the resilience or toughness her older brothers had shown.

I am glad that I am not a working mother of younger children today, for I believe that it is harder to find adequate child care now than it was 15–20 years ago. Women's Lib remains mostly sound and fury until means are provided to care for children properly and at a modest price.

My present job situation is a rough one. I am temperamentally unsuited to the arbitrary ordering about, regulations, and political maneuvering encountered by the government scientist at the so-called "lower echelons of line management." I wonder if there is not a basic incompatibility between the qualities required to create new ideas and the mold of the "good soldier" which one must force himself into to be rewarded and advanced in a civil service organization. Needless to say, I have neither advanced nor been rewarded within the organization, although I have had some exciting honors and opportunities from the outside, ranging from the fun of appearing on the Today Show on television to world travel, where I have made warm friends and colleagues in the Soviet Union, England, Australia, Italy, and Iran. Four years ago I was elected a Fellow of my professional society, and next summer I will participate in the Distinguished Visiting Professor Program at a western university.

In my job, I have found one main compensation, without which I would retire tomorrow morning, regardless of whether I could afford it. My small laboratory, which I have forged out of nothing and on a shoestring, consists of about 15 persons, all young, bright, creative, eager, and wonderful people, nearly every one of them under 35 years of age. Some are my own former students and some presently still are students, from the high school up to the Ph.D. dissertation level. Together and individually, we fly in research aircraft through thunderstorms and hurricanes. We carry out cloud-seeding programs, both for research and to help mitigate a recent destructive drought. We study the cumulus cloud engines that drive severe storms, with tools ranging from satellites through aircraft to computers, and turn out research papers, public talks, articles, and seminars at the rate of dozens per year. In 1971 our work was written up in publications ranging from *Medical Opinion and Review* through *Popular Science, Newsweek, Readers Digest,* and *The Wall Street Journal.*

It is a delight and stimulation for me to interact with these brilliant young people and to provide intellectual leadership and a quasiacademic atmosphere in order that they may develop their talents freely and fully. I have fought like an alley cat to secure them advancement and honors and have figuratively spilled my blood on the ground to shield them from the nightmare of the bureaucratic and political quagmire until they acquire the maturity and toughness to share this burden with me, as two of them already are beginning to do beautifully.

This part of my story always brings the question from the intermittent procession of interviewing female reporters: "How does a woman fare being the boss of so many men? Don't some or all of them resent it?" As I have grown older, I have learned to minimize this problem in two ways. The first is by selecting very young men to work for me. We all know that in America young men are conditioned to accepting an authority figure in the form of an older woman. Second, I delegate authority and allow each person as much freedom of choice and decision as he or she can cope with. This requires a judicious initial selection, in which I have been extremely fortunate.

Another question everyone asks is: From what sources or from what persons did I derive the intense motivation to persist through all these difficulties, and did it not require superhuman physical health and energy? The answer to the latter part of second question is negative; my energy level is high, but I have all along waged a constant battle with poor health and physical pain. The last seven years I have carried on in the face of frequent crippling migraine headaches; it is a source of some pride to me that, even so, I have missed fewer working days than the majority of my colleagues.

To analyze human motivation is far more difficult. As far as I can understand, my motivation arose early from the combination of a miserable and rejecting home environment with high intellectual goals in the family and school situation. I was the elder of two children. My unwanted and premature birth terminated my mother's promising career as a newspaper reporter. My brother, who followed five years later, was a wanted and much-favored child. Later, my mother returned to work part-time in public relations and became an ardent feminist and pioneer in the birth control movement. My father, whom I admired but rarely saw, was a brilliant newspaper editor and later rose in state politics, retaining, however, his infectious love for airplanes and aviation, which he transmitted to me via numerous plane rides beginning at the age of six.

I attended a wonderful private school for girls that nurtured and inspired me from second grade until I went to college. Every scrap of love and approval I knew as a young person came wholly from friends and teachers at school, who provided affection, guidance, and extremely high standards of scholarship, and who inspired curiosity concerning all intellectual pursuits. Even now, when all else fails, I can keep going from intellectual curiosity alone, with a desire to know more about virtually every subject, particularly history, archeology, and mathematics. I have also found a delightful escape in ballet dancing.

I first recall becoming consciously ambitious at the age of 14, when I vowed to myself that I was going to "get somewhere and be somebody." The "somewhere" and "somebody," however, were largely molded by events. Reacting away from the eastern seaboard social establishment of my childhood, I chose the University of Chicago for college, attracted by Robert Maynard Hutchins and his theories of education.

As I went away to college in 1940-41, the trauma of World War II struck hard. France fell, Britain fought for her life, and then Japan attacked Pearl Harbor; my world was in flames, and to remain in college seemed wrong if I could contribute my slight knowledge of airplanes and mathematics to the war effort. So at age 18 I seized the opportunity to enter the meteorology training program on the University of Chicago campus. Six other women joined with me. After our own nine months of training, our function was to train weather forecasters for the military services.

At the end of the war, like Rosie the Riveter, we women were supposed to go back to our mops and babies. When about three or four of the roughly 30 war-trained women wanted to go on to graduate school for master's or doctor's degrees in meteorology, our professors were considerably shocked. Some laughed, and a few in key positions were openly hostile.

My professor, a famous Scandinavian and the greatest living meteorologist, was a model (to me) whose creativity, expansiveness, and ability to combine and inspire people I am still seeking to emulate. He had no use for women in meteorology, however, and told me frankly that I would look both ridiculous and pathetic if I didn't really "make it big" after creating such an unconventional spectacle of myself and exacting such an unfair sacrifice from my husband and child.

Only after he returned to Sweden did I become the first woman to obtain a Ph.D. in meteorology. Nearly a decade later, when I visited him in Stockholm a month before his death, he said, "Well, you made an enormous contribution after all, so everything it cost turned out to be worth while." I am gratified that he made that conclusion before he died, but, ironically enough, I am no longer certain he was right.

In summary, I stand now at the stage where I, and many of those around me, ask whether or not it has all been worth while. From the casual viewpoint of an outsider, the accomplishments and the rewards appear formidable, but only I and those very close to me have any inkling of how staggering the cost has been. I am emotionally, physically, and spiritually near exhaustion from 35 years of colossal and constant effort. Right now it does not appear to me that either the scientific contribution, the position I have reached, or the rewards are enough to compensate for the terrible price exacted from me and from those close to me. Perhaps in one or two decades from now, as I approach retirement, I will have a fresh and more optimistic assessment of the benefit-to-cost ratio of my professional lifetime. I hope so.

Meanwhile, if there is any way in which my experiences could be made use of, to help younger aspiring women, I shall gain more confidence in the worth whileness of my efforts.

I will assume the most difficult possible situation for a young woman, namely, that she is determined to combine a career with marriage and motherhood, and that she is also determined to achieve at the highest level.* Omitting the obvious advice that she must exceed the male competition by several factors, I have boiled my recommendations down to three, as follows:

1. Cold-bloodedly seek a field so underpopulated, if possible, that employers are "scraping the bottom of the barrel." To my knowledge, all existing women meteorologists got in at the time of World War II, when hundreds of forecasters had to be trained and sent all over the world for military service. Few women are getting into meteorology today, when male Ph.D.'s are unemployed. Five to ten years from now, the huge World War II group will start retiring, and opportunities should again open up.

2. Forego false pride. Learn to type and to teach and to do both of these well, even if you must work without pay. You can always earn room and board by baby-sitting. I started as a volunteer secretary in the Office of the Aviation Director of my state. Later, I became his paid administrative assistant. From that platform I learned to fly, to write effective letters, to administrate, and to handle a budget. The contacts I made and the stimulation received from the job were so essential, that I doubt that I would be here today without them. Cultivate important contacts and references regarding your qualifications and never hesitate to use them. Never take no for an answer, at least for the first three times. Develop a thick skin toward being disliked by some—even many—people. This is bound to happen if you are successful.

3. Learn to put every minute of your time to good use. I have written some of my best scientific papers in the pediatrician's waiting room, on streetcars and airplanes, while furniture was being delivered, and in other people's boring seminars. If you must have uninterrupted peace and quiet, without emotional stress, to study or do your work—forget it. Always take work with you wherever you go. Be prepared for an 80-hour week and the prospect that you will be slaving when your friends are lying on the beach, playing bridge, partying, or in the beauty parlor. In the last analysis, then, you must love your work, for the sheer doing of it, as well as or more than anything else in life. I did, for many, many years.

---

* Those who initially forego one or more of these objectives will have a situation so much easier that my advice is less necessary.

Discussion

Lynn Harrington (*Purdue University, Lafayette, Ind.*): Dr. Simpson You seem to be exceptional among the speakers of the day. But I don't find you exceptional myself. I came from an incredible background, just as you did. I have a nonsupportive husband, in every sense of the word, and what I want to know is whether you consider yourself exceptional in regard to what has gone on here today.

Dr. Simpson: This is the first opportunity I have ever had to talk to other women who have faced the same problems, so I really have not decided whether I am exceptional or not. I think this is one of the functions this conference can serve: to find out what is exceptional and what is not.

I think perhaps the difference between you and me is simply a matter of age. I believe that when one is young, one is more full of hopes and optimism than when one is older.

PHYSICIAN AND PUBLIC HEALTH EDUCATOR

Mary S. Calderone

SIECUS (Sex Information and Education Council of the U.S.)
New York, New York 10023

How Was the Profession Chosen?

I was born in 1904 into a family of artists—my mother a would-be singer from the Ozarks in Missouri, my father, Edward Steichen, a young artist whose family had brought him from Luxembourg to the United States twenty-five years earlier. My first ten years were spent in France, first in Paris and then in a small village near Paris. Most of the people who came to our home were artists; I remember Isadora Duncan, Brancusi, Arthur Carles. Rodin was a name well known to me, but I don't remember him. I know now that we were poor, but we never felt poor in that little village, for by contrast with the rest of the people there, we were rich. Every winter my father came to the United States to sell a few of his paintings, so that we could live for another year, and the part he played in bringing modern art to the United States is well known, although I was not then aware of it. Every summer American friends and patrons came to visit us. The garden was lovely and there was much talk and laughter.

By the time I was sent to the village school at about nine years of age, I was reading voraciously; in fact, I don't remember ever *learning* to read. My reading consisted mostly of the then popular Andrew Lang Fairy Books (Blue, Green, Lilac, etc.). I was the older child; my sister was four years younger, and I was violently (literally) jealous of her, for I was lanky, with stringy, straight brown hair, and she was round and cuddly with golden curls. Intellectually, I seem to remember always understanding everything that went on around me, and I didn't feel very differently then than I do now. I had extremely powerful feelings of all kinds (including sexual), and my relationship with my father was exceedingly close. He was joyous and full of life and, most of the time, entirely fair in his discipline, and I identified with him very much. I never did get along with my mother, who simply could not manage me and, I much later learned in analysis, was very hostile to me after I outgrew babyhood.

The outbreak of World War I in 1914 caused us to flee France, and I had my first experience of an American country school in Sharon, Connecticut, where we were refugees in someone's summer home. With my French accent and independent ways, I seemed a strange child to my schoolmates. A year later I was, at 11, taken in by Dr. Leopold Stieglitz, the brother of Alfred Stieglitz, the photographer and editor, to live with them in New York while I went to the Brearley School. This is where my academic intellectual life and my interest in medicine began, for Dr. Stieglitz loved to talk over his cases with me. I often went on his rounds with him in his old Franklin car, and he would discuss them.

Between the ages of 12 and 16 I had the run of his library, and by 14 I had read all of Thomas Hardy, as well as Scott, Dickens, and so forth. Meanwhile, at the Brearley School I was admired as the brightest in the class, but I was not particularly liked, and of course I was always the poor relation among girls who were exceedingly well-to-do, with fine clothes, and this made things difficult for me. (I wore hand-me-downs until my second marriage, at 37). Nevertheless, I *was* admired, not only for my intellectual capacity but for my gifts in music and acting, and especially in writing. I left Brearley at the end of the eleventh grade (thereby missing American history for the second time) and went directly to Vassar because I was bored with high school, coming back to Brearley to graduate with my class. After the age of ten I never had my own home and family again, my mother and father having been divorced, although I did pass one or two years with my mother in my late adolescence before going to college, with constant friction and unhappiness. My relationship with my father always remained very close, although he was separated from me a great deal by his service during the First World War.

Preparation for a Profession

During adolescence and college it was taken for granted by everyone, including myself, that I would go into medical school. No one seemed to have any doubts at all that I would go, and, retrospectively, the most extraordinary factor I can now recognize is that never once while I was growing up do I remember anyone at any time ever suggesting that there was something I could not do simply because I was female. Everyone I knew or ever came in contact with simply took it for granted that whatever I wanted to do, I could do. At college, 1921–1925, I took premedical subjects, getting mediocre marks because they were boring to me, for as the Human Engineering Laboratory found in 1933, I was a typical "too many aptitude person." The good marks I got were always in English and in music, and I continued to act a great deal. None of this bothered anybody at all. No one asked why a girl who had received only A's in a very high-level school received mostly B's and C's at college. In the end, these marks were of little importance. By the close of my junior year I was so fed up and bored with chemistry that when I had finished all my premedical courses, I simply dropped everything scientific and, deciding to go on the stage, spent my senior year in acting, music, and English. Again, no one appeared particularly upset, although maybe some were and didn't say so, or if so, I've forgotten it.

In retrospect, the five people who most influenced my life were my father; my mother's sister with whom I spent many summers and who taught me the real joy of cooking, canning, and physical work in general; a very wealthy woman who was a dear friend and patron of my father's who "adopted" me, too, and who left me a bequest that eventually allowed me to go to medical school; a teacher at the Brearley School, Ann Dunn, famous for her wit, her toughness, and her extraordinary teaching ability, and another whom I shall discuss later. The quality that these five had in common with respect to me was their unique ability to discipline me emotionally and intellectually while conveying their total belief that, with my capacities generally, eventually I could and would do something worth while. They were also entirely able not to appear disappointed when for ten years I apparently was deflected from such positive goals by three years on the stage, marriage, two children, divorce, and trying to support us by selling in a department store.

The fifth person who had a tremendous influence was my analyst, a woman, who also believed in me, who was my good friend before and after analysis, and who eventually suggested that I take the Johnson O'Connor Human Engineering Aptitude Tests. This I did at the age of 29, and Johnson O'Connor discovered that I was, in his terminology, a "too many aptitude woman," an even more horrendous thing to be then than nowadays! Unless I used all of my aptitudes, I would continue to wander from one thing to another, becoming restless where aptitudes were unused. He clearly directed me back into medicine, which I managed to reenter at the age of 30 against considerable odds, and here again, the University of Rochester Medical School and my father and many friends lent support and encouragement.

Unique Problems Associated with the Chosen Profession

I would say that all my problems were associated with the period before medical school. From then on it appears, in retrospect, to have been mostly smooth sailing. I was totally celibate in the ten years between divorce and remarriage, lonely, and missing sex. But I graduated thirteenth in a class of 45, and after a year of internship at Bellevue Hospital I obtained a fellowship from the City of New York to study public health. My reasoning was simple: I did not want to leave my surviving daughter for the several years of residencies required for medical practice. She had already had to be separated from me for my last two years of medicine and my year of internship. The fellowship I received was exceedingly generous for those days—$200 per month, on which it was entirely possible to live, still always, of course, with the generous help of friends and my father, who were immensely pleased that at long last I was "finding myself" after what must have been to them some pretty discouraging detours. I apparently did well in my two years of public health training, during which I met and married my second husband. I do not remember any problems at all associated with the fact that I was a woman, either in medical school or in the school of public health. In fact, it was two women in the New York City Health Department, Dr. Leona Baumgartner and Dr. Margaret Barnard, who were responsible for my receiving the fellowship. In medical school, I was told ten years later that one of my professors had commented about me, "She never used the fact that she was a woman, but never forgot it."

Attitudes of Professional Colleagues (Men and Women) and of People in Social Situations

Neither of these topics arouses specific memories. Everyone seemed to take me for granted as a physician especially trained in public health. It has to be remembered, however, that the year I received my Master's degree in Public Health and would have been ready to go to work was also the year in which I remarried and became pregnant (intentionally) at the age of 37. At 38 I again dropped out of the professional world entirely, having four pregnancies and two more children by the time I was 42, and staying with them until the second one was in school. During this period I worked two or three hours a day as a school physician in my local community, but I didn't look upon this seriously as *work*. This was the period during which my husband was at the peak of his profession, which was also in public health, and I had my hands full with travel, a large house, entertaining, and the children—but I had adequate help. I always knew that eventually I would go to work sometime, but, perhaps significantly, this was the period I was known as "Mrs. Calderone," and people barely remembered that I, too, was a physician.

Love, Marriage, and Husband

It was curiously coincidental that the year that my husband retired after his distinguished career in public health (New York City Health Department, World Health Organization, United Nations Secretariat Health Services) was the year that my younger child was seven and I was offered the position of Medical Director of the Planned Parenthood Federation of America. It was some time before I became aware that it had been offered to me because no one else would take it, most male physicians looking upon it as a blind alley and professional suicide. I have always felt it was more than happenstance; the right person for the right job at the right time. Even then, commuting to New York, I still was working only half-time, and it was not until the younger child was fourteen and in boarding school that I began to work more intensively. For the next ten years I commuted every day without difficulty, and looking back it does not seem to *me* that my profession was in any way a handicap to my marriage, although my family probably feels otherwise. We were fortunate in being able to command excellent household help, and after his retirement my husband was occupied with his business affairs.

Children

My surviving daughter was eight when I decided to go to medical school, and she came with me. My first two years were spent in a small house in Rochester, with a housekeeper while she was in school, and I took a young teacher as a boarder to help pay the expenses. During my third and fourth year, however, and my year of internship, it was impossible to keep her with me, so I gave up the house and my daughter lived with an old friend in the East, where we knew many people, and went to an excellent day school. Although we spent all of our vacations together, except when she was visiting her father, I still feel sorry about it, wonderful as her foster mother was.

I had much more time with the second two children. I was always there when they left in the morning and there when they came home in the afternoon, and we spent our vacations as a family except when they began going away to summer camp because the isolation where we lived meant that there were few children for them to play with. It is curious, however, that they claim, retrospectively, that "Mother was always away." Maybe I was, psychologically, but *my* memory is of my very intense and caring feeling for them, and the intense joy that, at my age, I could still have the pleasure of bearing children, nursing them, and caring for them personally and entirely during their infancy and early childhood. When my youngest child was five, my oldest daughter gave birth to her first child! Again I cheated her, because I never was able to play the role of grandmother. In all, I've experienced seven pregnancies, four live births, and one induced and two spontaneous abortions as well as many illnesses and operations and the death of an eight-year-old child.

Personal Ambition

The only personal ambition I ever recollect having was that of doing something worth while, no matter what it was. I think I have (in fact, I *know* I have) difficulty in separating work from play, so satisfied am I with the kind of professional life I have.

Earning Capacity

My husband has always earned much more than I ever could, so this has never been a problem. I now recognize that in the job I held before SIECUS, my salary scale was ridicuously low for what I accomplished, and the amount of time I spent was far more than full-time after the first few years. The year that I resigned to help form SIECUS, I was replaced by two male physicians, each of whom earned more than I was earning after 11 years of service. This all speaks for itself. At SIECUS I have always received adequate compensation.

Evaluation of Self

I shall never be satisfied, even though I do not feel frustrated. At the age of 68

I must recognize that my feelings and character are still in the process of formation, and how much time do I have left? I have evolved more in the past eight years than in the previous sixty. My father is 93. He had two careers after retirement at 65. We are a long-lived family.

Conclusions

I don't feel that I made any sacrifices at all; it simply took me an extra long time to find out what I really wanted to do, and if that was an "extra" price, then it was well worth it. Perhaps my family made the sacrifices. I just don't know.

Advice to Other Women Entering Scientific Careers

No career should be associated with one or the other sex. Johnson O'Connor has shown that of 22 aptitudes, 14 are equal in both men and women, women excel over men in six, and men excel over women in two.* Although there are many things that some women cannot do that some men can do, the reverse is equally true, and it should also be remembered that there are many things that some men can do that other men can't do. If all girls could have the kind of upbringing I had, in terms of taking for granted that gender has nothing to do with what a female could or should do, or could not or should not do, things would be a lot easier for females all around, and also for males, who would then not feel so threatened when women started doing things well in fields that men had previously thought belonged entirely to them.

With slavery, those who enslaved were damaged, if in a different way from those they enslaved. So it is with men and women, who are people first, before they are men and women. There are as many points of difference between men and men and women and women as there are between men and women. For either sex to use these differences against the other sex is self-defeating for both sexes.

* Jon J. Durkin. 1971. The Potential of Women. Bulletin No. 87. Johnson O'Connor Research Foundation. New York, N. Y.

CHEMIST AND "ECO-FREAK"

Ruth Weiner

Chairman, Department of Physical Sciences
Florida International University
Miami, Florida 33144

My family background was probably more conducive than most to pursuit of a professional career. I was born in Vienna, Austria; my father holds both an M.D. and a Ph.D. in zoology, and my mother was one of the first women to receive a Ph.D. from the University of Vienna in a science (biology). My two grandfathers were both physicians (my father's father was Mrs. Freud's obstetrician!). In general, my family belonged to the upper-income Jewish society of Vienna; indeed, my paternal grandmother was extremely wealthy. My parents were religious freethinkers, to the extent that they formally disaffiliated with Judaism, and were political liberals. My mother was, until the Anschluss, a Social-Democrat member of the Vienna City Council.

I am the younger of two half-sibs: my brother is the child of my father's first marriage. It was always assumed that he and I would (1) pursue our education through some graduate degree (preferably in a science), (2) speak at least three languages fluently, and (3) play at least one musical instrument quite well. These, I might add, were the normal expectations for children of the social subgroup into which we were born. Our subsequent forced emigration to the U.S., and life there in moderate poverty for the first decade after immigration, made no difference in these expectations. In fact, we lived up to them. My brother is Dean of the College of Humanities at Montclair State College, New Jersey, and was for several years Chairman of the Department of Comparative Literature at the University of Massachusetts.

It was always assumed that I would pursue a scientific career, since I showed some talent in that direction, and I was strongly pressed to go into my father's field: medicine. I cannot say that I was *encouraged* to have professional aspirations, as much as that it was *assumed* that I would fulfill them. Indeed, throughout childhood I was quite strictly punished for less than superior academic achievement. I was simply too old to change my basic aspirations when I learned that American girls did not, for the most part, share them.

I am a product of the Baltimore, Maryland public school system, and my recollections are that I fought it every inch of the way. My high school (interestingly, a girls' public high school, one of two such in Baltimore, and with the best academic reputation in the city) discouraged pursuit of scientific professional careers: "Don't you want to go into nursing, instead?" Since I was already on the principal's blacklist because of various political views and general intellectual snobbery and nastiness, this attitude only encouraged me. At the University of Illinois, I was neither encouraged nor discouraged. I chose physics mainly because it was difficult and challenging, rather than out of any great interest. It never occurred to me until much, much later in life that one could enjoy intellectual pursuits and endeavors that *weren't* difficult.

I married at 18, so that almost all adult professional and social interactions came after marriage for me. My husband also always assumed that I would pursue a professional career, along with him. The question "Was your profession a handicap to love and marriage?" is meaningless for me. I would, however, agree wholeheartedly that marriage has been a handicap to my professional career. The one person who crystallized what is my present professional life is my husband's (and later, my) preceptor for the doctorate, who urged me to do what I wanted and go to graduate school.

The doors began to close to me after graduate school. I am now aware that there is considerable discrimination against women in chemistry at the point of graduate school admissions. I suppose that, at that time, in graduate school, I didn't think about it and accepted it as a normal state of affairs. In my last graduate school year, I did become aware that the reasons given for sex discrimination (girls marry and don't finish, girls don't use their degree even if they do finish, girls have babies and quit) were part of a vicious circle that included inadequate child care and enormous social pressures. I suggested a counseling service for female graduate students—a suggestion that caused considerable hilarity among my colleagues and professors.

My first child was born six months before I began graduate school; my fourth, one year after the Ph.D. Two of my children were contraceptive accidents, and would not have been born had there been any legal abortion available to me. If we can render one service to all women, everywhere, and especially those with professional aspirations, it is to legalize abortion on request by the pregnant woman. As long as the burden of contraception rests primarily on women, this is especially necessary.

Child care was difficult, and enormously expensive. Johns Hopkins University had a good day care center for children from 18 months on, which was my best experience with child care altogether. Other than this one experience, I always employed housekeepers, and was paying, in the last year of graduate school, 75% of my income for child care. Since my youngest child started first grade, I have employed no one for either child care or housekeeping, nor does my husband, now that we live apart. I did experience a great deal of guilt leaving my children to go to work, most of it, I now realize, brought on by comments of nonworking mothers such as those at nursery school: "Don't you think you are ruining your children's lives?" From my present perspective, now that they are eight through fourteen years old, they seem to be normal children, with a normal relationship toward me and their father. They are, perhaps, more independent and self-sufficient; for example, my thirteen-year-old bicycles to the orthodontist and they *always* walk to school.

As girls, they have perhaps one unique advantage: their father assumes that they have the same aspirations as do boys and that they would undertake no greater household responsibility than nor exhibit markedly different behavior from boys their age. Their attitude toward a professional mother is that this is the normal state of affairs for them. Their behavior and attitudes truly seem to be shaped more by their individual personalities and the way the six of us interact than by whether or not I have a full-time professional job. The two elder ones are extremely "liberated" young women, and are both explicit and vociferous about any sex discrimination that they observe at school or among their friends. I have perhaps been lucky in that they are all sound constitutionally, and are almost never ill. On the other hand, I also encourage them to ignore minor ailments. They have also been, of course, saddled with a mother who could never be "Room Mother," who could not always attend the school Christmas Play, who never made cookies for the bake sale, but does any of this matter in the long run?

I have never made a conscious effort to spend my spare time with my children, but both my husband and I generally do so. We are a close family, and we like to do things such as skiing and traveling as a family. I certainly enjoy my children's company, and this may, in part, be because I have not ever had it for 24 hours a day, day after day after day. Our social life, rather than our children's, is different from that of our colleagues. Because there is little time for household chores (and less inclination to do them) and little interest on either my own or my husband's part in the house and its setting, we live simply and somewhat shabbily. The place is generally a mess; we almost never entertain in the formal sense. Now that we have separate households, this is even more true. Both domiciles are still furnished in "early Salvation Army," and the sum of the two housing payments are about 12% of our combined incomes. If my children could point to one distinguishing feature of their lives as children of professional parents, it is that our housing and life style are well below the expectations in our income level.

When I had completed a year of postdoctoral fellowship, I went with my husband to Denver, where he had found a position at the University of Denver. We had decided that *he* should look for a job, but, if possible, should take one in a place where I would have opportunities also, and Denver seemed like such a place. In looking for an academic position in the Denver-Boulder-Colorado Springs area, I came on very restrictive and very overt sex discrimination. The University of Denver, where my husband was, would not even consider my application (nepotism, although a father and son had been department members in the recent past). The Colorado School of Mines wrote (although their policy has since changed), "We never hire women in the sciences." In general, the attitude toward a person seeking an academic job in a given place because her family is in that place is very negative. I finally got a position at the University of Colorado School of Medicine as a research associate, paid from grant funds. I really got this only because both the chairman and my subsequent coauthor were Johns Hopkins men themselves. After three years, by a stroke of luck, a position as assistant professor of chemistry at Temple Buell College, a woman's college in Denver, opened up. Since CU would not put me on hard money or a tenure track, I went to Temple Buell. I was considered by my preceptor at Hopkins to be a great success, because I had a tenure-track teaching position at a small college for women, one that is not, in my opinion, first-rate.

My experience at both the Medical School and Temple Buell demonstrated to me that fulfilment involved more interaction with people than was possible in a purely research position and a larger role in policy-making than was possible as a very junior faculty member. At TBC I was, fortunately, able to have positive power in making decisions about curriculum, new faculty, budget, and so on. It is a small college, and a faculty member's role in decision making depends rather heavily on his or her own initiative. The structure of the chemistry major program there is primarily my creation; there was no chemistry major when I went on the faculty.

My experience at TBC demonstrates the enormous importance of women as role models for women students. Prior to my appointment, all of the physics, chemistry, and mathematics faculty had been men. The highest professional aspiration voiced by any student then was to become a laboratory technician! Not only was I able to encourage the girls to go on toward a professional career, but I convinced my closest colleague in the Department that encouragement was both necessary and worthwhile. Although he was not himself prejudiced in any way, he had failed to realize that most girls need encouragement to overcome the tremendous internal pressures that have been built up in them.

Shortly after we moved to Colorado, and because I really felt somewhat unfulfilled in my work, I became active in what was then called the conservation movement. We are very active, out-of-doors people and enjoy all sorts of wilderness experiences, and in this sphere, I have developed a deep sense of responsibility of man toward the earth, and see a need to change some fundamental human attitudes. I also saw where, as a scientist, I could render some valuable services to the "lay" citizenry concerned about conservation.

In 1965, a group of us founded the Colorado Open Space Council. I have been on the board since its inception, and have served both as secretary (1966–67) and as vice-president (1970–71). In 1969 I became one of the founders and chairman of Colorado Citizens for Clean Air, and held this post until leaving Colorado in 1971. I served for two years as legislative chairman for the Open Space Council, and was appointed by the Governor of Colorado to the Executive Committee of the Colorado Environment Commission 1970 (one of two women on the 56-member Commission and the 11-member Executive Committee). I have given technical testimony on air- and water-resource problems before innumerable state legislative committees, and five times—twice by invitation – before committees of the United States Congress. I have helped write several laws, including the Colorado Air Pollution Control Act, and have received several state awards for my activity in the field of conservation.

In spring of 1970, while on a speaking tour for the Conservation Foundation, I spoke at a luncheon for a citizens' clean-air group in Miami. One member of the audience (whom I did not meet at the time) was Dean of the College of Arts and Sciences at my present institution—Florida International University. As a result of the speech, I was offered a deanship (which I turned down), and then the chairmanship of the Department of Chemistry, which I ultimately accepted. FIU has made a deliberate effort to hire women for upper-level administrative positions. For this reason, and because of my work in environmental concerns, they wanted me as chairman. My offer from FIU was totally unsolicited by me and came, I might add, as such a complete surprise that I never connected it with the speech I had given there.

What has happened to my family life as a result of my move to Miami has caused a great deal of private and public comment. Having myself been in the position of looking for an academic job while tied to a given geographic location, I did not want to put my husband, now professor of chemistry at the University of Denver, in that position. FIU has no nepotism rule, except that the case where one spouse has direct administrative authority over the other must be considered specially. I felt then, however, and I still feel, that insistence on a "package deal" would be unwise, would set a bad precedent, and would make everyone unhappy. Moreover, we were not sure that we were ready to transfer the entire family permanently from Colorado. Thus, we decided that, for the present, he would remain in Denver with two children, and I would take two with me to Miami.

Our situation certainly focuses a major problem for women (or perhaps one ought to say for married couples) pursuing professional careers. Unless we initiate jobs that are filled by a married couple rather than by a single person, we cannot guarantee a husband and wife equally satisfying professional appointments in the same geographic location, because there are so few positions available. Elimination of nepotism rules is vitally necessary, and will go a long way toward alleviating this situation, but it is no guarantee of good positions for a married couple.

The choice I made is one which a married woman (or man) would make only after many years of marriage, or when contemplating a permanent separation anyway. It has taught me much about the relative roles of married and single people in our society. I am very lonely, but that is largely because almost all social life takes place for couples. In a married society, the woman alone is a social outcast. If we adapted more naturally to the presence of unmarried, mature adults in our social gatherings, they would not be so lonely, and, I am convinced, the present pressure to be married would be greatly alleviated.

I achieved my present position by a fluke, but in part because I had sought and found fulfilment in an area that is now booming: environmental studies. I became an active leader in the conservation movement because opportunities in my chosen professional area—chemistry—were so severely curtailed by sex discrimination. This is the first time since graduate school that I have felt challenged by my job; I enjoy it very much.

The primary advice I would give girls contemplating a professional career is:

1. Be well prepared, but stay flexible. Few women or men end up doing what they had planned while in graduate school.
2. Maintain your humanity in dealing with people and follow your natural instincts, even though some things you do may be labeled "feminine."
3. Be prepared to work very hard, if you plan to have children. Equality in housekeeping roles is something we are still working to attain.
4. Don't sacrifice your ambition, aggressiveness, or intelligence for any of the standard feminine rewards like marriage.
5. Learn to deal casually with, or to ignore, sexism and discrimination.
6. Set high goals for yourself, and set them independently of your sex.
7. If you marry, marry someone in sympathy with those goals.

CONSUMER SPECIALIST

Esther Peterson

*Former Assistant Secretary of Labor
Consumer Adviser, Giant Food Inc.
Washington, D. C. 20006*

I was next to the youngest of six children—two boys and four girls — in the Eggertsen family of Provo, Utah. My mother was born in Denmark, where her family was converted to the Mormon Church. My father's parents were also converted in Denmark, but he was born in this country. Father was the superintendent of schools in a small university town (I remember telling people when I was very small that my father "owned" the schools), and mother added to the family income by taking in student boarders and roomers during university sessions.

Although we were never poor, our household was run on a tight budget, and everything we wore was painstakingly cleaned and mended to last for what seemed like forever. Everyone in the family, which included various cousins from time to time, had to work hard to keep the house and garden and small farm running smoothly. In those days, everything from rugs to jam was made at home. I remember well my first "boughten" coat. I was a college freshman. I always preferred the outdoor chores, and generally helped my father pick the fruit, feed the pigs, and gather the eggs. He was a kind, gentle man, my refuge whenever anything went wrong. He made me feel that I was very special.

Mormon youth were expected to "go on a mission" to preach mormonism. My parents gave each of us a choice: to go to college or on a mission, or both, if funds were available. We chose college. I never questioned the rigidity with which "women's work" was categorized when I enrolled at Brigham Young University to prepare to become a teacher. Teaching and nursing were socially accepted temporary jobs for women until wifehood was expected to take over, as it did with my three older sisters. It never occurred to me to be anything but a teacher; medicine and law were not for girls. But I have often wondered why I did not consider medicine. I remember being at the top of the class in physiology and anatomy, competing with boys who later on became M.D.'s.

While I was in high school, my father's health became very poor. He had to resign his superintendency and accept a less strenuous role, teaching. During this period, mother became director of an old folk's home to supplement our family income. By my senior year, my father's health became so poor that I taught his classes when he was forced to withdraw.

He died just after my graduation, and my mother urged me to give up my new job (teaching physical education, physiology, and "English" at the land-grant college in Cedar City, Utah) and come home to live with her. I wanted to be independent, and refused. After two years of teaching, I went East to Columbia University Teacher's College for a master's degree. There I met Oliver Peterson, who opened up a whole new world for me to see and react to—a world of sweatshop labor and social inequities. He took me to meetings, and I met dedicated people who wanted to help effect social change.

In 1930 I turned down offers to return to Utah with my master's degree, and I accepted a teaching post at the Winsor School in Boston, where my sister was teaching. The director of Winsor, an exclusive school for girls, was a most remarkable woman of great courage who became my mentor. When I wanted to involve myself in the cause of sweatshop workers, she gave me permission "so

long as your outside activities do not interfere with the quality of your teaching."
More than that, she sympathized with me and supported these activities at a time
when it was not easy to do so. She also defied the McCarthy-like hysteria of that
era and testified against the adoption of a loyalty oath for teachers by the
Massachusetts Legislature.

It was while I was at Winsor that I encountered another major feminine influence in my life, Hilda ("Jane") Smith, whom I met through Cornelia Anderson,
a fellow sports teacher. Miss Smith had resigned as Dean of Women at Bryn Mawr
College in order to direct and solicit funds for a summer school on the Bryn
Mawr campus for working women from the United States and the rest of the
world. I was excited by her account of the program and decided that that was
where I wanted to work. Oliver and I discussed it and found that we both could
serve there, and we did—he as librarian and I as recreation director. Here, during
six summer sessions, we met leaders from here and abroad and had close association with leading professors of the turbulent 30s. I developed a firm belief in
women's ability to help effect social change. I remember directing a play, "We
too are needed," in which the students acted out unwritten parts as "role players."

I left my job at Winsor and the "fabulous" salary it paid for those days ($3,200)
to work for much less as a labor organizer and educational director. I had found
my milieu: social and political activism. In retrospect, I realize that my family and
early church experiences helped prepare me for this, even though my politics did
not fit the mold. We were all taught social responsibility. Additionally, it was
natural for us to express ourselves in public, to sing and dance, and this helped me
in the early days of labor organizing and teaching. Under the aegis of some
Harvard professors of economics, I began to organize overworked and under-
paid people, textile workers, garment workers who did piece-work at home, as
well as fellow teachers who were beginning to overcome the traditional idea that
they were "above labor."

I recall no unique problem during this period associated with my desire to
work in this field of social activism. There were more opportunities to work than
I could accept, and men and women in the labor movement accepted my contribution. I remember some difficulty in being accepted by some leaders of working
people at first because I was an "intellectual," but this was quickly dispelled when
we worked together on concrete problems. I recall clearly being rejected by
many of my friends who felt that I had deserted the ranks of social acceptability
and joined questionable political groups; I was even accused of being a com-
munist by some.

Oliver and I had married in 1932, and then as now, he was my greatest support,
encouraging me, strengthening my confidence. Our four children were born
between 1938 and 1946, and during those years I worked part-time, arranging
it so that I would be at home as much as possible during the children's waking
hours. I don't believe it ever occurred to my husband to question my working,
even when I earned less than the cost of our household help. After our first child
was born, Jacob Potofsky of the Amalgamated Clothing Workers offered me a
job, which I accepted on the spot. A few years later, when my husband's career
took him—and us—to Washington, I became Amalgamated's Washington lobbyist,
working under the direction of Sidney Hillman. Although I had excellent household help, it was not unusual for me to take a preschooler along on my rounds
of Capitol Hill, or an infant to a labor union convention.

During this period I did considerable political work and was greatly influenced
by J. B. S. Hardman, Editor and Editorial Director for the union. I edited "Letters

for Roosevelt," expressions of factory workers I had found to be real and moving. I campaigned for Hillman's Political Action Committee. My children (three then) went to Utah with me in 1944, when I directed the labor work for the election of Senator Elbert Thomas. (Later, in 1958, I acted in a similar capacity for Senator Frank E. Moss.)

I don't know just how the children were affected by my working those years, although they seem to feel that it enriched their lives as it did mine. In 1948, we moved to Sweden, where my husband worked with great satisfaction as labor attaché in the American Embassy. The four years in Sweden and four more in Belgium were formative for all of us. Though I was not earning money during those years, I worked hard; in fact, I saw less of the children under the pressure of obligatory parties and dinners than I did while working at a paying job. However, I managed to study working conditions and women's participation during these years. I attended conferences and prepared a report in Sweden on household employment standards and in Belgium, one on women's role in bettering working conditions.

Upon our return to the States, I returned to the labor movement in the Industrial Union Department of the AFL-CIO, and it was there that I encountered unequal pay for equal work, discovering that I was being paid less than the man who had held the job before me. My appointment by President Kennedy as Director of the Women's Bureau and later as Assistant Secretary of Labor restored my faith in economic democracy, for I earned as much as any of my male counterparts.

Consumer work was something I did not anticipate as the next step in my career, but all the experience in labor and political work came into use to help establish a base of concern for consumer affairs. Obstacles I have encountered along the way have had little to do with my being a woman, as far as I can tell; they are the same kind of difficulties a man would have run into.

I have always felt the work I was doing was worth every minute of effort, and my husband and children always seemed to feel that way, too. Now I am enjoying the luxury of working in what is for me another country—management— in thoroughly interesting and challenging work. Now my only worry is that I might not get everything done that I want to do.

What would I tell a young woman starting a career? I would suggest that she get herself a thorough, liberal education; that she stay loose; that she be ready to shift from one job to another, from one field to another; that she strive to like the work she is doing or do something else more to her liking. If I had sat down in 1930 and tried to figure out where I wanted to go or be 40 years later and proceeded from there, I probably would not have had such an interesting time of it. I would emphasize that joy every day in a challenging assignment that has some significance for one's philosophy of life is more important than the size of the paycheck.

Most of the women I have known who worked after marriage have done so either because they had to for financial reasons or because they felt a need to use their brains and their talents. Either way, a job that summons up one's imagination each working day is the happiest answer to this need.

PART II

*Family Attitudes
and Relationships*

THE KENYAN CAREER WOMAN: TRADITIONAL AND MODERN

Beatrice B. Whiting

Graduate School of Education
Harvard University
Cambridge, Massachusetts 02138

Watching developing countries move rapidly from subsistence economy to modernization is enlightening; it is as if one could witness the course of our own history replayed. During a brief span of time, these societies are undergoing the changes that Western countries have experienced in the last 200-odd years—the same problems emerge, and women are faced with the dilemmas that still remain unsolved and that are the motivating force behind this conference. The first college preparatory secondary schools for Kenyan girls opened in the late forties. The first class of women students completed courses in University College, Nairobi, in the midfifties and received certificates in home economics. The first B.A.'s were granted in the late fifties and early sixties. The first woman lawyers were graduated from the University of Dar el Salaam in 1967; the first woman doctor trained in Great Britain started practicing in 1968. This year the first class of medical students, including several women, will be graduated from the University of Nairobi. There is a woman mayor in Nairobi, two women in Parliament, a woman magistrate, two or three women lecturers at the University—albeit in Advanced Nursing, Home Economics and Education. The great majority of the college graduates are teachers in secondary schools.

During the past six years I have had the opportunity of meeting and working with a number of Kenyan university women. I should like to present a summary of the background of these successful women and compare their experiences to some of the research findings of studies in the United States, in the belief that such a comparison may be enlightening.

The fathers of the successful young women I know were all Christians who had been taught by missionaries to believe that in order to be "civilized," one must be educated. These men have at least a primary school education. Many are teachers or preachers, the rest mostly successful farmers. When they attended their daughters' graduation, they discovered old friends among the other fathers. The mothers of the girls, by and large, had little if any formal education but believed along with their husbands that education was important for both boys and girls. Although being "civilized" was given as the paramount reason for sending children to school in their day, prestige and financial reward are most important. Educated children are a life insurance policy, someone to provide for the mother and father in their old age and to help see the younger children through school. During the period of rapid social change, the parents see education as equipping their children with skills that will ensure both their entrance into the modern world and access to the sources of power.

I would guess that there was little ambivalence in the support these young women received from their parents. The fathers worked hard to earn enough money to pay for school fees and uniforms. The mothers saw to the food supply of the family. Both parents awaited the results of the examinations with as much concern as their children.

The young women also mention the importance of older brothers and sisters who were successful. These siblings were role models and real life examples of the rewards of earning admission to secondary school and the university. They came home on vacations with tales of urban life and new knowledge. For some of the young students, the lack of success of older siblings had been a contributing factor in their fathers' pressing them the harder to get good marks.

In sum, the support by both the father and the mother and older siblings was consistent and positive, and the whole family was both proud and concerned with their daughter's success. As far as I can see, there was no thought that being educated was unfeminine.

During primary school, the girls remember some hostility or rivalry with boys, but it does not seem to have been a real worry. The secondary schools were segregated as to sex, so that for the next six years there was no competition with men.

Although I do not have extensive interview material, it is my impression that all the girls assumed that they would marry, have children, and have careers. Their mothers were seen as having jobs, since they were responsible for a major portion of the agricultural work, for raising the food for the family, and often for contributing money by selling extra garden produce. The maternal role model for the Kenyan girl is not that of a dependent housewife but one of a competent agriculturist and executive who directs the children in the work in the household and in the fields. The wives of successful farmers that I have met are women who seem to have high self-esteem. They are not afraid of directing others. They expect and demand the cooperation of their children.

As mothers of large families, they are respected by all men. Motherhood has a high status universally recognized throughout Kenya.

One of my informants remembers with entertainment the discussions between her father and mother as to which one should take the major credit for having such successful children. Her father had paid school fees; her mother had provided the food and taught her children to work.

The first indication of conflict for the successful young woman emerges in the university. By now we are talking about .5% of the women of Kenya. The competition with men in the classrooms and on examinations becomes a conscious problem. The young women remember discussions in which the men who were fellow students suddenly turned on them and told them they should not contradict men or behave in such an aggressive manner. Unlike the United States, however, where such derogation is often subtle and unconscious on the part of men, the Kenyan men spoke out. Both men and women in Kenya are raised to believe that men are superior to women and should dominate them. Women are expected to respect and show appropriate deference to men, not to speak loudly or boldly. Men do not hesitate to make their criticism known. The women are, therefore, completely conscious of the conflicts that competence created and discuss them openly with their women friends. They were unanimous in deciding that it is wise to find husbands who were more successful than they, since a man cannot tolerate a woman with more education or a better job.

Most of the college women marry while they are in the university or immediately after graduation. Most frequently, they marry men who have graduated from the university several years earlier and have jobs. After marriage these young women combine working with motherhood. Most have, or expect to have, a minimum of four to six children, and they all have salaried jobs—mostly teaching. Maternity leave is three months and is granted in all jobs.

That Kenya expects married women to have careers is demonstrated by the fact that the government offers scholarships to married women. Women who do not earn such support, however, are often financed by their husbands, who see the bachelor's degree as an investment.

The university graduate mothers do not worry about delegating child care to others. Their mothers who worked away from home in the gardens four or five hours a day had turned their children over as early as four months to older siblings or young uncles and aunts to be cared for. It is always possible for married women to get relatives from home or to hire women in the city to act as surrogate mothers. The Kenyan mother is not burdened by guilt, as is the American mother, when she sets off to work for the day leaving her children with baby-sitters.

These Kenyan mothers have little time for social life. They return home after work and devote the rest of their energies to the household. Their husbands frequently join other men in the evening. Since the social life of men and women has always been separate, this is not the deprivation it would be to a married American professional woman, who expects to share a social life with her husband.

Finding an appropriate husband is far more difficult than it was in traditional times, when husbands were selected by the bride's father. A woman wants a man who esteems himself and is not threatened by the status of his wife. The university graduate who chooses to go on for an advanced degree realizes that she is in a difficult position. In a society where men stress their dominance over women, she is ill-advised to marry a man with less education; hence the pool of potential mates is small. To remain unmarried, on the other hand, is difficult—far more difficult for a Kenyan woman, since traditionally all women married, than for a woman in the United States, where the status of spinster is acceptable. In Kenya, women who are not married are not respected by men, who see them as free sexual game. On the other hand, higher education is seen as a potential financial asset, and hence, from a strict materialistic point of view, a woman who earns a graduate degree is more valuable than her less well-educated peer.

What, then, are the similarities and differences in the problems of American and Kenyan educated women? What insights do we get from comparing their backgrounds and expectations? Are the experiences of the emerging professional women in Kenya repeating the history of women in the United States, or are there major differences?

In the first place, I would judge that education in general and education for women is more valued by the population of Kenya as a whole than it is or ever was in the United States. Historically, missionary influence and the role model of British Colonials both contributed to the perceived value. The present status system reflects this attitude. To be a university professor is considered one of the most prestigious careers that a man or woman can have. Certainly for the last seventy-odd years this has not been true in the United States, if it were ever so. In the U.S. scene, a professor who is an adviser to the president might approach the prestige of a bank president or corporation executive, but in general, college professors are not one of the top-prestige statuses.

The Kenyan mother and father who believe in education are backed by the value system of the society as a whole, and there seems to be none of the ambivalence about educating women that existed in the United States during the early part of the twentieth century.

In the second place, there is at present no ambivalence about Kenyan women's working. The role model of a successful woman includes productive work outside the home, delegated child care, and executive ability; hence, to pursue a career is not considered masculine, as it was and in some circles still is in the United

States. It is true that educated women in Kenya, as in the U.S., are primarily teachers, and that they may encounter trouble when they begin to spread out into other professions. In general, however, there has been less discrimination against women than in the early 1900s in the United States.

In the third place, motherhood is more highly valued in Kenya, and there is far less ambivalence about marriage. Women seem to want children genuinely and to see child-bearing as a means of attaining rewards—respect from men and from the society as a whole. They do not share the ambivalent feeling of the young college women in the United States. The status of a mother is not just given lip service; it is acclaimed, and women believe that it is of value. On the other hand, they do not expect so much from marriage as the American woman. Love and emotional interdependence are not essential to a successful marriage—rather, cooperation in the creation of a family of strong and successful children. Neither social life nor confidences need be shared between husband and wife. Each has a clearly defined role, a separate life, and a separate important job within the home.

In the fourth place, young women do not feel the competition from men until they reach the university, and therefore are perhaps more secure both intellectually and psychologically before the full impact of the overt conflict with men begins. The American girl faces the competition and antagonism from boys at the very time she is reaching menarche and beginning to see herself as a true woman. The American adolescent seems to have more difficulty accepting her femaleness than the Kenyan girl of the same age.

Last, and perhaps most important, the differential status of men and women is clearly defined, and there is no question that men are superior. Because there is no pretense about equality, as there is in the United States, Kenyan women are not angry about the status system, but at least for the time being, are able to work within the system in order to attain status jobs. Their energies are not dissipated by righteous anger, as are those of American women who are told from first grade on that they are equal to men but are treated in a manner that belies the statement. Since Kenyan women have always been treated as inferiors, they are not so surprised and upset by derogations. Furthermore, since the discrimination and hostility are more overt than in the U.S., they can identify the behavior and discuss it with other women. It has taken American university women one hundred years to be able to bond together to discuss male chauvinism and male discrimination. Kenyan women, because of the clear separation of the status of men and women, have had more experience both in handling the derogation of men and in bonding with other women. This leads to a strange paradox, and one which may prove true in other parts of the world; namely, that when there is a clear status difference between men and women, the self-confidence and self-esteem of women is less weakened by the antagonism of men in competitive situations, since they are less surprised and upset when the derogation is expressed. They are more able and likely to share their experiences with others and to help each other. They are less dependent on men, more used to the expectation that they will fend for themselves and provide for many of their own needs. Although they are expected to be submissive in their relations with their husbands, they are expected to be competent, independent, and managerial in their role of mother and farmer.

There is an interesting paradox in the struggle of women in Kenya (and for that matter, in all of Africa), in India, and in the United States for equal status. It may prove hardest for women to attain equal status in societies where there has been the myth of the equality of the sexes—societies where, by and large, the family is isolated and nuclear, and of necessity male and female roles within the household are more interchangeable. In these societies it is more difficult to define maleness and femaleness in the context of specific settings, as one does in Africa or India. In these countries a woman is submissive and passive in the presence of men but active, executive, and forceful in their absence. In the societies where there are clearly defined roles for men and women and a recognized status relationship, women have always been conscious of discriminatory practices and have learned to work within the system. They are fighting an enemy who is often open and direct in his confrontation. In our society we are still often fighting with unconscious enemies: identification with a father rather than a mother, rejection of the role model of a masochistic, housebound mother. Matina Horner's studies of the fear of success are the closest we have come to identifying the enemy of our equal status with men, and to date the enemy has only been identified in the unconscious or confronted in the conscious-raising small groups of the women's liberation movement. We are still not clear how we want to define femaleness, because we find it difficult to conceive of personality traits as varying with settings. A good woman can be an active executive in her job if not in her connubial bed.

FAMILY DYNAMICS AND
THE SUCCESSFUL WOMAN EXECUTIVE

Margaret M. Hennig

Director, Prince Program in Retail Management
Simmons College
Boston, Massachusetts 02115

It is difficult to give proper coverage in so short a space to a subject the understanding of which may be essential to enable women to contribute fully to life and knowledge in our world. Dr. Matina Horner of Harvard University must be given the highest credit for setting before all of us the evidence of the knowledge that women suffer from blockages and permutations of the achievement motivation. These, if removed, could unlock, once and for all, the achievement potential of large numbers of women in our society and could predict future generations of women whose scope of accomplishment is impossible to forecast. Because of space limitations, I should like, first, to summarize those of Horner's findings that relate most directly to my topic and then to report to you some findings from my research on *Career Development for Women Executives*.[8] What first drew my attention to the relationships between these two pieces of research was that the women executives I studied were clearly, at maturity, women who had possessed the achievement motivation and acted it out to the fullest, having reduced their feelings of anxiety that Horner finds in younger women, and without having suffered as acutely as many of her subjects when placed in competitive achievement situations with men. In this research it became clear that the women executives had been able, through family and peer relationships, to develop an integrated positive achievement motivation from early childhood, and in spite of meeting all the difficulties our society creates for the intelligent and achieving woman, never to let go of or reduce that basic achievement motivation. Let us look for a moment at Horner's findings.

What Is the Need to Achieve that We All Talk about?

Very simply, the need to achieve means that an individual has internalized a desire to achieve in situations of intelligence and/or leadership, and, acting out that achievement, the measure of its quality comes from a set of standards or yardsticks created by, administered by, and embodied or internalized within that particular individual.

Matina Horner, in viewing all the research on this subject prior to her own in the midsixties, found that it demonstrated a conspicuous absence of female subjects and, hence, findings about women. My own review supports this finding. In first raising the question of possible existing sex differences in achievement motivation, Horner took as her clue the conclusive findings of a number of researchers that women get higher test-anxiety scores than do men. Either consciously or unconsciously, a young woman apparently accepts our society's judgment that intellectual or professional achievement for a woman signifies that woman's concurrent loss of femaleness. As Horner says: "A bright woman is caught in a double bind. In testing and other achievement-oriented situations, she worries not only about failure but also about success. If she fails, she is not living up to her own standards of performance; if she succeeds she is not living up to societal expectations about the female role."* From this study came some of Horner's now well-accepted findings:

1. That achievement motivation in women is a double-bind situation;
2. That, hence, achievement is a source of high anxiety for many women;
3. That some women develop a "negative achievement motivation" or the motivation to avoid success or to stop it at a point of intolerable anxiety over conflict between achievement and femininity;
4. That even among women who do evidence achievement, they evidenced higher achievement when working alone, and not when in direct competition with males. Thus, in fact, because of the previous points, women will often consciously or unconsciously reduce their achievement when working in competitive situations with men.[2]

The women executives whom I studied were all presidents or vice-presidents of medium-to-large, nationally recognized business firms. All of these businesses were considered male-oriented, and all of these female corporate officers were in supervisory positions with direct power and influence over major decisions and policy-setting. The study encompassed their entire lives and career histories, and the method was simple, in-depth, clinical interviewing, accompanied by intensive factual data collection and analysis of a detailed autobiographical statement written by each subject. In 1968, there were approximately 100 such women in the entire United States, and 25 took part in this research. Thus the sample was very large, but the population was very small. In addition, as the first identifiable body of such women, this group probably encompasses many of the characteristics of pioneers; the most important was to have incurred the strongest attempt by the larger society to eliminate or confine it and, on the part of the women who made it up, the need to represent the extreme in all of their enabling characteristics. In working from childhood toward the goal of achievement and success in a career, there is complete evidence that these women experienced Horner's double-bind situation and that, in their early years, achievement was a source of potential conflict and possible anxiety. But this did not result in their developing a negative achievement motivation or fear of success, or in an avoidance or lowering of achievement in competitive situations with males.

The findings of my research place much of the explanation for this in the family dynamics during the childhoods of these women executives. Although I can offer only limited evidence that the absence of the dynamics I am about to discuss explains the absence of positive achievement motivation in women, there is strong evidence that their existence explains, in large part, the ability of this particular group of women constantly to evidence positive achievement motivation in their successful executive careers. In a control group of women who appeared overtly to match the top women executives in all factual data but who had never succeeded in rising beyond middle management, it was clear that the major identifiable difference between the two groups was in the strength, security, and health of their family dynamics during childhood. Let us move, then, to an examination of these dynamics, preceded by a few biographical facts about the women.

All of the subjects were born in the United States between 1910 and 1915; a war was developing and a climate of anxiety and austerity prevailed. All were first-born and female. Each was destined to be an only child or the eldest in an all-girl family of no more than three female siblings. All were born into upward-

---

* A bright woman is caught in a double bind. In achievement-oriented situations, she worries not only about failure, but also about success. (See Ref. 1.)

aspiring middle-class families residing on or near the eastern seaboard. All subjects, except three, had fathers who held middle-management positions in business. Three subjects were children of professional educators. All had mothers whose primary activity was within the home and family, but one mother was also a practicing educator. With the exception of two, the subjects' mothers had education equal to that of their fathers. In thirteen of these cases, the mothers had an education superior to that of the fathers. Of the 25 subjects, their parents' education ranged from the minimum of a high-school diploma to doctorates held by two fathers. Most of the parents had some educational or vocational training beyond high school. All subjects and their parents were American-born Caucasians, but no distinctive patterns existed in their religious preferences or heritage.

As is the rather typical finding in all research on professional women, all of the subjects were first-born, and, in this case, first-born in what were to be all-girl families. Douvan and Adelson, in their extensive studies of adolescents, reported the following:

> Anecdotal accounts, clinical observations and empirical studies concur: the first child is likely to be the recipient of pressures, hopes and anxieties that later children are more apt to escape. The parents will generally be overattentive and overambitious; excessively eager that the child validate their worth as parents, excessively fearful that the child may depart from some ideal standard, overstern yet overindulgent. . . . Firstborns are far more likely to achieve eminence and, in fact, are more likely to receive higher education.[3]

In general, then, they concluded that firstborns tend to be more active, more future-oriented, and more achievement-motivated. Realizing that such sibling placement has frequently resulted in this identifiable pattern of family dynamics involving both the child and the parents, it is more useful to think of the first-born syndrome as a special-child syndrome, since it is possible for other children in other sibling placement to experience these same dynamics (particularly a last child or a second child following a firstborn who has been a disappointment to his parents).

In recalling their relationships with their parents during early childhood, all of the subjects reported them as having been extremely close, warm, and attentive. While they saw their relationships with their mothers as having been typical of a caring and nurturing mother-child constellation, they viewed their relationships with their fathers as being atypical; that is, closer, warmer, more supportive, and, particularly, more sharing than those of most fathers and daughters. In this sharing, the fathers and daughters tended to share the fathers' personal interests, activities, and enthusiasms. The subjects also viewed the relationship between their parents as unusually strong both between the parents themselves and in the way that the parents related to them. They defined this as meaning that each parent liked and respected the other, and while each related to the subject in a different way, they shared similar aspirations for the daughter and strongly supported and reinforced each other's parent-child relationship. As one subject characterized this: "I had the fortune to have two full and complete parents. That is, both my mother and my father were separate real people and I had a separate and real relationship with each. Most girls have such experience of sharing common interests with their mothers, few share common interests with their dads." In other words, these young girls wished to and did develop integrated personalities; instead of rejecting either of the classic sex stereotypes, they explored both.

The explanation most often given for the family dynamics of an achievement-motivated woman is that she was raised as a boy. This explanation proves unsound in this research and is replaced by the idea that these subjects who were raised as sons might have been so without the abandonment of any parental support and recognition of the fact that they were girls. Therefore, while the mothers tended to represent the traditional feminine role model for their daughters, they also actively supported their child's total freedom of exploration of what were considered male roles. Concurrently, the fathers, who were actively participating with their daughters in frequent male activities, similarly supported their daughters' femaleness but demanded from them more than typical expansiveness of role-testing, activity choice, and willingness to engage in competition with both boys and girls. Both parents offered the daughter large amounts of evidenced personal satisfaction and pleasure for her accomplishments. However, even when the subjects were as young as four and five years, both parents sought to help their daughters internalize those satisfactions and pleasures. The young female was encouraged to set her own goals, establish her own standards for measuring the success of her achievement, and, hence, experiencing her personally determined rewards and satisfactions.

Another essential family dynamic in the childhood of women executives was the way in which they and their parents dealt with conflict that arose around gender-related role definitions. The subjects reported that until they began school, they were unaware that certain sex-related role taboos existed for males and females. Because of this, their first year in school was a particularly traumatic and potentially conflict-laden one in which they found themselves constrained or even punished for engaging in aggressive or active sports activities and behavioral styles that were quite natural to them. Rather, they were limited to more passive activities in both play and work. The parental response to this problem was to support the child uniformly and, at the same time, attempt to change the teacher's attitude or structural impediment at the school. Even if change didn't occur fully, the child felt herself upheld by her major sources of support and satisfaction, the parents and herself. Therefore, for most of the early years, the subjects were able to put aside the potent role conflict within the school. None of the subjects reported experiencing negative feedback from peers, male or female, until adolescence.

Although there is a great deal more evidence in my research to support and illuminate the strong and positive family dynamics in the childhoods of the women executives studied, some can be effectively summarized by looking at the major characteristics of the family constellation formed between the mother, the father, and the very young daughter.

1. Both parents valued highly for their girl child both femaleness *and* achievement, activity, and competitive success.

2. Both parents valued each other highly and reinforced each other's role choices and behavioral styles.

3. Each parent related to the other and to the child as separate persons, yet valued highly and supported each other's relationships.

4. The female child was treated by her family as a person who was a female but who had available to her all role and behavior options available to either sex.

5. The family constellation provided a security base and a source of personal reward, satisfaction, and reinforcement that allowed the young girl child to overlook or retreat from potential gender-related role conflicts.

6. Overall, the parents created a positive, supportive climate in which the girl child could explore, without limitation of gender-related constraints, numerous roles and behavioral styles that allowed the girl child to experience direct instrumental life at a very early age.

What was the result of such a family constellation? First, the girl child was allowed to experience active, self-directed instrumental life, or simply, to experience the achievement motivation in action. The result of this was to allow her to develop feelings of mastery and success at increasing levels of difficulty in a variety of settings that by no means excluded direct competition with young male children. Therefore, in relation to Horner's findings that many young women feel the need to reduce achievement in competitive situations in order to preserve their femininity, this was not the case with these girl-children. They were able to internalize achievement in a sufficiently supportive climate before they even became aware of the potential conflicts. Therefore, when the conflicts did arise, it was the conflict itself, rather than the achievement, that was perceived as needing to be eliminated.

Second, not only do many women get caught in the double-bind of achievement vs. femininity, but this is further complicated by the fact that there is an extremely high positive correlation between self-esteem and achievement. Unlike the early life experience of many girl children, these subjects spent their earliest years developing tremendous amounts of self-esteem related both to their parents' reinforcement of them and their own experiences of mastery and success. Further, from their earliest years, they learned to connect achievement and self-esteem directly, and when they became aware of gender-role taboos, being denied these roles served not to affect either their achievement or their self-esteem but, rather, to place their direct anger on what they perceived as a ridiculous direct constraint on girls; in other words, not on girls' self-esteem and not on the question of whether girls should achieve, but very directly on the choice-limitations to girls. Much later, in adolescence, these conflicts would more directly challenge the future women executives' ability to continue achievement motivation and maintain her self-esteem as a woman. Even then, the direct connection between her previous experience as a full person and a high achiever who was highly esteemed in those roles sustained her.

It was clear in my research that the family experiences of the childhood provided these women with such strongly internalized feeling of self-esteem and the positive feelings of achievement success in the direct instrumental world that they were less vulnerable to attacks on their femininity than they would have been from achievement failure. During those early experiences, they accepted such a strong concept of themselves as people that even years of later conflict and pressure to split them into two segments—the feminine affective person and the masculine instrumental person—could not cause them to reduce their achievement drive. And, finally, their very early experiences with competitive achievement with males (beginning with the father) helped them to overcome and feel comfortable in such settings in the future. They learned then and always believed that competition with others served only as a further stimulus to competition with themselves, which, in the end, whether male or female, was what they believed the achievement motivation was really all about.

References

1. HORNER, M. 1969. Psychology Today : 3(6).
2. HORNER, M. 1968. Sex Differences in Achievement Motivation and Performance in Competitive and Non-Competitive Situations. Unpublished Doctoral Dissertation. University of Michigan. Ann Arbor, Mich.
3. DOUVAN, E. & J. ADELSON. 1966. The Adolescent Experience. : 277. John Wiley & Sons, Inc. New York, N. Y.

4. FREUD, S. 1965. Femininity. Lecture XXXIII. *In* New Introductory Lectures on Psycho-analysis. W. W. Norton & Co., Inc. New York, N. Y.
5. ATKINSON, J. W. & N. T. FEATHER. 1966. A Theory of Achievement Motivation. John Wiley & Sons, Inc. New York, N. Y.
6. FRENCH, E. G. & G. S. LESSER. 1964. Some characteristics of the achievement motivation in women. J. Abnorm. Soc. Psych. **68**: 119–128.
7. MEAD, M. 1967. Male and Female. Wm. Morrow & Co. New York, N. Y.
8. HENNIG, M. 1971. Career Development for Women Executives. Unpublished Doctoral Dissertation. Harvard University Graduate School of Business Administration. Cambridge, Mass.

FAMILY CONSTRAINTS ON WOMEN'S WORK

Lotte Bailyn

Sloan School of Management
Massachusetts Institute of Technology
Cambridge, Mass. 02139

The "immediate objective" of the Conference on Successful Women in the Sciences was "to convene successful professional women . . . who have managed to work actively in predominantly male professions and to evaluate the parameters in their lives that were determining factors in their subsequent careers." But a second goal, one described by the planners as "ultimate albeit utopian," is "to salvage the tremendous natural resources currently being wasted by the neglect of talented women in our society."

There is no doubt that the first of these goals has been served. We are learning something about a group of exceptionally talented women. But will knowledge about this group of remarkable women generalize to the vastly larger proportion of less exceptional women whose waste of talent is deplored in the statement of the second goal? Partly, of course, it will—and in any case, the determinants of success of such an unusual group are of great interest in their own right. But exceptional talent is always a rare commodity, and if we want to understand the constraints operating on less remarkable but still talented, trained, and committed women, we may have to redesign our investigation.

Studies of women in the sciences, women actively engaged in the pursuit of a scientific career, deal with women who are exceptional not only in their energies and abilities, both scientific and managerial, but in family circumstances as well. Most studies comparing the careers of men and women in science consistently show that a much larger proportion of the women are not married. Generally, close to half the women scientists are unmarried; the figure for men is closer to ten percent. Further, even when married, the women scientists have fewer children: between one third and one half of such women's families are childless, whereas the childless men generally comprise no more than 10% of the total group.[1]

By studying such groups, we may miss the pattern of constraints operating on less exceptional women: women with families who are trained, and willing to participate in professional work, but whose contributions are not on the level of the most accomplished group of either sex. By identifying the constraints on the work of such women we may be able to localize those conditions in need of change, those circumstances which today still require exceptional individual effort to overcome. It is at those points that social intervention will be most fruitful in the pursuit of our "ultimate albeit utopian" goal.

For this reason I shall deal here not with a group of extraordinary women, but with a more varied group, a group of women that is defined only by the fact of marriage to educated men. It is among such women that we characteristically find the greatest waste of talent, and the factors that influence their participation or lack of participation in the occupational world may be very different from those that propel the most gifted group.

Speaking quite generally, we can identify three overall sources of constraints on women's professional work: those stemming from the woman herself, those from the professional world, and those from her adult family. The first — dependent on her early socialization by parents and teachers, and influenced by such circumstances as sibling structure and parental role models — encompasses such phenomena as the reduced expectations documented by Rossi and Davis, and the apparent difficulties of reconciling achievement and femininity, which have been investigated by Horner, Alper, and others.[2]

Constraints emanating from the professional world range from straightforward discrimination (the easiest to handle, to judge by the progress already visible under the prodding of the Department of Health, Education, and Welfare) to those more subtle and pervasive forces stemming from lack of female role models during training[3] and the fact that women are at a disadvantage in circumstances where advancement and importance in an organization are accomplished by means of ill-defined processes dependent on informal networks of association.[4]

Finally, a woman's adult family is the source of a number of constraints ranging from direct problems stemming from the number and age of the children she has, through the intermediary influence of a husband's attitude toward his wife's professional work, to more subtle forces stemming from the husband's own occupational role.[5]

Of these three sets of constraints, the current study emphasizes the third: specifically, the immediate family situation of women and the complex relationship between a woman's professional career and her husband's attitudes to his own work and to his family life.

The data used derive from an alumni survey of M.I.T. graduates from the classes of 1951, 1955, and 1959, men now in their late thirties and early forties.[6] The survey was designed mainly to trace the career patterns of M.I.T. graduates, but it included enough information about these men's wives and families to serve the present purpose.

More than 90% of the 1,351 respondents to the questionnaire are currently married. It is these 1,219 M.I.T. graduates, together with the data they provide about their wives, who comprise the sample on which this paper is based.

Most of these wives are not currently working: only 27% are employed at present (of which one third are working full time). But this is an overall figure and ignores two crucial influences on these women: their professional qualification and their current family situation.

As is evident in TABLE 1, a woman's education is strongly related to the likelihood of her working: no more than a quarter of the wives whose education did not exceed college are working, fully 81% of those with Doctorates are currently working in their professional fields (and of these, more than two thirds are working full time). Of course some women (and men) do professional work even without a Doctorate. Hence we add knowledge of occupational field to that of education to classify the wives into three levels of professional qualification: top professional, semiprofessional, and nonprofessional. All those with Doctorates, as well as those Bachelor's and Master's degree holders whose occupations are classified by their husbands as professional, comprise the top professional group; lesser professionals are those with Master's degrees as well as those college graduates without higher degrees whose occupations are listed as lesser professional; the nonprofessional group, thus, consists of all those who did not graduate from college as well as those with Bachelor's degrees who are not associated with professional occupations. The higher the professional qualification of a woman, the more likely she is to be working — a finding that belies, once again, the contention that professional training is wasted on women because they do not use it.

Second, TABLE 1 gives information on the work status of women with various numbers of children and with children of various ages. It shows that the absence

TABLE 1

WORK STATUS IN RELATION TO LEVEL OF EDUCATION AND CURRENT FAMILY COMPOSITION

	Percentage of Total Sample in each Category	Percentage of each Category Working	Percentage of those Working who are Working Full Time
Education			
HS graduate or less	15%	19% (N = 187)	31% (N = 35)
Some college	29%	23% (N = 350)	21% (N = 80)
Bachelor's degree	39%	24% (N = 477)	30% (N = 116)
Master's degree	14%	41% (N = 169)	34% (N = 70)
Doctorate	3%	81% (N = 36)	72% (N = 29)
Family Composition*			
No children	7%	60% (N = 90)	70% (N = 54)
One child	10%	28% (N = 122)	44% (N = 34)
school age	4%	39% (N = 44)	59% (N = 17)
preschool	6%	22% (N = 78)	29% (N = 17)
Two children	33%	25% (N = 393)	28% (N = 98)
youngest is school age	16%	31% (N = 188)	31% (N = 58)
youngest is preschool	17%	20% (N = 205)	22% (N = 40)
Three or more children	50%	24% (N = 604)	19% (N = 142)
youngest is school age	24%	34% (N = 285)	22% (N = 97)
youngest is preschool	26%	14% (N = 319)	13% (N = 45)
Total Group	100%	27% (N = 1219)	33% (N = 330)

* Ten people (including two working wives) did not give information about their children; they are excluded from this part of the table.

of children greatly increases the likelihood of working: 60% of those with no children are working, most of them full time. Once one has children, the number one has seems to affect one's work status less than does the age of the youngest (although the number is related to the extent to which the working wives are able to participate in full-time work).[7] For the present purpose, therefore, it is sufficient to differentiate among three different family situations: those with no children, those with children all of whom are already at school, and those with preschoolers. The likelihood of working decreases markedly from each of these groups to the next.

These two factors, then — professional qualification and family situation — are crucial determinants of whether or not this group of women is working. They are not independent of each other, of course: almost one fifth of the women with top professional qualifications have no children, in contrast to less than seven percent of the other wives.[8] Their joint influence on work status is assessed in TABLE 2.

It is obvious from the table that the only women with professional qualification who are not working in their fields are those with preschool children at home: only half of these are currently working. By contrast, almost all of those professionally qualified women without children are working full time; most of those with school-age children are also working, about half full time and half part time.

In the past few years, the prescription of discontinuous work for women — training first, then time out for children, followed by the resumption of work — has been seriously questioned, especially for women engaged in scientific work,[9] and the advantage of continuous work, even if on a part-time basis, has been stressed. Our data support this position. TABLE 3 shows that those women who worked when their youngest child was under three are much more likely to be working when their children are all older than three than are those who withdrew from work at that time. Further, the table indicates that whether or not the work at the early stage was full or part time makes no difference to their subsequent participation in work (although it does affect the extent to which their current participation is full time). By stressing the crucial nature of continuity of involvement, this finding underscores the importance of the effort of many women's groups to establish full status but part-time positions in the professions.

The fact that continuity in professional work is crucial makes it particularly important to investigate the constraints on professionally qualified women with preschool children, only half of whom are currently working in their professional fields.

Certain solutions to their dilemma are obvious. The easy availability of part-time professional work combined with good day-care facilities would, no doubt, increase this percentage considerably. But it is perhaps a mistake to feel that such managerial solutions are all that is necessary. Previous research has shown that combining two professional careers into a satisfactory family situation is not easy, and requires a certain amount of accommodation on the part of the husband.[10] If this is so, then no amount of external management will be sufficient to ensure the success of such dual-career families. TABLE 4, which relates such a woman's work status to characteristics of her husband — to the way he approaches his own work and its relation to his family — provides further evidence on this point.

Professionally qualified wives whose husbands are able to integrate career and family needs, whose satisfactions in life stem from both career and family and who are pleased with their jobs and with their family situations, are more likely

TABLE 2

WORK STATUS IN RELATION TO THE JOINT INFLUENCE OF PROFESSIONAL QUALIFICATION
AND FAMILY SITUATION

Professional Qualification	Family Situation			Total
	No Children	Youngest is School Age	Youngest is Preschool	
Top Professional*	95% are working of which 83% are full time (N = 19)	88% are working of which 52% are full time (N = 33)	51% are working of which 36% are full time (N = 49)	71% are working of which 54% are full time (N = 101) (8% of total group)
Semiprofessional*	44% are working of which 71% are full time (N = 16)	58% are working of which 35% are full time (N = 82)	29% are working of which 19% are full time (N = 109)	42% are working of which 32% are full time (N = 207) (17% of total group)
Nonprofessional	53% are working of which 62% are full time (N = 55)	24% are working of which 18% are full time (N = 402)	10% are working of which 11% are full time (N = 444)	19% are working of which 24% are full time (N = 901) (75% of total group)
Total	60% are working of which 70% are full time (N = 90) (7% of total group)	33% are working of which 28% are full time (N = 517) (43% of total group)	17% are working of which 20% are full time (N = 602) (50% of total group)	27% are working of which 33% are full time (N = 1209)† (100%)

* Women in these categories who are not working in their professional fields are not included in the percentage currently working: four women with top professional and ten with semiprofessional qualifications are currently employed, but not in work for which they were trained.

† Excludes those who gave no information on family situation.

TABLE 3

RELATION OF PAST TO CURRENT WORK STATUS
(FOR WOMEN WHOSE YOUNGEST CHILD IS OVER THREE)

Work Status when Youngest Child was Under Three	Percentage of each Category Currently Working	Percentage of those Currently Working who are Working Full Time
Worked full time	60% (N = 15)	78% (N = 9)
Worked part time	62% (N = 71)	23% (N = 44)
Did not work	24% (N = 689)	22% (N = 167)

to be working when their children are very young than are those of "noninte-grated" husbands.[11] But such integration between career and family on the part of husbands seems to imply some pulling back from the career-oriented attitudes usually associated with the occupational roles of educated men. It is those whose job satisfaction is high but not very high, those who value achievement but not too much, whose wives are most likely to be working. On the other hand, those for whom success at work is all-important, and who do not take family needs into consideration in job-related decisions, have wives who, although professionally qualified, are very unlikely to be working during the years when their family sit-uations are least supportive.

But complete withdrawal of the husband into the family is also no answer. Those men whose satisfactions in life are primarily derived from family, for whom career is not a major source of satisfaction, are particularly likely to have their professionally qualified wives at home, not working in their fields. Further, wives of men with great confidence in their abilities to identify and solve prob-lems — an assessment usually found among success-oriented men — are more likely to be working professionally when their children are very young; but so are those whose husbands are concerned with social problems, an attitude more often associated with less traditional occupational roles.[12]

The key seems to be balance, a balance of commitments — to work, family, society — without exclusive involvement in any one of these areas. Such an inte-grated life style on the part of the husband increases the likelihood that a profes-sionally qualified woman will work even when her children are very young, thereby providing the continuity of involvement that she needs for the full devel-opment of the professional part of her life.

Thus husbands' life styles create a significant set of constraints on a married woman's participation in the professions. It should be stated, however (and it is obvious from TABLE 4), that while important, the effect of this set of constraints, taken alone, is relatively small. An increase in the number of women who receive professional training, or the development of first-class facilities for the care of preschool children, or reduction in family size, including an increase in the num-ber of childless marriages—any one of these changes by itself would, no doubt, contribute more to the likelihood of women's careers than would a change in their husbands' life styles. But the husband's pattern of life remains fundamentally important because it sets a limit to the effect that the lifting of other constraints could have.

We started this paper with an account of exceptional women. We must end it with a word about exceptional people of either sex, exceptional in the contribu-tion they are able to make to science, both human and physical. It may be impos-sible for such people to live fully balanced lives, and perhaps we would all be losers if they were to attempt to do so. In recommending balance, therefore, we

TABLE 4

FAMILY CONSTRAINTS ON WORK OF FULLY PROFESSIONALLY QUALIFIED
WOMEN WITH PRESCHOOL CHILDREN*

	Characteristics of Husband	Percentage of the Wives Currently Working
1.†	Integrates family and work	59% (N = 17)
	Does not integrate family and work	45% (N = 29)
2.‡	Very satisfied with his job	38% (N = 8)
	Satisfied with his job	60% (N = 25)
	Not very satisfied with his job	40% (N = 15)
3.§	Very much values work achievement	48% (N = 21)
	Values work achievement somewhat	62% (N = 13)
	Does not value work achievement very much	50% (N = 14)
4.¶	Oriented to success but not to family	38% (N = 8)
	Oriented to family but not to success	56% (N = 16)
	Equally oriented to success and family	55% (N = 20)
5.**	Main life satisfaction from family, not career	25% (N = 12)
	Main life satisfaction from family and career	67% (N = 21)
	Main life satisfaction from career	54% (N = 13)
6.††	Possesses ability to identify and solve problems to great extent	72% (N = 18)
	Does not possess ability to identify and solve problems to great extent	38% (N = 29)
7.‡‡	Concerned with social problems	59% (N = 27)
	Not concerned with social problems	45% (N = 20)

* There are 49 people in this group. For any given category, this number is reduced by those not answering the relevant questions.

† Men are considered "integrated" if they listed "career or occupation" and "family relationships" as the two aspects of their lives that give them the most satisfaction; if they rated their satisfaction with their present jobs as at least four on a five-point scale; and if their ideal description of the relationship between work and family corresponds to the one they actually had.

‡ Based on the question on job satisfaction mentioned above: ranks 1, 2, and 3 are combined to form the bottom category ("not very satisfied with his job").

§ Respondents were asked to indicate on a five-point scale the importance to them of each of 22 characteristics of a job. The ranking to the following three items are averaged to obtain the score for achievement value: "challenging work to do; work from which I could get a personal sense of accomplishment; and considerable freedom to adopt my own approach to the job — to be creative and original." Those who rated each of these as very important (rank 5) are included in the top category; those who gave one of these items a lower ranking are in the middle category; all others are included in the bottom category.

¶ Orientation to success is measured by responses to two items: the extent to which the respondent feels he possesses "high aspirations for [his] career," the degree to which he says it is important to him to be successful in his work. Family orientation is also measured by two items: the item mentioned in the above footnote indicating the relative positions of career and family in the list of those aspects of life that give the greatest satisfaction, and the importance assigned to the following job characteristic: "job which leaves sufficient time for family and personal life." Those who indicated that it is important to them to be successful in work and who said they have high aspirations for their career are considered oriented to success; those who mentioned family as a source of satisfaction and who indicated that whether or not a job leaves sufficient time for family and personal life has some importance for them are considered oriented to family. Of those equally oriented to both success and family, five are oriented to neither (three of whose wives are currently working), and fifteen are oriented to both (eight of whose wives are working).

** Based on the question already mentioned. The first category includes those people who mentioned family but not career as the aspect of life that gave them most or next to most must not be led to condemn, on behalf of a general principle, the exceptional cases in which great imbalance has creative objective results and subjective satisfactions.[13] We must, in other words, make sure that one of the characteristics of the just society toward which we are all working is differentiation: the possibility for people with different needs and abilities to find and pursue the life style that maximizes their contributions to society and the satisfaction of their lives — whether they are women or men.

Acknowledgments

The author would like to thank Marc Gerstein, Susan Mattes, Edgar H. Schein, and Dany Siler for their help during the preparation of this paper.

Notes and References

1. E.g. DAVID, D. S. 1971. Career Patterns and Values: A Study of Men and Women in Science and Engineering: Chap. V. Bureau of Applied Social Research. New York, N. Y.; ROSSI, A. S. 1965. Barriers to the career choice of engineering, medicine, or science among American women. *In* Women and the Scientific Professions: The M.I.T. Symposium on American Women in Science and Engineering. J. A. MATTFELD & C. G. Van Aken, Eds.: Table 9, 72. M.I.T. Press. Cambridge, Mass.
2. ROSSI, A. S. 1965. Equality between the sexes: an immodest proposal. *In* The Woman in America. R. J. Lifton, Ed. Houghton Mifflin. Boston, Mass.; DAVIS, J. A. 1964. Great Aspirations: The Graduate School Plans of America's College Seniors: Chap. 3. Aldine. Chicago, Ill.; HORNER, M. 1969. Fail: bright women. Psychology Today 3: 36–. ALPER, T. G. 1971. Achievement motivation in college women. Paper read at ann. meeting Eastern Psychological Assoc. New York, N. Y.
3. E.g. ROSSI, A. S. 1970. Status of women in graduate departments of sociology, 1968– 1969. American Sociologist 5: 9–11.
4. EPSTEIN, C. F. 1970. Woman's Place: Options and Limits in Professional Careers: Chap. V. University of California Press. Berkeley, Calif.
5. These three sources of constraints are not independent of each other, of course. For one analysis of the interaction of some of these factors see R. RAPOPORT & R. N. RAPOPORT. 1971. Early and later experiences as determinants of adult behavior: married women's family and career patterns. Brit. J. Sociol. 22: 16–30.
6. This study was financed in part by a grant from the Carnegie Commission on Higher Education to the Sloan School of Management, M.I.T.
7. There were 22 women graduates in the classes surveyed, of which 15 answered the questionnaire. For these women it was found that the crucial difference was between those with one child and those with two or more: all of the alumnae who were single (N = 3), or married with no children (N = 1), or married with one child (N = 2), were fully involved in a career. Of those with two children (N = 5), one had full career involvement, two had no career involvement, and two showed a career pattern that was accommodative to family needs. None of those with three or more children (N = 4) had full career involvement, two had none, and two followed an accommodative pattern.
8. Nor are they independent of the constraints outlined above. The pursuit of professional training, for instance, would seem to be primarily dependent on early socialization, though experiences during training and the circumstances surrounding a woman's marriage no doubt interact with this primary influence in determining whether or not a woman will be professionally qualified.

---

satisfaction in life; the second category includes those people who ranked family first and career second; the bottom category includes those people who ranked career first and family second (N = 10; 5 working wives) as well as those who mentioned career in the first two choices but did not mention family (N = 3; 2 working wives).

†† Based on self-assessment of two abilities: "ability to identify problems" and "ability to analyze and solve problems." All those who indicated that they possess each of these abilities to a great extent are included in the top category; all others are in the bottom category.

‡‡ Based on two items in the list mentioned in the fourth footnote: "work that is relevant to social problems" and "job which allows me to make a contribution to society." People whose average ranking on these two items is over 3 are included in the top category; those whose average is between 1 and 3 are in the bottom category.

9. E.g. ROSSI, A. S. 1965. Women in science: why so few? Science **148**: 1196–1202.
10. E.g. RAPOPORT, R. & R. N. RAPOPORT. 1971. Dual-Career Families. Penguin Books. London, England; HOLSTROM, L. L. 1971. Career patterns of married couples. *In* The Professional Woman. A. Theodore, Ed. : 516!524. Shenkman. Cambridge, Mass.; ROSEN-KRANTZ, P. 1972. Egalitarian families: some clinical observations. Paper presented at invitational conference Women: Resource for a Changing World. Radcliffe Institute. Cambridge, Mass.
11. The marriages of such couples have also been found to be happier. BAILYN, L. 1970. Career and family orientations of husbands and wives in relation to marital happiness. Human Relations **23**: 97–113.
12. PLOVNICK, M. 1972. Social awareness and role innovation in engineers. Working Paper 604–721. Sloan School of Management, M.I.T. Cambridge, Mass.
13. BAILYN, L. 1971. Accommodation as a career strategy: implications for the realm of work. Paper read at ann. meeting Eastern Psychological Assoc. New York, N. Y.

FATHERS AND AUTONOMY IN WOMEN

Marjorie M. Lozoff

Wright Institute
Berkeley, California 94704

Exactly what constitutes "success" for women begs further definition. There appear to be several kinds of success, although here we will discuss only three models mainly characteristic of white middle-class or upper-middle-class college women. Some women achieve success in the development of personal talents at the same time that they enjoy viable, intimate relationships with men, women, and children. Other women have vigor and imagination in the areas of human learning and the professions but proceed ineptly in more intimate human relationships. Still others are women who see themselves as productive mainly in their homes and communities and prefer such success to paid employment.

From 1961 to 1965 we conducted intensive interviews with 49 able college women at the Institute for the Study of Human Problems at Stanford University, Palo Alto, Calif. These women were a random sample of a much larger group of students we studied with use of psychological tests and questionnaire self-reports of behavior and attitudes.[1] The 49 women were divided into eight subgroups on the basis of clinically derived evaluations of autonomy and conflict. Three of the subgroups epitomized, respectively, women who seemed destined for the three types of success outlined above.

About a fourth of the interview sample entered the university with enthusiasm about commitment to scientific careers. They were the products of their high schools' responsiveness to the "sputnik" challenge. Only about one-half continued in the sciences, and of this group several had lowered their aspirations regarding occupational goals. Since our research dealt with students interested in a variety of fields, the emphasis will be on success for able college women rather than primarily for women scientists.

Less than ten years ago, many women students appeared to restrict themselves regarding interests not directly related to role development as wives and mothers. Those students who were relatively free to concern themselves with development as persons instead of focusing primarily on feminine roles we described as *Autonomous;* other major groups were designated *Moderately Autonomous* and *Least Autonomous*. The degree of autonomy and the amount of conflict students experienced seemed closely linked to their relationship with their fathers, although other factors also were important.

Of the three subgroups on which I shall concentrate, *Autonomous Developers* had relatively positive identifications with both parents and envisaged lives combining growth-producing marital relationships with personal development. They placed less emphasis on careers than on personal growth and the development of talent. The "Supercompetents," on the other hand, strongly desired achievement in careers but encountered difficulties in personal relationships. These students had special difficulties with aloof and perfectionistic fathers. The *Least Autonomous* women students' definition of success involved vicarious identification with successful husbands and successful children. Their fathers' role primarily consisted in supporting the mother as she primed the daughter for success in marital sweepstakes.

Autonomous Developers (N-7)

Of the seven *Autonomous Developers,* three were involved in the arts, with college teaching and creative efforts their primary interests, two were interested in international service, and two in the field of clinical psychology and research. Having a job *per se* did not appeal to these students as much as the challenge of testing their intellectual and service-giving resources and participating in their own growth and that of others. Their motivations were more self-developmental than financial or status-directed.

In comparison with the other groups, these students ranked highest in SAT scores, particularly in their abilities in mathematics. High scores in Math SATS and Autonomy had parallel linear descent. The Autonomous also scored high in the Social Maturity Scale of the Omnibus Personality Inventory. This scale tapped tolerance of ambiguity, acceptance of one's dependency and sexual needs, tolerance of weakness in the self and others, avoidance of stereotyped preconceptions of the importance of authority, and avoidance of stereotypic attitudes about members of out-groups. The *Autonomous Developers,* compared with women in the other seven subgroups, were most likely to plan on graduate school, most likely to have disagreement with parents, least inclined to disagree with peers, and most apt to experience personal growth as the result of involvement with the problems of peers. They valued time alone for thinking and reflection and for pursuit of intellectual and artistic interests.

Most of these *Autonomous Developers* had dynamic, ambitious, brilliant fathers who married admiring and supportive wives. In many instances the daughters were attractive women at the same time that they were energetic, ambitious, and vigorous like the fathers. Of all groups, the *Autonomous Developers* had the largest percentage who described themselves on a Senior Year questionnaire as emotionally similar to their fathers and yet frequently in disagreement with them and their values. Such self-evaluation implied closeness and preoccupation with the fathers. Qualities that most of these women felt they shared with their fathers included outspokenness, stubbornness, and ability to understand behavior rationally and make intelligent plans. Most of these fathers were secure in their "masculinity," in their professions or occupations, and in their relationships with their wives. The men treated both daughters and sons with respect for their abilities and urged each child to develop according to her or his talents and inclinations. At the same time that these fathers encouraged the women students to develop competencies without linking any sex-role value, for example, to either traditionally feminine or masculine interests, they still treated their daughters in a way that conveyed to the students a sense of their value as women. As these students developed during college, they were remarkably unconcerned and unselfconscious about their femininity. They were primarily involved in relating to people, learning in and out of the classroom, and developing their talents. But the message they got across to other people was one of comfort with their sexual identity.

Probably as a result of their deep emotional involvement with their fathers, they were sensitive to paternal possessiveness or domination. Characteristically, they had great eagerness to work out their own life plans. By their senior years, most of them had satisfying occupational aspirations and were seriously involved with young men who encouraged them to continue self-development. Possibly because their parents had treated them as unique and valued individuals, they proceeded to develop with less destructive conflicts than was true of most of the other groups. The conflict that existed was open and vigorous, leading to clarification of values and facilitating the separation process for both parents and daughters.

The fathers of the *Autonomous Developers* perceived intelligence, energy, and talent in their daughters and pushed them to exploit these qualities. Their mothers, capable hostesses and respected and beloved wives of well-regarded men, provided a contrasting attraction that often contributed to a toning down of such ambitions. As freshmen, most of the *Autonomous Developers* described their mothers as inadequate, because they perceived them either as lacking forceful personalities or as viewing issues in an emotional, irrational, or uninformed manner. The students admired nurturant qualities like gentleness and generosity, but found irritating their mothers' perceived irrationality, submission to the fathers, and interest in high social status. The students equated femininity with indecision and immaturity; masculinity with competence and rationality. As they progressed through four years of college, however, their descriptions of their mothers began to include such characteristics as wisdom and strength of opinion. It may be that turbulence and concern connected with the growth of the daughters stimulated development in the mothers, but it also is possible that the daughters no longer needed to perceive their mothers as relatively colorless and ineffectual.

There was, however, much about their mothers' lives that disquieted them. One student commented: "The thing that depresses me most about married women is that they are not individuals." The comments and behavior of the women, including the *Autonomous Developers,* suggested that "fathers are not enough," that the dearth of adult women who comfortably pursued challenging careers neutralized the influence of fathers.

The Autonomous Conflicted (*N-16*)

Evaluation of the degree of conflict experienced by students during their four years of college resulted in the researchers' dividing the Autonomous women into two major groups: the *Autonomous Developers* and the *Autonomous Conflicted.* The former appeared to have sufficient friction in their lives to stimulate growth and development, but they were not overwhelmed by intrapsychic conflict or by family problems, as were the latter.

Ten of the 16 *Autonomous-Conflicted* entered the university planning to pursue careers in science or mathematics. The rigorous demands of the courses and the preponderance of males in their classes discouraged them; all but two students moved out of these fields by the time they graduated or left the University. Analysis of the college careers of the *Autonomous Conflicted* provide some interesting data regarding the fate of some of our most promising upwardly mobile students. Eleven of the sixteen were scholarship students, which meant for some that they were meeting the challenges of late adolescence in a university environment with values that differed in important ways from their home values. In addition, some lacked adequate finances to participate in the social and cultural activities of the university; this tempted and frustrated them.

One subgroup of the *Autonomous-Conflicted,* called the "Supercompetents," included students who enjoyed success in college that augured well for future professional success. They were vital and energetic. For the most part, these women encountered difficulties of an interpersonal nature. Their drive toward competence had a compelling, overcompensatory, sometimes joyless note to it.

The fathers of the "Supercompetents" were aloof, self-disciplined, and perfectionistic. Occasionally a Supercompetent student would mention having considerable difficulty with her father because both of them were stubborn; his disciplinarian tendencies were equaled by her dislike and resentment of disciplinary behavior. The Supercompetents' mothers appeared to them to be conciliatory and ineffectual. Several of them leaned on the girls for support, rather than offering them either protection against the fathers' demands or opportunity to identify with a strong feminine figure. In spite of this, more "Supercompetents" felt that they resembled their mothers than they did their fathers, and possibly this reflected their own submissive attitudes toward the fathers.

The fathers' demands for perfection from their daughters frequently had a narcissistic tinge to it. The young women seemed hesitant to rebel against their fathers' requests because of concern about the withdrawal of what little love they received. Possibly because of their relationship with their fathers, the "Supercompetents" either avoided association with young men or engaged in pal-like, competitive relationships.

Although they may have been submissive to their fathers and other authority figures, they were far from conciliatory toward peers and subordinates. One young scientist was described by friends as follows:[1]

> She is so ambitious that one cannot help but think it is overcompensatory. I can't imagine her relaxed and trusting anyone. She is remarkably neat, proud, well-groomed, efficient, dependable and service-oriented. Sometimes in her enthusiasm and self-confidence, she does not realize that she has offended or used others. . . . She is a person who tries to excel in everything she undertakes. As a person who never experienced failure or difficulty, she is not very sympathetic toward other students and at times is inconsiderate of them. She is obsessed with the idea of personal success and has spent her entire career in obtaining it.

Toward the end of her college career, she experienced considerable strain. Apparently she had incorporated perfectionistic, unloving, proud, demanding values for herself that had derived from her perception of her father's hopes for her, and had driven herself relentlessly. Partly as a result of a relationship with a young man, she became freer to be self-critical and to attempt change:

> I found out I couldn't do everything I wanted to do. I'd always thought I was some kind of a superman and could do anything and as much as I wanted. I guess I like me fairly well now. I didn't before but I told myself I did. Now the most important thing is being gentle to people. I valued the intellect very highly but I don't think I'm the greatest thing anymore. I still don't have the ability to open up to all kinds of people. I was an amazingly inflexible, rigid personality. It probably was because of my background. My parents were unfair, but to avoid getting negative responses I went to great lengths to suppress anything not in accord with their wishes. I made achievement a way to earn their affection. There was a lot of competition in our family. I think I built up defenses to avoid getting hurt when my family withdrew their love.

Fathers of the "Supercompetents" stimulated competence in their daughters by relentless demands and implied threats of loss of love. Competence resulted, but at great personal cost.

The Least Autonomous (N-15)

The *Autonomous Developers* and the "Supercompetents" at times during their college years were very unhappy young women, but they did feel free to develop talents and competencies unrelated to the role of wife and mother. The *Least Autonomous* followed a home-oriented model for success, which gave precedence to the development of skills related to domestic roles and minimized other aspects of self-development. Faculty and peers described most of these women as competent, well-organized, and reliable, but not imaginative or innovative. They scored lower on aptitude tests than women in the other autonomy groups. These students tended to choose fields where diligence and precision were rewarded, like languages, the teaching of grammar (rather than creative writing), and the care of handicapped or helpless children.

Seven of the 15 *Least Autonomous* came from privileged homes, and their main interest was to hand down to their children a comparable home life and opportunities. They showed rigidity or independence in the sense that they maintained a belief in the dignity of suburban living and conservative political, economic, and religious values in spite of assaults from liberal students and faculty members. Their fathers were successful business or professional men from families where rigid sex-role differences between parents existed. Fathers mainly supported their wives, whose important task was to guide the daughters toward appropriate marriages.

The role these women chose for themselves was to be attractive and supportive, and to enjoy growth and development vicariously through the achievements of their husbands and children.[1,2] One student commented:

> Once married, I do not intend to work. My duty is to my children and to give them all there is of myself and open the world to them. I think you're cheating yourself, your children or your husband if you do something that will take a large hunk of your time and demand commitment.

A main fear on the part of these women was of their potential dominance. This fear sometimes occurs in traditional families and grows out of the authoritarian nature of the personalities of the men and women involved. Some traditional, home-bound women try to suppress their dominant natures by dual means. First, they try to avoid any situation where they might compete with men, since they distrust their vitality and regard it as unfeminine. Second, they try to choose mates who claim superiority to women and who approve of dependent, flattering types of women. Sometimes such marriages work out well, but sometimes both parners are shortchanged. The husband may not be as strong as his facade appears, and he may have married his wife because he thought that she would constantly build up his masculine image. When he encounters the latent dominant strain in her, it becomes quite a blow to that expectation. On the other hand, for the woman who had hoped to rely on his forcefulness and dominance to keep her in a submissive, "feminine" stance, finding that the man has dependency needs and does not always want to be dominant can be frightening and disappointing to her.

Interviews on another research project with comparable women in their forties and fifties revealed that if a proper balance is maintained, if the husband is successful and faithful, and if their children are conforming and achieving according to parental expectations, those women perceive themselves as highly successful.[3]

In this paper, we have not discussed students whose development was impeded by conflict over family health and financial problems, students from supportive but unstimulating homes whose development was slow and cautious, and students whose parents' symbiotic relationships interfered with the development of independence or autonomy.[1]

Conclusion

Up to 1964 or 1965, things seem to have changed very slowly. This was called to my attention vividly two years ago when Susan Bell, a historian, showed me her manuscript about women in history who began careers in middle age. Her research into the lives of European and white American women, dating back to the fifteenth century, showed striking similarities to our sample of college women during the middle 1960s. It was the father or some important male who encouraged and guided women to persist in the development of their talents. These women who developed careers late in their lives and some in our college sample had in common mothers whose domain was the home and who protested their daughters' "unnatural" nondomestic talents.[4]

On the other hand, when women have career-oriented mothers, the daughters tend to develop a variety of talents and interests at an early age. Only a few of the women during the 1960s had mothers in careers not commonly thought of as feminine, such as social work, teaching, and nursing. Few had personal experience with professional women in other fields or women who combined careers with marriage. Thus the students had little familiarity with a variety of occupations or the excitement of simultaneously enjoying work and family. This left many of the students struggling with their perceived ambitions and talents as alien forces that had to be dealt with in a personally unique and often troubled manner.

No one likes to have his or her sexual identity challenged. Being a male or female is part of each of us, and a cruel aspect of past history has been the gender-linkage of personality traits. It has been cruel both in its limitations on independence and ambition in women and on sensitivity and emotional expression in men. When the fathers of young women, like the fathers of the *Autonomous Developers,* treated their daughters as if they were interesting people worthy and deserving of respect and encouragement, these fathers imparted to the women that their femininity was not endangered by the development of talent; that the fathers did not feel threatened by a female pushing forward with ambition. When they also treated their daughters with courtesy and affection as they encouraged development of talent, one could say that the fathers gave their daughters "permission" to be whole persons, to develop a variety of interests without concern that their femininity was at stake.

Productive as some gifted women may have been in the past, it is highly probable that they and other women would have achieved success with less conflict and pain if society had not ascribed gender qualities to fields of interest or to traits such as aggressiveness, ambition, independence, objectivity, and rationality. Although these qualities still retain a masculine flavor, this is diminishing as a male monopoly at the same time that the qualities of sensitivity, ability to express emotions openly, and ability to love, lose their primary feminine identities. A new dynamic force may be loose in our nation when women and men develop talents and emotions without constraint because of limiting definitions of masculinity and femininity.

The year 1965 seems like a long time ago when one considers the dramatic changes in attitudes about male and female roles. One could say that more easily available contraceptives and abortions, combined with pressures for population control, have changed the ecology of women's lives.

Now both men and women desire fewer children; for example, in 1965 two-thirds of our Stanford sample of men and women students wanted three or more children. In 1971 only a sixth desired three or more children, with about a tenth not wanting any children of their own. Technological advances in homemaking and increased longevity for women make the relatively childless home a less challenging lifetime work situation for many able, energetic women. Now women are more diversified and ambitious in their career aspirations; more women students anticipate contributing equally with men in providing for family finances and expect men to share responsibilities for household tasks. More women now than during the 1960s are having premarital sexual relations, thus satisfying impulse and curiosity without necessarily committing themselves at an early age to marriage.[5] Currently, women are turning more frequently to each other for support and guidance and are viewing their mothers' lives with attempts at greater empathy and understanding.

I cannot conclude without a word about changing perceptions about success. For some students in our study and for some young people of 22–30 whom I now teach, there appears to be determination to involve themselves only in what appears to be significant, socially useful, and personally fulfilling work. In science, students evidence increasing sensitivity to the potential value for humankind of their efforts, and eschew "success" unless it results from efforts that enhance human dignity, safety, and well-being. The quality of a culture may be judged by the relative ease with which the gifted and noble feel free to utilize their talents and energies in ways that harmonize with their ideal selves. Educational and social institutions also should guide individuals with lesser degrees of talent into activities that offer them opportunities to achieve satisfaction and to feel successful.

Reviewing the past suggests that "fathers are not enough"; that the influence of fathers in the high autonomy subgroups was neutralized by the absence of female careerists with whom young women could identify. A study of intergenerational mobility of children in Israel indicated that women with mothers in high-status jobs tended to follow their example, particularly if the mothers chose positions usually thought of as masculine. Another finding of that study affirming the importance of the mother as an identification figure and as the carrier of values and patterns of ambitions was the fact that both sons and daughters of women in high-status positions tended to achieve similar positions with greater frequency than was true of children of men in high-status positions.[6]

Hopefully, in the future, there will be a more encouraging atmosphere for the whole development of able young women. Hopefully, there will be more fathers, husbands, teachers, counselors, employers, and male friends who will encourage women to develop a variety of talents and provide opportunities for such development. And as many more women from all classes and races move into highly visible positions of decision-making and authority, opportunities will increase for future generations of young women to develop themselves fully and with less conflict.

References

1. LELAND, C. A. & M. LOZOFF. 1969. College Influences on the Role Development of Female Undergraduates. ED-026975. ERIC. Bethesda, Md.
2. LIPMAN-BLUMEN, J. 1972. Perspectives on the Development and Impact of Female Role Ideology. Presented at Radcliffe Institute Conference. Cambridge, Mass. April.
3. KATZ, J., M. COMSTOCK & M. LOZOFF. 1970. Educational and Occupational Aspirations of Adult Women. Report to College Entrance Examination Board.
4. BELL, S. Women who began careers in middle age: historical cases. In Women's Search for Autonomy (tentative title). J. Katz & M. Comstock, Eds. Van Nostrand-Reinhold. New York, N.Y. In press.
5. KATZ, J., M. LOZOFF & A. BOCHNER. Women and Men: New Roles and Relationships. Van Nostrand-Reinhold Inc. New York, N.Y. In preparation.
6. PADAN, D. Intergenerational Mobility of Women: A Two-step Process of Status Mobility in a Context of a Value Conflict. 1965. Publication of Tel Aviv University. Tel Aviv, Israel.

FAMILY ATTITUDES AND RELATIONSHIPS: A SUMMARY

Iolanda E. Low

Channing Laboratory, Boston City Hospital
and Harvard Medical School
Boston, Massachusetts 02118

Historically, we are in the midst of a third wave of the feminist movement that is concerned with far greater and more basic changes in the "status quo" of women than ever before in its 100-year history. Still concerned with political rights, professional opportunities, and legal and economic equality, women and some men are today trying to find viable, productive, satisfying alternatives to the stifling, sexual stereotypes of the past.

So rapid has been the change in thinking that just a few years ago at the 1964 M.I.T. symposium on American Women in Science and Engineering, the basic assumption was still to fit women and their dual responsibilities into the male-oriented and male-dominated scientific world. One panelist even stated that she had not found any problems or prejudices against women if they were extremely competent and hard working. To paraphrase the message: "Being number two, we must try harder!"

In 1970, The New York Academy of Sciences sponsored "The Impact of Fertility Limitation on Women's Life-Career and Personality." A different consciousness emerged: the workshop organized by Esther Milner questioned many of the previously held assumptions on sex roles and looked toward changes in society and institutions to salvage the tremendous human resources being wasted by the neglect of talented women in our country.

At that time, it may have seemed that the questioning and dissatisfactions were those of a few intelligent, overeducated, perhaps neurotic women. There can, however, be no doubt today that many women all over this country (some even opposed to female liberation) want to reexamine themselves as human beings, asking "Who am I? Can I be more?" and searching for broader horizons and clearer directions for their own and their children's lives. The evidence is in the lay press: Life, Newsweek, even Women's Wear Daily record the change.

At any rate, the stereotype of the female sex role, historically comfortable, emotionally laden, is obsolete. The data available underlines that this role is not good either for the individual or for society, and philosophically no longer acceptable from a humanistic and ethical standpoint.

This effort is trying to analyze those positive and negative aspects in our Western-oriented society that were determinants in the lives of individual case histories as well as in the lives of many productive, unusual women who are comfortable with their own sexuality without being overwhelmed by the feminine mystique of the 3 K's.

What are the determinants that, hopefully, will provide models and guidelines for the future? If we allow that the first five years, perhaps the first two, are the most important years in setting the mold for the future, an analysis of family attitudes and relationships is fundamental.

Past research in this area has been focused on successful men or on women fulfilling the traditional female role with and without careers. Such data as socioeconomic status, family stability, primogeniture, and educational level attained by parents are also relevant in predicting female success.

Analysis of family determinants concerning successful women, except for a few studies such as the Rappaports have done, is in its infancy. Two points merit further discussion:

One is in relation to the word "successful": — enough polemic has been engendered by that word already. The definition of successful "is strictly operational," as Dr. Kundsin pointed out, to identify women "who have made it up the ladder in male-oriented fields and are so identified by their peers." We can all agree that many more unusual women can be called successful if we use a more open-ended definition of success. We can encompass all those who have an inner sense of their own identity and worth as a person, self-esteem as a woman without reference to money or career accomplishments. Society needs more of these "successful" women, free in their choice of roles (including the domestic ones), flexible to the needs around them, freed of guilt feelings and expenditure of negative energy.

Second, although our title refers to women in science, the discussion really applies to all professional women and, it is hoped, to all women, irrespective of vocational, educational, or socioeconomic status.

The questions posed by our workshop included:

What qualities identify these successful women?

How were these achieved? What family relationships, attitudes, and relationships influenced the development? Can one implement the positive findings and defuse the negative influences in the future?

The family is involved in two crucial periods in a woman's life, and we must distinguish the two kinship units:

1. Her childhood family, crucial in her personality development and in setting her ideals, sex identity, and expectations.

2. Her adult family, wherein the roles of wife and mother are expressed; her choice of husband, not exactly independent of her past experiences, her desire for individualism and career become important parameters. And as life comes to a full circle, a new generation is influenced in turn.

The panel brought together investigators from the various areas of anthropology, sociology, and psychology to explore the family determinants.

In order to avoid any subjective misinterpretations as well as to preserve the individualiy of each presentation, the findings and conclusions are summarized, insofar as possible, in the original words.

Dr. Beatrice B. Whiting presented "The Kenyan Career Woman: Traditional and Modern." Her work in anthropology reminds one of a gold miner who sieves through the silt of time to find relevant nuggets. Does history repeat itself? Do these patterns have relevance to our present-day world?

Watching developing countries such as Kenya rush from subsistence agriculture to modernization is enlightening; one can witness our own history replayed over a brief period of time. The same problems emerge, and women are faced with the dilemmas that still remain unsolved and that are the motivating force behind this conference. Dr. Whiting presented a summary of the background of successful, university-trained women in Kenya and compared their experiences with some of the research findings of studies in the United States.

The support by both the father, who had at least a primary school education, and the mother, with little formal education, and by older siblings was consistent and positive; the whole family believed that education was important for both girls and boys, without any thought that being educated was unfeminine. It was the impression that all the girls assumed that they would marry, have children, and have careers. The maternal role model for the Kenyan girl is not that of a dependent housewife but of a competent agriculturalist and an executive who directs the children in the work in the household and the fields. Thus motherhood has a high status universally recognized throughout Kenya.

The first indication of conflict for the successful young women who comprise less than 1% of the women of Kenya emerges in the university. Both men and women in Kenya are reared to believe that men are superior to women and should dominate them, while women are expected to respect and show appropriate deference to men. The women therefore became completely conscious of the conflicts created by competence and discussed it openly with their women friends.

After marriage these young women have combined working with motherhood. Most have or expect to have a minimum of four to six children, and they all have salaried jobs, mostly teaching. These university graduate mothers do not worry about delegating child care to others. The Kenyan mother is not burdened by guilt, unlike the American mother when she sets off to work for the day leaving her children with baby sitters. It should be noted that many of these married women, as has always been the custom, seldom have a social life with their husbands.

What, then, are the similarities and differences in the problems of American and Kenyan educated women? In the first place, it seems that education, both in general and for women, is more valued by the population of Kenya as a whole than it is or ever was in the United States. The Kenyan mother and father who believe in education are backed by the value system of the society as a whole, and there seems to be none of the ambivalence about educating women that has existed in the United States. In the second place, there is at present no ambivalence about Kenyan women working. The role model of a successful woman includes productive work outside the home, delegated child care, and executive ability; hence, to pursue a career is not considered masculine. In the third place, motherhood is more highly valued in Kenya and there is far less ambivalence about marriage. The status of a mother is acclaimed, and women believe that it and children are of value. On the other hand, they do not expect so much from marriage as the American women. Each partner has a clearly defined role, a separate life, and a separate important job within the home, with love and emotional interdependence not essential factors.

In the fourth place, since competition with men is postponed until the university years, the young women are perhaps more secure both intellectually and psychologically before the full impact of the overt conflict wtih men begins.

Perhaps most importantly, the differential status of men and women is clearly defined, and there is no question that men are superior. Because there is no pretense about equality, as there is in the United States, Kenyan women are not angry about the status system for the time being. This is not the case with American women, who are told from first grade on that they are equal to men but are treated in a manner that belies the statement. Kenyan women, because of the clear separation of the status of men and women, have had more experience both in handling the derogation of men and in bonding with other women. This leads to a strange paradox that when there is a clear status difference between men and women, the self-confidence and self-esteem of women is less weakened by the antagonism of men in competitive situations. They are less dependent on men, more used to the expectation that they will fend for themselves and provide for many of their own needs. Although they are expected to be submissive in their relations with their husbands, they are expected to be competent, independent, and managerial in their roles of mother and farmer.

It may prove hardest for women to attain equal status in societies where there has been the myth of the equality of the sexes — where the inimical forces are hard to identify. Matina Horner's studies of the fear of success are the closest we have come to identifying the enemy of our equal status with men; we are still not clear how we want to define femaleness, since we find it difficult to conceive of personality traits as varying with settings so that a good woman can be an active executive in her job and also carry out her marital role.

Although Dr. Margaret Hennig has not as yet studied women scientists, she has examined in depth a most unusual sample in the administrative and managerial professions often labeled psychologically and physiologically unsuited for women. Since upward professional mobility, including scientific occupations, demands administrative and managerial skills, Dr. Hennig's data, presented under the title "Family Dynamics for Developing Positive Achievement Motivation in Women: The Successful Woman Executive," is both pertinent and "liberating." The women executives studied by in-depth clinical interviews were all presidents or vice-presidents of medium-to-large, nationally recognized, male-oriented business firms. All of these female corporate officers were in supervisory positions with direct power and influence over major decisions and policy settings.

In 1968, there were approximately 100 such women in the entire United States, and 25 took part in this research. It became clear that the women executives had experienced Dr. Matina Horner's "double-bind" situations but had been able, through family and peer relationships, to develop an integrated positive achievement motivation from early childhood, and that, in spite of meeting all the difficulties created by our society for the intelligent and achieving woman, never to let go of or reduce that basic achievement motivation. In a control group of women who overtly appeared to match the top women executives in all factual data but who had never succeeded in rising beyond middle management, it did become clear that the major difference that could be identified between the two groups was in the difference in their childhood and adolescent family dynamics.

A few pertinent illustrative details emerge from the analysis of their family backgrounds:

1. In recalling their relationships with their parents, they saw their relationship with their mothers as having been a typically caring and nuturing mother-child constellation, while they viewed the relationship with the fathers as being atypical; that is, close, warmer, more supportive, and, particularly, more sharing. The explanation most often given for the family dynamics of an achievement-motivated woman is that she was raised as a boy, "the surrogate son syndrome." This explanation proved unsound in this research and is replaced by the idea that these subjects, had they been raised as sons, would have been without the parental support and recognition of the fact that they were girls — a very negative experience.

2. The subjects reported that until they began school they were unaware that certain sex-related role taboos existed for males and females. Because of this, their first year in school was a particularly traumatic and potent conflict-laden one in which they found themselves constrained or even punished for engaging in aggressive or active sports activities and behavioral styles that were quite natural to them. The parental response to this problem was to support the child uniformly and, at the same time, attempt to change the teacher's attitude or structural impediment at the school. Even if change did not occur fully, the child felt herself upheld by her major sources of support and satisfaction, the parents and herself. Therefore, for most of the early years, the subjects were able to put aside the potent role conflict within the school until much later.

Although there is a great deal more evidence in Dr. Hennig's research to illuminate further the strong and positive family dynamics in the childhood of the women executives studied, they can be effectively summarized by looking at the major characteristics of the family constellation formed between the mother, the father, and the very young daughter.

1. Both parents valued highly for a girl child both femaleness and achievement, activity and competitive success.
2. Both parents valued each other highly and reinforced each other's role choices and behavioral styles.
3. Each parent related to the other and to the child as separate persons, yet valued highly and supported each other's relationships.
4. The female child was treated by her family as a person who was a female but who had available to her all role and behavioral options available to either sex.
5. The family constellation provided a security base and a source of personal reward, satisfaction, and reinforcement that allowed the young girl child to overlook or retreat from potential gender-related role conflicts.
6. Overall, the parents created a positive, suppportive climate in which the girl child could explore, without the limitation of gender-related constraints, numerous roles, and behavioral styles that allowed the girl child to experience direct instrumental life at a very early age.

It seemed clearly apparent in this research that the family experiences of those first five years did provide these women with such strongly internalized feeling of self-esteem and the positive feelings of achievement success in the direct instrumental world that they were less vulnerable to attacks on their femininity than they would have been from achievement failure. During those early experiences, they accepted such a strong concept of themselves as people that even years of conflict and pressure to split them into two segments, the feminine affective person and the masculine instrumental person, could not cause them to reduce their achievement drive. And, finally, their very early experiences with competitive achievement with males, beginning with the father, helped them to overcome and feel comfortable in such settings in the future.

Dr. Lotte Bailyn's name has long been at the forefront in research on women even if it had to be carved, like Adam's rib, out of male-oriented research.

In "Family Constraints on Women's Work," Dr. Bailyn touched on the dynamics of a woman's second family unit and the effects of those parameters, especially choice of husband, on her life-style.

The data used derived from an alumni survey of M.I.T. graduates from classes of 1951, 1955, and 1959, men now in their late thirties and early forties, included information about 1,219 wives and their families. These women represented a more varied group, perhaps more average and certainly with more wasted talents than similar professional, successful groups discussed previously. Only 27% are presently employed, but the overall figure ignores these crucial influences on these women: 1) professional qualifications, 2) current family situations, and 3) husband's attitudes and motivations.

1) The higher the professional qualification the more likely she is to be working.

2) With children, it is not their numbers but their ages that are significant determinants. In comparing family situations (those with no children, those with children all of whom are already at school, and those with preschoolers), the

likelihood of working decreased markedly from each of these groups to the next.

Thus from combining the above two factors it was obvious from the data that the only women with professional qualifications who are not working in their fields are those with preschoolchildren at home: only half of these are currently working. By contrast, almost all of those professionally qualified women without children are working full time; most of those with school age children are also working, about half full and half part time.

In the past few years, the prescription of discontinuous work for women — training first, then time out for children, followed by the resumption of work — has been 'seriously questioned, especially for women engaged in scientific work. Rather, the alternative of continuous work, even if on a short part-time basis, has received more emphasis. Dr. Bailyn's data support this position. It is continuity of some involvement that is crucial, not the extent of that involvement at any given time, a finding that underscores the importance of the effort of many women's groups to establish full status, but part-time positions in the professions. This fact, that continuity in professional work is crucial, makes it particularly important to investigate the constraints on those professionally qualified women with preschool children, only half of whom are currently working in their professional fields.

Certain solutions to their dilemma are obvious. The easy availability of part-time professional work combined with good day care facilities would, no doubt, increase this percentage considerably. But it is perhaps a mistake to feel that such external managerial solutions are all that is necessary. A two-career family requires a certain amount of accommodation on the part of the husband.

Wives of husbands who are able to integrate career and family needs — those, that is, whose satisfactions in life stem from both career and family, who are pleased with their jobs and with their family situations — are more likely to be working than are those of nonintegrated husbands.

It is those whose job satisfaction is high but not very high, those who value achievement but not too much, whose wives are most likely to be working. On the other hand, the wives of men for whom success at work is very important and who do not take family needs into consideration in job-related decisions, are very unlikely to be working when their professional qualifications are great but their family situation is at its most vulnerable. But complete withdrawal of the husband into the family is also no answer. Those men whose satisfactions in life are primarily derived from family, for whom career is not a major source of satisfaction, are particularly likely to have nonworking wives.

The key seems to be balance: confidence in one's cognitive abilities, usually found among success-oriented men, combined with a concern for society and one's contribution to the solution of social problems, an attitude more often associated with different, more innovative occupational roles; both are associated with comparatively large proportions of working wives.

Ms. Marjorie M. Lozoff has succeeded in combining career and marriage by a "horizontal," sequential approach rather than the combined career-models we are considering. Her productivity stresses that we must be flexible with options open to varied career patterns for women.

"Fathers and Autonomy in Women" dealt with data from intensive interviews with 49 able college women at the Institute for the Study of Human Problems at Stanford University. Conducted from 1961 to 1965, they were a random sample of a much larger group of students studied, using psychological tests and questionnaire self-reports of behavior and attitudes. Though some were committed to a scientific career, the emphasis of the data is on success for able college women rather than primarily for women scientists. The 49 women were divided into eight subgroups on the basis of clinically derived evaluations of autonomy and conflict. Three of the subgroups epitomized, respectively, women who seemed destined for the three types of success models mainly characteristic of white middle-class or upper middle-class college women. Some women achieve success in development of personal talents at the same time that they enjoy viable, intimate relationships with men, women, and children. Other women have vigor and imagination in the areas of human learning and the professions, but proceed ineptly in more intimate human relationships. Still others are women who see themselves as productive mainly in their homes and communities and prefer such success to paid employment. The degree of autonomy and the amount of conflict students experienced seemed closely linked to their relationships with their fathers, although other factors also were important. The three groups were succinctly labeled *Autonomous Developers, Autonomous Conflict-Supercompetent* and *Moderately* or *Least Autonomous,* respectively.

Of the three subgroups described, *Autonomous Developers* had relatively positive identifications with both parents and envisaged lives combining growth-producing marital relationships with personal development. They placed less emphasis on careers than on personal growth and the development of talent. The *Supercompetents,* on the other hand, strongly desired achievement in careers but encountered difficulties in personal relationships. These students had special difficulties with aloof and perfectionistic fathers. The *Least Autonomous* women students' definition of success involved vicarious identifications with successful husbands and successful children. Their fathers' role primarily consisted in supporting the mother as she primed the daughter for success in marital sweepstakes.

Ms. Lozoff then portrayed the various girls, their fathers, and the relationships with both parental figures.

The father relationship is described ideally as follows: The fathers of the *Autonomous Developers* treated their daughters as if they were interesting people worthy and deserving of respect and encouragement; these fathers imparted to the women that their femininity was not endangered by the development of talent and that the fathers did not feel threatened by a female pushing forward with ambition. When they also treated their daughters with courtesy and affection as they encouraged development of talent, one could say that the fathers gave their daughters "permission" to be whole persons, to develop a variety of interests without concern that their femininity was at stake.

Productive as some gifted women may have been in the past, it is highly probable that they and other women would have achieved success with less conflict and pain had not society ascribed gender qualities to fields of interest or to traits such as aggressiveness, ambition, independence, objectivity, and rationality.

The students in this study seemed to indicate that "fathers are not enough"; that the influence of fathers in the high autonomy subgroups was neutralized by the absence of female careerists with whom young women could identify. Findings from other studies that affirm the importance of the mother as an identification figure and as the carrier of values and patterns of ambitions showed that both sons and daughters of women in high-status positions tended to achieve similar positions with greater frequency than was true of children of men in high-status positions.

Mention was made of the dramatic, rapid changes occurring since 1968 in the younger generation of both sexes. Their life-styles and perceptions about success, especially in the sciences, will influence the development of able, young women.

Ms. Lozoff spoke hopefully of a more encouraging atmosphere with less conflict for future generations of all socioeconomic classes and races, for both men and women.

How do the workshop findings tally with our original case-sample of unusual individuals? Of the parental figures, 67% had predominantly positive attitudes toward their children and encouraged their ambitions; the 16 out of a total of 24 parents included 7 mothers and 9 fathers. In one case the maternal grandfather was the positive figure, while in others, a grandmother, aunts, and even older siblings played important supportive roles. One individual experienced negative attitudes from her father that, she felt, caused severe problems and delayed her career success; another woman who overcame rejection from both parents experienced considerable conflicts, especially in her marriages and family life. Dr. J. Russell, who analyzed this data, felt that if one had a matched socioeconomic control group, the correlation of success and parental support for the career group would prove to be very high indeed.

The husbands also were, and are, an unusual group; they were supportive and interested in their wives' lives and careers without playing "second fiddle." Both partners were autonomous individuals who could tolerate each other's shortcomings and problems.

The data presented here seems cold and distant, not at all representative of the love, esteem, energy, and drive that were present in many of the successful women's family relationships. We are very grateful and touched by their honesty.

It is quite exciting to see concepts that one intuitively supports confirmed by solid data from independent research groups.

1. A very clear picture emerges of the "successful" women: they are vital, independent, interesting, and interested individuals, with a balance between achievement and femininity. They were not devoid of conflict, but they could externalize their anger against what was perceived as ridiculous constraint on girls; their self-esteem remained intact and provided a solid foundation for their mental health.

These women clearly can provide the "role models" that younger women over and over again tell us are lacking, and that are needed in their own development.

How to foster such integrated human beings? How to nurture these qualities in the preschool child is a very relevant question.

2. The need for both parents in the rearing of "successful" women (and, I presume, men) is clearly brought out by these studies. The importance of the father-daughter relationship implies that men must be brought back to center stage in their roles and responsibilities of husbands and fathers, and not just as economic providers. This would considerably relieve the burden of guilt of the working mother.

The father- and husband-figures are also unusual people, sharing many traits with the "successful" women: autonomous, achievement-oriented but not success-driven, yet sensitive to interpersonal relationships, comfortable and unconcerned with their sexual identity, without the need to dominate.

3. Indirectly, this report focuses on the need for changing the male stereotype role in our Western society and other societies. This change, despite probable benefits in physical and mental health, will be the most difficult to achieve, since in essence it would involve modification and reassessment of institutions and of social attitudes and practices, particularly our concept of success.

4. In our quest for change, we have often focused on the benefit to the adult without evaluating the effect of changes on children. The need for both parents,

clearly documented by this panel, and perhaps the need of one-to-one supportive relationships, in growing up to provide the optimum milieu, means that we must carefully evaluate the effect of changes we may be proposing in child care, family arrangements, working patterns, and so on.

This kind of searching and evaluation for viable, alternatives will, hopefully, be a spin-off of this meeting. Any change that would benefit present-day women at the expense of another generation would not be real freedom at all.

5. Women and men, wives and husbands, mothers and fathers are intertwined in what some call a hate-love relationship. I think we have options in shifting the climate to a more positive frame of reference by considering and implementing some of the conclusions presented at this Workshop on "Family Attitudes and Relationships."

PART III

The Impact of Education

EARLY CHILDHOOD INFLUENCES

Jacqueline Melton Scott

Principal, Cambridge Montessori School
Cambridge, Massachusetts 02138

Looking back to my early years and the many positive influences generated by my mother and father, it is not a simple task to isolate the influences that have had the strongest impact in determining my success as a woman today. Although I was the only child of my parents, I was raised with four cousins. The most impressive factor was the ideology of my father, which was catalyzed by my mother and respected by those adults with whom we, as a family, were in close contact. His position was to encourage me to speak my mind. My mother's position as the catalyst in relation to his, was to allow me to do so, but to set down the ground rules. In other words, "Think before you speak." She believed that speaking one's mind was not merely a matter of what is said, but, just as important, the way it is said. How does this tie in with the subject matter of early influences determining the success of a woman?

My purpose is not only to sum up the influences that determined success for me, but to discuss these as factors that I believe contribute to the success of women in general. In so doing, it is my intent to relate these personal experiences to the basic philosophy of Maria Montessori in relation to her position of how the attitude and the environment of the adult can influence the development of the child in the preschool years. It is her principles that I have found to be an excellent model toward the child's development as a whole being. If the world is to change toward the goal of peace and understanding, then we, as adults, must look very closely at ourselves, for the truth is that as adults, we influence the lives of children either directly or indirectly. It is never too late to reassess ourselves in the direction of producing positive reinforcements toward the development of the child who is to become an adult.

During the preschool years, in our society, girls and boys are treated more as equals than they ever will be again. We must firmly establish this concept and extend it into the child's later development.

As I see it, the implications underlying the simple ideology practiced by my parents in child-rearing, and which I believe to be fundamental, are as follows: Through their encouragement of free expression of self, they enabled me to develop respect for self. By insistence on my mother's part to be reflective, she was helping me to create the internal order necessary to facilitate motivation and the ability to set realistic goals for myself. Through repetition and consistency in their approach, they aided in my development of self-confidence, and thus the process toward realizing those goals perceived for myself. Another factor that should not be overlooked is that my parents, through no preconceived plan, shared responsibilities in child-rearing. Mother worked during the day and my father went to work at night, but after dinner. Still another contributing factor was the fact that once a week we spent a day in communications. This day was my mother's day off, and we all spent the day together doing something as a whole family. This was a time of sharing, airing gripes, and just ordinary "catching-up." For many years I believed that those days (usually Wednesdays) were legal holidays.

During those early years, my mother taught me how to sew; my father and I sewed buttons on his shirts and my dresses or blouses when needed. Mother, through example, taught me care of my person and good grooming; my father taught me how to braid my hair. My father and I cleaned the house to surprise mother and then worked on the car. Mother showed me how to fix electrical appliances; my father and I prepared dinners. Mother taught me how to make cakes from scratch; my father and I painted rooms in our house. . . .

Unlike the early experiences related by some of the women in the Women's Liberation Movement today, mine was heavily reinforced with positive male and female input. From my parents models, I can honestly say that I derived no stereotypes for male and female sex roles. I could cite many more incidents in my early years to indicate how the natural phenomena of my parents' influences affected my life in relation to the creation of a positive identity and how I became devoid of stereotyped sex roles, but this concludes my beginning thesis.

Before continuing with the philosophy of Maria Montessori and how she viewed the attitudes of adults and the environment as contributing to the positive development of the child, I wish to summarize here the six factors that I believe contribute to the development of a positive self-image. They are as follows: 1) Free expression of self aids the development of respect for self; 2) reflective actions contribute to the goal of creating internal order, an element necessary to facilitate motivation and the ability to set realistic goals; 3) repetition and consistency contribute to the goal of producing self-confidence and to the ultimate realization of those goals; 4) shared responsibilities through adult and child participation reinforce respect for others; 5) communication develops love and understanding of each other; and 6) discouraging stereotypes for male and female roles create a positive identity.

Maria Montessori, in her philosophy, strongly emphasized the influence of the environment in the development of the child. What is meant here by environment is not just the physical environment of the child, but also the mental and social environment. The adult, being part of this environment, must be conscious of the child and of his ability at an early age to absorb his environment through sensory impressions, and later to imitate. This is quite a responsibility, if you look at this notion in its complexity. In other words, as an adult, one must be consciously aware of his influence on the child at all times. His attitudes and actions must be truly worthy of repetition, for one day the wrath of those unconscious actions of the adult will be reflected in the actions of the child.

It is interesting to note that the Montessori approach to education plays down that principle which is dominant in traditional education; specifically, Montessori emphasizes the process or the subconscious efforts toward the end of attaining the goals or skill, where traditional education emphasizes the goal or skill as a conscious direction. She refers to the subconscious efforts as being order, independence, coordination, and concentration, which are called "direct aims." The skill is referred to as the "indirect aim." Here is where I believe the key lies: children are not born as conscious beings, but have the potential to become such. The adult, on the other hand, has become conscious, and can bring to the child, through his subconscious, a conscious awareness. How we do this as adults is the task at hand if we are to aid the children toward positive total development.

Montessori states that the role of the adult is to help the child help himself. In order to do this, the adult must take a passive but conscious role with the implementation, being forever ready to step in when needed.

SEXUAL STEREOTYPES AND THE PUBLIC SCHOOLS

Florence Howe

Women's Studies Program
State University of New York/College at Old Westbury
Old Westbury, New York 11568

Plato was probably the first man in western civilization to guess correctly about the intelligence of women. In *The Republic,* he prescribes a similar education for both sexes, since he believed the intellects and general capacities of men and women were equivalent. Aristotle, Plato's student, learned little from him on this score, and women have been forever sorry that he was so weak a pupil, for Aristotle's views have prevailed. Aristotle ranked women with children and slaves. Like slaves, women might be taught something to make them of some use to men, but they were essentially unteachable in the higher sense, since, Aristotle believed, their rational faculties were innately of inferior quality. Since Plato's day, women have had several other friends, but I shall pass over them all to come to Jerome Kagan. In a recent issue of *School Review* devoted to women and education,[1] Kagan concludes a section of his article (on the "initial left hemispheric advantage" of female infants over male infants) in the following manner:

> Perhaps it is woman, not man, who is the intellectual specialist; woman, not man, who insists on interlacing sensory experience with meaning. These reversals of popular homilies join other maxims that science has begun to question. For now we know that it is the female, not the male, who is most predictable; the female, not the male, who is biologically more resistant to infirmity; the female's anatomy, not the male's, that is nature's preferred form. Man's a priori guesses about sex differences have reflected an understandable but excessive masculine narcissism.[1]

I state Kagan's hypothesis at the outset because, like much that is coming out of the women's movement, it upsets several traditional stereotypes that grip our schools and the education they offer to children. "Masculine narcissism" dominates our culture, controlling our language as well as our major institutions. Most completely, such bias controls the futures of young females and males.

In 1928, Virginia Woolf[2] speculated on the likelihood of Shakespeare's talent lodged not in him but in his sister. "What would have happened," she queried, "had Shakespeare had a wonderfully gifted sister, Judith, let us say." She imagined the life of a woman for whom no education would be provided, unless a friendly brother or parent chose to teach her to read. She continued to follow the girl through a life in which no doors, not even at the theatre, open to her: she is finally suited only for marriage and child-bearing. Woolf concluded that "any woman born with a great gift in the sixteenth century would certainly have gone crazed, shot herself, or ended her days in some lonely cottage outside the village, half witch, half wizard, feared and mocked at."

But how would Judith fare in the twentieth century? Writing about creativity a decade ago, Paul Torrance[3] suggested that as many creative girls as boys are born into the population at large. Creativity, Torrance speculated, is in no way sex-bound. Indeed, creative people, as he described them, are androgynous; their characteristics include traits associated typically with male stereotypes: aggressiveness, curiosity, and adventurousness; and those associated with female stereotypes: intuition, sensitivity, and perceptivity. What, then, happens to creative infants and children?

Somewhere in childhood, in schools and outside, Torrance continued, creative boys are taught to bury their sensitivity or at least to hide it from public view, although they are still "boyish" if they continue to be adventurous, aggressive, curious. It is possible, therefore, for the creative boy to retain the overt portion of his creativity, to practice his being, so to speak. Whether or not he is also sensitive or intuitive may not be obvious to the social eye. On the other hand, girls may be "tomboyish" only until puberty, and sometimes not even that long. The social pressures on them require the giving up of aggressive, curious, adventurous behavior; temporary or social burial of those traits is less plausible. The "proper" socialization of girls, Torrance concluded, probably precludes creativity—in invention or politics, say, though girls are now permitted to dabble in the arts.

The differences between sixteenth century Judith and a twentieth century Judith, I am willing to venture, are smaller than those between both Judiths and their respective brothers. Despite the fact that our daughters have gone to schools for more than a hundred years now, have sat beside their brothers for as many legally compulsory years, their education has not been that of "equals." The world we live in treats boys and girls as though they were two different species. If Kagan[1] is correct, we have spent two thousand years attempting to reverse biology, and in some respects we have nearly succeeded.

A review of the literature on sex differences and elementary schools reveals that research has focused not on the treatment of girls, but on the problems of boys. Studies aimed at explaining the reading disabilities of boys, for example, turn to female teachers or the "feminized'" classroom. According to a recent critical review of such research, "no evidence of sex bias was found in these investigations," despite initial assumptions that female teachers' prejudice against boys results in the inferior performance of boys in elementary schools. Indeed, one study found that women teachers favored boys![4]

It is true that two to three times the number of boys, as compared with girls have reading problems. It is probably also true that boys have a more difficult time adjusting to the demands for obedience, order, and neatness in the elementary school classroom. By the time they get to school, boys have been taught by other women, their mothers, to be aggressive and independent. Although these traits may cause them some difficulty in school to begin with, they are finally important ones for future success both in school and in the world outside.

Little girls come to school eager to learn and more capable than boys their own age, since they are as much as a year to eighteen months ahead of boys developmentally. They can please the teacher, since their mothers have taught them to be neat and quiet, to follow directions. They have had practice in watching and waiting—typical classroom activities—rather than in bouncing about, questioning, being curious or aggressive, in the manner of boys. What, then, happens to girls as the elementary years roll on? Boys are often said to "catch up" to girls late in those years, but in fact, except in sex-typed subjects like math and science, girls never really fall behind. Girls' high school grades are, by and large, better than boys'. The problem for girls is not achievement at all, but attrition or aspiration.

Aspiration is remarkably low throughout a girl's lifetime compared to a boy's. When 700 fourth, fifth, and sixth graders were asked what they wanted to be when they grew up, girls' responses fell mainly into four categories: teacher, nurse, secretary, mother. Significantly, there was no fantasy; they are the roles prescribed in the literature and curriculum of schools and in their immediate surroundings at school. On the other hand, 15% of the boys' responses were pure fantasy, the rest a broad selection of vocational possibilities.[6] In high school, girls' commitments to careers decline, and in college, women become increasingly interested—

between their freshman and senior years—in becoming housewives and mothers. By now we all know the statistics that report the discrepancy between the proportions of women going to college (42%) and those who complete graduate degrees (13%) or enter a profession like law or medicine or engineering (1%–7%). Despite both intelligence and achievement, one can only conclude from the literature and the statistics that girls and women are *programmed* for attrition.

For several years now, feminists have been surveying the elementary and high schools, as well as colleges and universities, for evidence of culpability. The reports are mountainous, especially of the male-dominated or male-biased curriculum. Culpability is not hard to find or to demonstrate. I am assuming some familiarity with these reports.[7] But I should like to illustrate what we can learn from analyzing several persistent stereotypes that function in schools.

First, a new and blatant example of male tyranny, female oppression. Begun just this school year, a new program called "Alpha One" teaches children to read by depicting all consonants as males and all vowels as females.[8] The boy/consonants, on first seeing the girl/vowels, say:

> A girl! A girl!
> Oh, go away;
> A girl's no good
> For work or play.

What are girls (or boys, for that matter) to make of that sentence? (What if we were to substitute "Black" or "Jews" or "Italians" for the word "girls"?) The girl/vowels in the text attempt to get boy/consonants to like them, or they seek the protection of the boys. The girls declaim: "Protection is what our short sounds need; the boys should protect us—is that agreed?" More often, girl/vowels complain and even weep: "Boo hoo, boo hoo, boo hoo, boo hoo," they cry to Mr. H., "We don't like what you want to do." Mr. H. wants them to "work harder for the consonants." Several of the consonant/boys claim particular vowel/girls as their own property, while Mr. R., in bullying fashion, forces girl/vowels to make special sounds just with him (as in the words "far," "or," "her"). Mr. R. threatens: "They'll be sorry if they don't agree."

If Alpha One seems a parody out of *Brave New World,* it isn't. Leaving aside all questions of linguistic veracity, the program offers children a summary of all that is wrong with male/female relationships; undisguised, it teaches little girls and boys that females are inferior to males. Indeed, in the text they are inferiors *of* males, their servants or slaves. Here is Aristotle among us, reborn.

While most children's readers and social studies texts are somewhat less overtly tyrannous, the stereotypes predict remarkably the limited perspectives of girls and women. A typical American family in readers and texts consists of four people and two animals: a father who works, a mother who does not, a brother who is always older than a sister who is always younger, and a dog and cat whose ages and sexes mirror those of the brother and sister. Brothers lead relatively active lives for school texts, in trees or games, performing before their sisters who are, as you might expect, admirers of male agility and inventiveness. Girls are prepared in all these books to be fumblers at physical activities, to function as listeners, watchers, waiters, rather than doers. Most of all, girls are prepared to be mothers, and mothers in school texts are also invariably docile. They spend their time as consumers or at home in aprons, waiting for Daddy. The absence of even token working mothers distorts reality beyond belief, since nearly half of all women work. What are children to make of such contradictions between their knowledge of life and the life presented to them in school texts?

If we move on and glance at high school literature texts or history, whatever the grade, we note two patterns dominating. Either women are present in dating, mating, or mothering roles, or they are totally absent. Few women writers are included even in anthologies, and, as several studies have demonstrated, the literary curriculum offers male lives in fiction or biography as though they were universal, and not simply male.[9] History provides probably the most notorious example of all, for it has no excuse for evading reality. And yet women are generally omitted even from labor history, even though the Lowell mill girls organized a strike as early as 1834 (they participated in one in 1824) and even though the history of labor cannot be truthfully told without an account of the sweat shops, fields, and mines in which women and children worked for as many hours as men, at half or less than half of their wages.[10]

Like the exclusion of women from history books and courses, there is a similar exclusion in the language. Children do not understand the allegedly generic term "man" or the use of "he" to mean, allegedly, "he and she." For children, "he" means the absence of "she," and "man" means male. Our language speaks of "manhood," "brotherhood," of "mankind," and of love for our "brothers" throughout the world. What are girls (or boys for that matter) to make of this? Can women reach "manhood"? Or do they never grow up? Manhood carries connotations of courage: are women never courageous? Does brotherhood mean that *men* feel a sense of connection and relatedness to other *men* throughout the world? Or, simply, that only men matter, that women do not? In a fourth-grade reader, boys who are building something they call an "Electro-Thinker" say to a girl called "Smart Annabelle," who stops to ask them some questions, "We are willing to share our great thoughts with mankind. However, you happen to be a girl."[11]

Finally, a potpourri of items that are essentially functionless in schools—practices that are remnants of sexual segregation or symbolic of male dominion. Dress codes, for example, inhibit the freedom of girls to run and fall, to climb, to do somersaults, to sit on floors. They serve no positive purpose in relation to the school curriculum, unless it is to disqualify girls from physical activities. Nor do separate entrances or sex-segregated lines at lunch for boys and girls serve a purpose. The patterns of segregated physical education and sex education or of shop for boys, cooking for girls, function, on the other hand, to promote an atmosphere of inequality, especially since facilities and rules are generally separate but unequal.

As if the foregoing were not sufficient, I shall add, for good measure, the results of a study of junior high school teachers' attitudes toward students. These were the adjectives chosen to describe good male students: active, adventurous, aggressive, assertive, curious, energetic, enterprising, frank, independent; to describe good female students: appreciative, calm, conscientious, considerate, cooperative, mannerly, poised, sensitive, dependable, efficient, mature, obliging, thorough.[12] (It's a pity that, in the manner of the notorious study by Broverman and colleagues of the attitudes of clinical psychologists, the experimenter did not also manage to get data on "the good student."[13])

It is quite understandable, from the mass of information on school life and curriculum, that women who score high on intelligence tests or who seem as college students to be creative do not accept traditional feminine roles and are likely to have been strong "tomboys." Those girls whose I.Q.'s rise between the ages of six and ten are as likely as boys to be aggressive, dominant, and independent.[14] Most girls, moreover, unlike boys, do not prefer the traditional roles of their sex, and why should they?[15] Men's lives, at least in literature and history, *seem* more interesting than women's.

What, then, should we recommend to schools? Androgyny, with males the dominant model? Should we aim at blurring all distinctions between the sexes—from dress to language to physical activity? That is certainly one perspective possible for the future. And it might result in the destruction of certain biases against women, for example, in the sciences. At the Woodward School, a private institution in Brooklyn where efforts are being made to move in the direction of sexual equality, girls have deliberately been selected to operate audio-visual equipment.[16,17] That is, one breaks stereotypes by reversing them.

On the other hand, there is more to be done than breaking or reversing stereotypes. We do not want passive boys, nor do we want to inflict on girls the hypertensions of competitive males. Indeed, an alternate perspective might project the deliberate use of separatism. Students might study stereotypes, partly in order to decide for themselves about patterns for the future; female students might learn about their history; boys and girls might meet separately for consciousness-raising to reach keen but kind perceptions about themselves and the opposite sex; the study of sex differences might be used as curriculum for teachers and students in a total institutional setting. What is it to be a woman? to be a man? In some respects we know little yet about those words, and the concepts are inclusive enough to incorporate most areas of knowledge.

In short, I hope that we have learned to avoid both mistakes of the first century of education for women. I hope that we will go neither the route of total separation nor attempt total assimilation. (We have managed neither women's colleges nor coeducational institutions very well up to now.) Both models are, I believe, not only impossible or impractical—in the abstract—but ineffective for education. I believe in differences; or rather, I believe that it is foolish to deny their existence—among individuals or between classes, races, sexes, groups of any sort. I believe that we may learn from the study of differences as much as we learn from similarities, and why not have it both ways? In this second century of women's education, perhaps women and men will study alone some of the time—to review their separate histories, to talk of their dreams and fears—and sometimes they will study together.

It is not too soon to begin thinking about what we will do if given the chance to change education. Last year, when I was preparing to talk with school superintendents, I could think of no single example of institutional change to point to; there had been no conferences on the subject of this section, and research essays like Kagan's were not appearing with the frequency that they are this spring. In the course of the year, there has been significant movement in at least a handful of small school systems around the country, the results of efforts by local feminists. I do not expect school systems to begin electing feminist boards of education or choosing feminist superintendents; there are two women superintendents among 13,000. But who knows what next year may bring?

Notes and References

1. KAGAN, J. 1972. School Review. February : 223.
2. WOOLF, V. 1954. A Room of One's Own : 70–74. Hogarth Press. London, England.
3. TORRANCE, P. 1962. Guiding Creative Talent. Prentice-Hall Inc. Englewood Cliffs, N. J.
4. GIRARD, K. L. Sex bias in research on sex differences: an essay from a feminist point of view. Unpublished. University of Massachusetts School of Education. Amherst, Mass.

5. FELSENTHAL, H. 1970. Sex differences in expressive thought of gifted children in the classroom. Aera. ERIC. Ed 039 106.
6. O'HARA, R. 1962. The roots of careers. Elementary School Journal 62(5): 277–280. (I am grateful to NANCY FRAZIER and MYRA SADKER's forthcoming Sexism in School and Society (Harper & Row, New York, N. Y., 1973) for this reference.)
7. HOWE, F. 1971. Sexual stereotypes start early. Saturday Review. Oct. 16. A full bibliography is available from The Feminist Press, Box 334, Old Westbury, N. Y. 11568.
8. NEWSDAY. 1972. Jan. 20. Bernard Kauderer, chief executive officer of New Dimensions in Education, Inc., Plainview, N. Y., is responsible for Alpha One. The firm is under investigation by The Suffolk County Human Rights Commission.
9. See, for example, ELAINER SHOWALTER, Women and the Literary Curriculum (College English, May, 1971 and reprinted in A Case for Equity by the National Council of Teachers of English, Urbana, Ill., 1971. Also see HOWE, F. 1973. Feminism, Fiction, and the Classroom. Soundings: An Interdisciplinary Journal.
10. See a new and excellent "compensatory" high school history text by GERDA LERNER, The Woman in American History. 1971. Addison-Wesley Publishing Co. Menlo Park, Calif.
11. WOMEN ON WORDS AND IMAGES – A TASK FORCE OF CENTRAL N. J. NOW. 1972. Dick and Jane as Victims. (25 Cleveland Lane, R.D. 4, Princeton, N. J. 08450. $1.50.)
12. KEMER, B. J. 1965. A study of the relationship between the sex of the student and the assignment of marks by secondary school teachers. Doctoral dissertation. Michigan State University. East Lansing, Mich.
13. See the classic experiment by BROVERMAN, I. K. *et al.* 1970. Sex role stereotypes and clinical judgments of mental health. Journal of Consulting and Clinical Psychology 34(1): 1–7.
14. See, for example, MACCOBY, E. 1963. Women's intellect. *In* The Potential of Women. S. Farber and R. Wilson, Eds. McGraw-Hill. New York, N. Y.
15. MINUCHIN, P. 1966. Sex differences in children: research findings on educational context. National Elementary Principal 46(2): 45–48.
16. BROWN, D. G. 1956. Sex-role preferences in young children. Psychological Monographs 70(14).
17. HARRISON, B. H. Feminist experiment in education. The New Republic. March 11: 13–17.

COLLEGE: WHEN THE FUTURE BECOMES THE PRESENT

Dorothy Zinberg

Department of Chemistry
Harvard University
Cambridge, Massachusetts 02138

As the data from women's career studies and anecdotes from personal experiences of women professionals begin to accrue, one of the questions that arises is not "Why are there so few successful professional women?", but rather, "How have so many been able to survive the vicissitudes on each rung of the career ladder?" By focusing on one of these rungs, the undergraduate college years, I should like to explore two of the developmental tasks that come to the fore at this time, particularly in the lives of young women who have been successful students in high school and who, on entering college, plan careers.

The tasks in the most generalized sense are: 1) to accomplish the social-psychological transition from late adolescence to young womanhood and 2) to narrow broader academic interests into an orderly pattern of career development. These complex, often conflicting tasks, which must be solved simultaneously rather than serially, make stringent demands on the affective and cognitive energies of young women students. In an attempt to forge a balance between competing demands, the undergraduate is forced into focusing her efforts on present concerns; for her the future becomes the immediate future, such as next term or next year, and the more distant future, toward which most career plans are shaped, she perceives only dimly.

We know there are significant differences in how these competing demands are experienced. Ethnicity, socioeconomic status, levels of parental educational achievement, ideology, and birth order are but a few of the variables which, along with individual personality, contribute to the perception and the resolution of the demands. We have just begun to recognize the complex interaction and pressure these variables exert under the deceptively simple title we give to the arena: college.

It is my purpose here to discuss the impact of the convergence during the college years of these two developmental conflicts, conflicts centered on personality and career growth, that force the present-time orientation. Although the male undergraduate has many similar challenges, the larger culture and the university support the priority of the vocational or career impetus for him. How he copes with career or future plans adds to his sense of growing maleness, autonomy, and adulthood. College for him can be and often is a unifying process. He knows that he might choose to drop out temporarily, defer graduate plans, spend several years searching for personal and work goals; yet in the long run, what he "does" will be the organizing principle of his adult life. The young woman, however, whose lifespan is more clearly demarcated by a limited period in which she can bear children, begins to feel that she is caught in a bind. Often this bind paralyzes her ability to focus on the future in other than fantasy terms related to the man she will marry. Her academic work becomes her career, and her energies are committed to performing well as a student without integrating her course work into ongoing, if often oscillating, progress up the ladder.

We know that some women have been able to resolve these conflicts. Considering, however, the amount of talent and potential among the female population, their numbers are few, and in many cases they have paid a high price for this resolution, either in their personal or their professional lives. The absence of any significant numbers of women in positions of leadership and top jobs[1] suggests that even those who chose not to marry or to marry but not to have children have not, for the most part, managed to become leaders in their fields. What we want to understand is how some young women have been able to resolve the strains and competing demands imposed by the apparent disjunctive linking of personal and career decisions during the undergraduate years. As one of the few successful English women scientists commented: "It's not being a top scientist that is a problem for women, it's getting to be one."

Except for retrospective accounts that suffer from the falsification we all enlist to give structure to our pasts, there is little longitudinal information available about the ways in which women have become successful in their careers. Longitudinal studies are expensive and time consuming. The few that have been carried out with scientists have not included women in their samples. In addition, it is impossible to predict who among a group of freshmen (men as well as women) are likely to have successful careers. Thus a proper study would require an inordinate initial $\underline{N}$ if the final sample $\underline{X}$ years hence were to include a fair sample of high achievers.

In the absence of such large-scale studies, one can at best expect only partial answers and tentative insights. It is my hope that I can suggest some of these by drawing on material I gathered for a formal study of Radcliffe undergraduate experience between 1962 and 1966, and since that time, less formally, as Dean, academic advisor, research sociologist, teacher, and friend to successive classes.

At no time was the goal to understand "success" but rather to identify what social-psychological factors were significant in the development of career plans. Therefore, what I shall try to do here is to link the observations from the past decade with the current career achievements of some of the women who participated in the study. I shall limit the discussion to women who are currently in medicine and the social or physical sciences, who define their work as a career rather than a job, and who, although under thirty, have by their accomplishments amassed the credentials that provide the external criteria of success—status and position. If the remarks suffer from excessive parochialism, it is not from bias but from a paucity of data and a somewhat blurred vision of what constitutes "success." I have, however, begun to observe in a sample of English women chemistry students that those few (and they are very few) who plan careers as scientists resemble their Radcliffe counterparts more closely than they do their noncareer-oriented classmates who envision marriage and childrearing as the core of their activities with a job, before and after, filling the interstices but not shaping their lives.

At the outset, we must recognize that there are several paradoxes implicit in the terms "Success" and "Career." For example, college, although looked upon as preparation for future life, is very much a career in itself. If a career can be viewed in part as achievement over time in a particular field, admission to an elite college can be considered the official stamp of intellectual recognition after four years of intensive training in high school. Without exception among the Radcliffe freshmen, every student mentioned during her initial interview that she had experienced excitement or pride at being accepted by Radcliffe, if not her own, at least that of her parents.[2] All these young women had had successful precollege careers as students, and academically, they usually maintained this success throughout college. Like all other groups of women in coeducational colleges, they outscored and outperformed their male peers and a higher percentage graduated with honors.[3] But as the growing body of literature on career achievement shows,[4] high grades in college do not, for the most part, correlate with professional achievment in later life. That begs the larger question: what does correlate with later success? Why is one type of success, academic, discontinuous with another, professional success? And what role does college play in determining the relationship between adolescent and adult success?

Ironically, "success," which like "career" has masculine connotations, derives from a Latin feminine noun. In its original use, "success" defined the end event of a series of events and necessitated the adjective "good" to define a positive outcome. However, by the nineteenth century, "success" had acquired its more vulgar meaning; that is, the gaining of money and position. In 1863 George Eliot wrote, "That argument of success which is always powerful with men of the world." So we see the familiar contemporary trilogy of success, power, and men linked to Victorian antecedents. A successful man is one who has achieved money and position, whereas, until recently, the successful woman, in most cases, has been the one who had the good sense to marry him.

If we turn from success in wordly terms and look to its social-psychological counterpart, self-realization or identity formation, we see once more the exclusively masculine interpretations these have been given. For example, sociologists view adult identity as "largely a function of career movements within occupation and work organizations," while psychoanalysts write that personality integration is usually achieved "preparatory to or coincidentally with occupational choice." Does this mean that if a woman chooses never to work professionally, she cannot hope to become a well-integrated adult? If she defers career plans until she raises a family, is she spending an extra decade as a psychological adolescent? If she follows the prescription for career development, is she becoming a man? It is easy to laugh indulgently and say, "Those quotes are from another era, the fifties and sixties." The world has changed profoundly, and the "climate of unexpectation," as Mary Bunting[5] described the world in which young women were socialized in the fifties, has improved. But has it?

In 1970, young women at Radcliffe read in the college newspaper the text of a purloined letter written by the Dean of Freshmen at Harvard. He said, in part:

> Quite simply, I do not see highly educated women making startling strides in contributing to our society in the forseeable future. They are not, in my opinion, going to stop getting married and/or having children. They will fail in their present role as women if they do.[6]

In 1971, the Harvard Director of Admissions, when interviewed about increasing the number of women at Radcliffe, stated:

> I think it unfortunate to reduce the number of men. It will mean less diversity in the class and, as a result, fewer interesting people.[7]

And in 1972, a vice-president at the same university, on hearing a young woman exclaim excitedly about her acceptance to Harvard Law School, snapped at her and said, "Forget this career stuff, in ten years, you'll be just like my wife . . . living in the suburbs with three kids."

The attitudes expressed by these men coexist with the genuine efforts by male faculty and administrators to increase the participation of women at every level of university life. Yet, we need only look at the percentage of women faculty members to see that the former assumptions are mirrored in reality. We still do not fully understand what has led women to accept these negative assessments of themselves. Through the efforts of HEW and a growing number of professional women's groups, the percentages of women in academic and other professions will increase, and with this increase more young women, seeing older women in professional roles, will begin to take their own career aspirations seriously. However, the undergraduate woman will continue to have the same psychological conflicts and reality problems to resolve. In the next decade, which might now be called a "Climate of Great Expectations," we may unwittingly be preparing many gifted young women for "Great Disappointments" if we do not thoroughly understand the kinds of personal dilemmas they still face, and through this provide the structural changes that will make it possible for them to follow careers if they choose to do so.

In 1962 I wrote: "We know that female adolescence has received less attention in the literature than has male adolescence. We also know that career choice plays a role in the lives of young women different from that of young men. And we have been told that there are discontinuities in a woman's education which leave her unprepared for the life she will lead. Because of these differences, we must assume that college women have different choices to make at each step of their development — choices which because of the shadowy nature of their futures . . . whom they will marry, where they will live, how many children they will have, how much money their husbands will earn, are more fantasy choices, more indefinite, more flexible and more negotiable than one would anticipate in an elite women's college atmosphere where the emphasis is on intellectuality and achievement."[2]

Now, ten years later, there are marked changes. More young women are planning careers; admissions to law and medical schools have risen; for an increasing number, marriage is not looked upon as an immediate goal; temporary alliances are not frowned on as intensely by society and, more importantly, by landladies; and, in many instances, new arrangements in life-styles and work patterns are being worked out in partnership with young men who are eager to expand their own horizons. The psychological impact of the pill has barely been discussed, yet its effect on male — female status relationships will undoubtedly be profound. It is too early to tell what the professional lives of these young women will be like. They are a minority, albeit a vocal and much publicized one. Nevertheless, the majority of current women undergraduates continue to share many of the same problems with students of a decade ago. Although more of them have come to college with career plans, the plans take on the same tentative, vague outlines as did those of their predecessors, and the future fades under the burden of immediate pressures. That even the more definite plans of the seventies begin to pale makes more obvious the extent of the immediate pressures that have been underestimated or at least not seen sufficiently clearly. The young woman must resolve both her sexual identity and her career identity at the same time. In the most basic sense, her feminine identity is already established, but the college years add the dimension of reality that challenges both her sense of self and her fears about her future. Although in high school her academic achievement has been rewarded (if only by admission to an elite college), it begins to loom as a threat to her femininity when linked with the need to consider a serious commitment to a career. It is not surprising to learn from recent studies of women undergraduates that, unlike their male peers, they become less happy over the four years,[8] and as seniors are less career-oriented than they were as freshmen.[9] Until recently one could say that as the young man came closer to graduation, his perceptions of himself in a work role were strengthened; the young women was more often ambivalent. Today, in the Humanities and the Social Sciences, more young men are beginning to resemble their female classmates; future plans are uncertain. The uncertainty, however, is less apparent in the Natural Sciences, where, as a woman undergraduate chemist observed recently, "The men are so sure of themselves and know where they're going, but the girls sound like their male friends who aren't in science." Nevertheless, the uncommitted young men know that at a certain time they will have to make a commitment to some sort of work, while the young woman translates her ambivalence to the need to make a commitment to a man.

Many women, some more overtly than others, regard their choice as being between marriage and career, or, more primitively, between femininity and masculinity. In Astin's study[10] of women doctorates, only 55% of the sample were married (this includes the divorced), while 86% of the general population of a similar age group were married, 6% were single, and only 4% divorced. The message is not unheard by late adolescents. They are not afraid of becoming men by devoting themselves to careers so much as afraid that they will lose the chance to develop into women, i.e., wives and mothers.

Obviously, those who are planning to work at jobs until they are married and then return to the work force after their children are in school and wherever their husband's work takes them and those who plan to write or paint and need few institutional supports are different from the preprofessional women I am discussing here. The latter make a commitment to a continuous effort over time and need to believe and behave in a manner that assigns a high priority in their future lives to achieving this goal. Unfortunately, the dichotomy "masculine-feminine" bears an overload of attached meanings and values that has distorted the biological differences implicit in the words "male-female." Although we wish to deny it, studies such as Matina Horner's work based on Thematic Apperception Tests and my own verbatim records of conversations and seminars at Radcliffe indicate that many women perceive their choice to be between the affective and the intellectual, as if the two were mutually exclusive. One young woman said: "Sometimes I say to myself at one o'clock in the morning, 'Shall I be an intellectual and read the book that was assigned for tomorrow's class or should I be a woman and put up my hair?'" Everyone laughed, but the comment touched a sore spot. Despite discussions about the integration of both these activities as aspects of personality development, it was difficult for these undergraduates to tolerate the possibility and to understand in a full sense that reading a book is just as feminine as setting one's hair. It is difficult because both of these activities are expected from a young woman simultaneously: she must be attractive and she must also understand the book. For the male student of the same age, reading the book is seen as part of a unifying process that leads to male adulthood; for the female it is sometimes experienced as divisive, because at this age, academic success begins to conflict with the wish to love, to be loved and, in time, married. After many years of being rewarded for high academic achievement, women undergraduates discover that top grades and specific career goals coupled with overt competition for awards and scholarships threaten their male peers and undermine their own developing sense of womanliness. It is not unusual to hear a gifted student say that she consciously refrains from speaking up in class lest she sound aggressive, i.e., masculine.

The would-be scientist, particularly in a coeducational college, has special problems because she has wandered into a male bastion, a fact that no one—from her freshman adviser who insists mathematics will be too difficult or her classmates who assure her that she will give up science as most girls do, or her professors who, for the most part, do not take her quite as seriously as her male counterparts—hides from her for a moment. That she is likely to be the only girl in an advanced physics seminar does little to dispel the maleness of her choice. For a few, this is of small concern, but they are in the minority.

For some the conflict is heightened, while for others, it does not surface until graduate school. How this comes about is highly speculative, but I shall try to put together a few pieces of the puzzle. Interest in science begins at an early age; many scientists report having decided on their careers before reaching the ninth grade. Although the preadolescent may know that the word "scientist" has male connotations, she is not personally involved, because her femininity is not as yet connected with her school work. The first year in college marks a new developmental phase for both men and women. Science loses the greatest percentage of would-be scientists by the end of the freshmen year. There are many reasons for this, but the one that contributes to a disproportionately high percentage of women's shifting out is the emergence of the conflict around femininity. Whereas many fields are stereotyped as feminine—nursing, education, and social work—science and engineering are perceived as masculine. In most books written about successful scientists, even those by women, the only reference to women in the index is likely to be under "wives of." And the few women scientists who do succeed are, for the most part, not visible in elite colleges. They are usually research assistants or associates, and only rarely the professor in charge of the large, first-year introductory courses. Little happens to counteract for the woman undergraduate the male image of science and scientists.

Among all women students, women science students have the highest achievement-motivation scores.[12] Science students, as a group, are high achievers and are also marked by a low interest in interpersonal relations, a tendency to deal with these relations in an inhibited fashion, and a marked willingness and often a preference to spend time alone. They develop more slowly socially, date less frequently, and marry somewhat later than their liberal arts peers. For some women science students who share these qualities, the conflict around their femininity does not emerge until later, and the undergraduate years are less troubled. Graduate school, however, presents a new threat. Again, we have little knowledge about the factors that enter into successful scientific careers for women, but we can speculate that some of the women who survive have had delayed developmental crises, and, consequently, when problems regarding their femininity emerge (and there is no certainty that they do for everyone), they have gained sufficient skill and competence in their scientific work to be able to separate, to some extent, the women-work dichotomy. Work has become an autonomous, conflict-free sphere of operation. But for the young women who are actively interested in getting to know and to spend time with young men during their undergraduate years, the conflict can be intense.

The definition of a scientist is usually in terms of what we have come to define (and, I think, incorrectly) as masculine; i.e., independent, rational, logical, distant, isolated, and so on. The very qualities that serve to strengthen scientific excellence are interpreted as either missing or, if present, deleterious to the development of a feminine self. "She thinks like a man!" — the highest accolade a male faculty member can bestow on a woman-science student, is received with mixed feelings by the young woman who both prizes and questions her apparent deviance.

What seems to mark those who have overcome many of the vicissitudes I have been discussing and who have climbed the next rungs of a successful career (assistant professorships and senior residencies) is that their work was and is a relatively conflict-free sphere of their personalities. Several of these women had personal problems of staggering dimensions: illegal abortions, affairs with married faculty members, deaths in their families, bouts of depression, severe doubts about their capacity to love or to accept love, crises about religious convictions—the list was endless and very human. Several of them did not have outstanding academic records, but they all were able to function academically, regardless of other strains. One young woman, now a physician, flew to New York on a Tuesday for an abortion in a hotel room and returned on Wednesday to take her final examination in organic chemistry. Although her life was in chaos, there was order and persistence in her approach to her work. She had not so much a commitment to a particular field as a need to do something well, to gain control over the material and through it to acquire a feeling of accomplishment. This is not a masculine (or feminine) trait, but rather an independent ego strength. We have come to associate a conflict-free sphere regarding work with men only because "career" has had masculine connotations. What these young women are exhibiting is a developmental achievement that has had the misfortune of being translated into sexual stereotypes when, in fact, it is unrelated either to masculinity or femininity.

No simple relationship between career success and marital status seems to appear. The woman mentioned above married to "settle" that part of her life. Some young women married classmates in medical school in an orderly progression of degree, husband, postgraduate training, and deferred child-bearing. Others made early marriages, often with the expressed wish of getting that part of their lives in order; some have already been divorced. But their careers are similar; very little has been allowed to interfere with their progress. From observing their lives, I believe that we have given too much credence to the idea that neurotic or other conflicts pervade all areas of the personality, thereby impairing productive professional lives.

Although we cannot expect the college to provide a means to resolve what are normal, developmental crises for young women, we can work toward developing an environment in which women are enabled to resolve their women-work conflict with more support from the system. The presence of increased numbers of professional women in universities and, one hopes, in business organizations will demythologize the masculine-feminine, independent-dependent, rational-emotional, competitive-compliant, active-passive dichotomy that has impaired both male and female functioning. Personality traits must be viewed as a spectrum instead of as polarities, in order that the sex-stereotyping traditionally associated with professional fields can diminish.

Many of the successful young women report the active interest of a faculty member in their future work. Someone has taken them seriously. It is difficult to tell whether the faculty member becomes interested in response to the student's enthusiasm and goal directedness or whether the faculty member initiates interest. One can safely say that for most male faculty members the young woman has to evince greater seriousness of purpose than a man to be sponsored. Unfortunately, until recently, few "successful" women scientists (with notable exceptions) have been active in promoting careers of other women. Although they might encourage undergraduates, they remain aloof from would-be proteges, preferring the specialness that accrues from being the only woman among many men. This, too, can and will change, particularly if both men and women faculty have the patience and willingness to learn about mutual misperceptions of the others' motivations and goals.

As young women's aspirations are raised, they will take themselves more seriously as preprofessional adults and will be judged accordingly. With more women on faculties, a heightened awareness of women's ambitions, and persistent legislative efforts, one can anticipate change.

One of the most important tasks will be to alter the young woman's time perspective by stressing during the early college years the importance of coming to grips with the reality that the future is long-term. She must realize that as demanding as the present and near future appear, there will be another future—a future of roughly 35 years when her children will be grown and those aspirations that led her to perform well enough to study in a leading educational institution will reassert themselves with the same demands for excellence and achievement. The young women who have begun successful careers have always recognized this in themselves. We must make it possible, through improved counseling, for many more to identify that part of themselves without feeling that their futures as women, married or single, are being impaired. Of course, not all women want careers, and we must not impose on all students a similar mold for aspirations. We need to provide an environment in which all choices become autonomous choices rather than responses to current social trends or outmoded masculine-feminine stereotypes.

The more radical changes will come from the minority who are experimenting with new marriage patterns, career sharing, joint child-raising, as well as from a cool assessment of the place that career should fill in one's total lifespan. Less extreme changes have already been effected in medicine and, to some extent, in the social sciences where part-time arrangements can be made. The natural sciences, however, will be the most resistant to change, particularly as entry to graduate school becomes increasingly competitive and the academic marketplace contracts. In addition, the constant change in scientific knowledge makes it difficult to drop out even for short periods without losing touch with the mainstream of significant research. Despite altruistic attempts to program part-time appointments, science departments will continue to choose full-time over part-time people, thereby discouraging both the young men and women who would want to experiment with new family-career arrangements. Universities might raise the status of the research associate and lecturer, but for the individual who aspires to the traditional model of success, a full professorship, the next decade promises little deviation from the traditional "male" model. Beyond this, because of the decreasing need for faculty, 90% of all science jobs will be outside the universities, largely in industry and government. This new reality, a startling departure from the expectations of most young scientists who envision a university-based teaching-research career, must also be reflected in college counseling and curriculum revision.

Young women with career ambitions must still resolve their personal and career identities simultaneously while adjusting to ever-changing career patterns. To enable them to develop the necessary future orientation despite the pressures of present-time demands, and to encourage them to persist in their academic efforts while developing broader options for successful scientific careers, may I suggest a cliché that can be called on in times of discouragement, discrimination, and downheartedness. Until such time as society, with our help, restructures its major social institutions in order to improve the quality of life for both men and women, we should seek solace in the timeworn truism: Nothing succeeds like success—the male model, that is.

References

1. FOGARTY, M., R. RAPOPORT & R. RAPOPORT. 1968. Women and top jobs: an interim report. PEP Broadsheet. London: Political and Economic Planning.
2. ZINBERG, D. 1966. The Career within a Career: the Freshman Year at Radcliffe. Unpublished Ph.D. thesis. Harvard University. Cambridge, Mass.
3. U.S. DEPT. OF LABOR. 1969. Trends in Educational Attainment of Women.
4. HOYT, D. 1965. The Relationship between College Grades and Adult Achievement: a Review of the Literature. No. 7. September. American College Testing Program Research Report.
5. TIME. 1961. Nov. 3: 68.
6. THE HARVARD CRIMSON. 1970. Nov. 6. CL.
7. THE HARVARD CRIMSON. 1971. Oct. 20. CLI.
8. CONSTANTINOPLE. 1970. Some correlates of average level of happiness among college students. Developmental Psychology 2: 447.
9. FOLGER, J., H. ASTIN & A. BAYER. 1970. Human Resources and Higher Education. Russell Sage Foundation. New York, N.Y.
10. ASTIN, H. S. 1969. The Woman Doctorate in America. Russell Sage Foundation. New York, N.Y.
11. SUNDHEIM, B. 1963. The Relationships between n Achievement, n Affiliation, Sex Role Concepts, Academic Grades, and Curricular Choice. Dissertation Abstracts 23: 3471.

PSYCHOLOGICAL BARRIERS TO SUCCESS IN WOMEN

Matina S. Horner*

Department of Social Relations
Harvard University
Cambridge, Massachusetts 02138

Mary R. Walsh

Boston University
Boston, Massachusetts 02215

Throughout history, society has viewed femininity and achievement as incompatible goals. As Margaret Mead has pointed out, "Each step forward as a successful American regardless of sex means a step back as a woman."

A brief review of the educational history of the past century indicates the conditions that have reinforced this deep-seated concept. When women fought to gain access to higher education they were confronted with the argument that college would conflict with femininity. In 1873, as women sought entrance into Harvard College, Dr. Edward Clarke,[1] an overseer at the college, published *Sex in Education,* in which he argued that feminine education could be gained only at the expense of woman's reproductive function. Clarke drew a vivid picture of what awaited the educated woman:" . . . those grievous maladies which torture a woman's earthly existence, called leucorrhoea, amenorrhoea, dysmenorrhoea, chronic and acute ovaritis, prolapsus uteri, hysteria, neuralgia, and the like." M. Carey Thomas,[2] the first president of Bryn Mawr, recalled in 1908 that women were haunted by "that gloomy little spectre," Clarke's book. "We did not know when we began," noted Thomas, "whether women's health could stand the strain of college education."

As women entered college in increasing numbers at the end of the century, it was clear that their health could stand the strain. But the concept of the incompatibility of achievement and femininity continued to follow their footsteps. Although M. Carey Thomas rejected Clarke's thesis, she too appeared to accept the notion that achievement could be realized only at the expense of marriage and family. In an article dealing with the future of women scholars, Thomas declared that they, like men, had to put their work first. Faced with the "horrible alternative" of marriage or one's profession, women scholars would choose to remain single and productive.

Thomas' position could not reassure those Americans who, along with Theodore Roosevelt, were concerned with "race suicide." Could the shrinking size of the American family—especially among the middle and upper classes—be traced to "over-educated" women? Defenders of women's education were forced to argue that femininity would not only survive, but would be reinforced by college. For example, when alumni criticized Cornell University for opening its doors to women, the school authorities were pleased to inform them that there was no danger of female "strong-mindedness. . . . It is simply a matter of course that the desire to please, which is natural among women, should lead them, when educated in the same universities with young men, to develop those qualities which appear well in the eyes of those about them." When Arthur Calhoun[3] published his

* Present affiliation: president, Radcliffe College, Cambridge, Mass. 02138.

popular *A Social History of the American Family* in 1919, he could look back on the experiment with satisfaction:

> College training gives a woman seriousness, a sense of values, self control, balance, breadth, and a philosophy of life. Her sense of maternal and connubial responsibility is quickened and strengthened and her reverence for the true meaning of the relationship is exalted. . . . College trained women have added to the maternal instinct a studied reverence for motherhood.

Nevertheless, problems remained. A number of women college graduates did not marry, and for many others there was an interval between graduation and marriage. Jane Addams[4] noted that this "want of a proper outlet" posed a serious threat to the health of women. "I have seen young girls," she wrote, "suffer and grow sensibly lowered in vitality in the first years after they leave school." A number of women like Addams found a socially acceptable solution in settlement houses, social work, and teaching: areas where the generally accepted traits of women, nurturance, protection, the fostering of growth in others, could be realized. Women had fallen into what Margaret Adams[5] has aptly described as "the compassion trap." Little has changed since that time. Educated women still tend to cluster at the bottom rungs of the ladder in the so-called helping professions, despite the wide range of skills and capabilities that they may possess. It has taken us a long time to realize how sadly we have wasted and under-utilized female potential in our society. And, as our data indicate, this has been at considerable cost both to our society and to the individual women involved. We have fostered an image of femininity that emphasizes tenderness and compassion at the expense of other valuable talents and emotions.

It has taken us an even longer time to become aware of the extent to which this image of femininity has actually been internalized, thus acquiring the capacity to exert psychological pressures on our behavior of which we are frequently unaware. Horner's research over the past eight years demonstrates that women still tend to view competition, independence, intellecutal achievement, and leadership as basically in conflict with femininity. They respond with anxiety to cues about successful women. Thus, despite the fact that our educational system purports to prepare both men and women identically for meaningful work, the data indicate the existence of internal psychological barriers for women, particularly for those who seek upper-echelon positions and training.

Evidence indicates that women who seek independence and intellectual mastery pay a high personal price for their defiance of prescribed sex roles, a price in anxiety. This idea is encompassed in the conceptualization of the Motive to Avoid Success. Horner[6] has argued that most women have a motive to avoid success—that is, a disposition to become anxious about achieving/success—because they expect negative consequences such as social rejection and/or feelings of being unfeminine as a result of succeeding.

This paper will focus on the causes and consequences of the continued presence of the motive to avoid success. We hope to demonstrate that despite the emphasis on a new freedom for women, particularly since the midsixties, negative attitudes expressed toward and about successful women have remained high and perhaps have even increased among both male and female subjects.

In order to substantiate the existence of the fear of success in women in 1964, 90 female and 88 male subjects at a large Midwestern university were asked to write imaginative stories about a successful person of their own sex. Analysis of fantasy material to tap motivational predispositions in subjects has been used successfully for almost three quarters of a century, since Freud and then Henry

Murray did their work in this area. In the Horner tests, females responded to the lead "After the first term finals, Anne finds herself at the top of her medical school class," whereas the males wrote to the lead "After the first term finals, John finds himself at the top of his medical school class."

More than 90% of the men responded positively to the cue, indicating increased striving, confidence in the future, and a belief that this success would be instrumental in fulfilling other goals. For example, one male respondent described John as thinking about his girl, Cheri, whom he will marry at the end of medical school, and to whom he can give all the things she desires after he becomes established. The few men who responded at all negatively focused primarily on the young man's rather dull personality.

On the other hand, 65% of the women at that time were troubled or confused by their cue. Their responses were filled with negative consequences for the successful female medical student, reflecting their belief that unusual excellence in women is associated with a loss of femininity and social rejection. In one typical story, Anne deliberately lowers her academic standing in the next term and does all she subtly can to help Carl. His grades go up; she drops out of school; they marry; and she concentrates on raising a family. Some of the young women stressed that Anne is unhappy, aggressive, unmarried, or that she is so ambitious that she uses her family, husband, and friends as tools in the advancement of her career. Others clearly could not cope with female success and resolved their anxiety by rejecting the cue. Thus, in one response Anne becomes a nonexistent person created by a group of med students who take turns taking exams and writing papers for the ficticious Anne.

The next important question was whether or not these differences in fantasy between the groups related in any meaningful way to performance in achievement situations or to background. It became quite clear from the data that the expectancy that success in achievement-related situations will be followed by negative consequences arouses fear of success in otherwise motivated subjects. This expectancy then inhibits their performance and levels of aspiration. For instance, young women high in the motive to avoid success were found to perform significantly less well under competitive achievement conditions than under noncompetitive conditions. The reverse was true for men as a group and for that relatively small group of women who were already low in fear of success. In other words, high-fear-of-success women seemed least likely to develop their interests and utilize their intellectual potentials when competing against others, especially against men.

In spite of high grade-point averages, these high-fear-of success women in the study gravitated toward traditional feminine careers of housewife, mother, nurse, and teacher. On the other hand, the minority of women subjects (those low in fear of success) were aspiring to graduate degrees and careers in rigorous scientific areas such as math, physics, and chemistry, despite the fact that their grades were not equal to their aspirations.

Since this initial study, the incidence of fear of success has been studied as a function of race and sex and across a wide range of ages and educational and occupational levels. The high incidence of fear of success in white women studied has not only been maintained but, in fact, has increased in most of the studies performed since the original 1964 research. Surprisingly, despite the growing interest in female liberation, recent data indicate the existence of something of a backlash phenomenon. The negative attitudes expressed toward successful women by white female subjects have increased from the 65% found in the 1964 study to a high of 88.2% in the data collected in 1970.[7] The pervasiveness of the fear of success is illustrated by the results of a study made at a major Eastern law school. One might expect women law students to have a lower level of fear of success, if not a positive attitude toward female achievement. Yet, 86.6% evidenced a high fear of success.

Our tests seem also to reflect the ongoing changes in society. In general, there has been an increase in the tendency of both sexes to view competition and/or the need for achievement negatively. Although these changes are usually viewed as a single entity, the greening of America or the development of a counterculture, the data suggest that significant sex differences remain. Recent research based on male responses to a cue involving a traditionally successful male figure demonstrates a sharp increase in fear-of-success-type imagery among men. Almost half of the young men in a 1970 study[7] evidenced fear-of-success imagery, in contrast to a figure of less than 10% of the male subjects in a 1964 study. The 1970 respondents tended to view the successful male in the cue as lacking social consciousness and possessing waspish or selfish personalities. While these responses indicate a change in the male view of male success, they also demonstrate that male attitudes toward female success remain constant. Whether men value achievement for themselves or not, they find female achievement drives threatening to their highly internalized cultural values and norms. Some men refuse to take female achievement seriously, while others exhibit more overt hostility. In response to cues about a successful female figure, only one third of the men in one study were able to accept the situation described, whereas the remaining two thirds felt it necessary to chastise her in any one of a number of ways including robbing her of her femininity. One young man described the female figure as paralyzed from the waist down, the victim of an automobile accident at age 16. Males in this category indicate a general fear that the woman will use manipulative skills and are suspicious that she will seek superiority rather than equality. Such men are quick to react negatively to female achievement. For example, recently a male graduate student told a group that he was interested in studying "achieving women." Afterward, the graduate student learned that one man in the group thought he was studying "cheating women."

On the other hand, there has been a continued persistence in the pattern of women to view achievement and femininity as incompatible. The only change has been in the content of the expressed anxiety; i.e., in the recent appearance of an association between lesbianism and successful achievement in their responses. For example, in 1969 a small pilot study[8,9] of sixteen women at an outstanding Eastern woman's college concluded that the students high in fear of success responded to this conflict in a predictable way. Just as the 1964 study had found that such women students veered toward traditional feminine majors, the more recent study likewise confirmed this trend. Women with a high fear of success lowered their aspiration levels as they moved from freshman through junior years. Instead of being politicians, they planned to work for politicians. Instead of going to law school, they decided to teach. These findings are interesting, despite the fact that it was a small pilot study. In general, this indicates that higher education for women is acceptable if the objective is to create a generally educated and thus more interesting and enlightened companion, wife, and mother. Difficulties arise only when the individual's objectives become more achievement- and career-oriented. The data show that those who showed evidence of anxiety about success and social rejection and had altered their career aspirations toward a more traditional direction came from primarily middle- and upper-middle-class homes with successful fathers. Until recently their families had stressed independence and achievement orientation, factors shown by McClelland[10] to be related to, and in fact to facilitate the development of, achievement motivation itself. Suddenly the young women began to feel the "double bind" in the culture's ambivalence about female achievement. They resolved the conflict by lowering their levels of aspiration. Those women low in fear of success came from lower class homes with mothers who were better educated than fathers.

The above findings are interesting to parallel with the data on blacks, which are now beginning to be analyzed. A recent study (Fleming & Horner[11]) found that black female students produced a 29% incidence of fear-of-success imagery as opposed to the 65–88% range found in the White female students. This low figure for black females is supported by other studies, one at an Eastern coeducational college and another at a teacher's college in Washington, D.C., which showed fear-of-success imagery from 35% to 40%. By contrast, the black males showed fear-of-success percentages ranging from 50 to 67. In a restricted sample of six competitively selected black high school males for an Upward Bound program in Washington, D.C., the incidence of fear of success was 83%. Even more distinctive are the themes revealed in the imaginative stories the students wrote about the achieving male or female figures. The differences reveal that by achieving success, white women are violating a socially prescribed norm, while black women are not. From the low numbers of black women who produce fear-of-success imagery of this type, an interesting question was raised as to whether the conception of femininity was different for black and white women, such that among black women independence and successful achievement were not inconsistent with being a woman. Important was the fact that the expected consequences of success for the two groups of women differed in such a way that fear of success was not aroused in the black women. Significantly, however, more recent research indicates that fear-of-success imagery appears to be rising among black women—possibly in response to pressures that black women should support their men. It is too early to determine how black women are modifying their behavior and whether they will internalize the same types of barriers to success that white women have developed.

It is becoming increasingly clear from our data that achievement motivation in women is more complex than simply the matter of whether or not women have internalized a more or less traditional view of the female role. A complex relationship or interaction appears to exist between the girl's internal personality disposition or motives and certain situational factors, which determine the nature of the expectancy a girl has about the consequences of her actions, and the value of these consequences to her in that situation. It is these latter factors that determine whether these internalized dispositions will be aroused and therefore influence behavior. Does, for instance, the girl care about the male competitor and the possible rejection she may get or the loss of self-esteem he will experience if she does better than he does?

It is clear from even these preliminary findings that women are paying a high price for their anxiety about success. Otherwise—able young women are prevented from actively seeking success; they perform at lower levels in mixed-sex competitive situations, and many who do succeed downgrade their own performances in the presence of males. Career aspirations are lowered, opportunities are narrowed, and, finally faced with the conflict between their feminine image and the development of their abilities and interests, many women simply abdicate from competition in the outside world. Just like Sally in the "Peanuts" cartoon, who at the tender age of five says: "I never said I wanted to *be* someone. All I want to do when I grow up is be a good wife and mother. So . . . why should I have to go to kindergarten?"

And there appears to be no successful escape. Unfulfilled abilities, interests, and intellectual potential give rise to feelings of frustration, hostility, aggression, bitterness, and confusion, which are clearly manifested in the fantasy productions of a group of young women. This was made clear by a comparison of the thematic apperceptive imagery written in response to the cue "Anne is sitting in a chair with a smile on her face" by women who had scored high in fear of success with the response by those women who had scored low. More than 90% of those low in fear-of-success imagery wrote positive, primarily affiliative stories centering on such things as dates, engagements, forthcoming marriages, and successful achievements. On the other hand, less than 20% of the 59 women who had scored high in fear of success wrote stories of this type. The bulk of their responses, if not bizarre, were replete with negative imagery centering on hostility toward or manipulation of others.

The kinds of stories characteristic of those written by the girls low in fear of success are exemplified by the following: "Anne is happy — she's happy with the world because it is so beautiful. It's snowing, and nice outside — she's happy to be alive and this gives her a good warm feeling. Well, Anne did well on one of her tests. . . . " Another girl responded: "She has just received a letter from the biological society of America. She is alone in the room. She did a wonderful experiment with a mutant mouse and broke through in biological science. . . . "

In comparison with these, the stories written by the girls high in fear of success were dramatically different and distressing. Consider, for example, the one that said: "Anne is recollecting her conquest of the day. She has just stolen her ex-friend's boyfriend away, right before the High School Senior Prom because she wanted to get back at her friend," or another, "She is sitting in a chair smiling smugly because she has just achieved great satisfaction from the fact that she hurt somebody's feelings. . . . " Another characteristic story originating with the high-fear-of-success girls is exemplified by the one in which "Gun in hand she is waiting for her stepmother to return home," or by "Anne is at her father's funeral. There are over 200 people there. She knows it is unseemly to smile but cannot help it. . . . Her brother Ralph pokes her in fury but she is uncontrollable. . . . Anne rises dramatically and leaves the room, stopping first to pluck a carnation from the blanket of flowers on the coffin."

At this point we can only speculate first about how much of what was expressed in the fantasy productions of these girls was a true reflection of their actual behavior of intents; and, second, if it was, what repercussions there might be. The psychodynamic causes and consequences of these differences are among a number of yet unanswered questions being addressed in ongoing research.

The results from some 1970 data gathered by Watson as part of a larger study, which show a significant relationship between presence of the motive to avoid success and reported drug taking, are relevant to these psychodynamic issues. The drug-taking measure involved a self-report questionnaire that dealt with the types of drugs taken, such as pot, speed, LSD, and others. Twenty-four of the 37, or 65%, of the college women in his study scored high in the fear of success. Of these, thirteen were heavy drug users and six moderate, and five never used any drugs. Of the thirteen girls low in fear of success, only one was a heavy drug user, five were moderate, and seven never used them. In other words, whereas

54% of the high-fear-of-success girls reported heavy drug usage, only 7.7% of the low-fear-of-success girls did so.

The causal direction of this observed relationship can only be a matter of speculation until further analyses are completed. Nevertheless, it is interesting to note that a recent congress of the World Psychiatric Association identified older women as the largest single group in the increasingly drug-dependent culture. Just what the functional significance of heavy drug use is for high-fear-of-success women remains a question that must be considered along with the rest of the data showing that negative consequences for women ensue when the expression of their achievement needs or efficacious behavior is blocked by the presence of the motive to avoid success. Consequent loss of self-esteem among these women is inevitable.

The issues raised in this paper are particularly important in light of the growing pressures on young women to have fewer children. Inasmuch as having children has been one of the major acceptable sources of self-esteem for women, it is necessary that other options for enhancing self-esteem be made available.

Achievement in the outside world is one such option that we have found is not at present a viable one for women because of psychological barriers like the motive to avoid success. It is clear that much remains to be done in order to respond fully to the issues raised and to understand the factors involved in the development and subsequent arousal of a motive to avoid success.

References

1. CLARKE, EDWARD H.   1873.   Sex in Education: or A Fair Chance for the Girls. James R. Osgood & Co. Boston, Mass.
2. THOMAS, M. CAREY.   1908.   Present Tendencies in Women's College and University Education. Publications of the Association of Collegiate Alumnae. Series III, No. 17. February.
3. CALHOUN, ARTHUR W.   1919, 1960.   A Social History of the American Family. Vol. III: From 1865 to 1919. Barnes & Noble, Inc. New York, N. Y.
4. ADDAMS, JANE.   1893.   Philanthropy and Social Progress. Thomas Y. Crowell & Co. New York, N.Y.
5. ADAMS, MARGARET.   1971.   The compassion trap. *In* Woman in Sexist Society: Studies in Power and Powerlessness. Vivian Gornick and Barbara K. Moran. Basic Books. New York, N.Y.
6. HORNER, M. S.   1968.   Sex Differences in Achievement Motivation and Performance in Competitive and Non-Competitive Situations. Unpublished Doctoral Dissertation. University of Michigan, Ann Arbor, Mich.
7. HORNER, M. S.   1972.   Toward an understanding of achievement related conflicts in women. Journal of Social Issues. In press.
8. HORNER, M. S.   1970.   Femininity and Successful Achievement: A Basic Inconsistency. *In* Feminine Personality and Conflict. Bardwick, Douvan, Horner & Gutman, Eds. : Chap. 3. Brooks-Cole. Belmont, Calif.
9. SCHWENN, M.   1970.   Arousal of the Motive to Avoid Success. Unpublished Junior Honors Paper. Harvard University. Cambridge, Mass.
10. McCLELLAND, D. C.   1961.   The Achieving Society. Van Nostrand. Princeton, N. J.
11. FLEMMING, J. & M. S. HORNER.   1971.   Sex and Race Differences in Fear of Success Imagery. Unpublished paper. Harvard University. Cambridge, Mass.

THE IMPACT OF EDUCATION: A SUMMARY

Mary G. Ampola

Tufts Medical School and The New England Medical Center
Boston, Massachusetts 02111

It is generally accepted that boys and girls are equal intellectually at birth. The *child's* concept of his or her competence is formed in infancy and either reinforced or damaged during the educational process, from nursery school to graduate school, and even beyond. Our participants have addressed themselves to the conflicts that arise during these years, and in many cases have made positive suggestions for reversing antiachievement trends in women.

I come to my intense interest in education because I see it as having been my way out and up: out of the mold into which my father (as with so many fathers) tried to cast me, a mold of antiachievement, antieducation for women, and so on. I was always told I could *not* do things.

For this reason, I am working hard to develop in my own three-year-old daughter a very positive sense of self. For example, I have said to her many times, when she was about to give up at a difficult task, "Leanna *can* do it, Leanna can do anything!". Now, I often hear her muttering while struggling at something, "Leanna can do it, Leanna can do it".

I worry, too, about role models as she grows up, and so I was particularly gratified when I recently overheard her inform her little girl playmate that "when you grow up, you will be Dr. — and I will be Dr. Ampola." She thinks that's what all mummies do. But whatever field she chooses, I hope she will aim high and do it well.

The first paper in Part II, was presented by Ms. Jacqueline Scott and entitled "Early Childhood Experiences." During the preschool years in our society, girls and boys are treated more as equals than they ever will be again. We must firmly establish this concept and extend it into the child's later development. The educational philosophy of Maria Montessori for the preschool years is an excellent model for the child's development as a whole person, male or female.

Ms. Scott summarizes the six factors she considers the major ones that lead to the evolving of a positive self-image: 1) Free expression of self, aiding the development of respect of self; 2) reflective actions, contributing toward the goal of creating internal order, an element necessary to facilitate motivation and the ability to set realistic goals; 3) repetition and consistency, contributing to the goal of producing self-confidence and ultimate realization of those goals; 4) shared responsibilities through adult and child participation, reinforcing respect for others; 5) communication, developing love and understanding of each other; and 6) the discouraging of stereotypes for male and female roles, creating a positive identity.

The second paper was given by Ms. Florence Howe and was entitled "Sexual Stereotyping and The Public Schools." The education we offer boys and girls cannot be described as "equal." The curriculum and other matters covertly or overtly teach children that females are inferior to males. The English language contributes sex bias; analyses of school texts and readers illustrate the dominance of stereotypes, in part through overemphasizing the marrying and mothering roles of women, in part through omitting the lives of working women in the present or in history. One significant effect of this male-biased curriculum and school life is the low aspiration of girls, which diminishes even further despite additional

145

education or actual achievement. Two models of change are projected for the future: An androgynous blurring of behavior and expectations in a deliberate attempt to destroy or reverse stereotypes, and a pattern of self-conscious and compensatory separatism, using for study stereotypes and sex differences themselves. Probably neither pattern by itself is sufficient, but instead, some careful combination of the two, will serve.

The third paper was given by Dr. Dorothy Zinberg, and the title was "College: When the Present Becomes the Future." In the college years, women are asked to do two things: a) make the social and psychological transition from late adolescence to young womanhood *and* at the *same* time; and b) narrow their broader academic interests into an orderly pattern of career development. But college demands that she focus on her studies (i.e., the immediate future), and the more distant future dims.

For males, what he "does" will be the organizing principle of his adult life. Women become very concerned about the limited period in which they can bear children. Relatively few women resolve these conflicts fully, successfully.

Many young women see the choices as between marriage and career or, as they themselves roughly translate it, between femininity and masculinity (or femininity and intellectuality). Too often, they see these choices as mutually exclusive. Academic success begins to conflict with love. After many years of being rewarded for high academic achievement, women undergraduates discover that top grades and specific career goals *threaten* their male peers and undermine their developing sense of womanliness.

Compared with ten years ago, more women are planning careers, and admissions to law and medical schools have risen; in many institutions new arrangements in life styles and work patterns are evolving in partnership with young men. But these are still the minority.

Astin's study of women doctorates[1] showed that only 55% were married (including divorces), while 90% of the general population of similar age was married (again, including divorces). Adolescents and young women come to fear that the doctorate means loss of the chance to become wives and mothers.

The would-be scientist has even more problems, because she has wandered into a male bastion. Although many girls enter college in the sciences, the greatest percentage is lost by the end of the freshman year. The reason is the emergence of their conflicts about femininity.

Among all women students, women science students *who continue* have the highest achievement motivation scores on testing. As a rule, they develop more slowly socially, and perhaps many of those who eventually complete graduate school have delayed their developmental crises and consequently have gained enough skill and competence in their scientific work so that it has become more conflict-free.

Studies of the careers of many successful young women in various fields seem to show that they are able to maintain an order and persistence in their work despite often staggering personal problems.

Dr. Zinberg suggests that colleges can help by enabling women to resolve their women-work conflicts with more support. The active interest of a faculty member, particularly a female, can be of particular help. The college must help the student to come to grips with the reality that, as demanding as the present and near future appear, there will be another future of approximately 35 years, when her children will be grown.

Not all women want or should have careers, but the goal is an environment in which all choices are their own, rather than a response to a current social trend or to stereotyped masculine or feminine ideas.

The final paper in the Education Workshop was co-authored by Dr. Matina S. Horner and Mary R. Walsh. The title was "Causes and Consequences of Existing Psychological Barriers to Self-Actualization." Throughout history, society has in some degree viewed femininity and achievement as incompatible. The authors trace the gradual change in attitudes from the late 1800s, when there was outright hostility even to college education for women. Later, women fell into what has been called the "compassion trap," and clustered into the so-called *helping* professions, e.g. Jane Addams and her Settlement House. This fostered an image of femininity that emphasized tenderness and compassion at the expense of other valuable talents and emotions.

Dr. Horner's work over the past few years demonstrates clearly that women still view independence, competition, and intellectual achievements as conflicting with their femininity. Her concept of the "Motive to Avoid Success" involves anxiety about success because of social rejection and feelings of being unfeminine as a result of achieving.

Despite the recent emphasis on a new freedom for women, negative attitudes toward successful women have remained high, and in fact have *in*creased. Among white females, Dr. Horner's group found 65% to have negative attitudes in her 1964 study, and by 1970 this had risen to more than 88%.

Among white men, fear of success imagery (for themselves) has also increased, from 10% to almost 50%. Recent studies of black female students, on the other hand, show that only 29% showed fear of success, as compared to the 65-88% in white females. For black males, the figures range from 50 to 67% in various studies.

It is clear that many women are paying a high price for these internalized anxieties about success. They do not actively seek success. They perform at lower levels in mixed-sex competitive situations, and those who do succeed, downgrade their own performance in the presence of males. Career aspirations are lowered, opportunities are narrowed, and finally, faced with the conflict between their feminine image and developing their abilities, many simply abdicate from the outside world and retire to the home.

One interesting recent study reported a significant relationship between the presence of the motive to avoid success and reported drug taking. Whereas 54% of the high-fear-of-success girls reported heavy drug usage, less than 8% of the low-fear-of-success girls did so.

There are growing pressures on young women to have smaller families. Since this has been a major source of self-esteem for women, other options must be available. Achievement in the outside world is one such option, but it does not at present seem to be a viable one because of psychological barriers like the motive to avoid success.

Reference

1. Asten, H. S. 1969. The Woman Doctorate in America. Russell Sage Foundation. New York, N.Y.

PART IV

Economic Factors

DEFINITIONS AND DATA FOR ECONOMIC ANALYSIS

Carolyn Shaw Bell

Katherine Coman Professor of Economics
Wellesley College
Wellesley, Massachusetts 02181

Among the social sciences, the field of economics has some reputation for being a particularly rigorous field. Partly, this reflects the quantitative nature of our data. A very famous British economist, A. C. Pigou, even defined the field of economics in terms of phenomena that could be measured,[1] although he warned that our measuring-rod was itself a variable. Modern economics consists primarily of investigating questions about measured quantities, and about the methods used to measure them. Recently developed mathematical techniques have been rapidly adopted to give our analytical models new elegance and sophistication. Partly, also, the rigorous nature of economics reflects its commitment to such analytical models, and to defining, strictly, the concepts used in these models. Some may sound familiar to other scientists — the notions of equilibrium, acceleration, circulation in a closed system, and ratchet effect; these and many others belong in the economist's tool kit.

On the other hand, few economists think of themselves immediately or primarily as "scientists." We are grateful to the National Science Foundation for including economics on its list of fields eligible for research grants, but only three economists belong to the National Academy, and none, so far as I know, has been considered for election to Sigma Psi, the honor society for more conventionally defined scientific fields. It follows that few economists have a working definition of science readily at hand. But in order to locate and analyze economic data for women in science, we require a delineation of the scientific fields.

As a first step, it seemed plausible to turn to another well-known definition of economics and adapt it to science. "Economics is what economists do, ergo, science is what scientists do." A directory or register of scientists, therefore, should provide a working definition by which specific individuals were included or excluded. Accordingly, I consulted *American Men of Science,* the latest edition being the eleventh, published in 1970. None of its seven volumes contains the slightest clue to the criteria used to determine the contents. Only the preface to the first edition, prepared in 1906, mentions this topic at all, and it does not give much of a definition of science. It contains, however, some useful insights for this particular data-problem; i.e., women in science. I quote:

> There is here given for the first time a fairly complete survey of the scientific activity of a country at a given period. . . . There are included in the directory the records of more than four thousand men of science, and it is believed that the entries are tolerably complete for those in North America who have carried on research work in the natural and exact sciences. Some are admitted who are supposed to have advanced science by teaching, by administrative work, or by the preparation of textbooks and compilations. There are also some whose work has been chiefly in engineering, medicine or other applied sciences, and a few whose work is in education, economics, or other subjects not commonly included under the exact and natural sciences.

... The names are included because they are supposed to represent work that has contributed to the advancement of pure science — the term being used in the narrower sense — or because they are found in the membership lists of certain national societies.[2]

The preface to the first edition then lists about 23 organizations, beginning with the National Academy of Science, whose membership provided the core of this directory.

The quotation is suggestive for two reasons. First, the conference on which this book is based and which is concerned with "successful women in the sciences" must perforce deal with data on women in the labor market, women with careers, professional women, educated women, and other categories associated with "being successful." It is impossible to focus exclusively on scientists, for lack of data. These categories of employed women, career women, and so on, crop up at many conferences today, including those on women in management, women in public office, women in higher education, in government, and in industry. And all such conferees, like those who compiled the first edition of *American Men of Science,* have to turn to existing data and put up with their definitions and sources whether or not they correspond to the subject under discussion. It is my intention to clarify and emphasize the limitations of our data, the definitions inherent in our data, and the implications of these definitions. I believe a close examination of the data and definition problem will reveal far more about the position of women than it reveals about the term *woman scientist.*

Second, the quotation is the only statement on methodology published in any of the eleven editions of *American Men in Science.* Unlike some scientific publications, the directory does *not* emphasize or even reveal its definitions or sources of data. *American Men of Science* — even though it is now changing its title to *American Men and Women of Science* — does not publicize the fact that it consists of arbitrary choices. This book, of course, resembles most other directories and lists of skills or professions: they are all compiled in a self-perpetuating way, and none includes a statement to this effect.

Data that are inclusive and unbiased cannot, obviously, be found in any such directory. For economic analysis, we should like a complete enumeration of the population of scientists (or a probability sample of this universe, with sex as one of the identifying characteristics).

Let us go back to basics and agree that science has to do with its Latin root, scientia, which means knowledge, and that scientists are those with a particular kind of knowledge. Does not the Census of Population, taken decennially, reveal anything about the knowledgeability of our citizens? In fact, no. The Census, which is the complete enumeration of all inhabitants required by the Constitution in order to apportion congressional representatives, collects these days many more kinds of data than merely this geographical count. Among the statistics produced are many tables entitled "Education." But another definitional problem immediately crops up. These tables, indeed all the data we have on education in this country, refer to school enrollment and the number of years of school completed. In effect, we are counting the term of sentence served by people, their entombment within the walls of schools, colleges, and universities. We can scarcely claim that such figures indicate the education achieved, or the knowledge acquired, during the period. In short, a census of the skills or qualifications of the population of this country has never been taken. It may be impossible to devise such a census, or unfeasible to administer one. But it is essential to realize, I think, that we simply do not know these basic facts.

We turn, then, to what data do exist and to the definitions we must put up with. Both the National Register of Scientific and Technical Personnel compiled by the National Science Foundation and the Bureau of the Census of the Federal government define scientists in terms of various occupational groupings. Because the Census covers many more occupations — that is, nonscientists — than does the National Register, its methodology deserves first mention.

There are ten major occupational groupings in the Census; these are sometimes further condensed into four: white-collar workers, blue-collar workers, service workers, and farm workers. The broad group applicable here consists of professional, technical, and kindred workers: within this classification appear such familiar categories as mechanical engineers, applied mathemeticians, surveyors, biochemists, and clinical psychologists. But the operative term in all these classes is the noun *worker.* All occupational data refer to people defined in terms of their work. To the extent that work opportunities and experience for women differ from those for men, the basic data will not be equivalent for men and women. The remainder of this paper will explore the concept of occupation for males and females in the United States and its implications for women in science.

Prior to 1950, at each decennial census enumerators were charged with finding and listing the occupation of each person "who followed an occupation in which he earned money or its equivalent, or in which he assisted in the production of marketable goods." The total group of such people were called "gainful workers."[3] The chief defect in the question was that it omitted any reference to time, so that various interpretations occurred. For example, some people who had retired or become permanently disabled reported their former occupations. A physician might well consider himself a physician even though he had given up practice. On the other hand, some people did not consider themselves "gainful workers" because they knew their employment was temporary. If they were students, they expected to return to their education; if they were women, they expected to become wives and mothers. The point is, of course, that no way exists to gauge the over-estimates or underestimates involved in the final totals. Furthermore, as occupations changed and as the life patterns of both men and women altered, people's interpretations of the question also changed. Any comparison of occupational statistics for two or more Census dates should contain detailed explanations of possible sources of error and a warning regarding the reliability of data.

From 1870 to 1950, then, a basic classification of the Census turned on whether people were gainful workers or not. To repeat, a gainful worker was one who followed an occupation in which he earned money or its equivalent. An economist could argue, of course, that women engaged in housekeeping and child-rearing and domestic economy were, in fact, earning, if only their keep. The board and room they received, the clothing and shelter and other amenities provided them by husbands or fathers, represented the equivalent of money wages paid to the hired housekeepers or laundresses working in homes. But the women concerned have not so argued. In 1900, for example, the Census recorded about 1.6 million private household workers out of about five million women workers (see Ref. 3, p. 74); and a population of 25 million women of working age (see Ref. 3, p. 15). If the economist's interpretation had occurred to a woman, chances are that she would not have had the temerity to voice it to the Census enumerator.

The gainful worker concept was abandoned in 1940 when a new definition of the *labor force* in the country was introduced. As a result the occupational data lost their previous sources of ambiguity, and acquired new ambiguities by being based on a universe known as the "economically active population" (see Ref. 3, p. 69). The primary sorting out of people that eventually leads to occupational data begins today, as it did with the revision of the forties, by classifying people with respect to the labor force. Formerly, the basic classification was gainful workers; now it is the labor force. This group consists of people who worked as paid employees, or in their own or family businesses, plus those who did not work but who made specific attempts to find work and were available for work. The current monthly figures on employment and unemployment come, of course, not from a complete enumeration but from a sample; the Census uses the same concepts but refers specifically to the four weeks preceding the survey.

For those who are not classified as employed or as unemployed, there remains the alternative classification, "not in the labor force." It becomes possible, therefore, to calculate labor force participation rates for various groups in the population, and to observe, for example, that since 1950 the percentage of men in the labor force has declined steadily, from almost 95% to 75%. Over the same period the percentage of women in the labor force has risen steadily from 34% to 44%.[4] How these two ratios are related and what causes labor force participation rates to change concerns a good many economists today.

Once the unemployed can be identified, they provide further details. They can be asked: why are they unemployed? have they quit? been laid off, or are they newly entering the labor market? And if the latter, they can be asked if they have ever been employed before. An affirmative answer here propels the respondent into a Census classification known as "currently unemployed with previous work experience."[5] Note that this is not the same as all *persons* with previous work experience. Not only does it exclude retired and disabled persons, it excludes people who have been working and who have gone back for further study, and it excludes people who have, perhaps temporarily, withdrawn from the labor force.

So the universe of the "economically active population" appears; it consists of all employed workers, plus those among the unemployed who have some previous work experience. And to be listed as unemployed, one must be available for work and actively seeking employment. From these people and *only* these people the Census gathers information about occupations. Both in terms of the numbers and proportions of people in various kinds of work and in terms of intertemporal comparisons, this method of collecting data avoids, of course, the ambiguities of the concept formerly used, that of gainful workers.

Before 1940, a student with a summer job as lab technician who expected to go back to school might or might not report himself as a gainful worker; now he has no choice. He is currently employed. Before 1940 the doctor who no longer practiced might or might not be included as a member of the medical profession; now he has no opportunity to say he's a doctor. He is not in the labor force. The implications for women should be clear. Unless she has worked in the previous four weeks or was available for work and actively seeking employment, a woman scientist would have no chance to report her occupation in terms of her training or professional qualifications.

The 1968 National Science Foundation report on *American Science Manpower* presents figures of scientists "not employed."[6] This category consists of those unemployed and seeking employment — roughly comparable to Census criteria for the unemployed — and those *not* employed and *not* seeking employment. Almost 30% of all the scientists who were "not employed" in 1968 were over 65; in Census terms they would nearly all be classified as not in the labor force.

Almost half are young people, with many more in the age group 25–29 than just younger or just older; in Census terms they would probably be classified as unemployed. Not much analysis is needed to realize that most of them, and certainly the men, have just completed training or have reached a new level of skill enabling them to shift jobs. If they are unemployed they are actively seeking employment. But women, who make up only 9% of the total number of scientists, account for 19% of those not employed, and it appears plausible that these women are, in Census terms, not in the labor force, rather than unemployed. That is, they are not available for work, nor are they actively seeking work.

The NSF report suggests that the Census probably underreports the number of women scientists; i.e., women who are qualified and have had experience as scientists. Being picked up in the Census occupational survey requires labor force participation, and to the extent that women scientists are not in the labor force at the time of an occupational survey, they cannot be counted. The same is true, of course, for other occupations, although the classification of professional, technical, and kindred workers includes most of the people with advanced training.

This examination of Census data may suggest that the National Register provides a much better data bank for analyzing the position of women in science than does the Census occupational material. In fact, the NSF and the Census Bureau have both relied on a classification by employment, as can be seen by investigating the primary sources for the National Register.

Each of the thirteen professional societies developed its own comprehensive mailing list containing members, nonmembers who have attended professional meetings, subscribers to professional journals, and members of alumni organizations. The NSF sent questionnaires to names on this list and built the register from the replies. In other words, like the first and subsequent editions of *American Men in Science,* the NSF *Register* depends heavily on existing organizations. Although each of the professional organizations has slightly different criteria for "full professional standing," they all employ both education and something called "professional experience," usually measured in years. Although I have not verified this with every society, it seems clear that such experience invariably consists of paid employment. Like the Census, then, the NSF *Register* in the end identifies a scientist as a *working scientist,* and a working scientist as one with paid employment. To the extent, therefore, that employment opportunities for women in science differ from those for men, it results not merely in wasted resources, individual hardship, excessive costs to society, and other dire straits; it also results in undercounting the potential scientific skills available. The actual disproportion between the number of men and women scientists becomes exaggerated, and the basic sources for all lists, data, and information must be suspect.

Two brief addenda about occupational classifications for both men and women. The insistence on paid employment or gainful work as a sorting device may lead some to a psychological or cultural analysis of the American scene, or to recalling the Puritan ethic or the pioneer necessity for self-survival. The economist has a simpler rationale for using this criterion of paid or gainful work. If people work, they produce something useful to, or desired by, themselves or others. But what the value of their output is, how much their work is *worth,* does not readily appear. Since economics deals with quantitative data, it does no good to measure hours of work without being able to measure the output involved. Economists have used market prices to solve this problem. If an employer pays $3.50 an hour, the employee must be worth 3.50 an hour. The buyer paying

$5.30 to the service station attendant who fills his gasoline tank must value his purchase at $5.30. The economist need not be concerned with subjective worth and objective value: market prices provide measurable data. It follows, therefore, that employment means paid employment. It does not mean, as is often charged, that economists either ignore or denigrate the value of housework, of washing and cooking and household chores performed by a wife, or of painting or re-modeling performed by a handyman husband. To date, economists have found no totally satisfactory way to measure such output, precisely because it is *not* sold on the marketplace for a specific price or wage; it does not represent gainful employment for money or its equivalent.

Second, the Census divides those not in the labor force into further categories. There are six of them: those attending school, those unable to work because of long-term disability, retired or elderly people, seasonal workers (if the survey occurs in an off season) or people working in a family business without pay for less than fifteen hourse a week, those engaged in housework in their own homes) and the voluntarily idle. This last category is usually residual: a respondent who does not give one of the preceding explanations for his status is deemed to be voluntarily idle. In recent years, the males in this group, which contains a dis-proportionate share of Blacks and ethnic minorities, have received some atten-tion from economists concerned with underemployment as well as unemployment. "Voluntarily idle" women have been excluded from these investigations chiefly because there are so few of them in the statistics. The majority of women not in the labor force, of course, have a well-recognized and defined occupation: they do housework in their own homes.

In fact, this occupational classification pervades most economic analysis of the employment of women, including those who are professionals and scientists. When economists look at data on women in the labor force, they sort by non-economic status. The primary classifications for women consist of single, married, mother of dependent children. Single women include never-married, widowed, divorced, separated. Married women are distinguished by the presence or ab-sence of the husbands. Finally, employment details exist for mothers of children, mothers of children under six, and mothers of children under three and by numbers of children in various age groups. No parallel data exist for the employ-ment of men classified as single, married, and the father of dependent children. In short, the data define a woman first in terms of marriage and motherhood, and only second with respect to her economic status. It is not denied that such classifi-cations provide highly useful information, or that marital status and child care have much to do with a woman's occupation. But the entire emphasis, the basic data, centers first on homemaking and only second on achievement in some other sphere.

The point can be clarified if we ask about the 34 million women who, in 1970, were classified as keeping house. How many of them are caring for husband? for parents or relatives? caring for children? for dependent children under six? under three? How many at home are "voluntarily idle"? No answers can be given. No analysis exists for the occupation of keeping house, the status of wife and mother. This need not be inevitable; in many societies the question for a woman is "Why aren't you working?" instead of "Why are you taking a job?" The fact that basic economic data delineate women in terms of marriage and the family leads to such titles as *Women's Two Roles*[7] or *Dual Careers*[8] for studies of women's employment. These wordings reflect, of course, the deep-rooted con-viction in our society that women have a primary responsibility for home and children, whatever their training, profession, or scientific bent. One must conclude that successful women in science, like successful women in other fields, must work out a life-style to cope with this assignment, whether by remaining single and avoiding it altogether, or by sharing with other family members.

With all their shortcomings, what do the data provide toward an economic analysis of women in science? The category *professional, technical, and kindred workers* (hereafter called *p.t.k.*) is the only useful one, even though it includes far more than scientists no matter how defined. Women in this group have a much higher economic status than those in other occupations. In 1970, the median income of women who work full time, year around, was 58% of what full-time year-round male workers received (see Ref. 9, p. 110). This proportion is the same as in 1939. Such full-time working women in the p.t.k. class earn much more — 67% of what men receive (see Ref. 9, pp. 117, 119). This fraction represents a gain since 1949. In 1970, some six million women supported their families. Most have children, some have disabled husbands or aged parents. Of these women, 375,000 fall into the professional, technical, and kindred occupations. Although a majority of the larger group (that is, the six million females who are head of the household) are employed, almost half their families have incomes below the poverty level. By contrast, the poverty rate among the p.t.k. women who are heads of households is only 5.6%.[10]

Aside from specific income figures, other data indicate a superior economic status for women in science. While only one out of five women works part time (at least on a voluntary basis), some 35% of female professional, technical, and kindred workers do so. It can be hypothesized that their higher skills enable them to earn, working less than full time, a higher income than that gained by other full-time women workers. The rate of involuntary part time among women far exceeds that for men, even in so-called "women's jobs" like clerical and sales positions. But not for p.t.k. women, where the number forced to work less than full time for economic reasons almost equals the number of men on involuntary part time.

Women scientists achieve their highest gains, at least in terms of income and status, in salaried positions rather than in self-employment. The median income for salaried men in p.t.k. occupations is closer to that for women than in almost any other field. It is not surprising that self-employed women professionals constitute a minority, and of this small group only a fraction work on a full-time basis. It follows that employment opportunities or their lack make up the chief determinant of economic success for women.

In order to emphasize the importance of employment opportunities, the impact of education may be considered. Scientists, of course, expect a close correlation between the specific positions available and their special training. One would also expect that the greater the level of training, the greater the productivity and hence the income earned. Then, in economists' terms, the higher salaries paid to holders of higher degrees would represent the payoff, the return on investment, to the graduate who has given up time and resources to further study. For women scientists, the income differential between two degree levels falls well below that for men. Furthermore, the payoff from further training for a woman consists, usually, of her arrival at the same position or income level as that of a man with less education. In this respect, women scientists are no better off than women in other occupations. Again, the primary definition appears to be sexual rather than professional or productive potential.

Reverting to Census data, median income figures show that a woman college graduate employed full time year round receives slightly less than the income paid to a full-time year-round male worker who has not completed high school. The median income of women with graduate school training does not differ significantly from that of men with a high school diploma (see Ref. 9, pp. 102, 106). One may hypothesize that the higher male incomes reflect years of on-the-job experience, and that married women, at least, have found it less possible to amass such experience. In short, the lack of payoff to women scientists and other women professionals may stem from a lack of employment opportunity. Data from the NSF Report support this hypothesis. The median income of full-time women scientists holding the doctorate falls below that of full-time men scientists with bachelors' degrees, except for a few social science fields where women Ph.D's receive smaller incomes than the men with M.A.'s (see Ref. 6, pp. 96–98, 253). On the other hand, that median salary for male scientists with a bachelor's degree conceals a pattern of lifetime earnings which, obviously, reflect experience on the job. Salaries for male B.A.'s are low during the years immediately after graduation and then rise gradually, coming to a peak with 30–35 years of professional experience. The median salary, in dollars, for all B.A.'s (both sexes) coincides with the median salary in dollars for all scientists holding the B.A. who have 10–15 years' professional experience (see Ref. 6, p. 121). The data also show that the professional work experience of women scientists does not compare at all to that of men: half those reporting full-time employment had less than 15 years' experience and only 3% of all women scientists had 30–35 years (see Ref. 6, p. 253). In short, the lack of payoff to women scientists probably represents the lack of employment opportunity.

Employment opportunities can be analyzed in terms of the jobs that actually or potentially exist, but the classifications so far discussed suggest, I think, that for women the opportunities for employment also reflect the ability to cope with the domestic responsibilities that society has assigned to them. Most American working women today, and certainly most working wives and mothers, hold their jobs for economic necessity; this cannot be said of most women scientists. Whether there are viable solutions to the homework and child care problems poses a different problem of economic necessity, and one that can be answered only by the individual involved. The effects of changed arrangements in the way of day care, a shattering depression that will provide a new servant class, the condominium boom evolving residential hotel-apartments to replace private homes, cannot be predicted by economic analysis because such arrangements require drastic social changes. Certainly the woman scientist in the foreseeable future cannot escape her definition in terms of marriage and the family. Whether she will accept this as sufficient remains to be seen.

References

1. PIGOU, A. C. 1921. Economics of Welfare. : 8. MacMillan & Co., Ltd. London, England.
2. AMERICAN MEN OF SCIENCE. V. 1906. The Science Press. New York, N. Y.
3. U.S. BUREAU OF THE CENSUS. 1960. Historical-Statistics of the United States, Colonial Times to 1957. : 68. Washington, D.C.
4. U.S. BUREAU OF THE CENSUS. 1970. Statistical Abstract of the United States: 1970. (91st edit.) : 213. Washington, D.C.
5. U.S. DEPARTMENT OF LABOR, BUREAU OF LABOR STATISTICS. 1962 to date. Employment and Earnings. Washington, D.C.
6. NATIONAL SCIENCE FOUNDATION. 1969. American Science Manpower. : 22.
7. MYRDAL, A. & V. KLEIN. 1956. Women's Two Roles. Routledge and Kegan Paul. London, England.

8. UNITED STATES DEPARTMENT OF LABOR. Manpower Administration. 1970. Dual Careers, A Longitudinal Study of Labor Market Experience of Women. Washington, D.C.
9. U.S. BUREAU OF THE CENSUS. 1971. Income in 1970 of Families and Persons in the United States. Current Population Reports, Series P–60, No. 80. Washington, D.C.
10. U.S. BUREAU OF THE CENSUS. 1971. Household Income in 1970 and Selected Social and Economic Characteristics of Households. Current Population Reports, Series P–60, No. 79. Washington, D.C.

EMPLOYMENT PROSPECTS AND ACADEMIC POLICIES

Hilda Kahne

Assistant Dean, Radcliffe Institute
Radcliffe College
Cambridge, Massachusetts 02138

The dramatic documentation of a general revolution of women at work is now giving way to more specific investigations directed to particular groups and concrete issues.[1] Women in professional occupations share a number of interests and common concerns with all working women and at the same time have distinctive characteristics, motivations, and work environments that contribute to their attitudes and experience with respect to work.[2] Within the professional category, they differ with respect to a variety of factors such as the number and kinds of work opportunities available, the degree of women's involvement in the field, and structural and policy characteristics that affect placement procedures and employment environments. Because of the increasing numbers of educated women and the expected continuing growth and importance in the civilian labor force of professional occupations in the years ahead, it is important to increase our understanding of employment issues and prospects in specific professional fields, both so that women can choose more wisely and so that academic policies affecting career choice and employment can be wisely developed.

This paper is concerned with employment prospects and possibilities for women in professional occupations, particularly women in the sciences, a traditionally male field encompassing in the available data the physical and biological sciences, mathematics, engineering, and often social sciences as well. An opening statement of educational and occupational trends and their potential impact on the employment outlook in the 1970s is followed by a discussion of the implications of these trends for women in science and for those interested in pursuing scientific careers. A final section of the paper considers academic policies designed to make more rational women's academic and career choices and to facilitate the placement of women in appropriate professional positions.

EDUCATIONAL AND OCCUPATIONAL TRENDS AND EMPLOYMENT OUTLOOK

While labor market forecasters predict a continuing increase in the relative importance of white-collar occupations in the coming decade, determined primarily by the growth in the professional occupations,[3] they also express concern about lack of employment opportunities for educated persons. Why this concern and seeming contradiction?

The answer is to be found partly in the greater expected growth in the supply of educated labor generally relative to the demand for it and partly in the changing expectations with respect to the nature and growth rates of specific professional occupations. Estimates of future demand-and-supply conditions in particular fields vary, depending on the time period studied, the specific field and kind of work involved, the level of education with which one is concerned, and whether one is talking about the impact of problems on educated men or women.

More and more we are becoming a society of educated persons. Between 1960 and 1969 the number of B.A.'s granted almost doubled, the number of M.A.'s increased 42%, and the number of Ph.D.'s increased 75%. In 1970 11% of persons 25 years old and over had four or more years of college; in 1960 the figure had been 7.7%.[4]

For women, there was both an absolute and relative gain in earned advanced degrees. Thus, in 1969 the 67,000 M.A.'s earned by women represented 36% of all M.A.'s earned, a rise of almost 4.5 percentage points since 1960. The 3,300 Ph.D.'s earned by women in 1969 were 13% of the total, an increase of 2.5 percentage points since 1960.[5] We know that the more education a woman receives, the greater the likelihood that she will engage in paid work.[6] Thus, the increasingly educated female population is one factor that helps to explain women's positive attitudes about paid work that are prevalent in the society today. During the next ten years, while the proportion of female M.A.'s and Ph.D.'s are expected to remain about the same as today, the numbers earning advanced degrees are expected to continue to rise.[7] There will continue to be an increasing supply of both educated men and women available and wanting to use their training in paid work.

What about the employment outlook in the years ahead? A recent study by the Department of Labor has analyzed occupational employment in 1968 and, based on a series of assumptions, has projected an employment outlook for college graduates in 1980. The study concludes that while there will be an overall balance in the supply and demand for college graduates, some imbalances will occur in particular fields.[8] The supply of mathematicians, life scientists, and elementary and secondary school teachers is expected to be significantly above requirements during this period, but in a number of occupations, including some scientific ones — chemistry, physics, engineering, geology, and geophysics — projected requirements are, in varying degrees, in excess of the estimated supply.

If, instead of talking about opportunities for all college graduates (combining persons at all degree levels on the assumption that evidence of college or graduate training is the important requirement), we review the outlook for doctorate recipients alone, then the situation with respect to employment opportunities probably can be described more accurately but also more pessimistically. High proportions of both men and women Ph.D.'s teach in colleges and universities, and for this reason consideration of the group must begin with a discussion of expectations about academic employment.[9]

The demand for college teachers, although influenced by a number of factors, is perhaps most profoundly affected by demographic trends that influence enrollment figures. The supply of potential teachers, on the other hand, while partly determined by demographic factors, is also affected by the interest, availability, and financial support of graduate training and by the general interest of advanced degree recipients in pursuing teaching careers. A number of independent demand-and-supply projections have been made, and though different specific figures emerge, depending on the assumptions of the particular study, they agree that while the number of new positions will increase substantially during the 1970s, growth rates will be lower than existed between 1960 and 1968, and as a result, the demand for new teachers will not increase so rapidly as the supply of potential teachers.[10] This probably will not result in widespread unemployment for the doctorate recipients, with their highly specialized skills, but for many of them their situations will require a reordering of priorities concerning desirable employment opportunities and career directions.

While expectations for academic needs are rooted in demographic considerations, those for nonacademic work relate to more tenuously based assumptions of growth rates. For example, fund expenditures for research and development work, both inside and outside of academia, are projected to remain at about three percent of the Gross National Product, but the proportion of personnel with Ph.D.'s is expected to increase. Nonresearch and nonacademic employment, on the other hand, is projected to increase at past rates or 25% more rapidly than past rates. Of those who take nonacademic jobs, a smaller percentage will engage in research and development work.[11]

This statement of the general employment outlook is particularly applicable to Ph.D.'s in the sciences. In these fields, both in academic and nonacademic markets, and in research and nonresearch capacities, the projected increase in requirements will not be sufficient to absorb the expected output of doctorate recipients. If past trends continue, the NSF anticipates an oversupply of about 40,000 of these science and engineering doctorates in 1980.[12] The data are a cause for sober concern and reflection about policies and priorities with respect to educational training and career directions.[13]

WOMEN IN SCIENCE

What are the implications of this employment outlook for educated women generally, and particularly for women in science and those contemplating careers as scientists? As members of the employed labor force, working women, no less than men, will be affected by the problems besetting some professional occupations in the 1970s. But because of the limited range of the professional occupations in which women concentrate, because of their low rate of participation in specific "highly educated" professions, and because of the heavy focus of those who are highly educated, in college and university teaching,[14] women are more vulnerable than are men to the current tight and fluctuating labor market. They are not for the most part entering those fields where shortages in trained personnel are expected. Unless women's professional participation becomes more diversified, the consequences for them as individuals and for the society may be compromising.[15]

Scientific fields represent one potential direction for expansion and diversification of women's interests. An addition to the pool of trained manpower in some scientific areas will provide needed talented personnel to fill job vacancies. At the same time it will ensure that the scientific aptitudes which many women have[16] do not go undeveloped.

Women are not strongly represented in scientific fields. The most informative and current indicator of numbers and characteristics of persons in science is provided by the National Register of Scientific and Technical Personnel.[17] In 1970 the Register identified 29,200 working women in these fields, 9.4% of the total. About three-fourths of the women scientists were concentrated in psychology, chemistry, biological sciences, and mathematics. For men, about the same proportion were distributed among a broader range of fields including physics and earth and marine sciences, in addition to the forementioned. Within each field the proportions of women varied. They accounted for at least 20–25% of persons in social science fields of psychology, sociology, and anthropology, but less than 10% of all persons in chemistry, earth and marine sciences, atmospheric and space sciences, physics; agricultural sciences, and economics (TABLE 1).

Doctorate degrees were held by 32.2% of the women scientists in the National Register (compared with 40.1% of all scientists).[18] Of all doctorate degrees held by women scientists, more than 70% were in the fields of chemistry, biological sciences, and psychology. By field, the level of training for women was highest in the social sciences and in biology, where the proportion of women with Ph.D.'s customarily was between 40% and 50% of the total. In other science categories,

TABLE 1

NUMBER AND PERCENTAGE OF SCIENTISTS BY FIELD AND SEX, 1970*

Scientific and Technical Field	Total	Sex					
		Male			Female		
		Number	Percentage of total	Percentage in Field	Number	Percentage of total	Percentage in Field
All Fields	312,644	203,351	100		29,293	100	
Chemistry	86,980	80,779	28	92.9	6,201	21	7.1
Earth & Marine Sciences	23,756	22,904	8	96.4	852	3	3.6
Atmospheric & Space Sciences	6,637	6,535	2	98.5	102	—	1.5
Physics	36,336	34,902	12	96.1	1,354	5	3.9
Mathematics	24,400	21,610	8	88.6	2,790	10	11.4
Computer Sciences	11,374	10,016	4	88.5	1,263	4	11.5
Agricultural Sciences	15,730	15,673	6	96.6	57	—	3.4
Biological Sciences	47,493	41,359	14	87.1	6,134	21	12.9
Psychology	26,271	19,944	7	75.9	6,327	22	24.1
Statistics	2,953	2,616	1	88.9	337	1	11.1
Economics	13,386	12,574	4	93.9	812	3	6.1
Sociology	7,658	5,929	2	77.4	1,729	6	22.6
Political Science	6,493	5,862	2	90.1	631	2	9.9
Anthropology	1,375	1,068	—	77.7	257	1	22.3
Linguistics	1,902	1,455	—	76.5	447	2	23.5

* Source: National Register of Scientific and Technical Personnel, 1970. ("Percentage in field" computed by author.) Percentages may not add to total shown because of rounding.

including mathematics and statistics, the percentage of Ph.D.'s among women was 25% or less.

Reflecting the disposition of women generally for teaching, 54.1% (compared with 41.7% of all scientists) worked in educational institutions, but only 12.5% (compared with 31.2% of all scientists) in industry and business. There was some variation of this figure among specific fields, most noticeably in computer sciences, where only 15% of the women worked in educational institutions and 53.4% in industry and business.

Among specific fields, the range of the median annual salary for women was narrow — between $9,400 (in agricultural sciences) and $13, 400 (in economics). For all scientists the range was $12,500 (in linguistics) to $16,900 (in statistics). But for every field, at each degree level it was lower for women than it was for all scientists.

What emerges in this picture of women scientists is one of a well-educated group (over 90% have advanced degrees) concentrated in a few fields, earning less than men in the same field with comparable degrees. They work primarily in educational institutions, although to a lesser degree than do women in arts and humanities.

The evidence we have from the 1950 and 1960 censuses about women working in scientific occupations shows no increase in the low proportion of women in science.[19] Today's figures appear to reflect the same situation that existed ten years ago.

Another way of looking at the expressed interest of women in scientific fields is to examine the degrees earned by women in these fields. We already have observed that the number of degrees at all levels earned by women has been increasing over time. What is interesting from our perspective, however, is that in a number of fields – engineering, chemistry, physics, mathematics – the number of women receiving B.A.'s increased at a slower rate than did the total number of B.A.'s conferred on women overall. The growth rate of B.A.'s among women in life sciences and in geology and geophysics exceeded that of the total growth rate of all female B.A.'s. Only for chemistry, life sciences, and mathematics were the number of degrees earned by women as many as 2,000 or more. In the other fields, both the numbers and proportion of B.A. degrees earned by women were very low.[20]

At higher degree levels, the proportion of degrees earned by women in scientific fields continues to be less than the overall proportion for all fields. In 1966–67, 25.6% of M.A.'s in biological sciences, 24.3% of those in mathematics, and 10.2% of those in physical sciences were conferred on women, compared with 34.7% of all M.A.'s. For earned Ph.D.'s, the figures were 15.2%, 7.1%, and 4.7% in biological sciences, mathematics, and physical sciences, respectively, compared with 11.9% overall.[21] Although the number of women doctorates almost tripled between 1960 and 1968, there was a constancy in the proportional distribution among fields. No more than 11% were awarded to women in physical science fields. In the biological sciences, the proportion ranged between 15% and 18%. The proportions in other areas, while larger, were equally constant: about 30% in education, 20–25% in social sciences, and 20% in arts and humanities.[22]

The increasing emphasis on the need for scientific expertise in the 1950s and 1960s did not seem to influence women in either their undergraduate or graduate school educational choices.

ACADEMIC POLICIES AND WOMEN IN SCIENCE

Perhaps, since the employment outlook in scientific professions is so uncertain, one should feel relieved that women are not gravitating to those scientific fields in which a surplus of well-trained persons is feared. Why should we be interested in stimulating women's interest in science and have a concern about increasing their opportunities in these fields? The answer lies partly in a desire to provide for women, as for other groups, an opportunity to pursue educational and work choice on an equal and competitive basis. Just as important, however, is the desire to provide for all members of society an increased well-being that results from having the best possible fit between the human resources available and the work that society needs done. Paid work, of course, is not the only way in which talented persons apply their education and training. But if choices can be more freely exercised, unencumbered by cultural stereotypes and discriminatory practices, the resulting benefits can be significant.

This paper began with an assessment of occupational trends and projections as a framework for considering particular policy issues. Given this frame of reference,[23] let us turn to a consideration of two areas where an expansion of academic interest and activity can help to move us in a desirable direction. While the suggestions are made in relation to scientific disciplines, their consideration and adoption are relevant for all academic disciplines.

Expansion of Activities of Academic Departments in Relating Disciplinary Study to its Applications in the Work World

The growing complexity and specialization of disciplines within academia have their counterpart in the nonacademic sector in a similar increase in the complexity of work and the speeding up of the dynamic process of change. Both within and outside academia there are problems, not only in keeping abreast of current developments in one's field but also in communicating and exchanging ideas with persons in related work. The difficulties experienced by the professionals are intensified for students who have less of a common base of knowledge and experience with persons outside academia. The current tight academic labor market only raises the pitch of an already loud and clear plea by students as well as by others for a clarification of the goals of higher education and of their relevance to the experiences to follow in life, including one's future professional pursuits. In view of this, it is indeed legitimate for students to ask how their present educational experience articulates with the work world of which they are to be a part.

Academic disciplines undoubtedly each have their own style of imparting some of this kind of knowledge to current generations of students. Additional assistance, however, could be helpful. For example, all persons who expect to work need to understand the functioning and projected development of the economy and need to have some perspective about possible occupational shortages and surpluses in the years ahead. Careful distinction must be made between short-run expectations and longer-run outlook. And care must be taken so that important decisions of academic concentration and career direction are not made solely on the basis of short-run job outlook.[24] But if students can have access to this kind of information, they will have gained one more valuable input, the relative importance of which may vary for each of them, to use in determining the relavance and direction of their academic work.

Students may also be less knowledgeable than we realize about the subtle differences in content among scientific specialties and about the different ways in which training can be applied. A theoretical physicist, who recently transferred from academic work to a position in an industrial firm, has commented: "In academia, I found theory to be the anchor point around which the rest of the field revolved. In industry it is a tool, useful and valued only if it helps in solving a specific problem." In another area, community and junior college administrators have expressed concern that their institutions are being viewed as possible temporary havens for unemployed Ph.D.'s. They rightfully point out that particular qualities of teaching and of course content are needed to meet the requirements of their particular student bodies, qualities that may be present but that are not guaranteed by the simple presence of a doctorate degree.[25]

In the 1970s it is expected that many new occupational alternatives will develop for science and engineering doctorates.[26] Students need to know more about these options and, indeed, are asking questions about the relevance of the advanced degree for doing the particular work they want to do. They should be informed about the content of the new degree offerings in bioengineering, the possible application of a combined medical and law degree, new course combinations that can lead to medical degrees, and the professional possibilities of applying science training, for example, to the education or publications field.

The point of all this is that there is a need for a more complete understanding about the economy's functioning generally, about how the nature and content of the work varies among different employing institutions, about what comprises the knowledge base of specific disciplines, and what comes under the umbrella of different occupational titles, whether they be in traditional or new professions. It is time for academic departments to address these questions in a serious and organized fashion in order that students can make more informed judgments about their education and work.

None of these needs is limited in their relevance to women. Nor are they substitutes for measures designed to identify women with scientific aptitude and to encourage them in developing their interest.[27] They are, however, particularly important for maximizing possibilities for that group of educated women faced with the necessity of making these decisions now. They are women who, until now, have often felt not only excluded from channels of communication about opportunities, but vague and unclear about the possibilities offered by the election of new directions. While women appear to be turning away from former traditional areas of concentration, we have as yet no evidence, other than in medicine and law, that they have chosen some positive new directions. Greater familiarity with options should encourage diversification among fields of study, including, presumably, the sciences. Academic advising could help in constructing this future.

Increased Academic Interest in Job Placement and Work Concerns of Women

Training is a necessary but by no means sufficient condition for finding a satisfactory job. For women, there has often been a traumatic transition from college, where admissions and scholarship committees generally have made equitable determinations among applicants[28] to the work world, where structures and attitudes have been more supportive, if not patently discriminatory in favor of men's work needs and life styles. The difficulties encountered in learning about job openings and in seeking letters of recommendation[15] are often repeated when women confront the work environment itself[29] and when they seek salaries equivalent to those of men with similar backgrounds and experience.[30]

These problems developed quite independently of academic institutions; their amelioration cannot be achieved solely as a result of actions taken by the academic community. But academic institutions can be an important force for improvement by making explicit the need for a positive policy with respect to employment issues and by initiating action with respect to some of these. For example, the help provided by academia in locating the first postgraduate position can be of critical importance for the entire future course of career development. Moreover, by demonstrating possibilities for flexibility in its own faculty and staff employment structures[31] and by stimulating an interchange of ideas and experience with other employing institutions, the academic establishment can heighten awareness of existing problems and suggest alternative approaches for their solutions.

A few years ago there was much discussion about the need to have available rosters of women in professional activities, both to identify them and to establish their qualifications and availability for jobs and advisory posts. Now that a number of these exist,[32] it is clear that without knowledge of existing job vacancies and selective recommendation from among the listed names, movement of women into the professional mainstream will be difficult.[33] College placement offices can, as they have in the past, supplement the academic departmental role of putting new graduates in touch with known vacancies. But the system as it works is neither equitable nor sufficient.[15] Faced with the realities of today's general economic conditions and employment policies and the limits imposed by family requirements on geographic location,[34] women need not only to be given more equitable consideration for the opportunities that become available but may also need more specific assistance in seeking out jobs compatible with other family demands. The kinds of measures and the desirable degree of liaison between the college placement office and the academic departments will depend on tradition and attitudes within the institution as well as on resources available to implement a program expansion. But the need for a more coherent link between education and its work applications is clearly present.[35]

None of this will work, however, unless the work world becomes more hospitable to women and to their increasing aspirations for professional as well as family lives. Equal opportunity for women will require not only that women's educational horizons be expanded, but that there be a corresponding broadening in the kinds of employment open to them—in private industry, in government, and in research laboratories, as well as in academia.[36] It will mean that administrative positions as well as opportunities in teaching must be available to them.[37] Salaries must become equal for comparable work. The introduction of flexibility in work structures and the greater availability of support structures must occur where potential benefits exceed costs.[38] Academic institutions can raise the issues, point the way in how to think about them, and provide useful structures for locating the critically important first postgraduate jobs. But the ultimate challenge lies in developing further and extending these possibilities to work centers, other than those of academia, where women of the future may also want and need to work.

NOTES AND REFERENCES

1. BAILYN, L. 1970. Career and family orientations of husbands and wives in relation to marital happiness. Human Relations 23(2): 97–113; COSER, R. L. & G. ROKOFF. 1971. Women in the occupational world: social disruption and conflict. Social Problems 18(4): 535–553; EPSTEIN, C. F. 1970. Encountering the male establishment: sex-status limits on women's careers in the professions. American Journal of Sociology 75(6): 965–982; GRAHAM, P. A. 1970. Women in academe. Science 169: 1284–1290; KAHNE, H. 1971. Women in the professions: career considerations and job placement techniques. Journal of Economic Issues 5(3): 28–45; PERRUCCI, C. C. 1970. Minority status and the pursuit of professional careers: women in science and engineering. Social Forces 49(2): 245–257; Symposium — Women and the law. 1971. Valparaiso University Law Review 5(2); WHITE, M. S. 1970. Psychological and social barriers to women in science. Science 170: 413–416; WILLIAMS, P. 1971. Women in medicine: some themes and variations. Journal of Medical Education 46: 584–591.
2. KAHNE, H. 1970. Women in professional occupations: distinctive qualities. Radcliffe Institute. Radcliffe College. Cambridge, Mass. Unpublished paper.
3. Professional and technical workers, accounting for more than one fourth of all white collar workers, almost doubled between 1950 and 1965. Between 1968 and 1980 the estimated increase of the group will be 50%, compared with 36% for white collar occupations and 25% for all workers. As a result, by 1980 white collar employment is expected to constitute 50% of all employment. Professional workers will increase from 13.6% to 16.3% of all workers. U.S. DEPT. OF LABOR, BLS. 1968. Occupational Patterns for 1960 and 1975. Bulletin 1599; U.S. DEPT. OF LABOR. 1971. Occupational Manpower and Training Needs. Bulletin 1701 : 8–11.
4. In 1970, 14.7% of men and 8.2% of women aged 25 and over had 4 or more years of college. In 1960, the proportions had been 9.7% and 5.8% respectively. U.S. DEPT. OF COMMERCE, CENSUS BUREAU. March, 1970. Educational Attainment. Series P–20, No. 207: 1.
5. U.S. DEPT. OF LABOR, WAGE AND HOUR ADMINISTRATION. 1969. Trends in Educational Attainment of Women : 15–16.
6. In March 1968, 71% of women with 5 or more years of college were in the labor force, compared with 54% of women with 4 years of college and 48% of women high school graduates. See Ref. 5, p. 10. A recent study of women Ph.D.'s found that 90% engaged in paid work 7–8 years after graduation. ASTIN, H. 1969. The Woman Doctorate in America : 56. Russell Sage Foundation. New York, N. Y.
7. U.S. DEPT. OF HEW, OFFICE OF EDUCATION, NATIONAL CENTER FOR EDUCATIONAL STATISTICS. 1969. Projections of Educational Statistics to 1978–79 : 67.
8. U.S. DEPT. OF LABOR, BLS. 1970. College Educated Workers, 1968–80. Bull. 1676.
9. Although figures vary somewhat by field, about 70% of working women work in academic institutions, mostly in teaching. In recent years about half of all first postdoctoral jobs have been as teachers in colleges and universities. During the 1970s it is expected that the doctoral degree will be held by 95% of newly appointed faculty members at

graduate institutions and by 62% of those at 4-year and 2-year colleges. WOLFLE, D. & C. V. KIDD. 1971. The future market for Ph.D.'s. Science **173**: 786–794; ASTIN, H. See Ref. 5; p. 10.

10. One estimate sees the annual increase in employment requirements between 1968 and 1980 at 2.7% for academic teachers, compared with a 6.8% annual increase between 1960 and 1968. U.S. DEPT. OF LABOR. 1970. Manpower Report of the President : 173; Cartter estimates that 40% of the new Ph.D.'s were needed to fill teaching needs in the period 1965–69. By 1975–79, the proportion needed will be only 27%. CARTTER, A. 1971. Scientific manpower for 1970–85. Science **172**: 135. Despite the conscious change in admissions policies in some graduate schools and the effect on graduate enrollments of the current stringency of fellowship money, overall graduate enrollments to date have continued to increase. Between 1968 and 1980 there is expected to be a doubling or more of the advanced degree output of M.A.'s and Ph.D.'s nationwide. U.S. DEPT. OF HEW. See Ref. 7: 41.

11. NATIONAL SCIENCE FOUNDATION. 1971. 1969 and 1980 Science and Engineering Doctorate Supply and Utilization. NSF 171–20; See Ref. 10.

12. The projected supply-utilization prospects among the fields, as well as for specific disciplines within each field, varies. According to the assumptions, projected 1980 supply and utilization in physical sciences are virtually in balance. For other scientific fields, the outlook is less favorable. Whereas today about two-thirds of science and engineering doctorates are engaged in teaching and/or research in graduate schools or are employed in nonacademic research and development positions, slightly less than one-half of those doctorates entering employment during the 1970's are projected to be in such positions. The rest will either be teachers of undergraduates or enter nonacademic employment other than research and development. See Ref. 11, NSF.

13. The experience of 1970 science Ph.D. recipients reflects these expectations. The job market was much tighter than in 1969, and while unemployment rates were much lower than those of all workers, they were not insignificant. Women fared worse than men. The proportion of Ph.D.'s continuing in postdoctoral work was greater than in earlier years. NSF testimony before NSF Congressional Subcommittee, Oct. 27, 1971.

14. Of the 29.6 million employed women in March 1970, 15% worked in professional and technical occupations, a broad Census grouping of some 70 specific occupations, only roughly correlated with college or graduate training. It is used as the best nationwide approximation of professional employment.

  Between 1950 and 1970 the numbers of women in the professional category grew, but until recently their proportion of the total declined. In 1970 the 4.3 million women in the group represented 38.6% of the total, still somewhat less than their proportion in 1950 but rising slowly and continuously throughout the past several years. In 1968 66% of women in the category were engaged in noncollege teaching or in health occupations. Among the "highly educated" professional occupations in 1960 (i.e., those where at least 15% of the women had 5 years of college), the "feminine" occupations (those in which 50% or more of all workers were women) included librarians, musicians, social and welfare workers, noncollege teachers, and therapists and healers. But despite increased enrollments of women in professional schools, as yet only 7% of the medical profession is female, 8% of persons in science, 3% in law, 2% in dentistry, and 1% in engineering. U.S. DEPT. OF LABOR. Nov. 1968. Fact Sheet on Women in Professional and Technical Positions; U.S. DEPT. OF LABOR. 1971. Manpower Report of the President: 215; data derived from 1960 U.S. Census. HEDGES, J. 1970. Women workers and manpower demands in the 1970's. Monthly Labor Review **193**: 24–26.

15. KAHNE, H. 1971. See Ref. 1.

16. U.S. DEPT. OF LABOR, MANPOWER ADMIN. 1958. Unpublished data from longitudinal maturation study. Quoted in HEDGES, Ref. 14, p. 20; LEWIS, E. C. 1968. Developing Woman's Potential : 45–46, 264–265. Iowa State Univ. Press. Ames, Iowa.

17. NATIONAL SCIENCE FOUNDATION. 1971. American Science Manpower. The compilation done by contract with the scientific societies in the past few years has included persons working in a number of social science fields, as well as those in physical, biological, and mathematical sciences. Figures in this section are computed from data contained in the report.

18. Figures were not available for male scientists separately. However, since women constituted less than 10% of the total group, percentages for the total reflect male experience. The high overall percentage figures for Ph.D.'s reflect the high proportion of persons with advanced degrees who are members of professional associations and hence are included in the National Register.

19. EPSTEIN, C. 1971. Woman's Place : 7. Univ. of Calif. Press. Berkeley, Calif.

20. U.S. DEPT. OF LABOR.   College Educated Workers. See Ref. 8, pp. 5–10.
21. U.S. DEPT. OF HEW, OFFICE OF EDUC., NATIONAL CENTER FOR EDUCATIONAL STATISTICS. 1967.   Earned Degrees Conferred, 1966–67 : 12–19.
22. Derived from data supplied by the National Academy of Sciences from the Doctorate Records File of the Office of Scientific Personnel of the National Research Council.
23. Projections, not to be confused with predictions, are a statement of what is possible, given assumptions about development trends. They can be useful bases for considering the impact of alternative policies on society's development, activities, and the well-being of its members.
24. The Engineers Joint Council reports a dramatic decline in engineering enrollments in the Fall of 1971, compared with 1970, greatest among freshmen but manifested at all educational levels. The decline was attributed to a student reaction to unemployment fears. While the recent short-run outlook for engineers has been bleak, long-run projections show an increased demand for engineering talent. The decline in enrollments will have serious implications for this future demand. ENGINEERS JOINT COUNCIL. 1971. Engineering and Technical Enrollments – Fall, 1971. New York, N. Y.
25. THE CHRONICLE OF HIGHER EDUCATION.   1972.   6(16): 1.
26. NATIONAL SCIENCE FOUNDATION.   1971.   1969 & 1980 Doctorate Supply and Utilization. See Ref. 11, iv.
27. ZINBERG, D. & P. DOTY.   Undergraduate Science Education, Carnegie Commission on Higher Education. In press.
28. COMMITTEE ON THE STATUS OF WOMEN IN THE FACULTY OF ARTS AND SCIENCES.   1971. Report. Harvard University. Cambridge, Mass.
29. COMMITTEE ON WOMEN IN PHYSICS.   1972.   Women in physics. Submitted to the American Physical Society.
30. NATIONAL ACADEMY OF SCIENCES.   1968.   Careers of Ph.D.'s, Academic vs. Non-academic. Publia. 1577: 91–98; See Ref. 1, PERRUCCI, pp. 250–253; See Ref. 6, ASTIN, p. 91.
31. BUNTING, M. I., P. GRAHAM & E. WASSERMAN.   1970.   Academic freedom and incentive for women. Educational Record. 51(4): 386–391.
32. Women in Physics. See Ref. 29; ASSOC. OF WOMEN IN SCIENCE. Roster of women in science, based on American Men and Women in Science (in preparation); SEVEN SISTERS COLLEGES. Roster of women doctorate recipients (in preparation). Compilations have also been completed by committees of social science disciplinary associations.
33. The comment has been made more than once by women, reflecting on their recent prominence as candidates for paid or advisory positions and their popularity for filling writing or speaking engagements, that their emergence into the professional world in a major way was initially made possible by the recommendation of another woman. Women still await their acceptance as serious professional colleagues, an acceptance that derives from more than the mere existence of rosters or even of affirmative action programs. One of the beneficial effects resulting from the increased appointment of women scientists to NIH advisory committees, additional to that of redressing earlier discriminatory behavior, is found in the positive image and role models such appointments provide, for men and women alike, of competent women scholars and the work they do.
34. Some professional couples today are working out their marital relationships with emphasis different from that of marital partners in the past. The greater equality they seek in the marital situation is often matched by a desire for equality in their respective professional work and its location. Some partners live and work apart and commute to be together for periods of leisure. Others jointly seek positions in an institution, and a few seek joint positions. All of these life styles represent important experiments, although none are yet sufficiently widespread to replace as the general mode the traditional pattern of the husband's work determining the family location. Other factors, however, such as the desire for proximity to an educational or cultural center, may place comparable restrictions on the job mobility of men and on their geographic location. U.S. DEPT. OF LABOR, BLS. 1970. Ph.D. Scientists and Engineers in Private Industry, 1968–80. Bull. 1648: 8.
35. Career-planning offices of women's colleges need closer inspection. They have traditionally served in a professional counseling and placement capacity, both for students and for alumnae, throughout their working lives. Their experience could provide useful data for developing more effective policies to assist both men and women college graduates.
36. Women in Physics. See Ref. 29.
37. In a recent conference on women in executive management positions, the point was made that in technically oriented industries, at least, such as those in electronics and engineering, it was necessary for persons in executive positions to be acquainted with technical aspects of the field as well as management techniques. It was this requirement that was

given as the cause of the small number of women in management positions. If true, as the number of trained women in sciences and technical fields increases, their appearance in higher management positions should become more common.

38. Part-time work is a possible structural change, suitable for some men as well as some women, that merits attention. The concept itself is a confusing one, and its practicality as a possible structure needs investigation. One study shows high proportions of women scientists, given the age distribution of the group, working full time. Another study points to the high withdrawal rates from work of women scientists and engineers. It has been observed that a number of highly competent women scientists work without pay on research projects, a practice neither beneficial for the woman professional nor for her male coworker. It would be interesting to learn the extent to which the lack of part-time opportunities explains these findings. See Ref. 2, KAHNE; SHARPE, L. M. 1970. Education and Employment : 59–60. Johns Hopkins Press. Baltimore, Md.; ROSSI, A. S. 1971. Women in science: why so few. *In* EPSTEIN, C. & W. A. GOODE. The Other Half : 113. Prentice Hall. Englewood Cliffs, N. J.

THE ECONOMICS OF WOMEN'S LIBERATION

Barbara R. Bergmann

Department of Economics
Director, Project on the Economics of Discrimination
University of Maryland, College Park, Md. 20742

It will take a lot of changes if equal participation in the American economy for women is to become a reality. In the feminists' vision of a better future there would be, with few exceptions, no "men's occupations" and "women's occupations"; women would get equal pay for equal work; they would do less unpaid work at home, and men would do more. I want to address two sets of issues concerning the postliberation world. First, I shall explore the nature and strength of the economic forces blocking the way to the development of a world in which women would have (and would take advantage of) equal opportunities for paid work. Second, I shall try to describe some of the changes in economic and social arrangements that a more equal participation of women in the economy and a more equal participation of men in the home would entail.

What's Blocking Women's Liberation?

Aside from inertia, there are four factors that have been alleged to be at work to keep things as they are: 1) discrimination against women in employment and promotion due to male prejudice or malevolence; 2) inferior job performance by women; 3) the disinclination of many women to enter into what they view as men's roles; and 4) the profits to be made by business from keeping women in their present roles. Although not all of these factors are of equal importance, as we shall see, they tend to reinforce each other.

When we speak of employer prejudice against women, we generally do not mean feelings of hatred or a desire to refrain from association with them. After all, most men are very glad to have a woman secretary right outside their office doors. The most important manifestation of employer prejudice against women is a desire to restrict them to spheres viewed as proper for them. Everybody knows which jobs are "fit" for women: domestic and light factory work for the least educated ones, clerical and retail sales work for the high school graduates and even some of the college graduates, and teaching, nursing, and social work for those with professional inclinations. We must look to the future researches of psychologists and sociologists to tell us why human beings enjoy enforcing and conforming to occupational segregation along sex (and racial) lines, and how the occupations "belonging" to each group are selected. But the enjoyment is clearly there. In Aldous Huxley's *Brave New World*—a novel truly remarkable for the number of ominous tendencies to which it correctly called attention—each occupation is performed by genetically identical persons in identical uniforms. Huxley was satirizing not only the misuse of science and the inhumanity of the drive for efficiency, but also the strong human liking for castes in economic life.

The economist Victor R. Fuchs of the National Bureau of Economic Research, who is one of the pioneers in research in women's role in the labor market, finds occupational segregation by sex to be far more extreme than occupational segregation by race. He says: ". . . one of the most striking findings is how few [detailed] occupations employ large numbers of both sexes. Most men work in occupations that employ very few women and a significant fraction of women work in occupations that employ very few men."[1] Fuchs attributes occupational segregation and the low pay for women it entails largely to the conditioning of women by society to avoid certain fields. A later study by Malcolm Cohen of the University of Michigan[2] attributes most of the pay differences between men .and women to "barriers to the entry of women into employment in higher paying jobs."

Up to now, the relative importance of discrimination in filling these high-paying jobs and the relative importance of women's failure to compete for them in explaining occupational segregation by sex have not really been carefully measured by anyone. In the end, it may prove statistically impossible to separate the precise importance of the various factors. There is, however, considerable evidence that discrimination is far from a negligible factor. Much of the evidence is anecdotal, but no less real for being so.

The economic results of occupational segregation for women are low wages. Women are relegated, for the most part, into those occupations where experience adds very little to the status and productivity of the worker as she advances in age. After a year or two, a secretary is about as good as she will ever be, while her junior executive boss, who may have the same formal education as she, continues to gain in confidence, knowledge, and expertise, and of course makes commensurate advances in pay.

Since the boundaries separating the men's occupational preserve from the women's are, economically speaking, artificial and not easily changed, the women's preserve may tend to get overcrowded, especially if the proportion of women in the labor force increases. This is exactly what has been occurring. Between 1950 and 1970, the number of men working increased by 15%, while the number of women working increased by 70%. (TABLE 1)

Into what kinds of jobs did these women go? Because of employer discrimination and their own limited horizons, millions of them went into the traditional women's preserve—clerical work. In that 20-year period, there was a very great increase in the number of women clerical workers: they more than doubled their numbers. About one quarter of women workers were in the clerical category in 1950, and by 1970 more than one in three working women were clerical workers. There was no change in the nature of the economy to require such a dramatic upsurge in clerical employment. On the contrary, computerization tends to reduce the demand for clerks. These extra women were absorbed through the classic mechanism of a flexible economy—clerks lost ground in pay, and took on work of a lower priority. That clerical jobs of a type filled by women became relatively overcrowded is shown by the fact that during this period, wage rates in this relatively poorly paid occupation lagged still further behind all other occupational groups for men and women (See last column of TABLE 1).*

Interestingly, some progress apparently was made in the professional and technical group and the service worker group during the fifties and sixties. Women increased their representation in these occupations substantially, yet enjoyed bet-

* While clerical workers have probably been in plentiful supply in the last two decades, "crowding" in an occupation in the sense we have used it here is not inconsistent with a "shortage" in the occupation. A shortage of nurses exists because the pay of nurses moves up sluggishly when demand gets ahead of supply. At the going price, nurses are hard to get because the number of nurses people want to hire exceeds the supply. But what supply there is of nurses has undoubtedly been increased artificially by the general exclusion of all but a handful of women from the medical schools and from administrative positions. If the pay of nurses were raised so as to equalize supply and demand, and thus eliminate the "shortage," that higher pay would still be considerably below what white males of equivalent talents and educational investment would get.

TABLE 1

EMPLOYED PERSONS BY MAJOR OCCUPATION GROUP AND SEX, AND WAGE CHANGES, 1950–1970*

Major Occupation Group	Employed Persons (Thousands)		Employment Change 1950–70 (%)	Average Annual Rate of Growth of Wages† (%)
	1950	1970		
Men				
Professional and Technical Workers	2,696	6,890	+155.6	5.0
Managers, Officials and Proprietors	5,439	6,896	+ 26.8	4.9
Clerical Workers	3,035	3,497	+ 15.2	4.5
Sales Workers	2,379	2,724	+ 14.5	4.3
Craftsmen and Foreman	7,482	9,737	+ 30.1	4.1
Operatives	8,810	9,539	+ 8.3	4.0
Nonfarm Laborers	3,435	3,499	+ 1.9	4.5
Private Household Workers	125	26	− 79.2	—
Other Service Workers	2,560	3,185	+ 24.4	4.2
Farm Workers	6,196	2,692	− 56.6	—
Total Men	42,156	48,686	+ 15.3	4.7
Women				
Professional and Technical Workers	1,794	4,431	+147.0	5.1
Managers, Officials and Proprietors	990	1,301	+ 31.4	3.9
Clerical Workers	4,597	10,337	+124.9	3.5
Sales Workers	1,443	1,990	+ 37.9	4.7
Craftsmen and Foreman	188	290	+ 54.3	—
Operatives	3,336	4,272	+ 28.1	3.7
Nonfarm Laborers	84	115	+ 36.9	—
Private Household Workers	1,758	1,559	− 11.3	3.6
Other Service Workers	2,092	4,954	+136.8	5.0
Farm Workers	1,212	472	− 61.1	—
Total Women	17,493	29,722	+ 69.6	4.1

* Sources: U.S. Bureau of the Census, Statistical Abstract of the United States, 1970 (91st edition), Washington, D.C., 1970, p. 225; and U.S. Bureau of the Census, Current Population Reprints, Series P–60, No. 69, "Income Growth Rates in 1939 to 1968 for Persons by Occupation and Industry Groups, for the United States," U.S. Government Printing Office, Washington, D.C., 1970, Tables 19–20.

† Compound rate of growth in wage or salary income of year-round full-time workers, 1955–1968.

ter than average increases in pay rates. I take this as evidence of expanding demand for women in these fields, possibly involving some desegregation of employment in the detailed occupations that make up these two large occupational groups.

Allegations concerning women's inferior job performance center in the lower commitment of some women to the labor market. Many women do leave jobs for prolonged periods to give birth to and take care of babies, or to follow their husbands to another city. At any given age they have less work experience than men of the same age, on the average. A great deal has been made of women's relative lack of experience, but the truth is that in the kinds of jobs to which women are mostly consigned, experience counts for very little in terms of skill or pay.

Women have been quitting jobs at a higher rate than men (the latest 1968 figures show quit rates of 2.6% per month for women in manufacturing and 2.2% for men). But calculations by Isabel Sawhill of Goucher College indicate that about half the gap in quit rates is due to the fact that women are heavily employed in the kinds of occupations where *men and women* tend to quit more often, while the men are heavily employed in the kinds of jobs in which stability of employment is rewarded.

Unfortunately, the dropout women give all women a bad name on the labor market. Unless the liberationists can succeed in making maternity leaves of more than three weeks unfashionable (as the bearing of three or more children has recently become unfashionable), the women who do want equality with men are going to continue to suffer guilt by association. There will also have to be a decrease in the propensity of men to accept a job in another city without consideration of the effect on the wife's career.

We come finally to the allegation, usually made by radicals out to discredit capitalism, that women's subjection is all a capitalist plot. Who benefits financially from the maintenance of the status quo? The most obvious beneficiaries of prejudice against women are male workers in those occupations in which women are not allowed to compete. This lack of competition raises pay and, in certain circumstances, may reduce unemployment in the occupation largely reserved for males. Of course, those wives who have a stay-at-home ideology also gain when women are excluded from their husbands' occupations. This undoubtedly accounts for some of the social pressure against women's liberation.

It is not, however, the male workers or their wives who do the discriminating. The employers of the male workers (almost entirely males themselves) are the ones who do the actual discriminating, although, of course, they are cheered on in their discriminatory ways by their male employees. The employers actually tend to lose financially, since profits are lowered when cheap female help is spurned in favor of high-priced male help. Thus, good strategy for the women's movement would be to fight against the exclusion of women from "men's jobs" and leave the equal-pay-for-equal-work battle until the former fight was won, by which time the pay issue might have solved itself. Whatever losses there are to discriminating employers are, in all probability, not very large. However, profits to discriminating employers from discriminatory hiring cannot possibly be an important roadblock in the way of nondiscriminatory treatment for women.

Will capitalism collapse if women don't stay home and spend their time purchasing consumer goods? In fact, women who stay home constitute a poorer market for capitalist enterprise's products than do women who go to work. Women who stay at home bake cakes and make dresses. Women who go to work patronize bakeries and dress shops more. A woman who leaves the home for a job will undoubtedly spend less time thinking about and seeking the detergent that will leave her clothes whiter than white, but she will probably buy the same amount of detergent, unless she starts patronizing a commercial laundry, in which case it will be the laundry that buys the detergent. Some nonworking women do make careers out of shopping and spend a great deal of money on items of doubtful utility, but the spending tendencies of most of these women would probably not be significantly reformed if they went to work. It is true that they would have to spend more dollars per hour, but they and their spendthrift male counterparts would have plenty of hours left, as we shall see.

To sum up, discrimination against women is an important factor in keeping women segregated by occupation and earning low pay. This discrimination does not, by and large, serve the economic ends of those who do the discriminating, although it does benefit male employees. The financial gains to those who do the discriminating are low or negative. The major cause served is psychological (it feels so good to have women in their "place"). The cavalier attitudes and low expectations of some women themselves concerning their paid work are also probably important and may help to rationalize some employer taboos against hiring women for occupations (such as executive) in which a considerable investment in on-the-job training by the employer is called for. In short, for the postliberation world to arrive, women's attitudes must be liberated and employers' attitudes must be liberated, but we may be able to do without a revolution that overthrows capitalism.

What Would the Postliberation Economy Look Like?

The success of the women's liberation movement would mean a radical reduction in the division of labor by sex, both inside and outside the home. It is difficult to imagine a "women's liberation" that did not include greater participation and success for women in the economy. Some of the ideologues of the movement have emphasized that postliberation woman should not adopt the aggressive habits of preliberation man, but it is difficult to envision success for women in the economic spheres from which they have been hitherto excluded without at least some movement in that direction.

The economic consequences of those changes in habit of both women and men that would constitute "women's liberation" would be enormous. We can assume it would be customary for all women who are not students to do paid work outside the home and for all men to do as much unpaid work inside the home as women will do. Both in paid employment and in unpaid work at home, there would be an end to the stereotyping of occupations and tasks as suited only for men or women.

One obvious consequence would be a large increase in the size of the labor force in paid work. If women had participated in the labor force to the degree that men of their age group did in 1970, the labor force would have been 30% larger than it was (TABLE 2). Certainly, a rapid growth of the labor force by anything like that extent would create grave problems of digestion for the economy, but the change in habits and the growth of the labor force are both likely to be gradual.

Gradual or not, any important increase in the size of the labor supply tends to

TABLE 2

FEMALE LABOR FORCE, CURRENT AND "POSTLIBERATION" BASIS
(THOUSANDS)

Age Group	Current Female Labor Force	Female Participation Rate	Male Participation Rate	"Post-liberation" Female Labor Force
16–17	1,268	33.2	43.1	1,645
18–19	1,914	53.0	66.1	2,387
20–24	4,929	57.7	86.9	7,423
25–54	18,192	49.9	95.8	34,926
55–59	2,554	49.0	89.3	4,655
60–64	1,607	36.0	74.3	3,317
65–69	662	17.7	40.1	1,500
70 and Over	396	5.5	18.1	1,303
Total	31,523			57,156

* Based on data of September, 1970. Source: U.S. Bureau of Labor Statistics, Employment and Earnings, October, 1970. Postliberation increase in women working = 81.3%; postliberation increase in total labor force = 29.9%.

create downward pressures on wage rates, and to raise profits. I would expect, however, that the increase in the number of persons on the labor market would be at least partially balanced by a fall in the number of hours worked, so that the labor supply in terms of person-hours might increase a great deal less than 30%. If the fall in the workweek just balanced the increase in persons working, we would have a 31-hour workweek (for both men and women, of course). This might work out to five six-hour days per week or to four eight-hour days. Quite obviously, both working men and working women would have more time than they do now to enjoy the pleasures of domestic life, and those wives who changed over from full-time housewifery to "full-time work" would experience less of a wrench than they would have to do under the present 40-hours-per-week regime in paid work.

One of the most dramatic effects of women's liberation would be the change in the size and pay of occupations from which women had been excluded or had excluded themselves. Assuming, for example, that the number of places in medical schools will, in the future, be responsive to the number of qualified applicants, the number of physicians might in time double or triple, and the income of physisians would surely come down, at least relatively. The benefits to nonphysicians in terms of better services and cheaper health care are quite obvious. The financial losses to the present members of the medical profession (and their stay-at-home wives) are also obvious, but even they might enjoy the shorter workweek and lower patient load.

After discussing women as physicians, it is only fair to discuss women as street-cleaners. The Soviet Union is always held up as a horrible example of what happens when women's liberation is tried; we have all seen the pictures of the elderly women, scarves tied around their heads, sweeping the streets in the Moscow winter. These pictures and their captions are supposed to make us feel sorry for those women in a way we would not feel sorry for male streetcleaners. But I don't think we should shrink from the notion of streetcleaning as an occupation appropriate to the physically fit of both sexes. Streetcleaning is probably healthier and more interesting than clerical work, and when these jobs are well paid they are much sought after.

We have made some rough calculations of the effect on wage rates that a relaxation of occupational segregation by sex would entail. We have assumed that women would compete on an equal footing with men of the same educational achievement. Occupations having similar requirements in terms of education, intelligence, skills, and experience would not have different pay scales, as they now do, depending on whether they are in the men's or women's preserve. Occupations previously reserved for women that currently command low pay would shrink in size as the rate of pay in them rose. Women would shift to those occupations previously reserved for men, which would increase in size and which would experience a fall in pay. For example, in jobs held by high school graduates with no college, we estimate that previously male occupations would increase in size by almost 50% and wage rates in these occupations would decrease by about 20%. Employment in previously female occupations would be cut about 20% and the pay would increase about 40%. Let me hasten to add that the decrease in wage rates projected for men would in actuality be translated, in most cases, into low or zero rates of increase, because the transition would occur only gradually and would be mitigated by increases in productivity. Despite this fact, our calculations suggest that women's liberation would bring a radical change in the lineup of occupational wage rates.

One of the benefits from the achievement of women's liberation would be a reduction in the incidence of poverty. One third of poverty families are those families which the Census Bureau defines as "headed by women." When a man leaves his family or dies, the family loses the worker who was discriminated against least. The low pay of most of the jobs open to women means that when the woman goes out to work she has a poor chance of earning an income above the poverty level. The boring nature of many of these jobs, plus the lack of incentive that the low pay entails, induces many women who have lost their husbands through separation or death to languish at home on welfare payments. Thus, in the United States, discrimination against women combined with a high incidence of marital instability have helped to increase the incidence of poverty. We have estimated that about two thirds of the poverty among black and/or female-headed families with working heads is due to discrimination.

The achievement of women's liberation obviously involves a changed distribution of work in the home. Arrangements may be made for outside paid help in cooking, dishwashing, shopping, child care, and cleaning chores, but family members are still going to have to do a considerable amount of unpaid domestic work. Norton Dodge's monumental study of women in the Soviet Union[3] shows that Soviet men have taken over some of the house work, but probably far from a fair share of it. Russian men who work an eight-hour day spend an average of 1.5 hours a day on household chores, while women who work an eight-hour day spend 3.7 hours a day on chores.†

In the United States, one effect of greater participation in paid employment for women might very well be an increase in the popularity of communal living arrangements. In addition to the virtue of broadening out the companionship of the family circle, such arrangements take advantage of economies of scale in meal preparation and child care.

But all of this is, as far as one can see, grossly unlikely. If the current level of interest in women's liberation were to continue for decades, then the transformations I have been describing would occur. But that is a very big "if." In the meantime, individual women who want to do work other than full-time unpaid domestic labor will just have to go on bucking the prejudice of employers, fighting their own laziness and sense of insufficiency, and nagging their husbands to help them with the dishes.

References

1. Fuchs, V. R.   1970.   Male-Female Differentials in Hourly Earnings : 12. National Bureau of Economic Research.
2. Cohen, M. S.   1971.   Sex Differences in Compensation. Journal of Human Resources. Fall.
3. Dodge, N. T.   1966.   Women in the Soviet Economy : 93. Johns Hopkins Press. Baltimore, Md.

† Of course, some Russian men have spouses who do no paid work, but almost no Russian women do, so the degree of unfairness revealed by the figures is somewhat less than it might at first appear.

WOMEN AND EMPLOYERS: THEIR RELATED NEEDS AND ATTITUDES

Felice N. Schwartz

President of Catalyst
New York, N. Y. 10028

An examination of the determinants of success among women who have made important achievements in science is interesting and provocative. But an analysis of the experiences of high achievers does not in itself enable us to understand the broad population of college-educated women or to help them meet their needs for meaningful work.

Barriers to the professional achievement of women have traditionally been so high that those who surmounted them must be characterized as superwomen whose intelligence, strength of character, and motivation were atypical. Undoubtedly, their abilities were nurtured by many factors in their life situations—the attitudes of their parents, the ambience of the communities where they grew up, or the values projected by the educational institutions they attended, for example. But the main determinant of each woman's success has been her extraordinary individual strengths.

By definition, the broad population of educated women does not possess extraordinary strengths; moreover, singular excellence should not be a prerequisite for professional achievement among women any more than it is among men. Therefore, to the extent that we wish to help women work at a level commensurate with their abilities, it is more productive to examine the total life situations and needs of *most* women than it is to dwell on the special conditions that enhance the ability of extraordinary women to achieve great success but will not, in themselves, enable the less-than-extraordinary women to pursue productive careers.

We must concentrate on the obstacles society has placed in the path of the general population of women and explore new ways to overcome them. Specifically, we must direct our attention to the career needs of women with family responsibilities. These women, who represent almost half the nation's investment in education, are, to a large extent, today barred from professional accomplishment.

This need not be the case.

For example, would you have predicted that 1,500 family women would apply for 50 half-time jobs as social workers and would do almost twice as much work per hour as their full-time colleagues?

Did you realize that by hiring educated family women to work part-time as teachers, with two women sharing one teaching job, a school system could largely eliminate the need to hire substitute teachers?

Would you deliberately fill 85% of the staff positions in your organization with part-time women workers because you were convinced, as I am, that you could get more able employees, higher productivity, lower turnover, and more creative input?

I propose to analyze the needs of educated family women and of employers, to note their overlapping interests, and to explore the newly anachronistic attitudes that prevent a necessary and mutually beneficial restructuring of work patterns. Such a restructuring is urgently needed if most women are to achieve professionally. Although single women and highly motivated family women who are not concerned with taking a primary role in the rearing of their children can work within the standard nine-to-five, 40-hour week, work arrangements, new concepts of jobs and work patterns are vital if we are to end discrimination against the general population of women.

Aside from the women whose marriage to a public figure is in itself a career or the women who find a fulfilling life in home-making alone, educated women today want to work outside the home. The desire for careers will undoubtedly increase in the future because woman's role has been fundamentally changed. The woman in early industrial society who found herself closeted with her nuclear family had legitimate cause for anger and frustration, but at least her extended maternity provided her with an identity. Today's educated woman, aware of the problem of overpopulation, tends to restrict her family to two closely spaced children; many choose to have one child or none at all. These women can no longer think of their lives as family based. Even if as many as seven of their 75 years are devoted to caring for preschool children, they must find an alternative focus for most of their lives in work outside the home.

These women represent an enormous economic opportunity to business. Given the necessary capital and a marketable product or service, a business needs an able and productive staff and a maximum demand for its product or service. The educated working family woman provides both.

Women who are not ambivalent about home and work obligations and who are seriously career-oriented can vastly increase the talent pool from which employers draw. The five most-qualified candidates drawn from a labor pool that includes all available workers from both sexes are likely to be more qualified than the five top candidates drawn from a sampling that includes the workers of only one sex. The employer serves his own interests in recruiting an able staff when he considers all women as carefully as men.

Moreover, family women who work tend to consume more than their stay-at-home counterparts. The working woman has a larger income as well as a greater need for clothes, transportation, conveniently processed foods, efficient utilities, and a myriad of other goods and services. As a consumer, she is an asset to business.

If women want to work and if working women can serve employers' needs for high-caliber staff and increased consumption, why have women not been absorbed into the work force at the same rate and at the same levels of employment as men? According to Alan Pifer, President of the Carnegie Corporation of New York, only 3.5% of lawyers, 2% of dentists, 7% of physicians, and less than 1% of engineers are women. Only eleven out of 731 tenured faculty members at Harvard are women, and two of the nation's 13,000 school superintendents are women. Why have women been so grossly underrepresented in responsible jobs?

Clearly, this is the result of role definition and discrimination, rather than any absence of intelligence or ability — witness the high representation of women in professional fields in Israel, Sweden, and the Soviet Union. In the past, society wanted women to stay at home in order to produce a maximum number of babies and nurture their large families. Because women were not entirely happy in this role, which society at large felt was indispensable, strong pressures were created to keep women at home. Both women *and* employers felt these pressures and acted accordingly. Women stayed home voluntarily and made the most of the homemaking role, or else they entered the work force with destructive conflicts about their roles as mother and worker, conflicts that seriously hampered their efforts to achieve. For their part, employers discouraged women from entering the work force or, conversely, encouraged them to stay at home. The stereotype that woman's place is in the home, the inflexibility of full-time employment practices, and the severely restricted range of professions deemed appropriate for women resulted in an underemployment that prevails to this day.

Now, however, the whole equation is changing: society wants a minimum of babies, and social pressures are beginning to work to discourage large families. The traditional female role is losing a great deal of its content, and a new set of expectations for women is developing. An educational effort is under way to counter the image of women as passive, supportive, intuitive creatures concerned only with the home, and to foster, in the minds of both women and employers, the realization that women can participate in the work force as effectively and creatively as men. Since motherhood can no longer be a full-time, life-time occupation, women must be encouraged to function without guilt in careers.

The failure to provide professional roles for educated women has had and will continue to have serious consequences. At the most basic level, society is crippled and the economy suffers when the vast reservoir of energy and brainpower of the country's educated women is insufficiently tapped. There are five and one-half million women college graduates and eight million women with some college training in America today. Women represent 38% of all college graduates and 34% of all graduate students. Obviously, America is not amortizing its investment in their education. Yet Peter Drucker, in *The Age of Discontinuity*, forecasts a 14% increase in brainpower positions in the nation within the next decade; the current waste of the talents of American women cannot be allowed to continue.

More dangerous, perhaps, is the threat to the family structure that is created when women are not given opportunities for professional achievement. Increasingly, young women realize that the family has become so small that it is not an adequate focus for a full life. Unless child rearing can be combined with a career, many women will totally reject the family unit. The pendulum has swung completely. The concept that women should stay exclusively at home not only cannot preserve the family unit; it threatens to destroy it.

Both women and employers are aware of the changes taking place. Women's consciousness of their new status has given birth to the feminist movement. Feminist efforts have awakened employers to women's need for professional growth, and opportunities have been opened further by effective legislation that outlaws much of the discrimination against women.

The stage for the transition from women at home to women at work has been set. The curtain is going up on the first act. Women who are prepared to make a full-time, life-long commitment to work, even those who are not superwomen, will be accepted by employers and given career opportunities equal to those of men. The needs of women and employers are recognized as overlapping; the anachronistic attitude that woman's place is in the home is giving way to the emerging awareness that employers will best be served by giving women full access to careers.

But Act One is a short act. It deals only with a small percentage of women who are prepared to make a full-time, life-time commitment to work. The real needs of the vast majority of women must also be considered. So far, these needs have not been represented, because the media-appointed representatives of women today are 1) the highly visible leaders of the vanguard of the feminist movement who are not family women and 2) successful female professionals who had to make full-time, life-time commitments to careers in order to achieve and who assume that serious professional women of the future will want to (and will be forced to) restrict the focus of their lives in an equally exclusive manner. But to refuse to recognize the biological and psychological distinction between the sexes and to deny the desire of women to take a primary role in rearing their children is to create a new monolith no less destructive than the shibboleth that woman's place is in the home. Unless society faces the reality that the majority of women want to combine family and work and will require part-time employment during one or two decades of their lives, most women will still be effectively barred from careers.

The major action of the play, then, is in Act Two, when accommodations in work schedules are made flexible so that women can work less than full-time. This is the most important act for employers and feminists alike. Right now the feminist pressure is so great that unless such arrangements for professional part-time work are made, employers will be unable to recruit enough able women to meet the requirements of new antidiscrimination legislation; if they insist on full-time women they will have to reach down to the bottom of the barrel. And feminists will have to realize that discrimination against women — the require-ment that they be single women or single-minded superwomen in order to have successful careers — will not end until women have the option to embark on careers before the birth of their children, contract their commitment when their children are small, and expand it as family responsibilities diminish.

For the first time since the invention of the full-time, life-time mother some eighty years ago, motherhood today can be a truly enjoyable, rewarding, and fulfilling experience for women because 1) it is limited to a very small period in a women's life and she can see beyond it to another phase of her life; 2) now that society no longer requires that she love every moment of the early family years she is less defensive and therefore free to express and come to terms with her frustrations and ennui; 3) her husband assumes a greater share of the re-sponsibilities of child care than men did a generation ago; 4) the growing evi-dence of the importance of the early years of the child's life upgrades the role of motherhood; and 5) these changes have in no way abrogated any of the intrinsic rewards of mothering.

For this reason, educated women, despite the license of the new society, are very likely to reject mother substitutes, whether home-based or institutional, and will choose freely to take a primary role in the rearing of their children. In the future, traditional sex roles may be so drastically restructured that men and women will take *equal* responsibility for child care, but, at least in the interval, women must have part-time career opportunities equal to those provided for both men and women who work on full-time schedules. A great deal of preparation, both for women and employers, is necessary. Women must shed their ambiva-lence toward careers, and employers must learn to make productive use of part-time workers at thoughtful levels.

But the effort is well worth the candle. In the ten years of Catalyst's ex-perience as a nonprofit, service organization dedicated to expanding part-time professional opportunities for women, we have found increasing evidence of high motivation, impressive abilities, and intensive application when women who want to combine family and careers are given the opportunity to work in thoughtful jobs. When members of the general population of college women are given the latitude to function comfortably both at work and at home, they become, relative to the general population of women who work full-time, superwomen in their own right.

For example, the caseworkers I mentioned at the beginning of this paper worked for the Boston Regional Office of the Masachusetts Department of Public Welfare. Not only did the half-time women handle 89% as many cases as their full-time colleagues, but they also had a turnover of only 13% compared with the average rate of 40%. Moreover, their clients, mainly AFDC mothers, often found they had more in common with the part-time workers who were family women; client and caseworker shared a common bond of maternity, and the clients felt more at ease talking with a contemporary rather than with a young social worker right out of college.

Teaching is another field in which part-time women have proved their ability to function as well as or better than their full-time counterparts. For example, women who shared teaching jobs in the Framingham, Massachusetts, school system found that partnerships allowed them more time for creative preparation and for better presentation, paperwork and evaluation. The traditional teacher's midday slump was eliminated because one of the partners was always fresh and fully prepared for a well-planned afternoon. And the emotional support the partners gave each other and the interaction and constant exchange of ideas gave an extra dimension to the teaching experience that is usually missing when one teacher must think and plan alone. Moreover, the child has double the opportunity for a successful relationship with his teacher, and two teachers give parents binocular vision of their children.

These are only two applications of the part-time concept, but they indicate the enormous benefits society at large can obtain if we allow capable, educated women both to enjoy the rewards of family life and to work at a professional level.

Toward this end, in September, Catalyst is launching a national program to provide vocational and educational guidance and occupational information through 54 publications and through individual guidance and group workshops at regional affiliates. Commencing with five and gradually extending to 100 affiliate relationships with established, newly-organized or emerging groups, these centers, coordinated by the Catalyst staff and serviced by a central computer, will also be able to facilitate cooperation and communication among women, educators, and employers seeking Catalyst's assistance.

In achieving success in her field, the superwoman helps all women. She is a demonstration of woman's capacity for professional excellence, as well as a model and inspiration for all women who seek careers. It is essential that superwoman continue to reach out and assist women who do not have their unique talents but who nevertheless have much to offer society. Woman today are more conscious than ever of their own intellectual and personal needs. Moreover, the changes that are taking place in woman's role are creating problems that will not go away; men and women are juxtaposed in every aspect of life, and not only do they not want to break the bond, they cannot. The juxtaposition will keep alive the will of both men and women to succeed in developing realistic and thoughtful job opportunities for family women. Only then will society benefit from the full utilization of the abilities of *all* educated women who seek to embark on successful careers.

PART V

Determinants in Individual
Life Experiences

HISTORICAL DETERMINANTS AND SUCCESSFUL PROFESSIONAL WOMEN

Barbara Miller Solomon
Assistant Dean of Harvard College
Cambridge, Massachusetts 02138

The life experiences presented here by twelve successful professional women are personal commentaries on female participation in a variety of fields. Trained in the physical sciences, or the social sciences, or the humanities, as well as in medicine and law, the twelve include three physicians working in public health programs, a chemist, a physicist, a meteorologist, a crystallographer, an electrical engineer, a consumer specialist, a horticulturalist, an architect, and an educator. For some, their work involves research exclusively, for others research and teaching, and for still others, administration.

The brief autobiographies give us important insights about what these women value in their lives. These accounts comprise a sample of exceptional twentieth-century women, exceptional even within the elite minority to which they belong, that of the most highly trained women of the United States. Their understanding of the factors contributing to their success is both exciting and sobering. There is, however, one serious limitation in the total sample: it includes only women who are married and have children. One is left with the impression that success in marriage and motherhood should be essential ingredients in the model of the professional woman. In considering how professional development is affected by marriage, we should not ignore how it is affected by being single; for this aspect we need the personal perspectives of unmarried women. We who are concerned with the past, present, and future participation of women in public spheres should support a variety of life patterns as models for those in the professions.

As a historian, it is my purpose at this conference to view the life experiences of the twelve married professional women in the broad context of the generations of women who have made a place for their sex in the professions. How do external conditions and events in the society affect the development of professional women? To what extent are their attitudes and experiences typical of earlier professional women and others in their own generation? To what extent do they share with their contemporaries the assumptions of the rest of American society? What has been and what is the meaning of success for these women? In a comprehensive study, these questions would be treated fully; on this occasion I shall deal with them only partially.

The individual life experiences of the participants at this conference span the twentieth century. Millicent McIntosh, Esther Peterson, and Mary Calderone grew up around 1920 and were in various ways connected with the older tradition of social reform, of which feminism was an integral part. Millicent McIntosh had the most direct link with the first proud academic women who were bent on improvement of their sex and of the whole society. Mrs. McIntosh has written that there was never a time when she did not expect to study, to prepare to save the world. Her message to educated women today is that if they are willing and able to work with self-discipline, they can do anything, provided they *really* want to. In these thoughts she transmits what her aunt M. Carey Thomas taught Bryn Mawr's women from 1885 to 1922.

A militant feminist, President Thomas was an archetype of the first trained academic woman. She herself had talked her father (against his will) into letting her attend Cornell (A.B., 1877) and pursue graduate study in Germany and Switzerland. She was the first woman from any country to receive the Ph.D. at the University of Zurich. She received the degree in 1882, summa cum laude. Obstacles were stimuli to her and others in the first generation of professionally trained women. It was not only that they were crusaders, but also they had been brought up to accept the rigors of hard thinking and hard work. Thomas identified herself with the rebels and nonconforming women who came before her in the nineteenth century.

The American revolution for women took root almost unnoticed during the 1820s and 1830s, decades of social and economic upheaval. The young republic was expanding with the internal migration of people westward and with the flow of European immigrants into the country. It was a competitive nation in which social patterns were not fixed. The goal of making the democratic ideal real absorbed the energies of reformers. Suffrage for white adult males was attained in state after state. Then there was concern with the extension of human rights to Negro slaves, to the insane, to convicts, to children, and to women.

In 1848 Elizabeth Cady Stanton and Lucretia Mott held the first women's rights meeting at Seneca Falls, N.Y. Their Declaration of Sentiments called not only for suffrage but also for the opening of the professions to their sex. At the time, leaders in law, medicine, religion, and collegiate education could not conceive of including women in those professions. But in this period of growth and change, the first feminists identified their cause publicly and added to the expectations of their sex. The year 1848 marked the formal beginning of a revolution that is still in process.

The first women's movement, like the present one, was consciousness-raising. It gave unknown mothers and daughters throughout the country new possibilities to which they might aspire.

Among them was a growing minority who gained expectations to advance as teachers through training at the college level. Oberlin had been founded in 1837 and was already open to both sexes, with academic restrictions, nonetheless, on the female students. Antioch and Ripon in the 1850s had coeducational patterns. Soon advocates of single-sex colleges responded to the increasing public demand for the higher education of women. Before the Civil War divided the nation, plans for Vassar were set; it opened in 1865.

The War itself brought women into the foreground as doctors, nurses, and volunteers in the work of the Sanitary Commission. The new forms of visibility for women in public spheres supported the burgeoning impetus for higher education.

In the following decades, coeducational institutions, new women's colleges, and some state universities such as the University of Michigan, the University of Wisconsin, and the University of Nebraska produced a generation of women students of which a tiny group wanted further academic and professional training. The challenge of breaking barriers for the A.B., Ph.D., M.D., and L.L.D. engaged the minds and spirits of growing numbers of enthusiastic young women; but they were still a privileged minority.

It would be a mistake to picture the college girls from the 1870s to the 1920s as totally dedicated to study. Most of them expected to marry and were enjoying an independent interval before matrimony, as M. Carey Thomas acknowledged with regret. But there were among them some serious students, independent and nonconforming in their ambitious goals. Dr. Alice Hamilton recalled that she and her sister Edith decided in the 1880s that they must train themselves because family finances were rapidly diminishing. "Our only hope of a wide and full life . . . lay in our own efforts. Edith chose teaching and began to prepare herself for Bryn Mawr . . . I chose medicine, not because I was scientifically-minded, for I was deeply ignorant of science. I chose it because as a doctor I could go anywhere I pleased—to far-off lands or to city slums . . . I should not be tied down to a school or a college as a teacher is, or have to work under a superior as a nurse must do."[1]

Increasingly from the 1870s to the first World War, the college generations believed that all things were possible for an American woman; that she could be self-supporting and useful to society. It was a golden day for spinsters. Jane Addams, Emily Balch, Vida Scudder, Lillian Wald, Grace and Edith Abbott, Alice and Edith Hamilton, M. Carey Thomas, and many others were settlement leaders, educators, doctors, professors. They exemplified new roles that offered dignified and valued alternatives to marriage.

Maria Mitchell, home-trained by her father, was the first woman astronomer in America. In 1847 she had made her great discovery of a comet. When Vassar opened in 1865 she joined the faculty. She became an innovative teacher: 25 of her students achieved the order of distinction, which placed them in *Who's Who in America;* they included such scientists as Ellen Swallow Richards in chemistry and applied science, Christine Ladd-Franklin in psychology, and Miss Mitchell's successor at Vassar, Mary W. Whitney.

From the 1870s and 1880s, other women of ability made niches for themselves in astronomy. Under the direction of Edward Pickering, in the 1880s the Harvard Observatory encouraged volunteers to measure the stars. More than forty who had some background in mathematics did computing and tabulating, patiently and steadfastly. In 1886 Pickering was able to expand his program in celestial photography and pay able young women 25 cents an hour, or maybe 30 cents, to work six days a week for seven hours daily. These assistants felt, however, that they were treated as "equals in the astronomical world," Annie Cannon noted.[2]

The most spectacular career of an assistant was that of Williamina Paton Stevens Fleming, a Scottish immigrant who, although pregnant, parted from her husband and temporarily became a maid in Edward Pickering's house.

The story goes that he was disgusted with a male assistant and vowed he could train his maid. She learned well, becoming a member of the staff in 1881; she proved to be an able researcher and administrator in charge of the women assistants. In 1898 the Harvard Corporation finally recognized her contribution with an official appointment, the first for a woman, as curator.

Her successor, Annie Jump Cannon, had gone to Wellesley, where, in the early 1880s, she studied with Sarah F. Whiting, professor of physics and astronomy, also a protégée of Edward Pickering. Annie Jump Cannon did not think about postgraduate work until her mother died. She returned to Wellesley as an assistant to Professor Whiting, then became a special student at Radcliffe before beginning her great career under Pickering. Miss Cannon's monumental work was in spectral classification. She classified the spectra of some 350,000 stars. The results were published in a nine-volume work called *The Henry Draper Catalogue* (1918–1924), to which was added the two-volume *Henry Draper Extension* (1925–1949). She held the post of curator of the observatory from 1911 to 1940.

None of these three women had Ph.D.'s; two were single, and one husbandless.

All gave single-minded devotion to astronomy and were appropriately honored by professional societies.

It would be a misreading of history to conclude, however, that there were no married women in the academic professions. Some who did not make getting a husband the central purpose of their lives were no less appealing to the right men. Ellen Swallow Richards and Alice Freeman Palmer are conspicuous examples. They provided a model of the professional woman different from that of M. Carey Thomas.

Ellen Swallow entered Vassar at age 25; she had earned the tuition through schoolteaching. Her professors made her feel she could do something "for science." "Thinking of that and of my astronomy and chemistry," she recalled later, she was "fast on my way to the third heaven."[3] Next she was accepted at Massachusetts Institute of Technology as a special student, the first of her sex. Unbeknownst to her, she was admitted without charge so that the president of M.I.T. could say that she was not a student! She met her future husband, Professor Hallowell Richards, in the chemistry laboratory. They were married in 1875 and had no children.

As a result of her work in collaboration with him, she became the first woman member of the American Institute of Mining and Metallurgical Engineers. On her own, in 1884, she set up a chemical laboratory for the study of sanitation, and in the 1890s gave leadership to the study of home economics and nutrition.

Alice Freeman, a graduate of the University of Michigan in the 1870s, started work for a Ph.D. in history. In 1882, at the age of 29, she became president of Wellesley. To the disappointment of feminists, she gave up the post five years later, in 1887, in order to marry George Herbert Palmer, a Harvard professor of philosophy. Thereafter she exerted even greater influence on women's education from her home in Cambridge. She advised President Harper of the new University of Chicago and served as its first Dean of Women from 1893 to 1895.

During the same years, the new field of ethnology attracted the interest of several women. Among those collecting ethnological data in the 1880s was Erminnie Adele Platt Smith, the first woman to be elected a Fellow of The New York Academy of Sciences. A wife and mother of four sons, she took her children to Germany for their education. She herself spent the time studying crystallography and German literature at Strasbourg and Heidelberg; she also completed a two-year course in mineralogy at Freiburg. A talented amateur and popularizer of anthropology, giving talks in her parlor, she was the first woman to engage in field ethnography. She recorded the legends of the Iroquois, which were published by the Bureau of Ethnology. She and Alice Fletcher were both influenced by Frederic Ward Putnam, director of the Peabody Museum at Harvard. Alice Fletcher, who also began as an amateur, became an advocate of Indian welfare. In 1886 her professional stature was such that the Secretary of the Interior sent her to Alaska and the Aleutians to study the needs of the aborigines. Years of research among the Omahas led to her scholarly study, *The Omaha Tribe*, in 1911.

Erminnie Smith, Alice Fletcher, and others are less well known than their dazzling successors, Elsie Clews Parsons and Ruth Benedict. Elsie Clews Parsons (Barnard, A.B., 1896, and Columbia, Ph.D., 1899) was married to a lawyer, Herbert Parsons, and bore six children. Marriage and motherhood did not deter her from academic pursuits. She wrote and lectured on sociology at Barnard from 1902 to 1905. Her views on the family shocked conservatives, but in her nonconformist thinking, she claimed nothing would stop women's progress. By 1919 her academic focus had shifted to the Indians of the Southwest, and she taught at the New School for Social Research. There Mrs. Parsons influenced Ruth Benedict (who soon inspired Margaret Mead at Barnard).

With some help from Elsie Clews Parsons and Alexander Goldenweiser, Ruth Benedict found her mentor in Franz Boas at Columbia. Completing her Ph.D. in 1923, she exhibited unusual creativity. Nonetheless, she advanced slowly, for years serving as Boas' poorly paid assistant. Only after separating from her husband did she become a lecturer, appointed annually, before moving on to the levels of assistant professor and associate professor by the 1930s. Her individuality as an anthropologist was definitively established with the publication of her first major work, *Patterns of Culture,* in 1934. After extending her research to the study of race (*Race: Science and Politics,* 1940) she worked for the United States Office of War Information from 1943 to 1945 in the field of overseas intelligence and foreign morale. She then took a year's leave of absence from Columbia to write the book that won for Columbia a large grant from the Office of Naval Research to establish, under her direction, a program of "Research in Contemporary Cultures." Only after she had begun to direct this significant anthropological research program did Ruth Benedict become a full professor in 1946, the year before she died.

In the evolution of each academic profession discussed here, university training gradually displaced private study. But in medicine, the field to which women felt an ancient, proprietary claim, the prejudices of the professional establishment made women dependent on heterogeneous forms of training. From the middle of the nineteenth century, those who wanted medical training missed no chance to study. Paradoxically, since they were usually ill-prepared, many in fact benefited from varied standards in the available medical courses.

The motivation of early women doctors was feminist in a very basic way. They wanted to improve the health care of their sex and of their children. The major problem facing the women was how to acquire adequate training. Elizabeth Blackwell's struggles are well known. She worked as a governess in the homes of doctors and steeled herself to read the medical books. She wanted to prove that a woman could be as good a doctor as a man, and to this end she forced herself to overcome her feeling of repugnance for the human body. She intended to place a barrier between herself and matrimony, and she succeeded. Liberal Quaker Philadelphia doctors helped her apply to respectable schools; Cornell, Harvard, and others all rejected her, but finally the rural Geneva College accepted her. She entered this less prestigious school in 1847 and studied abroad afterwards, before starting the Woman's Medical College of the New York Infirmary in 1868. Blackwell was not alone. There were other women equally determined to become doctors. Several of the pioneers in medicine have described their life experiences. One of these concerns the Quaker couple, Mary and Owen Thomas.

Mary Frame Myers Thomas, living in Salem, Ohio, had listened to Lucretia Mott at a Quaker Meeting in 1845, and after the birth of a third child at 29, she and her husband both decided on a plan of study with a preceptor. It took "the most vigorous discipline of my mind and systematic arrangement of time," she wrote a friend. She intended that her husband and children should not "suffer for any comforts a wife and mother owed them." (See Reference 3, p. 450.) After sewing their clothes for eight or nine months in advance and arranging for the care of the children, in September of 1853 she went to Philadelphia, where her half-sister, another married woman with an interesting life story, Hannah Longshore, was demonstrator in anatomy. Later Mrs. Thomas attended lectures at Western Reserve College, in Cleveland, Ohio, and eventually finished her degree at the Penn Medical University in Philadelphia. During the Civil War, Mary Myers Thomas served with her husband, by then an army surgeon. Afterwards she had a distinguished career in public health service in Richmond, Indiana.

Her half-sister, Hannah E. Myers Longshore, a sixth-generation Quaker, moved with her family several times, from Maryland to Washington, D.C., then to an Ohio farm. As a young girl she had wanted to be a doctor, but her plan to attend Oberlin was curtailed because of lack of funds. She married a teacher at New Lisbon Academy in 1841. Four years after marriage and after two children, she became apprenticed to her brother-in-law to study medicine. At 31 she was the mother of an eight-year-old and a five-year-old, and she enrolled in the Female Medical College of Pennsylvania (which her brother-in-law helped establish). She received her M.D. in 1851, at commencement exercises guarded by the police. She became the first woman doctor in Philadelphia and had a large private practice in addition to lecturing. She drove her own horse and carriage. She was successful as a wife and mother; her son became a doctor.

Such careers, and there were many others like these, show that discontinuities in education and professional training did not stop the first women in medicine, whether they were married, divorced, widowed, or single. For some, training had to be intermittent while they earned money to go on.

One of the few benefiting from social position and affluence was Mary Putnam, the precocious, intellectual daughter of the New York publisher, George Palmer Putnam. Self-willed, she began her medical studies at various American schools and spent five years completing her studies, from 1866 to 1871, in Paris. Few men could equal her in training. In 1873 she married Dr. Abraham Jacobi, a German refugee of the 1840s and a leading pediatrician. He was as strong-willed as she, but encouraged her career. Although she bore three children, she taught for many years at Dr. Blackwell's Woman's Medical College.

It took time for women to overcome the problem of receiving adequate, recognized training. In 1860 the schools approved by the American Medical Association would not admit women. The A.M.A. however, would not approve the so-called medical colleges for women started by their sex. It was a milestone when in the 1870s the University of Michigan accepted female students. In the 1890s Johns Hopkins and Cornell also opened their doors and brought the training of women up to the standard available to men.

Before long, a few women made brilliant contributions to medical research. Alice Hamilton (M.D., University of Michigan, 1893) found her specialty in bacteriological studies relating to industrial diseases and, as a result, was appointed assistant professor at Harvard Medical School, from 1919 to 1937. Florence Sabin (M.D., Johns Hopkins, 1900), the anatomist, became distinguished for her studies on blood in the 1920s and 1930s. Helen Taussig (M.D., Johns Hopkins, 1927) is noted for her heart research which has saved "blue babies." She became the first woman full professor at Johns Hopkins Medical School in 1959. Others in the 1920s and 1930s such as Josephine Baker, Connie Guion, Leona Baumgartner, and Margaret Barnard stand out among those who continued to enlarge the tradition begun by earlier women in the sphere of public health. In the 1970s Mary Calderone, Gertrude Hunter, and Judianne Densen-Gerber are part of that great tradition.

The 1920s, 1930s, and 1940s also witnessed the fruition of individual women as scholars in the arts and sciences. In 1920 the overall percentage of women Ph.D.'s was at its highest point, and at the start of the decade there seemed to be a momentum that would carry women further and further in academic and other professional activities. As we all know, this expectation was far from fully realized.

The statistics on women receiving Ph.D.'s from 1920 to 1945 show great differences in various disciplines. In some fields, such as the biological sciences, the proportion of female recipients rose to a peak between 1925 and 1929.[4] By contrast, the proportion of women receiving medical degrees during this period was fairly consistently at a low 4–6 percent. That proportion, however, expanded dramatically between 1948 and 1951, with 1949 being the highest year. This proportion decreased significantly in 1951.[5]

It is an oversimplification to conclude that women's aspirations declined after the suffrage movement attained its goal with the passage of the nineteenth amendment in 1920. During each war period, women profited by taking places in graduate schools that were filled by men in peacetime. The results are reflected in the increased numbers of Ph.D's granted to women in some fields for the years after World War I and after World War II.

The diminution of women's professional opportunities actually began in the 1930s. It is true that one of our participants, Esther Peterson, found her métier in the labor movement, in the depths of the Depression. But the Great Depression helped slow down the participation of women in graduate study. Marjorie Nicolson noted in 1937 that women were facing restricted admissions in graduate and medical schools, and that administrators justified the limited admissions of women on the basis of the fact that they could not be placed in academic positions.[6] In 1937 there were almost no openings for academic women, except in the women's colleges, which were few in number. Miss Nicolson, herself, however, became in 1941 the first of her sex to be named a full professor at Columbia University; her field was English literature.

The first woman professor of Harvard's Faculty of Arts and Sciences, Cecelia Payne-Gaposchkin, received a B.A. degree at Newnham College, Cambridge, England, in 1923, and a Ph.D. at Radcliffe in 1925. She served as an assistant on the staff of the Harvard Observatory from 1923 to 1938, as Phillips Astronomer from 1938 to 1956, and, at long last, became Phillips Professor of Astronomy and chairman of the department from 1956 to 1960. Married in 1934, she and her husband were a famous team in astronomical research. They also produced three sons, all of whom became scientists.

In the same years, from the 1940s to the 1960s, women as a numerical group (as opposed to individuals) fell far behind men as a group in terms of professional accomplishment. The reasons for this lag were complex, and are not yet fully understood. These years were filled with turmoil and unpredictable changes.

Yet, paradoxically, in the midst of the upheavals of wars, depression, and the uprooting of people, Americans in the second half of the twentieth century have had higher expectations for themselves and their children than ever before. For both sexes the pressures of this competitive society grew in many ways, but the pressures affected women differently from men. As graduate schools became heavily populated with male students, and as most professions became more highly structured in this period, it was more difficult for women to pursue graduate studies at their own rate in a flexible way. Interruptions in some professions were more detrimental to career development than they had been in the past. Among our twelve, Isabelle Karle, Mildred Dresselhaus, Betsy Ancker-Johnson, Joanne Simpson, and Ruth Weiner (in crystallography, electrical engineering, physics, meteorology, and chemistry, respectively) have kept on the regular tracks, and even they have experienced some of the difficulties of advancing within institutional structures, whether in government, industry or academia. By contrast, Ernesta Ballard chose the field of horticulture, in which she could train belatedly without a B.A.; she has flourished despite the discontinuity in her career development.

As educated men and women married earlier and produced larger families than in preceding decades, many wives in the 1950's combined motherhood with various kinds of employment, but without a long-range career commitment. For many more, wifehood and motherhood on a full-time basis received reinforcement from the interpreters of Sigmund Freud. Motherhood took on a new intensity, adding to the pressures on women. Argentinian-born Gretchen Minnhaer, as an architectural student, observed this fact with a surprise. She and the rest of the twelve have had to demonstrate that they value wifehood and motherhood as well as a career. At this time the association between spinsterhood and a career also helped deflate the aspirations of educated women. In comparison with earlier generations, the twelve professional women, especially those starting work in the 1950s, have had to be externally conforming (until recently) while committing themselves with the same professional dedication as their predecessors. They have understood and managed their priorities in an individual way for the benefit of themselves and their families.

As in the past, some of the twelve have had the advantages and disadvantages of membership in established, affluent families. Some were born into European professional families in which there were expectations for women as well as men. Others were daughters of immigrants who lacked economic or social advantages but believed that if they and their children worked hard they would get ahead in America. But as in earlier generations, the majority have middle-class and upper-class backgrounds, irrespective of their diverse ethnic and racial origins.

In the present, as in the past, the origins of professional motivation are varied. Few of the twelve had a clear notion of what they wanted to be until they were in college, and some not even then; however, they did know that they wanted to use their abilities in a worthwhile way, and they adhered to high standards. The majority never felt that being a woman should make a difference in their aspirations. That view is their legacy from the 1920s.

For all, the encouragement or discouragement of an influential person made an essential difference in their development. They affirm what is striking in history: that women's expectations have grown because some people and some institutions have believed in them. Whether during childhood, school days, college, graduate, or professional years, these women have had special encouragement from one or more people: father, mother, teacher, friend, or professional colleague; the continuous influence of husbands receives significant emphasis, more than it would have in the past. Only self-reliant women can respond effectively to such kinds of encouragement and support.

In the present, as in the past, successful women in the professions exhibit the same qualities as comparable men: determination, self-discipline, self-esteem, acceptance of hard work, and the ability to withstand discouragement. But the women need, as others have noted at this conference, a *superabundance* of these qualities, which are tested every step of the way in their careers.

In the 1970s when disapproval of women's aspirations is more subtle than blatant, society makes it all too easy for women to give up. Those in the professions still need to have what Maria Mitchell recognized a century ago: "extraordinary persistency" (see Reference 3, Vol. II: 555) and a good bit of luck.

References

1. HAMILTON, A. 1943. Exploring the Dangerous Trades. : 38. Boston, Mass.
2. JONES, B. Z. & L. C. BOYD. 1971. The Harvard College Observatory: The First Four Directorships, 1839–1919. : 390. Cambridge, Mass.
3. JAMES, E. T. & J. JAMES, EDS. 1971. Notable American Women. Vol. **III**: 143. Belknap Press of Harvard University Press. Cambridge, Mass.
4. HARMAN, L. & H. SOLDZ. 1963. Doctorate Production in United States Universities 1920–1962. : 50–53.
5. LOPATE, C. 1968. Women in Medicine. : 193.
6. NICOLSON, M. H. 1937. The rights and privileges pertaining thereto. . . . *In* A University Between Two Centuries. W. B. Shaw, Ed. : 414. University of Michigan Press. Ann Arbor, Mich.

MAKING IT: MARGINALITY AND OBSTACLES TO MINORITY CONSCIOUSNESS

Arlie Hochschild

Department of Sociology
University of California
Berkeley, California 94720

I should like to discuss not what makes a woman successful but rather, how being successful makes her feel less like other women. This was not stressed in the autobiographies we have read here. On the contrary, they often focused on their lonely migration into the male world of the physical sciences, and on the men who encouraged or discouraged them along the way. But in entering a male culture, they have left behind if not the female role (they are all wives and mothers), at least the female culture. This difficult transition creates personal problems that, to the women's movement, are social issues, and at the same time it leads many professional women to reject the women's movement. For example, in her autobiography one architect notes: "Now unwillingly, I seem to be part of the Women's Liberation Movement, a fact that I resent because I refuse to be bunched up under the heading 'women' and then see all the things I must be or do. . . ." In this she speaks for many professional women. Her feelings may be in response to a movement leadership ahead of its time, or a response to the media's focus on the trivial (e.g. bra burning), or to the necessity in any social movement of dealing with people in categories. But I also have a feeling that something else is going on, something that could explain why the very women who are most likely personally (or through peers, almost personally) to suffer prejudice and discrimination, often resist thinking of women as a minority group.

Minority Consciousness and Professionalism

A minority group is, according to the American sociologist Louis Wirth (cited by Hacker[1]) "a group who because of their physical or cultural characteristics, are singled out from others in the society for differential and unequal treatment, and who therefore regard themselves as objects of collective discrimination." By this definition, there is an objective and a subjective side, the fact of unequal treatment and the awareness of it. All the autobiographies show ample evidence of unequal treatment, but not all of the women define themselves as part of a minority group.

Few women in the society at large have minority consciousness. As late as 1970, a nationwide Harris poll found that three-fourths of women agree that "having a loving husband who is able to take care of me is much more important to me than making it on my own." When asked about the women they admire, most women mention those who have not made it on their own: Mrs. Robert Kennedy, Mrs. Joseph Kennedy, Mrs. Dwight Eisenhower, and Mrs. Lyndon Johnson. One quarter of female (and male) California voters would not vote for a qualified woman as the vice-presidential candidate, while fewer (11% of women and 17% of men) would not vote for a qualified Black man for that position.

Those at the very top of society and at the very bottom are probably the least likely to recognize women as a minority group. At the bottom, it is because the woman's husband is hardly better off, and at the top it is because the woman often assimilates to the male elite at the price of identifying with males and looking at women, in part, as a semialien group. Under certain conditions, this happens to virtually every ascending and assimilating group: the Indians under British rule, Jews in a Gentile community, the Black bourgeoisie in the United States, and the déclassé and detribalized natives in many countries around the world.[2] Somerset Maugham's short story "The Alien Corn" describes this experience for upper-class Jews among the English landed gentry, and E. Franklin Frasier describes it for the Black bourgeoisie.

It is not that the professional woman totally identifies with her male peer, for if in identifying with him she compared her experience to his, she might feel relatively deprived. Rather, she compares herself with other women who share her aspirations to assimilation and, compared with them, finds herself fortunate. Thus a sense of injustice, which might divide her from male peers, is overwhelmed by a sense of gratitude for what rewards there are for hard work.

Research suggests that there is wide-scale discrimination against women in the professions. In Helen Astin's study of all the female Ph.D.'s receiving degrees in 1957 and 1958, a third reported experiencing discrimination.[3] White found that half of his sample of more than 2,600 lawyers reported discrimination.[4] These autobiographies give evidence of discrimination, too (this monograph). While not part of a random sample, they suggest an ambivalence toward it that may be common to other women juxtaposed between the male and female cultures.

For example, Mildred S. Dresselhaus, one of the only women in the 110-man electrical engineering department of M.I.T., notes that her thesis adviser was "totally unsympathetic to career women" and left her to do her thesis work alone. but she also notes: "I cannot say that I face any unique problems in the profession because of my sex," and . . . "there is nothing in life that is impossible to accomplish." Again, Esther Peterson, former Assistant Secretary of Labor, mentions that in the AFL-CIO she earned less than a man who held the job before her, but she continues, "Obstacles I have encountered along the way have had little to do with my being a woman, as far as I can tell, they are the same kind of difficulties a man would have run into." Isabelle Karle, a physical chemist, notes that when she mentioned her intentions to go into chemistry in college, "my high school chemistry teacher . . . tried to discourage me by saying that chemistry was not a proper field for girls. . . . Although I graduated with highest honors, I was not encouraged in graduate studies at the University of Michigan. . . . No teaching assistantships were available in the chemistry department for girls," but she concludes: "Quality leads to success in the long run, resulting in a firmly established basis for recognition." Mary Calderone, a physician, describes trying to raise an eight-year-old daughter while going to medical school full time. During her third and fourth years and her internship, she notes ". . . it was impossible to keep her with me, so I gave up the house and my daughter lived with an old friend in the East. . . . Although we spent all of our vacations together, except when she was visiting her father, I still feel sorry about it, wonderful as her foster mother was." But she concludes, "I don't feel that I made any sacrifices at all. . . ." Ernesta Drinker Ballard, a horticulturist, commented that "Outside of writers of popular garden texts, I know of only two other women who have attained a position equal to mine in salary and responsibility," but also, "The fact that I have one of the top horticultural jobs in the country with no academic degree beyond an associate in science degree shows that horticulture holds out rewards to anyone with above average ability, a determination to work harder than most people, and a basic knowledge of the subject." Gretchen Minnhaar comments, "Being a woman in a liberal profession is really an asset; it opens doors that a man with my same background would find difficult to get in," but also, "I cannot look for a more interesting job in another city since my husband has first choice." Most of the autobiographies show a sensitivity to the problems, but the concluding summaries often belied the earlier evidence of the disadvantages.

The professional woman is the "cutting edge" of the female minority group, and is thus more "marginal"[2] than women who live in the more "segregated" female world of suburban den mothers, volunteer work, and bridge parties. Like other marginal peoples, she is not totally rejected, but *partially* rejected.* This partial rejection takes various subtle forms, two of which are "de-feminization" (where her ties to other women are cut) and "de-professionalization" (where her ties with male colleagues are cut). In either case, part of her identity is rejected by others, with whatever good intent, and by herself, however unwittingly.

De-feminization can take the form of a compliment: "She's a fine analyst. She doesn't think like a woman." Or "She writes clearly. She writes like a man." To the extent that this seems like a compliment, she experiences distance from other women. The second process, "de-professionalization," undermines her professional identity just as the first process undermines her sexual identity: "She used her sex to get her promotion," or "She's the wife of so and so. You can see his influence in her book." Often the woman must choose, at a party, between "de-sexualization" (she sits talking shop with the men) or "de-professionalization" (she sits talking babies with the women). This is because, in combining both roles, she finds herself deviant. Other women she meets at professional parties are likely to be housewives without profession or single professionals; roughly half the women in science are single.

In fact, in order to maintain a professional identity she must sometimes prove herself different in some ways from what other women are thought to be like. She does her own subtle "defeminization." If other women are undependable, and unpredictably quit work to have babies, she is different. If other women do not think analytically or can't do math, she is different. If other women are less committed to their work, she is different. If other "different" women are manlike and make poor colleagues, she is different from them. This is close to the "de-Blacking" that Black professionals undergo: if other Blacks are lazy and careless, this one is not. If other Blacks are dirty and messy, this one is neat and clean. If other Blacks talk too loudly, this one talks softly. If other Blacks are incompetent, this one is competent. If other Blacks are neat, hardworking, soft-talking, and competent but overly sensitive about their race, this one is different and easy to get along with.

It is not simply that the professional woman must be more dedicated, reliable, and productive *than men,* to get the same recognition;[2] it is that she must be more dedicated, reliable, and productive than what people in general and employers in particular expect *other women* in the professions to be. For example, Ernesta Drinker Ballard, a noted horticulturist, notes: "It took me fifteen years to convince people that I was not a super garden clubber." Men must prove themselves too, but they need not contrast themselves with a negative stereotype of men.

The identity of "the exceptional woman" is probably rarely a ploy or conscious tactic to "divide and rule" women. Typically, proof is required by very well-

* As Arnold Green notes (cited by Hacker, Ref. 1, p. 68): "It is those Negroes and second generation immigrants (and we can add, women) whose values and behavior most approximate those of the dominant majority who experience the most severe personal crises. . . . The classical marginal man symptoms appear only when a person striving to leave the racial or ethnic group into which he was born is deeply identified with the family of orientation and is met with grudging, uncertain, and unpredictable acceptance, rather than with absolute rejection, by the group he is attempting to join, and also that he is committed to success-careerism."

meaning men and women who are "on your side" for reasonable reasons. An employer is sensible, in fact, given the stereotypes, few jobs, and many applicants, to ask for proof of exceptionalness. It is her deviant status that is at the heart of the "you-are-different" problem.

Another form of partial rejection comes not from male colleagues but from other women: secretaries who are less willing to do work for a woman; housewives, especially older, well-educated, nonworking women who, discontented with their own lives, have a keen eye out for the faults and problems of married professionals; antiprofessional members of Women's Liberation; and some students. In a study of undergraduate women, the sociologist Goldberg[5] gave two sets of the same six articles to 140 female university students. In one set the author's name was given as Joan McKay, and in the other, as John McKay. The female students judged the articles by John, in 44 out of 54 cases, as the more persuasive, profound, competent, and well written. The finding held for "male" fields (e.g. city planning) as well as for "female" fields (e.g. dietetics).

There are many possible responses to these partial rejections. One frequent one is the intellectual *nouveau riche* syndrome, common to other marginal persons under similar cross pressures: "I am *so* a professional. In fact, I'm more professional than any man." This may result in academic overcaution in writing and in overidentification with the professional organizations and subculture. The man, not ground down by the cross pressures of "desexualization" or "deprofessionalization," can afford to be more casual and "hip" about his status (the wearing of beards, sloppy clothes, and so on), since no one questions it. Another response is superfemininity, expressed in extreme elegance in dress and unusually soft voice or appeasing manner.

For some women there is another factor, too. Partial rejection is also partial acceptance, and being a minority has not only its punishments but its rewards. There is a sense of specialness, even when she plays it down, that comes with being "the only woman" or "the first woman." The first astronaut to the moon is, after all, more special than the eleventh. And this too can divide her from other women by giving her, ironically, a stake in her minority status, in the sense that her reward is based on what other women are not doing. For the profession it may be useful to have a woman who feels this way, since that one woman may resist, even more than some men, the entrance of other women into the field. But many probably feel as the physicist Betsy Ancker Johnson does: "I would like to be known, if I'm known at all, for my contributions to physics research and teaching, and not for being 'a woman in physics.' " Like the Black doctor who wants to be known for the doctorness, not the Blackness, she, reasonably enough, wants merit to count.

The evidence, however, suggests that woman will not be accepted until we are no longer a minority, until it is no longer so unusual. An example of such evidence comes from Marlaine Katz' replication of Matina S. Horner's recent classic study of women's motivation to avoid success.[6] Katz[7] had 169 undergraduate men and women complete a story based on one of the two following cues: "All Anne's classmates in medical school are men. After first term finals, Anne finds herself at the top of her class." and "Half of Anne's classmates in medical school are women. After first term finals, Anne finds herself at the top of her class." There were no differences for women students between the stories where Anne is alone and the stories where she is one of 50% women students. But for male students there were large differences. When Anne was one of 50% women students, the stories reflected acceptance, but when she was the only woman, they mentioned how distractingly pretty she was, or how she got boyfriends to help her on the exams, and in general they saw femininity as incompatible with success.

This illustrates one way in which the women's movement is in the interests of professional women, even the elite among them. If she genuinely does not care about being partially rejected, or about being known as "the woman" this or that, then the woman's movement may be of only passing interest. But if she does care about this, then it might be wise to see her situation in the larger social perspective.[8,9] But, ironically, she may see the woman's movement as yet another threat to "de-professionalize" her when, as I have pointed out, similar pressures already come from employers and colleagues. Her sex is already a point of latent tension and to "come out" as a feminist, even a sweet and reasonable one, only feeds into the existing fear that one is, in the minds of others already "bunched up under the heading 'women'."

The well-known educator Millicent MacIntosh notes (this monograph): "The querulous members of the movement have failed to recognize one basic fact about women: provided that they are willing and able to work hard, with self-discipline, they can do anything they *really* want to." There is a difference between these personal qualities and the "open-caste" ideology built upon them. The ideology can ironically help maintain the sex roles that obstruct success, just as the open-class ideology sustained the hopes of the lower classes without really altering the class structure. Implicit in the Horatio Alger ideology is that it is *only* a question of talent and hard work, that the contours of sex roles themselves are no obstacle, that male careers are suitable to men of moderate to extraordinary talent but suitable only to women early labeled as "extraordinary." The "exceptional woman" can then be used as a weapon against women not yet defined that way. It suggests that social movements boost only the weak and infirm. It ignores the fact that most professional women, like these, have been able to devote time to their work by giving over part of their motherhood to other (usually lower-class) women whose role remains unchanged. Buttressed by the Horatio Alger ideology, and eschewing the woman's movement, deviant women often maintain their deviance and forestall the full acceptance they seek.

To endorse or join the women's movement, the professional woman must overcome ideological and structural obstacles to identification with other women. These present obstacles may be compounded with earlier ones, too. Many professional women were motivated in the first place not only by the positive goal of a career, but by the negative goal of not being a "mere" housewife. It is perhaps hard to feel empathy for the problems of those who have at one time been an "antimodel."

The autobiographies say little about this, so I am unsure of how much the dropping of the female culture is a determined defection or how much a busy professional schedule simply crowds out the traditional female activities. Dr. Karle mentions that she does not go to neighborhood coffee groups, do volunteer work, go bowling, or play bridge. She minimizes nursing duties (since her children seldom get sick), and her shopping and meal preparation would be an inspiration to Frederick Taylor. Dr. Dresselhauss describes herself as "running the house with my left hand." I have noticed among other professional women a reverse pride in a slightly sloppy or casually adorned house, but, to be honest, I don't see it here, except perhaps in Ruth Weiner's note that her home is furnished in "early Salvation Army."

The obstacles to minority consciousness add up, and the consequences are harmful. There is tentative evidence that some professional women help inadvertently to keep other females out of the professions. Academic women, for example, may be harder on female students than on male students. Unpublished data from a sample survey of students at the University of Chicago show that both male and female faculty support the graduate aspirations of male students more than those of female students. Twenty-seven percent of female versus 46% of male students say male faculty are "very favorable" to their graduate aspirations. But the female students also get less support than male students do from their *female* professors. Twenty-seven percent of girls but 35% of boys get support from female professors.[7]

The women whose life stories appear here are, as the introductory quote suggests, at best ambivalent about the women's movement, and I have suggested some reasons why. To buck the pressures to disaffiliate from other women would be, in my view, their crowning achievement, even, ironically, the real sign of arrival. It would be especially meaningful in light of the relative decline (in comparison with men) of the income, education, and proportion of women in the professions over the last 25 years.[10]

References

1. HACKER, H.   1951.   Women as a minority group. Social Forces **30**: 60–69. Oct.
2. STONEQUIST, E. V.   1937, 1961.   The Marginal Man. Russell and Russell Inc. New York, N. Y.
3. ASTIN, H.   1969.   The Woman Doctorate in America. Russell Sage Foundation. New York, N. Y.
4. WHITE, JAMES J.   1967.   Women in the law. Michigan Law Review **65**(6): 1951–1122.
5. GOLDBERG, P.   "Are women prejudiced against women?" TRANS-action, Vol. 5, No. 2 (1968) pp. 28–30.
6. HORNER, M. S.   1968.   Women's Will to Fail. Psychology Today **3**: 36–42.
7. KATZ, M. L.   Female motive to avoid success; a psychological barrier or a response to deviancy? Unpublished manuscript.
8. LAW, J. L.   A feminist analysis of relative deprivation in academic women. Unpublished manuscript.
9. EPSTEIN, C. F.   1970.   Women's Place. University of California Press. Berkeley, Calif.
10. KNUDSEN, D.   1969.   The declining status of women: popular myths and the failure of functionalist thought. Social Forces **48**:(2). Dec.

PSYCHOLOGICAL DETERMINANTS

Jane V. Anderson

Department of Psychiatry, Harvard Medical School
Boston, Massachusetts 02115

The women who have presented papers on their "Individual Life Experiences" have provided a unique opportunity to see how they have struggled to resolve various issues and conflicts in their lives for a relatively happy outcome. For a psychiatrist, who is used to working with people whose individual life experiences have led to less happy end results, having a chance to study and reflect in detail on what these women have described about their lives gives vital information about what makes for growth and fulfillment in contrast with arrest of development, and frustration.

Being Regarded as a Deviant

In terms of psychological determinants that have enabled these women to function effectively professionally, the most important one appears to be their capacity to cope emotionally with being reacted to as a deviant. The concept of the professional woman as deviant has been set forth by Dr. Cynthia Fuchs Epstein, sociologist, in her book *Woman's Place*.[1] She states: "The attitudes of social scientists have lent considerable legitimation to the popular suspicion that women who seek an independent identity outside the home are women with problems and that women who don't feel a strong drive to establish a family first and foremost should wonder what is wrong with them. Many women who in recent years sought the solution to their discontent on the analyst's couch often heard their own worst fears corroborated and were persuaded to try to cast their lives more contentedly in the feminine (read "domestic") mold. . . . Women in male occupations or with male-typed aspirations . . . hear accusations that they are not feminine. The accusation is usually powerful and debilitating to the woman." Epstein goes on to say that if a woman chooses to make a serious ongoing professional commitment in her life, "given these popular images and cultural definitions, . . . she is . . . a deviant case by the standard of what is normal in her society."

The speakers themselves have given a number of examples of having been reacted to as deviants. They have experienced this reaction in their education, work, and personal relationships.

In the sphere of educational experience, Ancker-Johnson particularly eloquently captures the inner anguish of being regarded a deviant. "As a result of this idyllic climate for learning [in college], I was totally unprepared psychologically for what followed. . . . During my first year of graduate school, what seemed to me like an infinite number of professors, teaching assistants and colleagues, none of whom were women, told me that women can't think analytically and therefore I must be husband hunting." She describes being regarded as "a 'wierdo' because I was a woman studying, of all things, experimental physics. . . . Consequently, I was never involved in the informal study groups that graduate students form and find so very helpful in the learning process." She concludes: "The essentially universal experience [of women physicists] . . . includes unnecessary, painful periods of isolation and suffering from the stereotype many [men] in the field have regarding women."

In terms of work experience, Ancker-Johnson again gives a very graphic picture of what she had to contend with emotionally when she became even more deviant by being not only a woman, but a pregnant woman on her job. She states: ". . . it became easier with time to convince employers that I was an acceptable risk but trauma still lay ahead. I had my first baby as an industrial research physicist, and it was an unnecessarily unpleasant experience. My private life was delved into by half-a-dozen executives in interviews that no one should have to endure. Finally, I was told, perhaps in jest, that the decision to lay me off over my protest went all the way to the Board of Directors. . . . I wasn't even allowed to enter the laboratory building for three months before the birth to hear a talk or get a book out of my private collection without special permission of the laboratory director. In order to understand something of how I felt, a member of the majority would have to have had an advanced case of leprosy."

Perhaps the most severely painful aspects of being reacted to as a deviant come in the realm of personal relationships. Ancker-Johnson once more records: "It did happen that some of my . . . dates, upon learning of my major and my interest in going to graduate school, dutifully informed me that my chances of finding a husband were nil." This kind of experience, particularly troubling for a young woman in her late teens or early twenties, has led to the sudden denouement of aspirations for a scientific career in more than a few. But if a woman manages not to be dissuaded by such threatening comments and goes on to have a family and profession, there may be more to come. Weiner notes: "I did experience a great deal of guilt leaving my children to go to work, most of it, I now realize, brought on by comments of nonworking mothers, such as those at nursery school: 'Don't you think you are ruining your children's lives?'."

Minnhaar sums up the issue most succinctly in the concluding statement of her paper: ". . . when I chose my way, I never thought that my sex made me different. It was not until I came to the United States that I realized that from a mundane architect, I was transformed into a pioneer."

Ability to Function Autonomously

But what has made it possible for these women to keep going in the face of repeated, painful rebuffs and frequent, negative feedback from their environment? I would like to suggest that it is their capacity to function in an emotionally autonomous way. By this capacity I mean a person's ability to provide positive feedback to oneself when the environment is indifferent or oppositional. The ability to function autonomously is in turn directly proportional to the extent to which a person has successfully relinquished dependent ties on parenting figures.

So long as a woman still is not sure enough of herself to give up a dependent relationship and still needs positive affirmation from the environment, her ability to move ahead, when reacted to as a deviant, often is seriously curtailed. If the goals she has set up for herself bring her into conflict with the environment, she often gives up these goals in order to live her life in such a way as to get more approval and a more positive and supporting response from the environment. Such a course of action, however, often leads to stunting of her own personality development and can result in a premature closure of her personality structure. If, when a woman meets opposition to her professional aspirations, she gives them up and "decides" to get married and have children, her approach to femininity is primarily a defensive one. It is based on a position of psychological weakness rather than of psychological strength.

A crucial factor in a person's relinquishing childhood and dependent ties is his or her ability to carry out a process, which Dr. Margaret Mahler, a psychoanalyst and researcher in early childhood development, has described as "separation individuation."[2] This process entails emotionally separating from parental figures by giving up dependent ties to them and thus being free to acknowledge and develop one's own individuality, independently of what the environment's response may be to it.

Dresselhaus has described very clearly what is meant by the capacity to function autonomously. About her graduate school experience, she comments: "Although my thesis adviser was totally unsympathetic to career women, *this had very little effect on me, because I did my thesis work pretty much on my own with essentially no help from him. . . .* I started working on a problem . . . and there was nobody around that could provide me with much help. *So I had to depend on myself,* which was fine with me." (Italics added.)

About a work situation later on, she writes: "Although women were treated very well at Lincoln [Lab], there was one constant source of harassment that . . . I faced, and that had to do with [my] working hours. . . . [I] always arrived at least one hour late for work because of [my] commitments to [my] young children. Although this time-clock routine was very irritating to me, *I refused to change my ways. This was going to be my life style, and the administrators had to accept it.*" (Italics added).

The Facilitating Environment

The next question that must be asked, however, is what enables a woman to reach the point in her psychological development where she is able to function autonomously. The answer, I believe, is that of a "facilitating environment." Dr. Donald Winnicott, a pediatrician and psychoanalyst, has set forth this concept in his book *The Maturational Processes and the Facilitating Environment.*[3]

What, then, are some of the significant components that go into creating this kind of environment? They include: 1) the parenting in infancy and early childhood that gives a young child an inner sense of being an inherently good, cherished person; 2) encouragement for and tolerance of manifestations of increasing autonomy and unfolding individuality; 3) availability of figures of identification. A specific factor that may particularly influence the first two is the number of siblings a person may have and his or her birth order among siblings. For a future professional woman, a factor of special importance is her mother's and father's attitude toward her having a profession.

In terms of parenting that gives a young child an inner sense of being an inherently good, cherished person, Hunter gives an excellent example: "To my father and mother, it was important that people are what they are—and that being who and what I was good. As a woman, I was told, I would be able to do whatever I wanted. I was taught that my skin had a beautiful color. *This constant, implicit reinforcement of positive self-image was my parents' most valuable gift to me.* [Italics added.] I grew up loving my color and enjoying the fact that I was a woman."

Karle provides an example of parental encouragement of increasing autonomy and unfolding individuality. She writes: "My parents constantly encouraged my younger brother, who is now an engineer, and me in our school work, even though they understood very little about science."

McIntosh gives striking examples of the importance of availability of figures of identification. Her identification with her mother and a maternal aunt most probably had a profoundly facilitating effect on her development, first, into a headmistress of a girls' school, and then, president of a women's college. She states: "My mother went to the newly opened Bryn Mawr College in its first class.

. . . Her energy, her hard work in behalf of unpopular causes, made the deepest impression on me. . . . It was she who was the earliest and most profound influence on my life." A second certainly was her aunt, M. Carey Thomas, who was President of Bryn Mawr College, when she herself was a student there.

A questionnaire was sent to the women and data was obtained on the number and nature of their siblings and birth position. (See TABLES 1, 2, & 3.) They have an average of 2.2 siblings, with 58.3% having only one sibling. Of the siblings, 65.4% are brothers, and 34.6% are sisters. Fifty percent of the women are firstborn. The fact that 58.3% have only one sibling and 50% are firstborn seems to indicate that the number of siblings and birth position probably are of significance for this particular group of women.

In this same questionnaire, the women were asked to rate their mothers' and fathers' attitudes toward their having a profession. They could rate it positive, negative, mixed, and neutral. (See TABLES 4 & 5.) Among the mothers, seven were positive, none negative, four mixed, and one neutral. The fathers' attitudes were nine, positive; one, negative; one, mixed; and one, neutral. These findings, with 16 out of 24 or 66.6% of parents with a positive and only one parent with a negative attitude, appear to have a high degree of significance in terms of providing these women, in their younger years, with a most important facilitating component in their evolving sense of self.

A facilitating environment is important, however, not only in early childhood,

TABLE 1

BIRTH POSITION, NUMBER OF TOTAL SIBLINGS,
BROTHERS, AND SISTERS: RANKING OF WOMEN

Birth Position	No. of Women	% of Women	No. of Total Siblings	No. of Women	% of Women
1st	6	50.0%	1	7	58.3%
2nd	2	16.6%	2	1	8.3%
3rd	2	16.6%	3	1	8.3%
4th	1	8.3%	4	1	8.3%
5th	1	8.3%	5	2	16.6%
No. of Brothers			No. of Sisters		
0	1	8.3%	0	7	58.3%
1	7	58.3%	1	2	16.6%
2	3	25.0%	2	2	16.6%
3	0	0.0%	3	1	8.3%
4	1	8.3%			

TABLE 2

BROTHERS, SISTERS, AND TOTAL SIBLINGS*

	Number	% of Total Siblings
Brothers	17	65.4%
Sisters	9	34.6%
Total Siblings	26	100.0%
Average Siblings per Woman	2.2	8.5%
Average Brothers per Woman	1.4	5.4%
Average Sisters per Woman	0.8	3.1%

* Overall tabulation and average per woman.

TABLE 3

BIRTH POSITION, NUMBER OF TOTAL SIBLINGS, BROTHERS, AND SISTERS*

| | Birth Position | Number of Siblings | | |
		Total	Brothers	Sisters
Ancker-Johnson	3rd	2	2	0
Ballard	4th	4	2	2
Calderone	1st	1	0	1
Dresselhaus	2nd	1	1	0
Hunter	1st	3	1	2
Karle	1st	1	1	0
McIntosh	3rd	5	4	1
Minnhaar	1st	1	1	0
Peterson	5th	5	2	3
Pour-El	1st	0	1	0
Simpson	1st	1	1	0
Weiner	2nd	1 Step	1 Step	0

* Tabulation by individual women.

TABLE 4

PARENTAL ATTITUDES TOWARD A WOMAN HAVING A PROFESSION*

| | Attitudes | | | |
	Positive	Negative	Mixed	Neutral
No. of Mothers	7	0	4	1
% of Mothers	58.3%	0.0%	33.3%	8.3%
No. of Fathers	9	1	1	1
% of Fathers	75.0%	8.3%	8.3%	8.3%
No. of Parents	16	1	5	2
% of Parents	66.6%	4.2%	20.8%	8.4%

* Overall tabulation.

TABLE 5

PARENTAL ATTITUDES TOWARD A WOMAN HAVING A PROFESSION*

| | Attitudes | | | | | | | |
| | Mother | | | | Father | | | |
	+	−	Mixed	Neutral	+	−	Mixed	Neutral
Ancker-Johnson	x				x			
Ballard		x				x		
Calderone		x			x			
Dresselhaus	x				x			
Hunter	x				x			
Karle	x				x			
McIntosh	x				x			
Minnhaar		x			x			
Peterson	x				x			
Pour-El		x					x	
Simpson			x					x
Weiner	x				x			

* Tabulation by individual women.

but throughout life. From what almost all these women have described, very significant figures in their adult years, who have provided ongoing facilitation, have been their husbands. These men appear not only to have the ability to tolerate but also to take pleasure in and actively support the professional functioning of their wives. They seem to have themselves achieved a high level of autonomous functioning. They do not need their wives as *in loco matris* nor is their masculinity apparently threatened by their wives' professional activities and intellectual achievements. Ancker-Johnson observes: "My husband is man enough not to be threatened by his wife's awareness of electrons; indeed he takes for granted that her interest in them can be just as deep as his in differential geometry, without adversely affecting her femininity nor disqualifying her for the role of wife and mother. Clearly his attitude and encouragement have played a key part in making possible the life I lead."

Effects of a Nonfacilitating Environment

Before leaving the topic of facilitating environments, three instances among the life experiences of these women, where a significant component of the emotional environment during their developmental years was negative, will be discussed. The three instances are the overtly hostile mothers of Calderone and Simpson, the general parental attitude, and, particularly, Ballard's father's attitude, which was negative toward her professional aspirations. Ballard's life history is the most instructive in demonstrating how deeply unconscious processes can have an extremely disruptive effect on a woman's attempt to pursue a profession.

The two women among the group to describe mothers who were overtly hostile to them are Calderone and Simpson. In addition, they share three other experiences in common. First, both of them have had periods in which, in different ways, they had serious doubts about where they were going in their lives. Second, they are the two who have been divorced. Third, they are the only ones who describe having been perceived by their children at times as being "distant."

Simpson forthrightly has shared with us her present anguish about whether or not "it has all been worthwhile." She feels the most disheartened of the twelve speakers. The burden of having been a deviant and having to function in a nonfacilitating environment over the years weighs most heavily on her. She also describes the most negative early environment. She indicates much rejection, particularly by her mother. Her life history is a good example of how important the quality of early life experience can be in determining how well a woman will be able to survive psychologically the negative experiences she may have professionally later.

Ballard's life experience raises many interesting questions. One wonders, had she grown up in a different family environment, whether she might have gone to college and undertaken a profession prior to the age of 31. At that point, the dream of a happy marriage, four healthy and wanted children, a lovely house in the suburbs "suddenly . . . ended, and I realized that I would never be satisfied until I proved to myself and to the world that I was not just someone's wife or someone's mother but a capable person in my own right. . . ."

But problems still lay ahead. They seemed to be associated primarily with Ballard's relationship with her father. As already noted, he was the one parent of the 24 who had a negative attitude toward his daughter's having a professional commitment. Of her early relationship with him, she recalls: ". . . My father paid little attention to me; . . . I resented [his] refusal to appreciate what I could do, a refusal traceable not to his appraisal of me as a person, but to his appraisal of women generally. From the time I learned to talk, my father made it plain that women were clever and lovable and might be useful, but they did not have men's brains or men's capacity for objective achievement. After living with this view of my sex for thirty years, I became determined, first at the subconscious level and later consciously, to prove him wrong." But six weeks after she began her studies, Ballard developed physical symptoms. Medical tests were negative. She was referred to a woman psychiatrist.

She writes about this experience that gradually she realized "the secret knowledge that I was about to repudiate many of the goals I had been brought up to accept and the dawning realization of the deep wounds inflicted on me by my father's view of me as a woman were the roots of my physical symptoms. I felt selfish and guilty because I was pursuing my own goals and rejecting my father's beliefs. When my doctor helped me to understand these things, the sense of selfishness and guilt receded and my ailments gradually went away."

"Biological Reductionism"

But how to characterize this viewpoint, which Ballard's father and many others hold? It might be called "biological reductionism." It is a point of view that tends to regard a woman as if the only part of her anatomy of consequence to her personality and sense of self is her reproductive system. It overlooks another significant portion of her anatomy, her brain and its functional component, mind. It does not take into account the fact that the urge to question, to reason, to know, must be adjusted to in its own way, as much as the urge to experience sexuality and to procreate.

Peterson refers to women working because they feel a need to use their brains and their talents. Calderone has described the problems she had because of having a large variety of aptitudes. Minnhaar states that inteilectually "I had a need and searched for fulfillment."

But for these twelve women who have responded to the need for an active mental life, how has doing so affected their sexual and procreative functioning? They all are married, have at least one child, and an average of 3.5 children per woman. From what they have described, in almost every case, their professional functioning appears to have enhanced their relationships with their husbands and children, rather than having had a negative effect. Hunter comments: "To date, I have been able to progress in my chosen profession, and to do so in a manner consistent with a happy and satisfying domestic life." Dresselhaus states: "My marriage has been an exceedingly happy one. . . . I would say that my children have gained more than they have lost because of my professional career. . . ."

Conclusion

The late Dr. Elizabeth Zetzel, psychoanalyst and psychiatrist, wrote in her book *The Capacity for Emotional Growth*:[4] "The most mature woman . . . does not rely entirely on [people] as the source of gratification and pleasure. She has also achieved personal areas of active gratification and mastery. The healthy . . . woman should be able to combine successful marriage and motherhood with some sort of personal career."

In order for them to do so, I have suggested the importance for these women of having grown up in a facilitating environment that enables them to reach a level of autonomous emotional functioning. This capacity, in turn, makes it possible for them to function effectively in all areas of their lives, even in the face of being reacted to, professionally, as a deviant. Without this capacity, it is not possible for most women to function successfully in a profession in the United States today because of the persistence of the attitude of "biological reductionism." This attitude denies that women, as well as men, share in common the unique characteristics of our species, *homo sapiens,* which enable it to ask: How? Why? What?

It is this ability, however, which makes possible science and scientists. And so, as we move toward an ever-deeper probing of outer space and continually more refined understanding of that which is life itself, most hopefully, the human creatures, man and woman, increasingly can work together, not in a spirit of mutual antagonism, but of mutual respect—a respect generated by their common awareness that the capacity to wonder, to ask, and to seek for answers is not uniquely male or female, but one of the most awesome aspects of being human.

References

1. EPSTEIN, C. F. 1971. Woman's Place. : 31–32. University of California Press. Berkeley and Los Angeles, Calif.
2. MAHLER, M. S. 1968. On Human Symbiosis and the Vicissitudes of Individuation 1: 7–31. International Universities Press, Inc., New York, N. Y.
3. WINNICOTT, D. W. 1965. The Maturational Processes and the Facilitating Environment. International Universities Press, Inc. New York, N. Y.
4. ZETZEL, E. R. 1970. The Capacity for Emotional Growth. : 285. International Universities Press, Inc. New York, N. Y.

EDUCATION: A NURTURANT IF NOT A DETERMINANT OF PROFESSIONAL SUCCESS

Mary I. Bunting*

President, Radcliffe College
Cambridge, Massachusetts 02138

It has been a sobering experience for me to be asked to think about educational determinants in the lives of professionally successful women. Not that such women can do without education any more than they can do without their daily bread. In fact, they make particularly good use of the educational opportunities available to them and often seek them out with unusual determination. There is, however, little evidence in the life histories presented to us that formal educational experiences or influences were the critical determinants in the career decisions or the eventual success of these women. Education was a resource they used well, rather than a force that directed or shaped their lives.

This does not mean that education could not play a far more significant role, but I know of no school or college that has developed professional women as successfully as the little town of North Brook, Illinois, has developed women speed skaters. Using the talent at hand, without fancy recruiting, North Brook produced skaters who won three Olympic gold medals last January in international competition. There is a lesson here. As John Gardner said, "A society gets the kind of excellence it values." North Brook valued speed skating.

Similarly, I know of no formal educational institution that has contributed to the professional success of its students the way Dr. Molitor's laboratory at Merck Institute contributed to the success of the high school graduates and dropouts who were hired to work in its animal room in the 1930s. The first twelve all became productive scientists, eleven of them eventually earning Ph.D. or M.D. degrees or both. Again, there is evidence of powerful career determinants, but I do not know of comparable clusters of professionally successful women, or men, emerging from our schools and colleges. Rather, in the case of women, the complexities have been such that it has taken a kind of genius to achieve levels of success to which many could undoubtedly attain if circumstances were more favorable.

When it comes to the production of professionally successful women, perhaps the best, and the worst, thing that can be said about American education is that it hasn't tried. With a few exceptions, notably M. Carey Thomas at Bryn Mawr, our educational institutions, public and private, have not even pretended that the production of professional women leaders was a major objective. Given prevailing attitudes, such a goal could have frightened away many applicants and added to the isolation and burdens of those who did dare to attend.

The climate is improving as conferences like the one on which this monograph is based and the rap sessions of the young attest. The thoughtful discussions of long-range plans that are now taking place between young men and young women in our colleges presage a new era. Those of us who have been working to raise sensitivity to male chauvinist remarks and practices and who are truly concerned about removing deterrents to women's success must watch lest our testimony become the most discouraging thing youngsters hear. All too often recently, I have visited in homes where well-meaning mothers urged their little daughters to

---

* Present affiliation: Princeton University, Princeton, N. J. 08540.

do and dare but exposed them day after day to remarks about sex barriers and discriminatory practices. Constructive action is one thing, but endless complaining is not likely to produce tomorrow's leaders.

Not only has American education failed to conceive of women as an important source of professional talent but its structure and processes have actively discouraged their aspirations. Emphasis on grades and daily performance rather than on social and intellectual problems to be solved, the scarcity of female role models or truly supporting male teachers, rigid schedules and entrenched practices and attitudes that are basically antiintellectual and antidemocratic as well as sexist all serve to channel female students away from intellectually demanding fields of work. In terms of structure, American education has been set up and operated as a race track or a maze where success is judged by the speed with which the course is completed. Those who have nearly everything going for them are well served, but the gaps widen. Education has not been the door to opportunity for the disadvantaged but the great sorter-outer, and all too often the sorting has been done through admissions and other forms of tracking. Relatively little attention has been given to providing the conditions most favorable to the growth and development of those who are not in the front ranks. Even our so-called experimental schools have generally had their set approaches. Clearly, the promise of democracy cannot be realized until our educational institutions are converted into gardens where the needs of individuals are studied and their capabilities valued and challenged.

It must be recognized, however, that misguided gardeners can ruin valuable plants just as surely as can poorly designed systems. In our better schools and colleges, it is the teacher more often than the system that rejects the bright girl, often without realizing what has happened. I shall never forget eating luncheon with a group of scientifically talented high school students at the 1964 M.I.T. Symposium on American Women in Science and Engineering. I had just participated in an opening morning session that had emphasized the importance of high motivation and follow-through. I had thought it rather inspiring until I saw the dark faces around that table and realized that they reflected each girl's sad conclusion that science was not, alas, for her. They were not that sure of their motivation. Had they been boys, would we not have spent that first morning sharing the excitement of recent discoveries with them, drawing them into science, letting their motivation build, instead of worrying them about it? If we women who planned the conference could be so inept, no wonder that men often err.

Our life histories do indicate that subject matter, aided now and then by enthusiastic teachers and a favoring environment, can reach through to individual students and spark or trigger a lifelong intellectual interest. The extent to which such exposure initiates a career drive as distinct from determining its direction is not clear, but the importance of such experiences cannot be doubted. The trouble is that they occur so rarely. Can it be that a work experience under a master teacher such as Dr. Molitor would be far more effective than attendance at any lectures he might give? Once ignited, can otherwise indifferent students make good use of traditional education? Or was it essential that the animal-room boys continued to work with Dr. Molitor, at least through the early years of their part-time formal education?

What does seem very clear to me is that the emphasis on liberal as distinct from career learning in our colleges has been a great disservice to young women. The search for identity might better be recognized as a search for a meaningful role, and most people need to find something more focused than the "life of the mind" as such if they are to use their minds to advantage. A burning interest is far more likely to suggest intriguing connections with other subjects than to blind one to their significance. If there is anything that our life histories verified, it is the relative breadth of the interests of successful professional women.

What will be the effect of women's studies on women's careers? I doubt that the availability of such courses would have made much difference to the women whose testimonies we have heard, but I do believe that their existence, and eventually the inclusion of appropriate material about women in regular courses in history, economics, literature, social studies and the arts, will help to change the climate of unexpectation that did not alter our sample of successful women but undoubtedly discouraged many of their contemporaries. College is the time in life when bright young people make and remake career decisions. It is when young women, at least those in coeducational colleges, face career choices realistically. Thanks to women's liberation and the courses and conversations it has fostered, they can now do so more openly and with more alternatives and encouragement than in the past. Additionally, the study of women is itself an exciting focus. Those of us who have seen previously tepid students become self-directed historians, psychologists, or sociologists under its stimuli can only applaud.

What can I bring to the problem before us from my own experience as an educator? In effecting social change, as in any scientific investigation, one selects the most significant problem that one thinks one can resolve with the skills and resources at one's disposal. By 1960, when I went to Radcliffe, I was convinced that the most serious problems in women's education stemmed from the fact that in this country women, no matter how bright and well educated, were not really expected to contribute significantly to intellectual advances in any rigorous field of study or action. Tinkering with curricula or guidance procedures could only add to the general confusion. Something had to be done to break the logjam, and that meant changing attitudes. An experimental approach seemed logical and more likely to find supporters than a campaign of persuasion. With the backing of the Radcliffe trustees and generous donors, we established the Radcliffe Institute as a laboratory in which to work on the problem.

Our first experiment was a very simple one. The Program for Independent Study offered financial assistance and other aids to women in the Boston area who had projects on which they wished to work but who had been handicapped by lack of time, the unavailability of university resources, or by more subtle forms of isolation. Did such women exist? Could we release them to be productive? Would they then be in a position to move ahead on their own? Would the fact that we valued what they did with their trained minds help to change people's expectations? Working in the gray area between college aspirations and proven performance, we wished to find out whether there were roadblocks which, if removed, would enable qualified but stymied women to become professionally successful. If so, earlier educational investments of impressive magnitude would have been brought to fruition, able individuals would achieve satisfaction rather than frustration, their examples would become incentives rather than warnings to younger women.

Our program was designed primarily for married women with children, although never restricted to them, because we believed that married women do have special problems and that until it is demonstrated that women with families can contribute effectively in demanding professions, younger women will continue to face cruel decisions, and single women to experience senseless discrimination.

Working cooperatively with our experimental subjects, we endeavored to find out how best to help them. Note that we did not set their goals or establish any deadlines. The married woman with children who chooses a demanding intellectual task is abundantly motivated. What we did offer was the recognition that came with selection; money, if needed, to free their time; a study or studio or laboratory; access to libraries and computers; a chance to audit courses; and opportunities to confer with faculty members at Harvard and with each other. Some 35 to 40 women have been Fellows in the Program for Independent Study each year since 1961, most Fellows working part-time over a two-year period. We have learned a great deal from their applications, their experiences as Fellows, and their subsequent careers.

Without question, there is a reservoir of able, educated women who, with just a little encouragement and assistance, are ready to demonstrate their productivity and then move into significant jobs in college teaching and other professions. Furthermore, it is not just among housewives that one finds examples of frustrated careers. A great many professional women lack the opportunities they need to procure advanced training on schedules compatible with the needs of their families, or are unable to demonstrate their ability to do productive intellectual work of high caliber on their own. Two findings have implications that merit widespread consideration. First, as long as able and responsible women wish to combine career and home responsibilities, institutions should schedule educational and job opportunities adapted to their needs. Second, during periods when their time for outside work is limited, women should take special care to use their time to advance their careers. A young scientist or scholar may feel that she can give only 20 hours a week to work away from home for a period of years. If she accepts a part-time teaching position and pursues it year after year without carrying forward her own research, she will be in no position to request promotion when she does wish to resume full-time work. I think also of a young lawyer who felt she could not combine law practice with her family responsibilities but devoted her time to writing a definitive book on South American tax laws, and of the young doctor who, in addition to her part-time clinic job, developed expertise in the health problems of travelers. Both had something special to offer when they were ready to work full time. Similarly, if it can be managed, it can be far more important in the long run for a young mother to spend her available time studying than to use it in a routine although remunerative job. Institutions as well as husbands must reexamine the assumptions that ask the wife not only to care for the children but also to spend her free time furthering his career rather than her own.

In addition to Independent Study, the Institute has set up fellowship programs to assist mature women with children who wish to continue advanced studies on part-time schedules and who need financial assistance to do so. In the case of medical women, the Institute has also negotiated with hospitals and deans to arrange suitably flexible schedules for them. From these experiments, as well as the Program for Independent Study, we now have impressive evidence that the momentum gained when a mature woman is helped to carry out an ambitious career plan is not later dissipated. Virtually all of the 300 women we have assisted have continued in their chosen professions. Younger women may become dropouts but not those whose career interests survive marriage, which is a useful finding. Furthermore, most of the Institute Fellows are convinced that the assistance they received was of critical importance to their career development. For them, the chance to continue their education or demonstrate their productivity seems to have been a career determinant.

This is not the place nor am I the person to assess the Institute's findings in detail, but drawing somewhat from its experiences with the developing careers of professional women and from the testimony of the successful women who have shared their life histories with us, I should like to make a few tentative observations.

I am impressed, as others on this panel have been, by the many differences in the backgrounds and life patterns of professional women. Clearly, one must be very careful about generalizations, recognize them as hypotheses, and verify each with care before using it to predict the performance of individuals or the value of educational measures. Thus, for example, a relatively high proportion of the first group of Institute Fellows had missed a year or more of school or college. Was this happenstance? Have any comprehensive studies been made of the effects of absence from school on girls? Did these women make special use of their free time, and if so, does this provide clues that might be utilized educationally? And so forth.

There were only two generalizations that I could draw with any confidence from our life histories. Both have been mentioned by previous speakers and neither can be considered an educational determinant in the usual sense. The women from whom we have heard and also those who apply to the Institute all seem to have been encouraged from a very early age to think of themselves as individuals rather than as conforming members of a group. I believe this is critically important, and that all too often our educational institutions act to negate individuality, especially in the case of little girls, thereby serving as determinants of success. One of the best ways to build a strong self-image in early childhood, as in later years, is to discover and foster the interests and strengths that the individual has, being careful not to fan any tiny flame so vigorously that it is extinguished, which can happen; independent study for those who are ready for it at any age; significant group projects in which each person plays a role, as in Dr. Moliter's laboratory, for those who are not yet self-propelled. Schools can help, but so can observant families, friends, and neighbors. All too often, even in well-educated families, little girls' hobbies are squelched.

What if there were schools and colleges that admitted and retained students, as the Institute does, primarily on the basis of projects on which, along with other studies, they wished to work? Perhaps it would result only in a lot of phony projects, but it might be worth a try and could be an interesting place to teach.

The second generalization in which I feel some confidence is the importance, given the unfavorable intellectual climate in which we live, of the backing that their husbands gave to our panel of successful women. It is no accident that so high a proportion of married women who do have successful careers enjoy such support. What can we do in education to produce more such husbands? I might add here that perhaps the most important reason for admitting men to good women's colleges is the exposure the men get to able women in an environment in which women's intellectual interests and capabilities are valued.

It would be of interest to learn about the family background and education and views of the husbands who have contributed so importantly to the careers of the successful women from whom we have heard. In our eagerness to free women for leadership we need not forget the importance of supporting roles. The supplementary study of these husbands could add insights of several kinds.

Support is important and it can come from many sources: families, schools, and husbands, but also aunts, uncles, neighbors, the press. How do we build a greater sense of caring as well as respect for individuality into our educational systems? If the determinants of success are primarily psychological and sociological, then education must be designed and run to foster the desired attributes. I believe today's young people have this in mind. Caring and respect for individuality are high on their agenda even while they are tormented with doubts about professional success.

Finally, our ignorance about the determinants of professional success for women is obviously colossal. Let us respect that ignorance. If we don't know just what to recommend, neither does anyone else know just what will not work. Experimentation is in order, as well as careful evaluation and conferences such as this one, which help us take stock and stimulate us to carry on.

PART VI

Related Problems of
Professional Women

PREGNANCY AND ABORTION: IMPLICATIONS FOR CAREER DEVELOPMENT OF PROFESSIONAL WOMEN

Malkah T. Notman

Harvard Medical School
Boston, Massachusetts 02115

Pregnancy

For the professionally active woman, her pregnancy often provides the first challenge to a life-style that may have functioned well and adaptively until that time. When she discovers she is pregnant, she has to make a choice whether to have the child or whether to have an abortion. Marriage may be included in this decision. Most professional women who do have children are married. Although increasing numbers of unmarried mothers elect to keep their babies rather than offer them for adoption, their educational and class background is generally different from that of career women. This, therefore, is not a widely accepted alternative for the women with a career.

Having a baby then brings a whole range of consequences. Some are related to the experience of the pregnancy and some to the impact of the child on family roles and responsibilities.

Many of the discussions about femininity and feminism these days waver between assertions that women are no different from men in any respect that really matters on the one hand, and to pleas for appreciation of those qualities which are specifically feminine on the other. Certainly in most professional occupations there are few ways in which women must inherently function any differently than men in regard to the actual character of their work. There are, however, many ways in which they may choose to arrange their lives differently from the prevailing patterns for men. The most marked of these concern their family relationships and the most compelling have to do with the care of children.

Numerous obstacles complicate a woman's gaining access to a career and then achieving recognition and the standard rewards or professional advancement within it. The problems posed by the external barriers of overt discrimination, subtle prejudices, and the inner conflicts such as those concerning the competitiveness and aggressiveness necessary for successful achievement may be solved in a number of ways, varying with the individual backgrounds and personalities of the woman involved. One possible option a woman has is to minimize the distinction between the sexes; that is, to work "like a man." She can insist on equal hours and on undertaking work of equal challenge, and can try to participate fully in all the informal exchanges of information, banter, and social communication. We have heard a good deal about the dubiousness of accepting these masculine role models, but it does remain difficult to modify or abandon them if one is after success. Whatever possibilities exist for managing this solution for the women graduate student or young professional become smaller or vanish in some fields once a woman plans to have children.

She has the theoretical option of insisting that there be no differences in her work conditions except for maternity leave and the immediate postdelivery period for a short while afterward, or she can ask for "special" consideration that takes some account of the integration of work with the human needs of her family and herself. The latter is actually not always feasible. Flexible work arrangements may not exist in certain work settings, particularly in the sciences, and the woman may be reluctant to "buck the system" and thus make herself more conspicuous and vulnerable. She often feels guilty at needing something "special" in the way of arrangements, because this is regarded as a disruptive rather than as a legitimate aspect of one's life. She is then forced into an either-or decision: either she adopts a discontinuous work pattern and stops for a few years after the baby is born or she makes a commitment to a full work schedule where she may inhibit her own full response to her pregnancy and its meaningfulness for her. This, in effect, devalues both the particular rewards of her life that childbearing can represent, and the child as well. In addition to its unavailability, men's and some women's depreciation of part-time work contribute to the dilemma.

The particular alternative ways of working out one's family roles are very difficult for the woman to conceptualize in the abstract before a baby is born. Partially this is true because plans theoretically conceived do not always take into account the real strains, pleasures, and tasks of parenthood. Most women bring to this role complex and sometimes confused expectations and fantasies of what it means to be a mother and care for a child. These derive in part from her own experiences and memories of being mothered, which are not always conscious. Another reason for the difficulty in anticipatory planning has to do with the growth that takes place during pregnancy—not only in girth, but also psychologically. A first pregnancy holds considerable developmental potential in the transition a woman makes to being a mother and caretaking person.

It is interesting that woman students who are contemplating careers have difficulty thinking through how the family-career integration is to be managed. They suggest innovative and interesting ideas, but often these are unrealistic, sometimes almost mathematical in their concepts of the division of time. If the woman students become interested in how other professional women have managed, this can often help lend some reality to their plans. The value of a variety of role models provided by women in the professions with a range of different life-styles has been properly stressed in many discussions of this problem.

The birth of a child puts a strain on what may, up until then, have been a successful arrangement with the husband, because prior to this point it is more possible to function in essentially parallel ways, with sharing and rearrangement of responsibilities. When a child is involved, however, and the issues of who is to provide care and how this is to be done become an insistent reality, many deep-seated expectations of each other's roles come into play. These deeper feelings may conflict with newer ideas, derived from ideological considerations or rational plans. For a woman to work seriously, some resolutions of these conflicts must be achieved in at least a relatively harmonious fashion.

Past identifications with parents and other important figures play a crucial role in determining the concept each person has of how one behaves as a woman—or a man—and how these should interrelate. Pregnancy stirs up these old identifications; particularly important for the woman is her relationship with her mother, which is revived emotionally. On the verge of being a mother herself, her mother's life-style assumes particular importance. She may feel conflicted at choosing a solution different from her mother's, or disturbed at what might seem to be outdoing her in status or achievement. She may feel uncertainty about her career plans, arising from the new appeal of her mother's pattern.

Pregnancy does obviously differentiate men from women. The experience is something potentially shared with all women. Although the care of a child can be divided with her husband and others, the bearing of a child is a woman's experience alone. There is evidence from the life histories of women who have chosen the socially deviant path of intellectual interests and serious commitment to careers that as girls they felt outside the more generally accepted group, which stressed prettiness and popularity. Residual doubts or uneasiness about her femininity may even seem to be confirmed by success in scientific pursuits. Faced with these feelings, even if they are not very prominent, pregnancy can bring a sense of being like other women. Surprising pleasure may accompany sharing this experience and having a common bond with "those other" women. If womanhood, femaleness, or femininity brings conflicts, and if it is disturbing to be linked with "those other" women, the pregnancy will be a trying time and may be avoided.

Pregnancy may threaten some well-established patterns. Psychologically and realistically, a woman is often more vulnerable during pregnancy; she may find herself more volatile, more fatigued, and be less in control of her body. This experience may be very threatening to someone whose self-image is based on being strong, competent, and in control. In the process of developing a career, many women develop defenses that make unacceptable anything appearing to be weakness in themselves, even the temporary symptoms of a pregnancy. These feelings may lead a woman to resist modifying her life patterns while she is pregnant and force herself to carry on just as before. Of course, many women feel no need to modify anything, since they feel well and prefer to work. But flexibility in making this choice is important.

For many women the pregnancy provides their first experience with being a patient—and a participant in the nonmutual relationship that some obstetricians seem to encourage. The passivity and dependence connected with being a patient runs counter to their other modes of functioning, which have been adaptive in their work development. It is frustrating for someone oriented to solving problems and valuing knowledge to be treated as someone who does not need to know what is going on in her pregnancy.

The pregnancy may also be the first encounter with such an intimate responsibility for another human being. The impact of the first child and the consequent expansion of the family unit is considerable. New responsibilities are added, often precipitating a realignment of roles and priorities. The range of plans that seemed theoretically possible in earlier thinking narrows down to those necessary to meet the real needs of a real child—but heavily affected by deeply held expectations of how to raise it. These may be difficult to modify by good intentions alone. Experience is important. The complexity, juggling, and ingenuity needed are considerable. Certain personality traits become particularly valuable for both parents. Among these are tolerance of conflict, ability to forego perfectionism, and the capacity to concentrate in the face of distraction. It would be valuable to know more about those personality traits which facilitate the integration of family and work.

Even where a husband and wife adopt a pattern of real sharing it is usually the woman who assumes the responsibility of the overall planning and availability to the child. Men tend to perform specific caretaking functions—feeding a baby, bathing, story-telling, and so on. Our clinical impressions suggest that the woman's role is conceptualized as providing the primary care for very young children. It is usually the woman who feels she has to find coverage for herself if she works seriously, and usually the woman who feels the conflict and guilt at working. This conflict is present especially when children are young and separation is traumatic, but also persists when they are older.

Abortion

When the pregnancy is unwanted, the implications of the availability of abortions for facilitating a woman's choices of the timing of the phases of her career and freeing her for professional activities are clear. Several colleagues and I are now completing an intensive study of the outcome of therapeutic abortion in 100 women in Boston. Thirty-eight percent of these randomly selected women sought abortions for reasons related to work or educational conflict, although these may not have been the only reasons in each case. After the abortion they did return to work or school.

There are many reasons for an unwanted pregnancy to occur besides accidents. Becoming pregnant has complex meanings that may be only partly related or actually unrelated to the wish for a child. It is one way of establishing one's fertility, of indicating potential creative productivity, or of confirming femininity. Our data and the work of others indicate that even women who actively and unambivalently seek abortions sometimes feel pleasure at the idea of having become pregnant. Six months after the abortions, many women feel that the whole experience has increased their view of themselves as women. Most of the women in the study did not feel that their wish for the abortion was connected with any serious doubts about their capacity to be mothers, but to the undesirability of a particular pregnancy at a particular time.

Becoming pregnant, deliberately or inadvertantly, may be a way of avoiding difficulties within a career, or an expression of the anxiety a woman faces at the point where she is about to make an important move. It is not uncommon to encounter women who were about to return to graduate school or start work on a long-delayed book or other project, who then become pregnant. Some women want to change their direction when their youngest child is in school. Having no clear training, or being frightened about how to catch up with years missed, they may find themselves pregnant, which leads to a more familiar role. (Twenty-eight percent of our patients had as their youngest child one who was older than seven years. Thus the pregnancy would have brought them back into a new period of motherhood of young infants when this period had already once been passed). They thus can escape the strains of competition and the complexities of resolving the family-career dilemma, the frustrations of difficult work, or the problems of dealing with one's ambiguous status in a largely masculine field.

Conscious or unconscious ambivalence about her career which might have led a woman to an unwanted pregnancy does not then present the same barrier to further career development as it might if abortion were unavailable. A woman who feels unready or unwilling to have a child at a particular time does not have to live with the results of only one part of her ambivalence.

Where abortion laws are restrictive, and even where they are relatively permissive (that is, where they state that abortion may be done to save the life and protect the health of the mother), the woman must convincingly present herself as ill and threatened in order to qualify. This situation rewards illness and weakness, and supports willingness to manipulate and pretend in order to secure the assistance a woman feels she desperately needs. We saw the dilemmas resulting from this approach when the requirements were more strictly enforced in Massachusetts and there was no legal abortion nearby. Some women faced enormous difficulty in presenting themselves as weak or desperate, particularly those whose successful adaptations included pride and strength in their academic or career roles. This posture runs counter to those personal resources which had been important in their previous responses to critical experiences. Consequently, they then exposed themselves to the risks and embarrassments of illegal abortions.

Students looking for ways to solve the problems of integrating family and career, or of simply developing their own patterns of functioning in the professional world, look to models of other successful women in their fields. Just as with the other aspects of professional experience, they want to see "how it's done." To see that a respected colleague or friend makes a decision to have an abortion and that this is a manageable experience, although this may not be public information, is important in the student's awareness of alternatives that might be available to her at a time she might be in a similar dilemma.

The possibility of a safe, dignified abortion openly chosen confirms a woman's self-image as someone who is valued not only for her child-bearing role. Whether a particular woman ever has an abortion is not as crucial as her awareness of the possibility of having one. The existence of a choice supports the validity of other priorities. If a pregnancy does interrupt another set of priorities, and if it is clearly possible to abort it safely, thus providing a real alternative to proceeding with it, this weakens the expectation that women's only true fullfillment leads to once again putting the "mother" role first. In my experience, this alternative self-image as a person with other legitimate activities can be very supportive in lessening the guilt women feel when they do place nonfamily commitments high. The concept that a woman's role is not necessarily the home, although she may enjoy her home and care deeply about her family, is reinforced by the awareness of having made an active choice to be there. Those women who do not feel they are suitable or optimal for motherhood do not then feel so downgraded and unacceptable.

Many of our patients who seek abortions have described the change in their relationships with their husbands and children afterwards. Most marked is the improvement in relation to children when the crisis precipitated by the possibility of having to meet a new set of demands is relieved. They value the existing children, and they can deal with them more effectively when there is some support for other aspects of their lives. The legitimacy of the abortion can be important here. The hospital or other respectable institution lends sanction to the decision. A permission granted by a psychiatrist may have some benefit in the implicit approval this creates. Anxiety as to whether the abortion will create some permanent physical damage can be an expression of guilt about the abortion and can be experienced as a punishment for doing a wrong. This anxiety can be reduced by the safety of the setting or even by its ordinariness and the acceptance and understanding of professional people in the environment.

It is interesting that many women, particularly those who are well educated, may feel guilty and ashamed over the pregnancy rather than the abortion. They feel, "How could I have gotten myself into this?" They nevertheless do act impulsivley sometimes, irrationally at others, and have accidents as well.

Our preliminary data indicate that many variables are related to the balance of the outcome. Social and situational variables are perhaps as important in determining the result as is the personality of the woman.

There is evidence, furthermore, that an abortion may have a specifically positive effect on the resolution of the crisis of unwanted pregnancy. This positive outcome is not only due to the relief of immediate pressure, but can be maturational in the long run. This maturational potential is probably related to the experience of making the decision. Many women, in looking back on this period, feel that this is a highly significant decision, often the first major decision they made autonomously. Participation and support from lover, husband, counselors, or friends are helpful, as is the possibility for carrying out the decision in an atmosphere of safety and acceptance. But the responsibility lies with the woman herself. Handling it successfully has an important long-range effect. Career decisions usually involve a high degree of independence and self-determination. We have heard how important it has been for the women scientists whose life histories were presented to be able to tolerate being considered deviant. Actions that are personally appropriate may be considered very deviant socially. Among certain groups of women, decisions such as having an abortion are accepted and, in fact, the rule, but not for everyone. The abortion experience may increase the capacity of the woman to deal with other decisions, leading to increased autonomy and individuation. The decision often seems to be a pivotal point in the move away from a dependent relationship with parents, even though we also have evidence that those women who have troubled relationships with their mothers have more distress, shame, and defense afterward than those who do not. Obviously it does not always work that way. An abortion may represent a conflicted, regressed, guilt-laden experience. Or one may need to repeat the expression of the underlying conflict and become pregnant again—only to wish to undo again. Our experience is that the intensely disturbing experience is rare. There have been few serious reactions, except in disturbed patients. Repetition probably is most frequent when there are defenses preventing a conscious confrontation with the issues involved—a problem not unique to abortion.

Perhaps the most important effect of the availability of abortion is the control of a woman's reproductive life, which it makes possible for her. Obviously this is provided by contraception in a more sound, sensible, rational, preventive form. But people are not all rational nor are they all single-minded. Not everyone uses contraception effectively at all times. The possibility of another point of decision-making permits a multiplicity of solutions for optimal development of the individual needs of everyone: mother, father, and children.

Suggested Reading

BIBRING, G. L. 1959. Some Considerations of the Psychological Processes in Pregnancy. The Psychoanalytic Study of the Child **14:** 113–121. International Universities Press. New York, N. Y.

NADELSON, C. & M. NOTMAN. 1972. The woman physician. J. Med. Ed. **47:** 176–183. March.

NOTMAN, M., A. KRAVITZ, E. PAYNE & J. RUSSELL. 1972. Psychological outcome in patients having therapeutic abortions. *In* Proc. Third Internat. Cong. Psychosomatic Problems Obstet. Gynecol. : 552–554.

PAYNE, E., A. KRAVITZ, M. NOTMAN & J. RUSSELL. 1972. Therapeutic Abortions: Outcome Study of 100 Cases. Presented at 125th Annual Meeting of American Psychiatric Assoc. May. Dallas, Tex.

RAPOPORT, R., R. RAPOPORT & M. FOGARTY. 1971. Sex, Career and Family. P.E.P. Monograph. George Allen & Unwin Ltd. London, England.

THE PROFESSIONAL WOMAN AS MOTHER

Lois Wladis Hoffman

The University of Michigan
Ann Arbor, Michigan 48104

In talking about the professional woman as mother, one could deal with the effects of the career on her mothering, the effects of motherhood on her career, or the effects of combining these two roles on her personal satisfactions. Most of my focus will be on the first: what kind of a mother is she, and how have her children turned out? But let me discuss the other two briefly, for they provide an important context for my major points.

The dysfunctions of motherhood for the pursuit of a career have been pointed out by Bailyn,[1] Epstein,[2] White,[3] and others. We are handicapped in our career advancement by geographical restrictions, family obligations, guilt, and prejudice. The husband's career considerations have been given priorities not only because of his insistence, but also because of our acquiescence. We have been assigned, and we have accepted, the major responsibility for child care and the household operations. As Rossi[4] has indicated, some men also have not pursued their careers with single-minded devotion, but have allowed their family concerns to temper their ambitions. But this is far more true for women. Furthermore, women have had that mixed blessing—the chance to drop out without censure. We have all returned from a bad day at work to a chaotic household and wondered why we ever left the kitchen. We are harassed, overworked, and in desperate need of a housekeeper.

But for all of this, we may have fared better with respect to personal satisfactions than had we chosen one of the alternative paths that were available. This is not to say that there is no room for improvement, but the life that includes a commitment to the several roles—wife, mother, and professional—may be the richest of all. There are a number of recent empirical studies indicating that despite all of the difficulties, the bright and educated women who have combined all three look back with considerable satisfaction and a minimum of regrets.[5-8] Birnbaum,[8] for example, compared a group of mothers who were also faculty members of a large university with unmarried faculty women, and with a group of mothers who had graduated from college with honors but who had pursued neither further education nor a career. The groups were comparable with respect to age—mainly in their early forties. Of the three groups, the nonworking mothers were the ones with the lowest self-esteem and the lowest sense of personal competence, including even sense of competence about child-care skills. These women also felt least attractive, expressed most concern over self-identity issues, and most often indicated feelings of loneliness. The subjects were asked what they felt was missing from their lives and the predominant answer from the two groups of professional women was *time,* but for the housewives it was challenge and creative involvement. The single women, in this study as in others,[9] held higher professorial ranks than the married professionals. Both professional groups indicated high self-esteem and a sense of competence, but the single women were lonelier and somewhat less comfortable in their social relationships.

The data indicate then that the woman who has combined a career with marriage and children has not pursued her career with the total undeviating involvement that has characterized men and single women. She has, in many cases, withdrawn from full career commitments when her children were young, returning to these commitments as they matured.[5,10,11] Her life has had more variety; growing old has not meant simply a dimnution of her powers, but instead she has experienced greater flexibility in responding to the various possibilities that life offers at different stages in the life cycle. This may seem a waste from the standpoint of a society oriented exclusively to productivity in work, but to many it seems a more fulfilling life. I am not even sure that it is a waste in terms of the criterion of productivity, for the woman with the combined roles may retain an enthusiasm and creativity in her work even in her very mature years, when many men who have constantly pursued their careers become bored, stagnant, and bureaucratized.

In turning now to the major focus of this presentation—the effects of the mother's professional role on the child—there is a remarkable lack of data. In part, this is a methodological problem. Studies that have examined the effects of maternal employment on the child usually locate a group of children around the same age, half of whom have employed mothers and half of whom do not, and compare the two groups. Since more than half the mothers whose youngest child is in school are employed, finding these groups is no great problem. But to find a group of children of the same age whose mothers have *professions* is obviously more difficult. In fact, I know of few such studies. We shall have to rely on those that have compared employed and unemployed mothers' children among the highly educated, or middle class. This can be supplemented with studies that have questioned professional mothers but have not obtained direct data on the children.

Ten years ago I published with Ivan Nye a book on the working mother.[12] The working mother had been considered quite a devil, and a great deal of the research reported in the book had originally been undertaken in the hope of documenting the ill effects of maternal employment. But the data simply would not cooperate. Examined as a general phenomenon, the standard study with adequate controls yielded no significant differences between the children of working and nonworking women. That should not have been a surprise. Maternal employment is too heterogeneous a variable to study. To see the effects, we have to break it down, for the effects will be different in the working class than in the middle class. They will be different if the mother works out of necessity than if she works out of choice. The effects will be different for young children than for older, for girls than for boys. The hours she works, her child-care and household arrangements, her attitudes about her role, all will be important. But even those studies which introduced such breakdowns found few negative effects and several positive ones. There was one study, however, that suggested a bit of caution.

This was a study that I did of working mothers of elementary school age children. The working mothers were divided into those who liked their work and those who did not. Each was compared with a nonworking mother family that was matched with respect to social class, size of family, and other pertinent factors. As you can guess, the women who liked their work were more typically—though not exclusively—the middle class, and better educated. The results indicated that when the working mother liked her work she often seemed to feel guilty, and she compensated for her employment to such an extent that she may have even gone too far. For example, her children helped *less* around the house than did the children of the nonworking mothers. There was much in her relationship with her children that was very positive—she expressed more positive affect, used less coercive discipline, she felt less hostility toward her children and more empathy—but in many cases she was somewhat overindulgent, and the children reflected this in their peer interactions and school performance. They played more with younger children than with their age mates; they were less likely to initiate interaction with their classmates; their academic performance was not up to par. These are almost the only negative effects of maternal employment found in the middle class to date, and they appear to result not from employment *per se* but from guilt about employment. This pattern was not extreme, and it was not found in a study of working mothers with adolescent children. It is important, however, because it indicates it may not be employment one has to worry about, but guilt about employment.

With the exception of the finding just mentioned, there is little evidence that maternal employment has a negative effect, and considerable support for the idea that it has a positive effect, particularly on girls. The daughters of working mothers are more likely to choose their mothers as models and as the person they most admire. Adolescent daughters of working mothers, particularly in the middle and upper socioeconomic groups, have been found to be active, autonomous, girls who admire their mothers but who are not unusually close-tied to them. For girls of all ages, having a working mother contributes to a concept of the female role that includes less restriction and a wider range of activities, and a self-concept that incorporates these aspects of the female role. They usually approve of maternal employment, plan to work when they grow up and become mothers, and, if they are old enough, they are more often employed themselves.[12]

A few years ago a study by Goldberg[13] indicated that undergraduate women tended to undervalue journal articles when authorship was attributed to women. Recently, Grace Baruch[14] replicated this study. She found that the tendency to undervalue the works attributed to women was less than in the earlier study, and that the daughters of working mothers showed no such tendency. That is, the daughters of working mothers, unlike those of nonworking mothers, did not assume that women were less competent than men. In this study, the college women who wanted to combine motherhood with a career most often came from homes in which the mothers had *successfully* combined the two roles. But simply having a mother who was employed was enough to affect the daughter's judgment about the competence of women, and this, of course, implies a positive effect on her self-concept.

If we focus on the daughter's academic and career achievements, we find further evidence of the positive effects of having a professional mother. A number of investigations[8,15,16,28] have found that highly achieving women and women who aspire to careers, particularly to less conventionally feminine careers, are more likely to be the daughters of educated women and the daughters of employed women.* The high-achieving woman has a high-achieving daughter. There are several reasons why this may be the case. Various studies suggest that the optimum conditions for a high-achieving female include the presence of a model, and the model of the professional woman is more relevant to academic and achievement goals than is that of the nonemployed housewife. The optimum conditions for achievement also include independence training, which is particularly important because many girls are handicapped by overprotection and encouragement of dependency. And finally, optimum conditions include a good relationship with a father who encourages the girl's independence and achievement while accepting her as a female.[5,17] All of these conditions are more likely to exist in the family with a professional mother.

* Birnbaum's[8] married professional women are themselves the daughters of educated, employed women. However, the pattern for single professionals is somewhat different, as indicated in both Birnbaum's data and Astin's.[10]

Nor is this simply conjecture. We have already discussed the professional mother as model. Regarding the encouragement of independence, the study by Birnbaum[8] mentioned earlier compared the two groups of mothers, professional women and intelligent nonworking housewives, with respect to their attitudes about their children. The professional mothers indicated pleasure in the child's growing independence. For the nonworking mothers, on the other hand, the child's movement toward independence was disturbing, perhaps because their own importance diminished as the child needed them less. Overprotection by the nonworking mothers was also suggested by the fact that they seemed to worry excessively about their children's health and safety, and they stressed self-sacrifice as a major aspect of motherhood.

With respect to the last-named factor that contributes to the development of achievement orientations in women—having a close relationship with an encouraging and supportive father—there are data also. Many studies have found that the husbands of working women are more actively involved in the care of the children, and other studies show that the active involvement of the father has a positive effect on both male and female children. Furthermore, the data indicate that the husbands of professional women are more likely to respect competence and achievement in women.[7,12,18-20]

There is very little else by way of solid data that differentiates the children of professional from nonprofessional mothers. For example, I have not discussed the effects on sons simply because we have not yet learned what these effects may be.†

There are, however, some hints about possible effects from the studies that have compared professional mothers with able women who are full-time housewives. Several studies, for example, have indicated that the woman who does well in college but does not pursue a career pins her achievement needs on to her children seeking vicarious satisfaction through their achievements.[8,15] Although her achievement frustrations are not great when her children are young, they tend to increase after a few years.[21] Several studies indicate that about twelve or more years after marriage‡ her need for achievement rises; her self-esteem is low; her feeling of self-sacrifice is high; she is prone to depression; she worries about her competence in general and particularly as a mother; she is very anxious about her children and guilty about occasional losses of her self-control.[8,22,23] Despite her eagerness for her children to achieve, she is, as already pointed out, ambivalent about their growing independence. Surely this situation—the plight of the bright, nonprofessional mother when her children have reached school age—does not seem conducive to rearing healthy, competent children of either sex. When the professional mother is feeling harassed and guilty about her employment, she might consider the alternative.

We do not have data on the effects on the child of the various career patterns that professional women have chosen. How important, for example, is the fact that so many professional women have reduced their work load when the children were young? Is the prevalence of this pattern one of the reasons why maternal employment has not been found to have adverse effects? What, indeed, is the

† There are a few limited studies. For example, in a study of a small sample of gifted boys, the low achievers had more employed mothers, but the high achievers had more *professionally* employed mothers, and another study which did not separate boys from girls found the children of professional women had better reading skills than a matched sample of full-time housewives.[30]

‡ More specifically, about fifteen years after college graduation.

effect of the mother's career pursuits on the very young child? We simply do not know. Those who oppose professions for mothers are quick to generalize from the studies of maternal deprivation showing that infants reared in inadequate institutions without any stable one-to-one relationship with an adult suffer serious affective and cognitive deficits. These early and important studies, however, do not provide automatic condemnation of day-care centers, various alternative foster-care arrangements, or even of institutional care itself if the institution is appropriately set up. Research suggests, for example, that putting a small number of babies in the attentive care of a single person mitigates many of the adverse effects. So does increasing the stimulation potential of the physical environment. In any case, the connection between the sterile, understaffed, institutional environment and the setting provided by the professional mother seems remote to me.

On the other hand, we do not know what the effects of the mother's career are on the very young child or what the effects are of the various possible child care arrangements. No one has studied them.

And now, if you feel that I have painted a bleak picture of the state of our knowledge about the effects of the mother's career on her child, let me add still further to that impression; for much that we know may be made obsolete by the recent changes in sex-role prescriptions.

The existing research, such as it is, is for the most part based on women who have been married about fifteen years or more. We had our babies during the time well characterized by the term *The Feminine Mystique*. From the midforties until recently, large families were desired and motherhood was extolled as woman's major role whether she was a professional or not. Freudian theory, or at least the emphasis on the crucial importance of the mother in molding the personality of her child, was at its peak, and the Bowlby and Spitz views on maternal deprivation added a shocking imperative to the mother's presence. This may have made those of us who pursued careers feel guilty, but it may have also alerted us to compensatory responses that had a very positive effect on our children's development. Thus, if the data show, and I think that on the whole they do, that we have done quite well as mothers, maybe it is because we tried extra hard.

On the other hand, we were harassed! Not content with being professionals and mothers, we wanted to be gourmet cooks, hostesses, supportive wives, and femme fatales. The major problem reported by the professional woman in several studies has been the management of the household. The difficulty of finding a housekeeper really was the single most predominant complaint of the women Ph.D.'s studied by Astin.[10] And our husbands may have helped more than the husbands of the nonworking women, but by no means was there equal responsibility for housework and child care.[6,7]

Much in this situation, however, has changed in recent years, and it is only with great caution that we can generalize from the existing data to the case for the new career women. For one thing, there will be more of them. Data collected each year on incoming freshmen at several colleges and universities show a continual increase in the percentage of women planning to combine careers and motherhood.[24,25] These younger women who will pursue careers may be quite different in values, self-concepts, and expectations.

If they marry, they will very likely marry a different kind of man than any we might have married, one for whom achievement and career lines are much less central. When Horner[26] did her research in 1965 on the motive to avoid success, this motive characterized women, but not men. In an exact replication, at the same school, we found just six years later that men were as likely as women to show evidence of a motive to avoid success. The percentage of men showing this motive had increased from 8% in 1965 to 78% in 1971. The dynamics of this motive in men is probably very different from what it is in women, but the finding does reflect a real change in men's orientations toward academic and career goals. We older women often gave our husbands' careers precedence over ours, in part because we felt it was a more intrinsic part of his self-concept. College men today are very different in this respect. This may augur well for the young woman who wishes to combine the mother and professional roles. The true sharing of household tasks, child care, *and* career commitment by man and wife may well be a viable possibility, whereas this has been only rarely the case until now.[6,7,20] Furthermore, if these women do become mothers, the styles of mothering may also have changed. Child-care centers may be more available and more acceptable. The pattern of women interrupting their careers for the early child-rearing years may diminish.

Finally, not marrying and not having children may be more psychologically available options than they used to be. In a recent study at the University of Michigan we found that ten percent of the undergraduate women said they wanted no children§ and the same percentage was found by Lozoff[27] at Stanford. This is not a high percentage, but it is considerably higher than previous comparable figures.

These changes must be kept in mind when we consider the data on the professional woman as mother. Very likely it will be easier to combine the two roles, for there will be more social acceptance and institutional supports for doing so. Earlier I indicated that balancing a career commitment with family and affective concerns has resulted for many of us in a richer and more fulfilling life. I think the possibility of achieving such a balance will be greater for the young professional woman of the near future, and for her husband as well. Needless to say, the lives of many men would also be enriched if they too had combined roles.

§ These figures are higher if we include those who said they wanted only adopted children.

References

1. BAILYN, L. 1964. Notes on the role of choice in the psychology of professional women. Daedalus. Spring : 700–710.
2. EPSTEIN, C. F. 1970. Woman's Place: Options and Limits in Professional Careers. University of California Press. Berkeley, Calif.
3. WHITE, M. S. 1970. Psychological and social barriers to women in science. Science 170.
4. ROSSI, A. 1971. Assessing women's history: our feminist predecessors. Presented at Center for Continuing Education of Women. University of Michigan. Ann Arbor, Mich. Oct. 19.
5. GINZBERG, E. 1971. Educated American Women: Life Styles and Self-Portraits. Paperback. Columbia University Press. New York, N. Y.
6. POLOMA, M. M. 1972. Role conflict and the married professional woman. *In* Toward a Sociology of Women. Constantina Safilios-Rothschild, Ed. Xerox College Publishing. Lexington, Mass.
7. GARLAND, T. N. 1972. The better half? The male in the dual profession family. *In* Toward a Sociology of Women. Constantina Safilios-Rothschild, Ed. Xerox College Publishing. Lexington, Mass.
8. BIRNBAUM, J. A. 1971. Life patterns, personality style and self esteem in gifted family oriented and career committed women. Unpublished doctoral dissertation. University of Michigan. Ann Arbor, Mich.
9. SIMON, R. J., S. M. CLARK & K. GALWAY. 1970. The woman Ph.D.: A recent profile. *In* The Impact of Fertility Limiation on Women's Life Career and Personality. E. Milner, Ed. Ann. N. Y. Acad. Sci. 175(3):.
10. ASTIN, H. S. 1969. The Woman Doctorate in America. The Russell Sage Foundation. New York, N. Y.

11. FELDMAN, S. D. 1971. Girls stay away from the boys: marital status and graduate education. Presented at Pacific Sociological Assoc. Mtgs. Honolulu, Hawaii.
12. NYE, F. & L. W. HOFFMAN. 1963. The Employed Mother in America. Rand McNally. Chicago, Ill.
13. GOLDBERG, P. 1967. Misogyny and the college girl. Presented at the meeting of the Eastern Psychological Assoc. Boston, Mass. April.
14. BARUCH, G. K. 1972. Maternal influences upon college women's attitudes toward women and work. Developmental Psychol. 6(1): 32–37.
15. TANGRI, S. S. 1969. Role innovation in occupational choice. Doctoral dissertation. University of Michigan. Ann Arbor, Mich.
16. ALMQUIST, E. M. & S. S. ANGRIST. 1971. Role model influences on college women's career aspirations. Merrill-Palmer Quarterly 17(3): 263–279.
17. HOFFMAN, L. W. 1972. Early childhood experiences and women's achievement motives. J. Social Issues 28(2): 129–155.
18. DIZARD, J. 1968. Social Change in the Family. Community and Family Study Center. University of Chicago. Chicago, Ill.
19. MACCOBY, E. E. 1966. Sex differences in intellectual functioning. *In* The Development of Sex Differences. E. E. Maccoby, Ed. Stanford University Press. Stanford, Calif.
20. RAPOPORT, R. & R. RAPOPORT. 1972. The dual-career family: A variant pattern and social change. *In* Toward a Sociology of Women. Constantina Safilios-Rothschild, Ed. Xerox College Publishing. Lexington, Mass.
21. VEROFF, J. & S. FELD. 1970. Marriage and Work in America. Van Nostrand Reinhold Co. New York, N. Y.
22. BARUCH, R. 1967. The achievement motive in women: Implications for career development. J. Personality and Social Psychol. 5(3): 260–267.
23. CHESSLER, P. 1972. Women and mental illness. Presented at Conf. on Women: Resource for a changing world. Sponsored by Radcliffe Institute, Radcliffe College. Cambridge, Mass. April 17 & 18.
24. CROSS, K. P. 1971. Beyond the Open Door. Jassey-Bass, Inc. San Francisco, Calif.
25. UNIVERSITY RECORD. 1972. ACE on "typical" freshman — M. Frosh: still ambitious but success not utmost. University of Michigan. Ann Arbor, Mich. Apr. 3: 3.
26. HORNER, M. S. 1968. Sex differences in achievement motivation and performance in competitive and non-competitive situations. Doctoral dissertation. University of Michigan. Ann Arbor, Mich. University Microfilms.
27. LOZOFF, M. M. 1972. Changing life styles and role perceptions of men and women students. Presented at Conf. on Women: Resource for a changing world. Sponsored by Radcliffe Institute, Radcliffe College. Cambridge, Mass. April 17 & 18.
28. LEVINE, A. G. 1968. Marital and occupational plans of women in professional schools: law, medicine, nursing, teaching. Unpublished doctoral dissertation. Yale University. New Haven, Conn.
29. FRANKEL, E. 1964. Characteristics of working and non-working mothers among intellectually gifted high and low achievers. Personnel and Guidance J. Apr. : 776–780.
30. JONES, J. B., S. W. LUNDSTEEN & W. B. MICHAEL. 1967. The relationship of the professional employment status of mothers to reading achievement of 6th grade children. California J. Educ. Research 43(2): 102–108.

MARRIAGE WITH A SUCCESSFUL WOMAN: A PERSONAL VIEWPOINT

Shepard G. Aronson

New York University
School of Medicine
New York, N. Y. 10016

I assume I've been asked to tell you what it's like to be married to a successful woman because I've been married to one for a long time, am a notorious proselytizer on the joys of marriage to a successful woman, and have a first-hand knowledge of the determinants that have made my own wife and my marriage truly successful by anyone's standards.

Come to think of it, I was married previously to another successful woman, so I qualify doubly. Also, I've been a practicing internist for more than thirty years and a consultant in endocrinology and in diabetes, as well as a family internist. So I've had occasion to discuss many problems of diverse types with women of all ages, from before the menarche to beyond the menopause.

Finally, perhaps I owe the honor of being the only male participant in this two-and-a-half-day symposium to my experience in the women's equality movement. I was the first board chairman of the New York Chapter of the National Organization for Women, and I've been an outspoken battler for N.O.W.'s goal of "equal opportunity for women in truly equal partnership with men." If, occasionally, I let slip the word "lady" or—even more unforgivable—"girl," this lapse merely indicates the verbal programming of my unenlightened generation rather than any emotional prejudice.

Invariably the first question asked about marriage to a successful woman is: How does it affect the husband's self-esteem? Does he feel threatened if she is *more* successful than he is? Suppose she brings in more money than he does—how does this affect the marriage and the relationship? I was on a TV show a few months ago that posed similar questions to four couples, all of whom had been married many years, and of whom both the husbands and the wives were successful. The consensus was that, if both the husband and wife are successful by their own standards, and not necessarily the materialistic standards of the world, the marriage can be a fulfilling one. If the husband is secure within himself, sure that his contribution to the marriage and to society is a valuable one, he does not feel threatened. Rather, he is as proud of his wife's accomplishments and recognition as she is of his. It is a mutually nurturing relationship. The moderator of the TV show asked, "How would you feel if your wife made more money than you do?" The unanimous reply from these four husbands was "Relaxed! Since we share and share alike, it doesn't matter who brings in the money." The suggestion that they might feel belittled by their wive's incomes brought incredulous smiles to the faces of these accomplished men.

Another time, I was on the Susskind Show needling David Susskind on his attitude toward women. Making common cause with me was Tim Cooney, bright, concerned, very much a man, and also the husband of Joan Ganz Cooney. Joan is the originator and producer of *Sesame Street,* administrator of a $13-million-dollar budget and boss of more than 200 employees. Tim, at that time, was working without salary as head of an important Harlem project, training minority groups to exert political pressure in order to obtain better housing for themselves. He was not at all abashed by the fact that his wife was bringing in nearly all of the family income. He looked upon her salary as an opportunity that enabled him to make a serious contribution to society. Tim joked that he was like "the wife who does volunteer work." It was obvious from his confident composure that neither Tim nor Joan measure masculinity with a monetary yardstick.

On the other hand, in my practice I have seen marriages founder when the wife found success in a career outside the home. It has been my observation that such marriages were not solid to begin with. The husband's contentment depended upon an "I'm better than you are" attitude, however hidden or sublimated it might have been. This reflected what Dr. Don Jackson has termed a Stable but Unsatisfactory Marriage and, in terms of more or less orthodox Freudianism, was often based on an anal-sadistic attitude of the husband toward the wife. Such a marriage tends to founder eventually if the wife rebels against her submissive role. The "I'm better than you are" attitude usually results in the unvoiced reply, "I'm equal to you—and probably superior". In the 1930s, the anthropologist Gregory Bateson described behavior of this kind in tribal life in New Guinea. Whole tribes would attempt to prove that they were as good as, or better than, neighboring tribes. Each action called forth a reaction, first from one tribe, then from another. The same thing can happen in married life or, actually, in any relationship between two people when one wants to exert mastery.

J. Sterling Livingston of the Sterling Institute conducted a survey of successful women in radio and TV and the characteristics that differentiate them from their less successful sisters. "Success" was defined as:

1. An income of $15,000 at age thirty or $10,000 below age thirty.
2. Supervision of relatively large numbers of subordinates.
3. Title and job description indicating relatively high or responsible position.

His conclusions: A woman's career success is correlated with the belief that she can control her environment and effect change. The most successful women were least controlled by their environment, and more by internal factors. Successful women think of themselves as originators. They initiate action and accept responsibility for the result. They attempt to solve, rather than avoid, problems. They believe they can make future events happen by their own efforts. Successful businesswomen obtain satisfaction from influencing other people, and have developed the skills to do this.

Other investigations into power motivation have isolated two types: First are *personal* power adherents who view the world in win-lose terms. These are authoritarian personalities who make themselves feel stronger by making those about them feel weaker. Second are *socialized* power advocates who have a win-win view. They satisfy their power needs by influencing individuals and groups to be more effective in achieving group or organizational goals. They tend to make other people feel stronger, rather than weaker.

The more successful businesswomen have higher socialized power motivation, are less authoritarian, and are more skilled in interpersonal relationships. The investigators speculated that a highly competent businessman in a senior position can "get away with" satisfying his own personal power needs, but a woman would encounter much more resistance and negative reaction. They conclude that high socialized power may be a key variable for predicting the success of women in business.

Lastly, a profile study of the successful female manager is very similar to that of male manager. Neither one is very much interested in establishing and maintaining close, warm relationships with the people around her or him in the business world. The male entrepreneur is somewhat higher in motivation toward achievement and lower in power motivation than is his female counterpart. This suggests that the male entrepreneur is slightly more interested in the task, whereas the female is slightly more people-oriented. But contrary to the popular stereotypes, Livingston found that the successful women in this sample were more interested in having a positive influence on those around them than they were in close personal relationships.

I propose for your consideration that a woman with these propensities and abilities who ends up a homemaker, with only her family to influence and with little or no opportunity for achievement, will exert power within the family structure that might lead to disaster. A family situation is not sufficient outlet for her manipulative and power needs. She may seek to manipulate her husband and children, provoking resentment and rebellion. Ordinarily, what one achieves from the family is nurturing support and emotional outlet. These are not the needs of a successful woman. She wants *influence*. If she can satisfy this need for influence through a career, she can make the best of wives. If she is frustrated in a career, she may bully her family and also torment her husband if he fails to provide her, through his own career, with the status and power she needs.

It is my contention that one is more apt to find a mutually supportive, open, and honest relationship when the wife is given the opportunity to prove her worth as an accomplishing person, not only during the few years of nest-building and motherhood, but also when those years are over. Then she needn't struggle in the home for status. She has achieved that status in the outside world; actually, this makes it easier for her to assume status in the home and in the marriage.

On the other hand, if she is caught in a sadomasochistic relationship (and in these relationships the woman is more often the masochist) it may be difficult or impossible to continue this relationship later if the woman gains recognition outside the home, so the marriage dissolves.

All this does not mean that I believe that a woman must work outside the home if she doesn't want to, any more than a *man* must strive for material success if he prefers other values. As long as the couple works out a *modus vivendi* allowing each person to flourish, that is a good arrangement. In the early years of a marriage, a woman may want to concentrate her emotional resources on the mother-infant relationship; she may not have enough time or energy for a career. However, with the newer attitudes blossoming between young couples, and husbands sharing housework and child care, today's young woman may be able to free her energies earlier for career fulfillment. If she can do so, I believe it can lead to a more exciting, a more varied, and a more mutually satisfying marriage.

The next questions that arise are: Doesn't the competition involved in pursuing a career make a woman too aggressive? Doesn't it force her to be competitive? Doesn't it make her too masculine? Certainly there are a limited number of careers that a woman, or a man, for that matter, can pursue to eventual success without displaying aggression.

We shouldn't shun the word "aggression" as a pejorative one, but we should decide when aggression has usefulness, and why it is supposedly good for a man but not for a woman. What does it mean for a woman to be—in quotes—"masculine" and what does it mean for a *man* to be "masculine"? Wouldn't society benefit if traditionally masculine and feminine attributes were distributed more evenly between both sexes?

Not to belabor the point too long, aggression can be a positive or a negative attribute for either men or women, depending upon how and to whom it is displayed. Those of us who have outgrown the need for a baby doll at home, or a mammy-servant we can lean on, can accept an accomplishing woman. If a husband demonstrates to his working wife that he appreciates her endeavors and applauds her success, there is no reason why she should bring the aggression necessary for her success at work into the home. She can leave her competitiveness at the office. And that applies to the wise husband as well.

Believe me when I tell you it is possible to have a marriage where neither mate is the boss but where both are partners. This makes for a harmonious home, helps keep both spouses' blood pressures normal, ulcers from forming, and heart attacks from occurring.

I would not ignore the importance of genetics or cholesterol, triglycerides, smoking, and so forth, in the genesis of myocardial infarction, but I believe that, over the long run, psychological factors are of at least equal importance. Psychological factors can bring out genetic weaknesses that might remain latent, can raise blood serum cholesterol levels, and can cause a person to smoke, or to smoke too much. A man or a woman may be able to withstand eight hours of aggression and competitiveness at the office but may break down if the eight is added to another eight at home.

In other words, if a large percentage of men in this country became less competitive and aggressive and a large percentage of women became competitive and aggressive enough to develop careers for themselves, the health of society and individuals would benefit.

Two masculine attributes I would warn women to avoid. The first is the development of a beer belly. The second is afternoon befuddlement caused by "tee many martoonis" at lunch. Most women executives and blue collar workers have avoided these noontime temptations. Ms.'s, keep up the good work.

One all too real problem that may arise in the home of a successful career woman is her absence from that home. Many careers necessitate attendance at business meetings, conventions, and so on. Of course, the traditional husband in America must be away from home frequently. If the marriage is a solid partnership, such absences can be borne with equanimity. If there are two incomes supporting the household, there will probably be enough money to hire some outside service to help perform either mate's work at home while he or she is away. This money cannot be spent grudgingly, but must be considered a desirable and necessary outlay.

Dr. Margaret Hennig of Simmons College studied top women executives and found that many of them did not marry until after age 35, that they then married superachievers, and that their marriages have been notably happy even when the pressures of business careers kept the couple from seeing each other more than once a week. (Of course, most of these women either had no children or had grownup stepchildren.) I'm not presuming to advise that absence is advisable; I'm just indicating that it is possible to have a happy marriage even if one spouse has to be away from home for considerable periods. As long as the other spouse, man or woman, knows that the absence is necessary for the fulfillment of the marital partner and respects this necessity, absence can be borne with no ill effects.

On the other hand, if the marriage is a happy one, one would expect the responsible spouse to minimize time spent away from home; to leave before the convention ends, if possible; to skip nonessential meetings that require extra time "on the road." Sometimes setting a realistic goal can help: "Dear, you're going to see less of me for the next two years. I've been elected President of the American Toothpick Publicity Directors' Association and I'll have to attend the national, state, and local conventions and make various speeches, but I promise to cut them as short as possible. Let's plan an especially interesting vacation when the whole family can be together, to make up for this lost time." Trying to make believe it isn't happening just creates resentment and confusion.

When one is married to a successful woman, it is necessary to keep remembering that she has not been conditioned to accept "female" career roles such as housewife instead of breadwinner, or secretary instead of boss. Dr. Hennig has pointed out that extremely successful women have had extremely close attachments to their fathers and their fathers' careers. Daddy is also usually a manager. The young woman ends up with a highly developed sense of self-esteem. If the husband now indulges in male chauvinist actions or words, that lowers her self-esteem; such a wife may react with hostility, as well she should. You can lead such a wife to dishwater but she won't like the sink.

When you're married to such a woman, you have to learn to balance minor inconveniences against the greater well-being of the marriage and the relationship. In my own home, for example, I've been waiting for many months for new dining room draperies. I've even offered to select them myself. Offer rejected. But I have set a goal: one month after my wife's term as Chair-one of the Board of N.O.W. is finished, I expect new drapery material to be chosen and the material to be in the hands of the maker. Is anyone listening?

Many successful women—including my own wife—are still in a transitional stage. They have freed themselves from ancient clichés about the nonfemininity of female achievers in a "male" world. But they still have not outgrown completely their early programming against asking their husbands to share domestic duties. Their philosophy in this regard might be summarized thus: "I don't want my own career to burden my husband at home." Because of their conditioning, they try to run the home by themselves. Guilt feeling might arise if their husbands had to undertake some work in the home. As a result, they are sometimes double-working wives, overtired, underslept, and unconsciously or consciously resentful. They must learn to ask their husbands to share specific duties in the home, and husbands of these women should learn to *volunteer* for household chores to spare their wives from undue fatigue and resentment.

This problem is certainly *less* prevalent among younger career women who have undergone the consciousness-raising of the Women's Rights Movement. They demand help at home from their husbands. But the interesting thing about a successful woman is that she may very well run a home efficiently, since she is an intelligent person and good manager. She will bring into the home some of the qualities and techniques that have made her successful in business. At least this is my experience in my own home, where I see many office techniques adapted to household management—typewritten to-be-done lists, mass purchasing, no overconcern with trifles, entertaining handled with the efficiency and aplomb of a meeting with clients but with much more warmth, relations with the school and teachers guided with the skill of an experienced public relations counsellor, planned division of responsibilities between all members of the family, pads and pencils at each of our phones, and plenty of phones, and plenty of business handled over the phone instead of in person.

Dr. Don Jackson has said that many different patterns of marital relations appear to function successfully, but nearly all happy marriages have certain elements in common. First, the spouses in a good marriage respect each other; the greater the number of areas of respect, the more satisfactroy the marriage is likely to be. Second, the spouses are tolerant of each other. Seeing themselves as fallible and vulnerable, they can accept shortcomings in their spouse. Third, each spouse makes the most of the assets in a marriage and minimizes its liabilities. They communicate and negotiate quid pro quos. They recognize that because no marriage relationship remains static but is a changing entity, the spouses must be working to improve the marriage until the day they die. The key words, then, are *respect, tolerance,* and *effort.* This applies to marriage to a successful woman as well as to any other marriage.

Some women who foresook the occupation of "just a housewife" and gained success outside the home learned that their husbands afforded them new respect, tolerance, and effort. These men esteemed their wives more because—to put it bluntly—they were earning money and therefore had tangible proof that society valued their achievements. Also, these husbands found their wives more interesting because they could now share anecdotes from the business world and "speak their language." On the other hand, certain husbands unconsciously wish to humiliate a wife who gains recognition in the outside world. These men can lavish a wife with benevolent affection only so long as she remains true to her role of the little woman at home whose chief satisfactions derive from pleasing her husband.

We must go back into the history of marriage to find out why a work such as this should even think of discussing successful women and their marriages. Why is a successful woman unusual enough to justify a weekend's time for so many busy participants?

Judging from anthropological studies, it is likely that early associations with any sort of permanence between men and women were polygynous or polyandrous, with incest taboos in directly ascending and descending lines. This strengthened group relationships by allowing males to avoid battling over their own sisters and mothers and gave them a group of males, brothers-in-law, who could be their companions in hunting and in battle. Monogamy was probably unknown, or the small bands would not have survived. It takes 12–18 months for a female to become pregnant again after a successful insemination, the life span was probably under thirty years, and less than half the children survived infancy. If monogamy had prevailed in very primitive days, the human race would have died out. The males remained away from the settlement for many months of the year, reducing the number of pregnancies sharply. Family groups were a survival mechanism. Love didn't enter into the picture. In fact, primitive vocabularies have no word for love.

Love became popular in the Middle Ages when the ladies of the castle had little work to do, performed mostly administrative duties, and soon became narcissistic, sumptuously adorned, and bored. With the Crusades taking most of the men away for years, stay-behind troubadors began singing songs of romance, men who remained at home tried to keep the castle ladies amused and content, and the chastity belt was invented. Of these phenomena, the least successful was the chastity belt. Available men did manage to keep the ladies content with extramarital sex, the troubadors sang of it, and the ladies institutionalized it. They called this institution "love". Under the leadership of the Countess of Champagne, they agreed upon a Code of Love in the Spring of 1174. It states there can be no such thing as married love; it exalts jealousy (a reaction to the culture's adultery and promiscuity), defines love as a conquest and yet abjures force as a prelude to true love, and waxes poetic over the autonomic nervous system symptoms in the love condition; that is, pallor, quickening of the heart beat, insomnia, and loss of appetite.

The word "courting" reminds us of the origin of the phenomenon of romantic love. To this day, the male utilizes the conventions of romance while courting the female, but then abandons the role of courtier when he finally assumes the new role of husband. The man then becomes dominant and, if encouraged, tyrannical.

When the two World Wars and the periods between them and since indicated to women that they could do practically anything as well as men, women began to demand equality within marriage and out. Add to this the diaphragm, the pill, and the I.U.D., and women saw the possibility of becoming man's equal in all spheres of living. When a male interviewer questioned a young woman executive's ability to hold a certain job because she might become pregnant, she waved her diaphragm under his nose and said "In the past fifteen years, I've become an expert in using this thing!"

The modern women's rights movement began with the explosive popularity in 1963 and thereafter of Betty Friedan's "The Feminine Mystique," with the Equal Pay Bill of 1963 and the Civil Rights Act of 1965, and with the founding in 1966 of the National Organization for Women. My wife and I attended that historic founding convention (so did our young son and daughter, incidentally), and we both became active in N.O.W. on national and local levels. As the largest and most influential women's rights organization, N.O.W. boasts 15,000 members throughout the United States, approximately ten percent of whom are men. Add to this the members of other like organizations, nonmembers who go along with the principles, and a good proportion of the younger generation, both male and female, who take equality for granted and practice it, and one can see evolution— more likely, revolution—in the making.

Two other events in history have kept women in an inferior position to men. For reasons difficult for me to understand, religions have always been run by men. Even when they exalted women, it was not as equals but as virgins, as temple prostitutes, or as high priestesses whose lives were strictly regulated. Perhaps the most effective antifeminist influence was the Roman Catholic Church, starting at the time of the Holy Roman Empire. Not that its principles were as male chauvinist as the worship of Baal, with its ritualized temple prostitution; it was just that the influence of the Church became so widespread in our Western civilization. Marriage was made a Holy Sacrament, although there is no proviso for this in either the Old or New Testaments. The priests and politicians who ran the Church defined what a woman might or might not do. Everywhere women became chattels with no semblance of equality before the law. As the power and influence of the Church waned, restrictions on women also lessened somewhat. But unfortunately, many thousands of discriminatory laws and customs still remain with us. The U.S. has been called "a Wasp country ruled by Catholic laws."

The second force that influenced marriage and women adversely was the Industrial Revolution, which took the husband out of the home for up to 12 hours or more per day, so that the great burden of running the home and raising the children began to seem the natural lot of women. Slum living fell upon us. Families were splintered by desertion, disease, disillusionment. Impoverished women in impoverished families did, of course, work for pay as cogs in the Industrial Revolution, usually under inhuman conditions for mercilessly low salaries. But gradually women began to study and to aspire, hoping to earn through their paid work a better life for themselves and their families. Since the measure of a "real man" as breadwinner was no longer his ability to hunt or handle heavy farm tools but was the amount of money he could bring home, women began to find that they too could bring home money. In other words, work roles for the two sexes became interchangeable. This has threatened the traditional institution of marriage as a source of physical and psychological nurture for both spouses and their offspring.

As the husband of a successful and liberated woman and the father of two bright, liberated children, let me put to you *my* conviction, that no other institution on earth can sustain and delight two human beings so fully and for as long a period as a modern, loving, sharing monogamous marriage.

Recently, according to *Life* magazine, I was supported in my evaluation of monogamous marriage by another very successful woman (apart from my wife who *insists* on monogamous marriage). Dr. Marina Whitman, Ph.D., summa cum laude, full professor at the University of Pittsburgh, and Nixon's recent appointee to the three-member Council of Economic Advisers, was quoted as saying, "I am a strong proponent of the monogamous or nuclear family." She adds, and I believe that this applies to all husbands of successful women, "Obviously you have to be a strong person with a strong sense of yourself to put up with me."

A successful woman must be a *strong* woman. She experiences not only the same stresses that men experience in the twentieth century rat-race; she also is subject to special stresses because she is a woman. She is accused of being masculine, of pushing too hard, of not needing the same income as a man because she has a husband to help support her. She may enter the work world late, after her family has grown up; she may have to relinquish her job because her husband moves to another town; she may work for a sexist boss or have sexists (male and female) working for her; and she may have a male chauvinist husband or lover.

Dr. Elizabeth Jeffress, in addressing an Industrial Health Conference, pointed out that these problems can be expected to continue until *both* boys and girls are educated for parenthood and also for responsible work outside the home. She suggests that work schedules be based on the task accomplished rather than on the time spent. Other experts have suggested that teams could share jobs, perhaps the husband working mornings and the wife afternoons. Or perhaps two women could share a job, each one putting in perhaps five hours a day, so that the enterprise receives even more than the usual eight work hours from the team. At least one employment agency in New York, working on this principle, has achieved good success placing part-time clients. These innovations can reduce the stresses on both men and women who work. Reduce the stresses and you will have better employees, better businesses, *and* better marriages.

Two women investigators, Honzik and Bayley of the Institute of Human Development in Berkeley, Calif., have demonstrated that mothers who are highly active and energetic had children who were more likely to score high on mental tests. These mothers were apt to be better educated. The closeness of the mother-son relationship in the early months was the one best predictor of a boy's test performance at age eighteen. So, to the men in the audience, one would recommend that you pick yourselves highly energetic, well-educated wives who are capable of setting up a close relationship with your sons and, if your genes are any good, your sons will do just fine on I.Q. tests — if that's what you want. And to the women, these same investigators found that a girl's intellectual development was likely to be increased when, during babyhood, her father had a close, warm relationship with both his wife and his daughter. They point out that it was the father's *interest* in his daughter's accomplishments rather than his expression of affection for her that seemed to count, especially from ages seven through adolescence. During the preschool years, the relationship between *mother* and daughter was the more influential. Dr. Wanda Bronson of the same institute noted that children seem to take on characteristics of the parent of the same sex and to reject or be unaffected by the characteristics of the parent of the opposite sex. Expressive, aggressive boys tended to have the same type of father, and expressive girls mothers of the same type.

The work of Bettye Caldwell and Julius Richmond of Syracuse University might have been describing my own wife and children when it pointed out that children reach a higher developmental level if their mothers:

1. Gave them more warmth and affection.
2. Specifically expressed a desire that their children do well in school.
3. Showed an ability to strive for the care of their children and to respond adaptively to the suggestions of child-care authorities.
4. Maintained physical order in the home.

I submit that all these qualities could describe either a mother who stays home or an alert, successful working wife.

The University of Chicago group, under Dr. Fred Strodtbeck, discovered that brilliant adolescents were found, on the whole, in families where relationships were warm and helpful. The high I.Q. family can define and solve problems better and can resolve differences, especially the complex conflicts of adolescence. Dr. Strodtbeck also indicated that it is easier for children in high I.Q. families to identify with parents of *both* sexes, not only with the parent of the same sex. These brilliant children developed to a high degree the characteristics of the role commonly ascribed to the opposite sex but, at the same time, were not any less like the parent of the same sex. They had a wider variety of roles open to them. Isn't that what we all want for our children? Marry a brilliant partner, be warm to your spouse and children, and reap the benefits.

WOMEN IN ACADEMIC LIFE

Patricia Albjerg Graham

The Education Program, Barnard College and the Department of Philosophy and
Social Sciences, Teachers College, Columbia University
New York, N. Y. 10027

Discussions about the status of women in higher education have become as contagious as cholera and just about as popular with predominantly male faculties and administrations. The scarcity of women in the upper echelons of academe has triggered heated arguments not only from women's activist groups but also from male faculty and administrations facing investigations from the Department of Health, Education, and Welfare.

The discussion that follows is a reflective one, not a report of research findings. This discusses specifically two crucial junctures in an academic career: the transition from graduate student to faculty and from faculty to administration. These are important for both men and women in the academic world. They present peculiar difficulties for women.

The most important single observation about women in the academic world is that their numbers decrease dramatically as the importance of the posts increases. For example, women constitute 44% of the undergraduates, 13.5% of the doctorate recipients, and about 2% of the full professors at leading graduate schools of arts and sciences, and none is president of a major coeducational university. When women are found on college faculties and administrations, they tend to be concentrated in those fields thought to be particularly suitable for women, i.e., social work, education, home economics, nursing, and library service. In administrations they are most likely to be located in offices of Deans of Women or Deans of Students. Each of these fields tends to be low in status in the hierarchy in the university.

In the process of academic careers there are (generally) two particularly critical junctures. The first is the transition from graduate student to faculty. The second is from faculty to administration. By no means all faculty members make the shift from teaching to administration, but most top academic administrators have progressed through faculty ranks. Some general considerations of these status transitions apply to both men and women.

For example, it is quite common at the beginning of one's teaching career to be both a graduate student and a faculty member. This is a period when the transition from student to faculty is obscure. Unlike physicians and lawyers, who enter their professions with degrees achieved, many young men and women begin their college teaching careers before they have completed their doctorates. This double status, however, is not expected to continue very long if the young college teacher expects to stay and advance in the profession. Once the Ph.D. is achieved, the part-time lecturer or the full-time instructor expects to be promoted immediately to assistant professor. (This rank usually means full professional and faculty status, the assistant professor having completed the transition from graduate student to faculty rank.)

* This is a revised version of "Status Transitions for Women Students, Faculty and Administrators," which will appear in the forthcoming *Academic Women on the Move,* edited by Alice S. Rossi and published by the Russell Sage Foundation, New York, N. Y. One section also appeared in "Women in Academe," *Science* 25, September 1970, and is reprinted with permission of the publisher.

Just as there are persons who are both graduate students and teachers, there are also persons who are both teachers and administrators. When a professor is a department chairman, he is usually both teaching and administering. In many colleges the academic dean teaches a course or two in addition to carrying out his administrative responsibilities. One difference is that once a graduate student attains a Ph.D., he never reverts to student status again. An administrator, on the other hand, may and frequently does resume a full-time teaching position.

The transformation from graduate student to professor, particularly when accompanied by completion of the Ph.D., is universally regarded as an enhancement of one's status; it is a clearly vertical move in the status hierarchy. There is less general agreement that the move from faculty to administrative position is a comparable enhancement of status. Just how vertical the movement, how high the elevation, depends on the particular institutional context and the type of administrative position to which the faculty member moves. The offer to a professor of the presidency of a good college or the influential deanship of an important school of a major university is still regarded in most academic circles as highly desirable. But there are many other administrative positions in academe about whose incumbents it is sometimes uncharitably observed, "He's all washed up as a scholar, so he's taken a deanship." (In those cases the individual's status is not significantly improved by accepting an administrative position.)

One final observation about status transitions for both men and women: In order to become a faculty member, one must have been a graduate student, but to become an administrator, one need not have been a faculty member. There are many administrative jobs in colleges and universities for which the entry requirements do not include college teaching, but there are no faculty jobs that do not require graduate study. Therefore, not all administrators have themselves made the status transitions of graduate student to faculty and faculty to administration. Thus, faculties are composed of persons who have had a common prior experience, graduate school, but administrations are not comparably homogeneous. They are made up of persons of more varied academic attainments and experiences. Ordinarily, however, the top academic administrative positions are held by former faculty members. The status transitions discussed here, then, apply to all faculty members but only to some administrators.

The circumstances that affect women seeking to move from graduate student to faculty to administrative status include all those endemic to the general academic situation alluded to earlier. Some distinct problems emerge only for women.

The status of women in academe, generally, reflects the larger society's expectations for women. These conventional expectations include the belief that while they are young, they are likely to have status comparable to that of men their age, but as they grow older the discrepancy between women's status and that of their male agemates increases dramatically. With advancing years, the men move into positions of higher status and the women largely remain behind in the lower echelons of academe. There are at least two general explanations for the slowness of the advance of women in any institution compared to that of men as the ages of both sexes increase. When both men and women are young, they are, professionally speaking, expected to occupy positions subordinate to older, more experienced, more distinguished practitioners in their fields. But as men grow older, they attain levels of equality with their senior colleagues with relative ease. It is much harder for a woman to do this. The social expectation, conscious or unconscious, is that she remain in a relatively subordinate status. To society at large, her increase in age does not seem inconsistent with this. In a world of highly competitive jobs, men are expected to move naturally into situations where an assertive posture is necessary for survival. But when a woman adopts that posture, everyone, including other women, puts down his or her paper and stares.

Another factor contributing to the expectation that women will remain in relatively subordinate positions is that in academe, as in nearly every field in which men predominate, important jobs have been defined with men in mind. It is often taken for granted that a major administrative job requires collateral duties in the form of entertainment, the dispensing of which it is assumed will be handled by the incumbent's accommodating *wife*. The traditional idea of what can be expected from a young assistant professor just out of the Ph.D. program is clearly a male-oriented concept. Very heavy pressure of duties for the new faculty member — teaching, preparing new courses, getting on with that first book or set of articles — are required at the same time that women would normally be bearing children. If women are to share places in the academic structure with men on some kind of reasonably equitable basis and are not to be left behind as years of service accumulate, the conditions of the academic job will have to be redefined with particular attention to the limitations of time normally imposed where the fulfillment of expectations is concerned.

There are fewer problems today for a woman who wants to achieve the status of a graduate student. Those graduate school professors who used to vow that they would not have a woman graduate student in the department have either retired or shut up. Once in a while a remnant of that anachronism may be picked up. Recently, a young woman, elected to Phi Beta Kappa in her junior year at a women's college, spent her senior year away at a coeducational institution where her new husband was also a senior. In her senior seminar in English there, it was clearly acknowledged that she was the outstanding student in the class, although all the rest, including the professor, were men. At the end of the term, her professor queried all the students about their plans for the following year, encouraging them in their decisions about graduate study in English, professional school, and so on. When he came to the young woman, he smiled and said, "Well, we all know where you'll be next year, at home looking after your husband." She was stunned by his assumption that her academic days were over, that simply because she was female and married she should have no further formal study. In fact, she had received a national fellowship for graduate school and was intending to work for a Ph.D. in English.

The shift from college to graduate school is in some ways a difficult one for young women, for at that juncture many recognize for the first time that their future careers may be very different from most men's. Nonetheless, the shift from undergraduate to graduate status for women does not entail the larger psychic shock that often comes later, frequently during the period of graduate study when the young woman contemplates her first professional position. A graduate student, after all, is a student; studying while either an undergraduate or graduate student involves one in a fundamentally nonassertive role, and this is one that society expects women to take. For many young women, graduate study is an intentional prolongation of that life to which they have already adjusted, the student life. Under the sheltering wing of a university, a graduate student is able to postpone those difficult decisions about job and future career, which have always been troublesome. They are particularly troublesome for young women, for the standard conveyor belts that take young men up into professional life are not yet adjusted to receive women.

At the end of graduate school studies, presumably upon or near the completion of her doctorate, the young woman is no longer able, whether she wishes to or not, to cling to the comfortable status of student, a searcher of truth at the foot of the wise professor. Such a posture appeals to some young women and to an even larger proportion of those professors (generally male) at whose feet she searches. It is not surprising that male professors regard with enthusiasm the prospect of bright, young, and often attractive women earnestly following their academic researches along lines suggested by the professors. Who of us would not rejoice in intelligent and eager students appreciatively exploring our ideas?

But when the young woman ventures into the job market to secure a teaching position in a college or university, she faces the classic obstacles that have limited women's full participation in American academic life. First, she must contend with the myths that surround women's careers. It is conventionally assumed that the young academic woman will not be as steadfast in her commitment to her job as a man — an assumption that ignores the research of Helen Astin, who found that 91% of the women receiving doctorates in the mid-fifties were employed seven years later.[1]

Another myth is that women in higher education may be good teachers (look at their large numbers in the elementary and secondary school ranks!), but they do not do research, and research is indispensable to a career in the senior ranks of scholarship. That such a conclusion is unwarranted is shown by numerous studies, at least one of which points out that women Ph.D.'s, head for head, actually publish more than men Ph.D.'s.[2] Other studies indicate that academic women, classical victims of heavy teaching assignments, publish despite this handicap.[3] The question cannot be settled by tabulating mere numbers of items on bibliographies; for indexes are no guides to quality. Further, many cases of women who could publish but do not do so with the frequency of their male colleagues can be explained in terms of pressures society exerts or fails to exert on women because they are women.

A third myth surrounding potential women faculty members is that if they are married, they cannot be expected to undertake really demanding professional positions. A chairman of a history department at a West Coast state university recently explained: "We just have difficulty believing that a married woman is really serious about her job. Surely she is more interested in her family." He added that in his department they were quite willing to appoint single women (presumably those whom they deemed unlikely to marry), but they were dubious about the married ones.

Most of the problems affecting the single woman Ph.D., such as the pressure to publish, also apply to the married woman Ph.D., often in heightened degrees. There is no question that the married woman Ph.D. must run a more difficult course than her unmarried counterpart. Recent studies indicate that single women Ph.D.'s are indeed hired in the more lucrative jobs so that they can earn an average of $2,000 more annually than married women Ph.D.'s, and this is no myth but a sign of real obstacles in the path of married women who wish to be college or university teachers.[4] This pay differential just cited is partly related to the higher proportion of older women in the single group and to the fact that some of the married women studied were employed part-time. Further, although Lindsay Harmon's studies have shown that women who were married at the time of receipt of the Ph.D. had academic records that were superior to the men's, the fact is that a much higher proportion of the single women Ph.D.'s achieved full professorships than did the married ones, a fact that tells us it is the married woman Ph.D. who faces the more formidable hurdles as she enters the job market. The percentage of women Ph.D.'s who marry has been increasing over the last 35 years, but the percentage of those who are unmarried is still startlingly high. Of the women who received doctorates in 1935, 47% never married. Except for the '50s, the percentage of those remaining single dropped about two percent every five years. In 1969, the last year for which figures were available, 40% of the women Ph.D.'s have never married.[5] The increase in the number of married women Ph.D.'s is not rapid, but it is real, and it is the married scholars who face the more serious problems of advancement in Academe.

Academic women are often ambivalent about academic success, as Horner has observed, just as women generally are ambivalent about success. This may be particularly true of married ones. A young married woman Ph.D., leaving graduate school behind her and entering full professional status as a college or university teacher, is often concerned not only about whether she should succeed herself but also about what effect her academic achievement will have upon her husband, who is likely to be in one of the professions himself, sometimes in her own field. Most women in this society are reluctant to achieve positions of higher status than their husbands, particularly when both are likely to be employed in the same line of work. A male professor of economics may find it amusing and enhancing to his own ego if his wife is a successful artist or actress, but it is more difficult for most men and women to accept if the economics professor's wife is herself a more able economist than he. When she receives a grant or fellowship for their joint sabbatical and he no grant at all, tensions may arise, or so many believe.

One way of ensuring that the academic husband's status will be higher than his academic wife's is to let the husband's job opportunities determine where the family lives. When that is the case, as it nearly always has been, the wife is left to find whatever job she can in the area of her husband's teaching institution. Generally, high-status institutions of learning do not look with enthusiasm on attendant wives seeking academic employment in their preserves. For many universities, proximity and availability of a married woman academic whose husbands they have hired are almost handicaps for consideration for first-rate appointments. The dean or chairman's attitude often seems to be that the best candidate is the one who must be lured with difficulty from a distant institution. The Ph.D. wife, who lives in town, may be useful for pinch-hitting in the department occasionally when it is short-handed, but she is usually not regarded as a full-fledged professional. Let her go and find a job at the local community college, or maybe the high school can use her! The married young woman's lack of mobility (or *perceived* lack of mobility) is much less serious when she is still in graduate student status. It is easier to find an acceptable graduate program where her husband goes than an acceptable teaching job. The situation is far more serious if the young woman is already a college teacher, and it is most serious of all with a potential woman administrator, married, following her husband to the place of his academic employment. For, in her case, the opportunities of match between candidate and job are most limited.

Another obstacle to the married woman Ph.D. (or more rarely, her husband) is the nepotism rule, written or unwritten, that still prevails on many campuses. Although more and more institutions are now willing to accept two members of the same family teaching in one institution, few regard with enthusiasm the prospect of husband and wife serving in the same department, particularly if both are on professorial lines. Since many academic women have met their husbands in graduate school (the proportion of women Ph.D.'s married to other Ph.D.'s in the same field is very high in all fields except education, where the women are less likely to be married), the probability of husbands and wives being in the same field is very high. In such cases, rarely is the wife given the superior appointment. Typically she takes a job in another, less prestigious institution or works part-time as a "research associate" at her husband's college or university.

Everyone in the academic world is familiar with the horror stories that circulate about a department that has disintegrated as a result of factions caused by having a husband and a wife who, as a pair, dictated policy for all the other department members. Some alarming instances of husband-wife domination of a single department have undoubtedly occurred. There is also the tenure problem. Many departments are reluctant to hire a young couple at the assistant professor level for fear that both (or even worse, that only the wife and not the husband) will meet the standard for tenure six years later. "What can we do?" they ask. "We can't possibly promote her and not him. It would ruin their marriage!" Of course, there are reasonable measures that can be taken to prevent or mitigate these rare occurrences. The couple can be warned upon appointment at the assistant professor level that tenure may not be possible for either or both of them. The department need not reach any advance conclusions, nor should it take it upon itself the shouldering of any responsibility for the security of their marriage.

What is often overlooked in discussions of the dangers of nepotism are the advantages that accrue to the universities that practice a policy of hiring, promoting, paying both husband and wife at position-levels fully appropriate to their training and talents. The potential for institutional loyalty among such couples is very great, simply because such couples recognize how few institutions reward husbands and wives with appointments that match their qualifications.

For couples in the same field, cooperative research is a real possibility. For all, however, probably the greatest gain is the recognition that both the husband's and wife's academic aspirations are being taken seriously by the university, thus undercutting the likelihood of the domestic tension that often occurs when the wife feels that her professional interests are being ignored. Such a couple is likely to give the university better service than either spouse would if the other were unemployed.

Even at those universities that do hire husband and wife at the professorial levels, the chances are not very great that salaries will be equally appropriate to their rank and qualifications. This is sometimes done deliberately, on the assumption that husbands without working wives need more income than a couple including a working wife. Other times the discrimination affecting both husband and wife will reflect the lack of mobility of the couple if it is well known in the profession that neither will move unless an opportunity is available for the other in the same locale, though not necessarily in the same university. Finally, many such husband and wife teams are themselves reluctant to press for salaries commensurate with others of similar qualifications in the department, simply because they are sensitive to the fact that the university is sending two checks to their family and only one to most others.

A notorious problem that young married women face as they enter the field of higher education professionally is pregnancy and maternity, although the interruption of professional life thus entailed may seem less serious an obstacle than the trauma the situation may produce in the male administrators of the institution employing the young woman. Although university administrators are accustomed to coping with male professors who suffer nervous breakdowns, coronaries, or sudden surgery, they are frequently aghast at the need to establish policy guidelines for pregnant faculty members. One reason why institutions may find the professor with the coronary a less perplexing problem than the professor expecting a baby is that he is likely to be a senior man in the institution whom the administration knows well; the pregnant professor, on the other hand, probably is in the junior academic rank and has not yet become well acquainted on the campus. Moreover, male administrators tend to assume that the responsibilities of child care that follow upon pregnancy must be assumed *in toto* by the mother, after the fashion of their own wives in the years when their children were small. For such male administrators, then, implementing a progressive maternity-leave policy entails a serious challenge to the social customs that have governed their own personal lives. Working out such a policy is seldom an easy task for these administrators.

The problem of pregnancies and the entailed maternity leaves for women faculty members is probably not one of disruptively great numbers. Since only a little more than half the women holding the doctorate are married, the pool of married women Ph.D.'s is about seven percent of the total Ph.D. group. True, the assumption that only *married* women Ph.D.'s will have children has been challenged, and properly so. Colleges and universities of tomorrow will have to adjust to certain changes in sexual attitudes, some of which will include claims to the right of a single woman to have a child if she wants to do so. But the number of these cases will probably remain small, and by far the largest number of professional pregnancies will be consequences of more or less traditional marriage arrangements.

Women Ph.D.'s tend to have fewer children than women generally. Their childless ratio, according to one study, was double that of the national norm. Those who did have children had fewer (two) than the national average of two and six-tenths. So it would seem reasonable to conclude that the assumption of many male administrators that married women faculty will spend most of their time procreating rather than publishing is unwarranted.

Nevertheless, there are significant numbers of young women faculty members with children, and these children are frequently born when the woman is not yet distant from the line dividing graduate school from full-fledged professional teaching. For the married woman professor with a child or two, a very serious problem exists: lack of time. There are just not enough hours in the day to do all she must. A recent UNESCO study revealed that the average working mother had 2.8 hours of free time on a typical weekday, compared with 4.1 for the working father.[6] In other words, women holders of the doctorate in the United States spend an average of about 28 hours/week on household tasks. Although we are fond of talking of the great advances made by technology (or gadgetry) in freeing women from domestic tasks, the working mother's concern for her children is not eased by her automatic washer-dryer or her dishwasher. None of her electrical household appliances will take care of a sick child. What that mother needs, and what she finds increasingly difficult to find, is household help, persons who are competent and reliable, who will help her in caring for her children and running her house. Day care centers are certainly needed, but even they do not solve the problem of vacuuming the living room and changing the beds, not to speak of dealing with a child with a feverish cold or a routine case of mumps.

Related to the problems of time and inadequate household help is the suburban syndrome, in which these problems are accentuated. More and more Americans live in outlying urban areas, and it becomes progressively harder for wives to find jobs that do not take them physically away from their homes for long periods of the day. Often a woman must spend three hours each day commuting to her academic institution, returning home to perform the customary domestic chores; the amount of energy she has left at the end of a day is small indeed. What time or energy has she left for her research and other scholarly activities? In suburban communities domestic help is notoriously difficult to find. Complicating the picture even further is the usual social custom of such residential areas, where people generally entertain at dinner parties in their own homes. In a city it is still possible to go to restaurants or concerts with one's friends without appearing inhospitable, but in many suburban communities there are no convenient public facilities where one can spend a pleasant evening. The home, and the overtired woman, are expected to provide the serene environment in which friends can spend a delightful evening. An obvious solution is simply to reduce one's social life to the barest minimum, but this too common way of dealing with the problem works hardships on the professional woman's family and on the woman herself.

Most of the problems limiting a woman's progression through professional ranks similarly retard her entry into administration. A graphic example is Columbia University, the institution that has granted more doctorates to women than any other in the country. Currently, 38% of those entering graduate studies and 19% of those completing the Ph.D. program are women, while only 3.5% of the full professors and none of the top administrators at the level of dean or above is a woman, except Martha Peterson, who is president of Barnard College, the women's undergraduate college of the University.

As the Columbia example shows, there are exceedingly few women in administration, and those who are, are likely to be assigned to "women's" tasks. The top woman administrator in most American coeducational colleges and universities is the dean of women, now often styled "Associate Dean of Students." This woman is likely to be one of those administrators who has not followed the faculty-to-administration path. On graduation from college, she has probably done specialized graduate work in guidance or student personnel administration, taken a low-level and peripheral job on the administrative staff of a college or university, and has reached the position of dean of women without ever having been a member of the teaching faculty. Such a background is not likely to permit her to move into a major power position within the university. Most of the women in administration, then, are to be found outside the faculty-to-administration track on which the male administrators run; they have had no faculty experience, nor are they regarded by the faculty as occupying high-prestige positions in the college or university hierarchy. Within the last year (1971–72), a number of institutions have begun to promote junior women faculty members to junior administrative positions. Whether or not they will eventually move into senior positions remains to be seen.

Of those women who *are* members of the teaching faculty and who by that fact constitute themselves possible candidates in the professor-to-administrator pool, the question why they do not move to upper-level administrative positions in greater numbers may be raised. There are several inhibiting factors present. A woman may shrink, consciously or unconsciously, from the inevitable isolation she will feel when she joins an all-male group of top administrators. Then, too, the pressures for women to forsake the classroom for the carpeted, curtained office may simply be much less than they are for men. First, for most women professors there is less financial incentive to enter administration, since very few women professors have sole or even principal economic responsibility for entire families. Second, because of the difficulties attending women's graduate study, it is quite possible that the relatively few women who receive doctorates are more intent upon a scholarly life than some men who seek degrees deliberately as a union card, not only to faculty membership but also to administrative posts. Third, many women, particularly those with families, may resist being drawn into the "office" regimen of administrative work with its less flexible schedules and inevitable time-consuming absences from home. The overall demands on a woman professor's time are great in terms of classroom teaching, lecture preparation, and research work, but these activities can often be scheduled at times and places convenient to the woman. And she does have her summers relatively free. Such is not the case with the woman administrator, who is expected to spend 9 a.m. to 5 p.m. in her office (or in other administrators' offices) five days a week, 48 weeks a year. Nor does a woman administrator have a wife to assist her in those social and community obligations so often regarded as a male administrator's collateral duty.

Violation of cultural stereotype may be another factor working against women faculty members moving into upper-level administrative positions. The general expectation of our society and institutions is that women can make their best contributions in positions subordinate to men. Hence the university administrator's job descrption is almost invariably drawn with a man in mind, particularly a married man with a wife available for auxiliary social support. Moreover, in the councils of high administrators, men are expected to be independent and assertive. But when women display that property they are thought to be "tough and bitchy." Perhaps some women executives *are* tough and bitchy, but it is quite possible that these same traits found in a man would be labeled "clear-headed, firm, and attentive to details." Tolerance for men's behavior is a good deal broader than it is for women's. Men are permitted their noisiness and crochets, but women are expected to maintain a much more precarious balance between conspicuous competence and tactful femininity. Manifestations of independence' and autonomy are expected in a male executive; their presence in women makes some male colleagues cringe.

Relevant here are the widespread beliefs that men will not work for women and that women may not wish to. Grounds for these common assertions are not frequently cited, and facts often point the other way. For example, at two colleges that have regularly had woman presidents, Barnard and Wellesley, men have consistently numbered between 40% and 50% of the faculty, and have never seemed to mind in the least serving under a woman president. It is often charged that women will not support female candidates for administrative positions, and there may be some truth in this contention. Men who try to enlist the aid of successful women in promoting other women for similar responsible positions are occasionally surprised to discover that women at the top are reluctant to help their "sisters" up the ladder. One may regret but still understand this. The few women who have "made it" may prefer to believe that they have succeeded strictly on the basis of their own merit and that any failure to succeed on the part of other women is simply due to lack of merit. As a consequence, such women are often resistant to any special efforts to recruit more women to top administrative posts. Men will quickly use these women's reluctance to support other women as adequate justification for not supporting them either. Some counterweight to this discouraging tendency has been achieved in recent years by those younger women who have come up from the ranks and who are displaying greater support for their "sisters."

A woman at a high administrative level deals principally with men, since they form the vast majority of senior academic administrators. Such men have rarely worked with women *their own age* in positions of responsibility equivalent to or superior to their own. Many academic men have not worked with women on an equal basis since their undergraduate days. At the very beginning of their careers, perhaps, some men may have worked with women on levels of relative equality. But in their middle and later years the gap between the two sexes in the professional field widens rapidly. From the persepctive of a senior university administrator, most of the women a man sees are secretaries, clerks, and junior faculty and administrative staff. Therefore, when a woman mounts to high administrative rank, she faces a complex task. Not only does she have a new job to learn and new relationships to cultivate, she must also legitimize the authority of her office, and gradually break down the resistance of her male associates to take supervision and direction from a woman. It is not easy for many men to change their customary expectations that women are bossed, not bosses. One department chairman recently commented about a woman professor who had shifted to a high administrative rung of the ladder, "She has been promoted and now works with the administration and therefore no longer has the point of view of either the faculty or women." Presumably, with the promotion she had become neuter.

Such a situation is no longer acceptable. Senior academic ranks and administrative posts should not be posts so demanding as to force a woman to lose both her humanity and her femininity. No wonder many able women are discouraged from making the shift from faculty to administration. The potential for such loss of administrative talent is considerable. It is a rare person, male or female, who is able to handle a responsible administrative position without being threatened by its latent dehumanization. The problems are particularly acute for a woman who is considering, and is being considered for, a high administrative post in academe.

In such circumstances, then, it is not surprising that few women find their way into top faculty and administrative spots, even if we count the very recent efforts of a few universities to appoint a woman to previously all-male central administrations. If society is to take the educational opportunities of its women as seriously as it does those of its men, it must broaden the options open to women. From the entering student to the top administrator, academic institutions must become truly coeducational. Tokenism has no place at any level of higher education today.

References

1. ASTIN, H. S. 1969. The Woman Doctorate in America: Origins, Career, and Family. : 57.
2. SIMON, R. J., S. M. CLARK & K. GALWAY. 1967. Social Problems. : 13, 221.
3. ASTIN, H. S. & A. BAYER. 1973. Sex discrimination in Academe. *In* Academic Women on the Move. A. S. Rossi, Ed. Russell Sage Foundation. New York, N. Y.
4. AMERICAN SOCIETY FOR MICROBIOLOGISTS. 1972. Loretta Leive presentation. Philadelphia, Pa. April 24.
5. HARMON, L. R. 1968. Careers of PhD's, Academic v. Nonacademic, A Second Report on Follow-ups of Doctorate Cohorts, 1935–60. National Academy of Sciences. Washington, D.C.
6. THE NEW YORK TIMES. 1967. March 5.

SEX HORMONES AND EXECUTIVE ABILITY

Estelle R. Ramey

Department of Physiology and Biophysics
Georgetown University School of Medicine
Washington, D.C. 2007

"She thinks like a man."

Translated, this means: This female has somehow overcome her gender disability and seems to be able to use her neocortex in rational decision making. Therefore, she may be designated as an honorary *Homo sapiens*.

"That's just like a woman."

Translated, this means: This female manifests the characteristic cerebral defects of the XX chromosomal behavior determinants. She is largely restricted to decision making via limbic system-hypothalamic neuronal pathways with little evidence of neocortical influences. Therefore, she is more accurately classified as *Homo emotionalis* or *Homo gonadis*.

Freud put it more succinctly when he said, "Anatomy is Destiny." This middle-class Victorian genius identified the female reproductive system as the inexorable vise that kept women emotionally unstable, submissive, passive, masochistic, and devoid of creative intellectual potential.[1,2] Freud's distorted view of female psychology was the most palatable of all his theories to the society of his day, because it appeared to give a physiological basis to the prevailing theological and cultural attitudes toward women. Seventy years later, it remains his most comforting pronouncement to many scientists, physicians, politicians, professors, university presidents, business executives, husbands, and lovers. It has, sadly, been embraced also by the very women who are bound by its chains. And it is a lie.

The female as a defective male has been bred into the bone of our culture.[4] Even those who reject the penis-envy construct that is central to Freud's hollow woman find solace in his *a priori* opinions about the psychologic inferiority of the female. Others, like Erikson, place her identity in the "inner space" of her uterus and her human destiny in her tail rather than in her head. And now, a bastardized endocrinology is being invoked to keep her in her place. A physician made headlines recently by calling attention to the "raging hormonal imbalances" every month which make women unfit for jobs of top responsibility.[3] Those who have lunar cycles thus become lunatics every month and cannot be trusted with the important affairs of the world. They can be relegated to only the trivial tasks of rearing the next generation.

The basic assumption that illumines all this mutually destructive nonsense is that males are biologically superior to females in every aspect of human function except the bearing and nurturing of the young. As a corollary, these special female attributes are assigned conflicting and dubious social values. On the one hand, motherhood is a noble state (if there is a man in the house), and on the other hand, any slob can have a baby and momism (see *Portnoy's Complaint*) is the curse of mankind.

The biology and psychology of the human female has been fixed like a bug in amber to conform to unproved and unprovable theories about the effect of female hormones on behavior. The Devil can quote endocrinology as well as scripture. When the pseudoscientific maunderings are cleared away, however, there is an interesting body of information about hormones and human behavior. It is known that, like the male, the female is exposed to a continually changing internal milieu of hormones.[5] It is also known that, like the male, the behavioral response of the female to these hormonal changes is in large part conditioned by her adaptive needs, experience, and cultural strictures. Animal studies even in the area of measurable metabolic responses can be extrapolated to humans only with the greatest caution. Species differences are often profound, and at the level of psychosexual responses, the extraordinary preeminance of the human neocortex makes a hash of the simplistic conclusions of many ethologists and anthropologists. Playful ducks and male-bonded baboons do not seem to be accurate prognosticators of the lack of "territorial imperative" evidenced by the South Vietnamese, for example.

Frank Beach, in a review of the neural and chemical regulation of behavior,[6] expressed this cogently: "It is reasonable to assume that the evolutionary increase in experiential control of sexual activities is an outcome of the increasing importance of the neocortex as a mediating agent. Evolutionary shifts in the physiological control of sexuality are most evident in our own species. Here one sees the greatest degree of diversity. Exclusive homosexuality, complete reversal of sex roles, sexual responsiveness to immature individuals, to animals or even to inanimate objects, total sublimation of the sex drive — these and many other uniquely human manifestations are possible only because the experiential component plays a dominant role in shaping human sexual behavior. The primary importance of individual experience is in turn due to reduced reliance upon gonadal hormones and increased intervention of the cerebral cortex."

It is the human cerebral cortex, not the endocrine system, that confers the almost infinite variability characteristic of human responses to environmental stimuli. It is also the neocortex that can distort and manipulate information to create myths and stereotypes. The stereotype of woman as the second sex, biologically fragile, unstable, intuitive, and irrational, and the stereotype of man as the primary sex, biologically strong, stable, hard-headed, and rational belies the empirical and experimental data available. For the little it is worth as commentary on Adam's Rib, it is the female sex that is primal.[7,14] The early embroyo is female until the fifth or sixth week of fetal life. A testicular inductor substance must be generated at this point to suppress the growth of ovaries. No ovarian inductor is required for female differentiation, because all mammalian embryos of either genetic sex have the innate capacity for femaleness. Eve, and not Adam, appears to have been the primeval human that God had in mind.

In passing, it might be added that it was Eve, not Adam, who showed the earliest signs of scientific curiosity and aggressive questioning of the status quo.

The endocrinology of the fetus does indeed determine the maleness or femaleness of the child in terms of the development of primary and secondary sex characteristics. The crucial question, however, is: What are the innate and immutable behavioral characteristics of the adult that can be attributed to the hormonal differences in the two sexes? The extensive work of Money and Hampson and others at Johns Hopkins reveals the complexity of gender identity and behavior in human beings.[8,9] Hampson and colleagues conclude that: "In the human, psychologic sexuality is not differentiated when the child is born. Rather, psychologic sex becomes differentiated during the course of many experiences of growing up, including those experiences dictated by his or her own bodily equipment. Thus, in the place of the theory of an innate, constitutional psychologic bisexuality such as that proposed by Freud — a concept already questioned on theoretical grounds by Rado,[10] among others — we must substitute a concept of psychologic sexual neutrality in humans at birth. Such psychosexual neutrality permits the development and perpetuation of diverse patterns of psychosexual orientation and functioning in accordance with the life experiences each individual may encounter and transact."

These scientists go on to detail their evidence for this statement from the study of patients born with profound gonadal abnormalities, such as human hermaphroditism. The term "hermaphrodite" is used here to describe not only patients with completely ambiguous external genital development but also a variety of individuals with a contradiction between the predominant external genital appearance and the sex chromatin pattern, gonads, hormones, or internal accessory structures. These biologic states are compared with the gender roles assumed by the individuals so afflicted. The investigators define "gender role" as: "all those things that a person says or does to disclose himself or herself as having the status of boy or man, girl or woman respectively. It includes but is not restricted to sexuality in the sense of eroticism. Gender role is appraised in relation to the following: general mannerisms, deportment and demeanor; play preferences and recreational interests; spontaneous topics of talk in unprompted conversation and casual comment; content of dreams, daydreams and fantasies; replies to oblique inquiries and projective tests; evidence of erotic practice and finally, the person's own replies to direct inquiry." These surely constitute our social interpretation of what is a man and what is a woman. In humans, the attempts to correlate these "typically" male or female gender roles with the basic physiology of gonadal development have not been notably successful. On the contrary, the data available on humans with gonadal or sex hormonal anomalies suggest that psychosexual orientation cannot be attributed to two separate predetermined instincts[11-13] — one male and one female.

The terms "innate" or "constitutional" or "genetically determined" often are used to account for behavioral differences that emerge in the two sexes with such seeming spontaneity and predictability that it seems inconceivable that they might result from experience and learning. Yet the effect of chromsomal influence on adult psychosexual behavior is of itself of no specific significance if the gonadal development is defective. In humans, there are many examples of a discrepancy between the chromosomal configuration and the fetal differentiation of ovaries or testes with the concomitant secretion of the appropriate sex hormones. Money concludes: 'No matter what the genetically determined anticedents and components of gender-identity differentiation, the postconceptual and postnatal determinants can, in test cases, completely override them. The syndrome of androgen insensitivity (testicular feminization) in genetic males provides a graphic example of the extent to which the genetics of sex chromosomes can be overridden in gender-identify formation."[11]

Such an individual is usually identified as a girl at birth and often is diagnosed as a genetic male only at puberty when she fails to menstruate and the physician belatedly discovers the male genetic identity. Such a human grows and develops with a self-image identical with that of the societal description of a woman. She-he typically marries a male and gives loving mothering to adopted children, since, of course, she-he is infertile. This individual does have some estrogen secretion from the testes, but the establishment of physical characteristics does not require this contribution of the female hormones.

As described by Ehrhardt and associates,[12] in a condition known as Turner's Syndrome the child has an inborn genetic anomaly and has virtually no evidence of either male or female gonadal development. These individuals lack a second

X chromosome totally or in part. They may thus be considered as XO. Nevertheless, they grow up unequivocally female in their gender roles and gender identity despite the absence of estrogens. They look like girls at birth and are reared as girls. They remain feminine in their self-image. Ehrhardt concludes: "Any attempt to attribute gender identity in human beings simply to either genetic, hormonal or social-environmental factors must result in oversimplification and misconception."

The question, however, that has occasioned the most soul searching and rage has been the role of testicular hormones or other androgens in conditioning behavior that is supposed to be typically male. The data from animal experiments and human fetal anomalies suggest strongly that fetal androgens influence the functional anatomy of the developing brain.[14-21] In rats, it has been shown that when radioactive male hormone is given either directly to the fetus or to the pregnant mother, the hormone is taken up in several organs including the hypothalamus. If the exogenous hormone is given within a critical period of fetal development, the hypothalamic nuclei that regulate cyclic release of pituitary gonadotropic hormones in the female appear to become masculinized. As a consequence, cyclic release of the gonadal hormones is not manifest in the female adult. The sexual behavior of such animals tends also to be somewhat disoriented, even though the external genitalia appear normal.

The extrapolation of these data to primates is not so easy. For example, in humans or even in the rhesus monkey, fetal exposure to androgens does not seem to interfere with the subsequent gonadal cyclicity of the adult female.[22] There are, however, some behavioral aspects of in utero exposure to excess androgens that have been reported in primates.

Recently, Ehrhardt and coworkers[13] described a series of 15 girls who had been masculinized in utero as a result of cogenital virilizing adrenal hyperplasia. When the condition was recognized at birth, the necessary surgical and hormonal corrections were instituted early, and the child was more or less restored to her genetic sex in terms of secondary sex characteristics and internal hormonal milieu. Nevertheless, these girls are reported to be more interested in so-called boys' sports and toys. They were more frequently identified as tomboys by their parents. Significantly, there was no evidence of a higher degree of lesbianism or aberrant sexual behavior than in control groups of women. They are described, however, as being more "career-oriented." An examination of the data reveals that of the fifteen girls studied, seven were thought at birth to be hypospadiac males with cryptorchidism. Presumably, the proud parents had been initially told they had a son. The sex assignment was changed within the first seven months in this group, but it is a matter of some importance that in these, as in all the other cases, the sex ambiguity was a problem for the parents from the time of birth. The effect of parental concern about the true sex identity of these children, despite medical corrective procedures, must inevitably have conditioned their behavior toward the child and the child's response. For example, the data reveal that in at least half the matched control group of normal children, sex education was derived in large part from communication in the home, while the adrenogenital children reported as the chief source of information the hospital input. These children were examined frequently with regard to their genitalia and could not have escaped the knowledge that they were not entirely the little girls that their parents might have wished for.

How is one to interpret the finding of a greater career interest in these young girls as compared with normal adolescent girls in this society? For Freudians it is tempting to postulate that fetal masculinization of the brain induces the development of a special neuronal pathway for "career orientation." It is more likely, however, that a girl who sees herself as less desirable as a woman than her peer group may seek other avenues of ego development. Of far greater interest in elucidating the ultimate effect of male hormones on behavior and achievement is the fact that most women with those "masculinized" brains do not, in fact, go on to typically male roles in society, but retain tenaciously the conception of themselves as women.[9] They play out the normal female roles, male brains notwithstanding. This is especially significant in light of the recent reports that excess androgens, progestins, or progesterone in fetal blood seem to be correlated with higher performance on all aspects of intelligence testing.[25,26] Males or females with the adrenogenital syndrome who were exposed to high androgen titers in utero have been shown to have a statistically significant elevation in verbal and spatial intelligence scores as compared with the normal population. Androgens after birth seem to have no such effect on performance.[25] The results of prenatal treatment with progesterone in girls who were not masculinized also point to a higher than normal IQ as a consequence of the effect of these female hormones.[26] The academic achievement of these individuals was also higher than that of the controls.

These observations are important in their implications as regards the extremes of human intelligence, both high and low. They shed little light, however, on the phenomenon of females or males with very high IQs who never achieve much of note in this society. For women, in particular, this is of the greatest importance, because for them the possession of an extraordinary intellectual capacity has seldom been the high road to achievement. Lewis Terman's study of exceptionally gifted boys and girls gives ample proof that whatever the genesis of a first-class brain, hormonal, genetic, or environmental, a female sex-identity seems to make creative use of that brain unlikely. The smartest women in Terman's series got married and vegetated pretty much like the not-so-smart ones in the general community. They did not become Supreme Court Justices.

Human behavior thus transcends natural endowment in an extraordinary way. An early study by Hampson and associates[9] demonstrates this forcibly. He followed the psychological development of 31 patients with virilization due to the adrenogenital syndrome and was led to the conclusion that "in the human, psychosexuality is not differentiated when the child is born." The group they studied was, in fact, far more traumatized by sexual ambiguity than Ehrhardt's patients. Hampson's female patients had lived for years with the external sex characteristics of the male: the enlarged clitoris, male hair distribution, male body configuration, and so on. They were all brought up as females, however, by parents who were told that their children were genetically female. In this series, the contradiction between sex rearing, sex appearance, and hormonal milieu was not corrected until the girls had achieved a precocious puberty. Despite this prolonged exposure to excess androgens both in utero and postnatal life, Hampson reports: "Of the 31 patients whose sex hormones and secondary sexual body development contradicted their assigned sex and rearing, only 5 became ambivalent with respect to their gender role."

The remarkable fact of this study is that the other 26 patients in this group "established a gender role consistent with their assigned sex and rearing, despite the embarrassment and difficulties of living with contradictory secondary sexual development." Obviously, these women must have had enormous problems in dealing with their paradoxical appearance. It is also of interest that another group of 11 females with the same degree of virilization who were reared as boys went on to establish a typical masculine gender role and orientation.[9] They were thus eligible for leadership and decision-making roles. Hampson's studies reveal that reassignment attempts after the first year of life, whatever the hormonal or genetic status, lead to a permanently poor psychosexual adjustment.

It should be noted that because of the lateness of surgical correction of the external genitalia of the girls in Hampson's study, many exhibited an enlarged clitoris during the most significant years of their psychological development. Yet these patients tested out later as typical American women in virtually all aspects of behavior, life goals, and self-image. What price penis envy?

None of this is to deny that sex hormones play a role in conditioning aspects of behavior in humans as well as in other animals. The problem is to separate the imprinting due primarily to hormonal mediation and the imprinting due to early experience. Even in lower animals, where parent-offspring responses are considered to be innate, unlearned behavior, it has been shown that appropriate response of the young to members of their own or other species is not preestablished.[23] Lorenz[24] points out that a greyleg gosling that has lived a few days with its parents will never react to a human as a transfer object. But goslings that are taken from their parents immediately after hatching and are cared for by humans will never follow a mother goose. They follow only humans. It is the ability to respond to the early environment that is innate, not some mysterious foreordained attachment of offspring to parent.

There is good evidence that androgens tend to increase libido in both men and women. Both women and men secrete the entire spectrum of steroid hormones. Males have higher androgens and lower estrogens than females, but both require androgens for normal sex drive. The adrenal cortex of the female secretes androgens, and the adrenal cortex of the female tends to be larger than in the male. Are the androgens that are normally secreted in her adrenal cortex male hormones? Since their secretion in excess produces "masculinization," the answer is a qualified yes. But since this "masculinization" is readily overridden by her psyche, the answer is a qualified no. When Fisher[27] injected sodium testosterone into the midlateral preoptic region of the hypothalamus of male or female rats, he could elicit male sexual behavior. That suggests that testosterone is a powerful male hormone that overrides previous brain imprinting. Well, yes and no. When Fisher injected testosterone into the medial preoptic region of the brains of males or females, he elicited typical maternal behavior. That is a rather odd effect for the most potent male hormone. Its possible meaning for human behavior is discussed in a perceptive paper by Money.[27] There may be a potential dimorphism in the human brain that is activated or suppressed by sex hormones or there may not. Adult human behavior and achievement cannot, however, be explained on this basis.

John Money and his coworkers have worked with the problem of gender identity and hormonal milieu for many years. In one of his papers[11] Money describes a boy and girl; both were genetically male, and both were subjected to the same fetal-hormonal environment. They were somatically similar in infancy and childhood but were subjected to very different parent-child and environmental experiences. With appropriate medical management the girl became a woman, and the boy a man. Money concludes: "This remarkable antithesis in psychosexual (sexobehavioral) differentiation is indicative of a general principle: namely, that gender-identity differentiation is phyletically programmed in the human species to take place largely after birth, and also to be dependent to a large degree on stimulation from and interaction with, the social environment."[11]

Given all these complexities of human development vis-a-vis sex differentiation, it is not surprising that selection and interpretation of data can be made to prove any point of view. For example, Maggie Scarf in *The New York Times Magazine* (May 7, 1972, p. 30) concludes that Freud was right, and hormones are indeed destiny because of the critical role they play in prenatal life. She quotes many of the excellent animal experiments to support this thesis and also some of the data on testosterone levels in homosexual humans. The problem of extrapolating from animal to human data has been mentioned above, but it is the interpretation of the human studies that requires comment. Despite the fact that some of the investigators quoted (Ehrhardt and Money, for example) have repeatedly commented on the postnatal environmental programming of behavior in humans, the emphasis in Scarf's article is almost entirely in the direction of immutable predestination. In the original papers of Money and Ehrhardt on the effects of androgens and progesterone on IQ, for example, the data show (and the authors emphasize) that the elevation in IQ is across the board and does not differentiate between verbal and mathematical skills. Yet Ehrhardt is quoted in Scarf's article as suggesting that the data on excess prenatal hormones might support the difference in verbal and spatial skills that are said to exist between females and males. Their data support just the opposite conclusion.

The data on testosterone levels in homosexuals are also a matter of dispute. Money, in reviewing the data, concludes: "One may fairly safely interpret today's clinical evidence to mean that sex-hormone levels of adulthood have very little to do with the etiology of homosexuality."[22] Certainly the high incidence and social acceptance of homosexuality in societies such as ancient Greece and Hitler's Germany would suggest that this kind of sexual behavior does not require an abnormal hormonal balance. Similarly, the administration of male hormones to either male or female homosexuals may increase libido (as it does in heterosexuals), but the direction of the sex drive is not altered.

The characterization of testosterone as the "take charge" hormone is also an engaging notion to many investigators. Aggression and leadership in humans or in subhuman primates have been studied with this bias and the results have been interpreted in many ways. One of the problems rests with the parameter chosen for study—in this case, plasma testosterone levels. Behavior characteristic of aggression is associated with changes in virtually all neuroendocrine systems. Adrenaline and noradrenaline, cortisol, thyroxine, glucagon, and the pituitary hormones, to mention a few, are altered by a variety of environmental factors that are the cues for aggression and "leadership." Gonadal hormones are additional variables in this complex system. The animal studies themselves demonstrate that testosterone levels in individual primates can be associated with pecking order only under certain conditions. The same monkey with high testosterone levels when he is at the top of the hierarchy can be shown to have low testosterone levels in a different social order. In other words, it looks as if the high testosterone levels do not determine ranking order or leadership, but the behavioral coordinates of being top monkey may change testosterone secretion along with many other physiological parameters.

Stress itself may significantly lower testosterone secretion as the adrenal corticoid secretion is elevated. Does this mean that those men who daily do battle with the competitive environment of the high reaches of business and government have chronic undersecretion of testosterone? If this were the case, then measurement of testosterone levels in our great leaders might lead one to conclude that low testosterone levels are the stigmata of leadership. This obviously makes nonsense of the complexity of human motivation and achievement.

Conversely, when apparently normal women show the symptoms of high intelligence, aggressive competitiveness, and a capacity for leadership, does this reflect an unusual pre- or postnatal exposure to high androgens? There is nothing to support such a concept. At a guess, the measurement of 17 ketosteroid excretion in such women is highly unlikely to reflect this simple association. Most such women are able to conceive and bear children, and this is the proof irrefutable of the predominance of female hormones.

The relatively greater aggressive behavior reported for male rats[17] can be interpreted simplistically to mean that women are naturally gentler creatures than men. Was Joan of Arc a woman when she rallied the French against the English and raised the siege of Orleans? Was Kenau Hasselaer a woman when she and her band of women fighters held out against 30,000 Spaniards in the 16th century? Are the Viet Cong women who lead companies in battle, really women? Or the women guerrillas of the IRA, or the women fighters of the anti-Nazi underground, or the women who fought with their Israeli men in 1948? We have no data on their androgen levels, but it is probable that these women secreted more estrogens than androgens. Human aggressivity is whatever a society says it is and leadership is in the minds of those who are led.

In all this miasma of claims and counter claims about the role of sex hormones in determining human behavior, there are no data to show that males as a group are more intelligent than females, or that there is any area of psychic response unique to either sex. For those who would use animal and human data to suggest that subtle but important contributions to behavior are made by the sex hormones, there can be no definitive proof to the contrary. Males are different biologically from females. They are also different sociologically. Men become United States Presidents and women do not. But then women do become Premiers of Israel and India and Ceylon. Endocrinologists have nothing to contribute to the explanation of these national differences.

In the modern world of extended life spans, where females outlive males by about seven years, an argument could be made that biology is on the side of the sex with the blood vessels that stay patent longer. But old men run the world. If testosterone levels are criteria for leadership, it is therefore no surprise that things are in such a bad way.

There can be no better conclusion to this rather pointless argument than to quote from the brochure that advertises a new book to be published in the fall of 1972. The authors are the great authorities in this field, John Money and Anke Ehrhardt, and the book is called *Man and Woman, Boy and Girl.* These experienced investigators are described as having reached the following conclusion: "In general, the authors' research suggests that there are as great differences between individual men and individual women as there are between members of opposite sexes. They conclude, therefore, that the social roles of men and women should be related to individual needs, rather than to membership in a sexual caste."

To the question: Which has the best hormonal basis for leadership and achievement, man or woman? The meaningful answer can only be: Which man and which woman?

References

1. FREUD, S. 1933. New Introductory Letters on Psychoanalysis. W. W. Norton and Co. Inc. New York, N. Y.
2. FREUD, S. 1905. Three Essays on the Theory of Sexuality. Imago Press. London, England.
3. RAMEY, E. R. 1971. What did happen at the Bay of Pigs. McCall's. Jan.
4. SALZMAN, L. 1967. Psychology of the female. Arch. Gen. Psychiatry 17: 195.
5. PUBLIC HEALTH SERVICE. 1970. Biological Rhythms in Psychiatry and Medicine. Pub. 2088.
6. BEACH, F. A. 1958. Neural and chemical regulation of behavior. In Biological and Biochemical Bases of Behavior. Univ. Wisconsin Press. Madison, Wis.
7. SHERFY, M. J. 1966. The evolution and nature of female sexuality in relation to psychoanalytic theory. J. Am. Psychoanal. Ass. 14: 28.
8. MONEY, J., G. H. HAMPSON & J. L. HAMPSON. 1957. Imprinting and the establishment of the gender role. Arch. Neurol. Psychiat. 77: 333.
9. HAMPSON, J. L. & G. H. HAMPSON. 1961. The ontogenesis of sexual behavior in man. In Sex and Internal Secretions. W. C. Young, Ed. Williams and Wilkins. Baltimore, Md.
10. RADO, S. 1940. A critical examination of the concept of bisexuality. Psychosom. Med. 2: 459.
11. MONEY, J. 1970. Matched pairs of hermaphrodites: Behavioral biology, sexual differences from chromosomes to gender identity. Engineer. and Science 33: 34.
12. EHRHARDT, A. A., N. GREENBERG & J. MONEY. 1970. Female gender identity and absence of fetal gonadal hormones: Turner's Syndrome. Johns Hop. Med. J. 126: 237.
13. EHRHARDT, A. A., R. EPSTEIN & J. MONEY. 1968. Fetal androgens and female gender identity in the early treated adrenogenital syndrome. Johns Hop. Med. J. 122: 160.
14. JOST, A. 1961. The role of fetal hormones in prenatal development. In The Harvey Lectures. Series 55: 201. Academic Press. New York, N. Y.
15. HARRIS, G. W. 1964. Sex hormones, brain development and brain function. Endocrinology 75: 617.
16. MONEY, J. 1965. Influence of hormones on sexual behavior. Ann. Rev. Med. 16: 67.
17. CONNER, R. L., S. LEVINE, G. A. WERTHEIM & J. F. CUMMER. 1969. Hormonal determinants of aggressive behavior. Ann. N. Y. Acad. Sci. 159: 760.
18. MONEY, J. & A. A. EHRHARDT. 1968. Prenatal hormonal exposure: Possible effects on behavior in man. In Endocrinology and Human Behavior. R. P. Michael, Ed. Oxford Univ. Press. London, England.
19. MONEY, J. & S. MITTENTHAL. 1970. Lack of personality pathology in Turner's Syndrome: Relation to cytogenetics, hormones and physique. Behavior Genetics 1: 43.
20. FEDERMAN, D. D. 1967. Abnormal Sexual Development. A Genetic and Endocrine Approach to Differential Diagnosis. W. B. Saunders. Philadelphia, Pa.
21. NEUMANN, F. & W. ELAGER. 1966. Permanent changes in gonadal function and sexual behavior as a result of early feminization of male rats by treatment with antiandrogenic steroid. Endokrinologie 50: 209.
22. MONEY, J. 1970. Sexual dimorphism and homosexual gender identity. Psychol. Bull. 74: 425.
23. LORENZ, K. 1935. Der Kumpan in der Umwelt des Vogels. J. Ornith. 83: 137.
24. SCHILLER, C. H., Ed. 1957. Instinctive Behavior. Int. Univ. Press. New York, N. Y.
25. MONEY, J. W. 1971. Pre-natal hormones and intelligence: a possible relationship. Impact Sci. on Soc. 21: 285.
26. DALTON, K. 1968. Ante-natal progesterone and intelligence. Brit. J. Psych. 114: 1377.
27. FISHER, A. 1966. Chemical and electrical stimulation of the brain in the male rat. In Brain and Behavior. R. A. Gorski & R. E. Whalen, Eds. Vol. 3. The Brain and Gonadal Function. Univ. Cal. Press. Berkeley, Calif.